SEA WARFARE, 1939-1945

SEA
WARFARE
1939-1945

by JOHN CRESWELL, *Captain, R.N.*

UNIVERSITY OF CALIFORNIA PRESS   /   BERKELEY AND LOS ANGELES   1967

University of California Press
Berkeley and Los Angeles, California

Cambridge University Press
London, England

Revised and Augmented Edition
© 1967 by The Regents of the University of California
First edition published in 1950 by
Longmans, Green & Co., Ltd.

Library of Congress Catalog Card Number: 67–17111
Designed by Hans Wehrli
Printed in the United States of America

T*o*
the Memory of
JOHN CATTERALL LEACH
Captain, Royal Navy
who lost his life while commanding
H.M.S. Prince of Wales
December 10,
1941

Preface

TO REVISED AND AUGMENTED EDITION

S INCE THE ORIGINAL version of this book was written many further works have been published on the maritime operations of World War II. To the three volumes of Professor Morison's work which were then available a further twelve have been added to complete his detailed and comprehensive history. On the British side the three volumes (the third in two parts) of Captain Roskill's official history, *The War at Sea*, were published between 1954 and 1961. These, with the addition of Volume I of *The War against Japan* by Major General Woodburn-Kirkby, also in the British official history series, provide all that any writer can need to ensure himself against errors of fact, and it is mainly in the light of them that I have revised my text. A large number of minor corrections have been needed and in a few instances the accounts of operations have called for revision of the deductions drawn from them.

Though it is with these authoritative works that I have been mainly concerned, there have, of course, been many others, varying widely in scope and scale between, for example, Winston Churchill's *The Second World War* in six volumes and Millington-Drake's *The Drama of the Graf Spee and the Battle of the River Plate*. These, too, have been taken into account.

In the original preface, printed below, I noted the possibility of including a more operational account of the Battle of the Atlantic when full information was available. This it now is, notably in Captain Roskill's great work and in Dr. Rohwer's "The U-Boat War against the Allied Supply Lines" (Chronicle VIII in Jacobsen and Rohwer, *Decisive Battles of World War II*). But so numerous are the events recorded that any attempt to reduce them to a satisfactory narrative on the scale of this book would evidently be impracticable. It has therefore seemed best to leave this aspect of the war in the generalized form in which it was originally written, with such corrections as the above accounts enjoin.

In addition to correcting the original work I have endeavored, on the valuable advice of Professor Arthur J. Marder of the University of California, Irvine, to broaden the background by including some passages on the prewar strategical outlook of each navy. These and some brief character sketches of the admirals who did most to influence the course of the war, which he also suggested, seem needed now that more than two decades have elapsed since hostilities came to an end.

The battle charts are based on information derived from the charts in British admirals' dispatches and from Professor Morison's *History of United States Naval Operations in World War II*, and were drawn by Surrey Art Designs of Oxshott, Surrey, England.

J. C.

Cattistock, Dorset, England
July 1966

viii

Preface

TO THE FIRST EDITION

T HOUGH MUCH INFORMATION about the war of 1939–1945 has still to be made known, enough has now been published to enable its course to be outlined with moderate assurance. An attempt has therefore been made in this book to give an account of the war at sea in its true proportions. As is natural, the view-point is mainly that of the Allied navies; but it is my hope that this has not led to any serious distortion of the picture. When the events of the maritime war can be examined in the light of the official histories which will deal with them in more detail, it should be possible to see more clearly why various things happened; but it seems unlikely that the general lines of the story will be much altered.

The published sources available as the foundation of an account such as this are of diverse types, but among them they cover most of the ground. Everything that was made public at the time is admirably summarized and arranged in Philip Graves's *Record of the War* (in twenty-four volumes published quarterly by Hutchinson and Co., 1941–1947). Many valuable booklets were published by the Ministry of Information during or just after the war—e.g., *East of Malta, West of Suez*; *The Mediterranean Fleet, Greece to Tripoli*; and *The Battle of the Atlantic*. General Eisenhower's *Report to the Combined Chiefs of Staff* appeared in 1946. And latterly a large number of Admiral's Despatches have been published in the *London Gazette*. Many books too have been written on various aspects of the war; and of particular value are the lectures given at the Royal United Service Institution by distinguished officers who had played prominent parts in the operations they were describing. On the German side there are the *Minutes of the Fuehrer Naval Conferences*, translated and edited by the Admiralty and United States Navy Department jointly, which

ix

are of the highest value as an authority despite the unevenness of the picture they present—for these conferences were held irregularly and do not include every important naval affair.

For the war in the Pacific the sources available in England are far less numerous than those for the Atlantic and Mediterranean, but several of them are particularly well informed and comprehensive: Fleet Admiral King's *U.S. Navy at War, 1941–45* (his three published reports to the Secretary of the Navy combined in one volume); *American Sea Power since 1775* by Professor Westcott and his colleagues of the U.S. Naval Academy, giving an excellent narrative of events; *The Influence of Sea Power in World War II* by Captain W. D. Puleston, U.S.N., with its clear account of Japanese strategy to which I am much indebted; and two books on Leyte Gulf, *The Battle for Leyte Gulf* by C. Vann Woodward and *The Japanese at Leyte Gulf: The Sho Operation* by James A. Field, Jr., both of which combine careful analysis with graphic description in so admirable a manner that any other writer touching on these operations will always owe much to them. From these, from the volumes so far published of Professor Morison's *History of United States Naval Operations in World War II* and Captain Karig's *Battle Report*, and from Admiral Spruance's lecture on *The Victory in the Pacific* at the Royal United Service Institution (October 30th, 1946), the main features of these campaigns are now clear.

Though it is my hope that the reader will gain an idea of the comparative importance of the various operations in relation to the maritime war as a whole, it has not been possible to indicate this merely by the space devoted to each. In particular it has seemed best to generalize the account of the German submarine campaign and this has resulted in relatively fewer pages being devoted to it than to the operations of the larger ships. When the full story of this intensive and prolonged battle has been published, both from the Allied and the German side, it may be possible to construct an account that will give a more precise picture of the operations while still keeping to the general scale of a short history such as this. In the meanwhile I have thought it best to deal with the campaign on general lines rather than to illustrate it with sample convoy battles or other episodes, which at present would have to be selected rather at random—for such a treatment would, I believe, tend to throw the main picture out of focus. I hope, though, that enough has been said in the chapters on this subject to emphasize the supreme importance of the Battle of the Atlantic.

In somewhat less degree the same remarks apply to the operations of Allied submarines and the attacks of Allied shore-based aircraft on shipping where these were continuous rather than episodic in nature.

Here too a more precise picture may eventually be possible, but until fuller information is obtainable it seems best to deal only with the general nature of these operations and their aggregate results.

In trying to get a true picture of events it has been my good fortune to have the valuable help of several friends. Commodore G. W. G. Simpson, who was in Malta through the difficult times of 1941–42 in command of the 10th Submarine Flotilla, has thrown much light on the Mediterranean war; the advice of Admiral Sir Victor Crutchley, V.C., has enabled me to see my way more clearly through the Solomon Islands and New Guinea campaigns; and Commander M. G. Saunders of the Foreign Documents Section of the Admiralty has supplied me with some details of the cruises of German ships. In addition, through the kindness of a mutual friend, I have been so fortunate as to be put in touch with Vice Admiral Forrest P. Sherman, U.S.N., formerly Deputy Chief of Staff to Admiral Nimitz, who has generously given his time to commenting on the Pacific chapters and has thus enabled me to correct some mistakes. That these officers are in agreement with all I have written I cannot claim, but that my book has gained great benefit from their advice I am sure.

October 1949

Contents

Maps

Battle Charts

1

NAVAL STRATEGY BEFORE 1939

THE INVASION OF Germany from the west in the spring of 1945 and the surrender of Japan in the summer of that year were each preceded by a series of amphibious operations of a magnitude, frequency, and overall perfection such as had never been approached in any previous war. In both theaters landings against opposition had followed one another in steady succession ever since 1942. In the west, the landings in Algeria and Morocco were followed by the invasion of Sicily and the hard-fought struggles of Salerno and Anzio, operations that were in some sort preliminaries to the tremendous and almost miraculously successful invasion of Normandy in June 1944 and the subsequent landings on the Riviera. In the Pacific the landing on Guadalcanal in August 1942 was the first step in depriving the Japanese of their conquests and in carrying the war to the threshold of Japan itself. The recapture of Guadalcanal was followed by further landings in the Solomons, in northern New Guinea and the Bismarck Archipelago, and on Morotai in the Moluccas, while another stream of assault operations was flowing over the atolls and islands north of the equator: Tarawa, Kwajalein, Eniwetok, the Marianas, and the Palau Islands. Arrived thus on the outskirts of Asia, the two streams joined for the reconquest of the Philippines and the capture of Okinawa.

The sum of these amphibious operations in Africa, Europe, and the Pacific employed a large proportion of the Anglo-American effort; their success was essential to victory, and for success a high level of cooperation among navies, armies, and air forces was needed. In many other operations, too, there was close interaction among the services. It was therefore not unnatural that combined operations were often said to excel all others in importance. It was even said from time to

1

time that all operations were now combined operations, with the implied corollary that the warfare of one service alone hardly justified any broad examination.

Such a view, however, would be a long way from reality. Though all naval operations of World War II fit into the overall picture of grand strategy, there were many, some of great importance, which were designed and executed with little reference to the other services, excepting always in the case of the British Navy the cooperation of those Royal Air Force formations that are allocated to maritime warfare. The Battle of the Atlantic, for example, though affected by the bombing of Germany, can well be examined without direct reference to the operations of armies and air forces, other than Coastal Command and the air components of the Allied navies. And on the Allied side the supply of munitions to North Russia was a purely naval affair insofar as fighting was concerned. So too was the American submarine campaign against Japanese warships and seaborne supplies, a campaign of remarkable success against both types of target, but one that could be so little publicized at the time that the magnitude of its contribution to Japan's downfall was not readily appreciated. And even in those operations where naval, land, and air forces were closely interwoven, the naval aspects may still be profitably studied as such, provided due regard is paid to the part played by the other services. The latter requirement is comparatively simple when dealing with the most spectacular and difficult of all forms of combined operation, a landing against opposition. It is less obvious but still important when dealing with those many operations in which the actions of naval forces are still strongly, though less intimately, affected by the needs and actions of armies and air forces.

These are the facts that justify a study of the maritime operations of 1939–1945 from the naval angle: from a point of view compounded of sea experience and a knowledge of past naval events. For such a study it is as well to start by considering what that point of view was in 1939: how the accepted doctrine of naval warfare had been built up and where it then stood.

The main purpose of a navy had long been understood: to safeguard the passage of one's armies overseas; to defend territory against seaborne invasion; to throttle the enemy's seaborne trade and supplies and to defend one's own trade and supplies. The two former objectives, as the more purely military, were originally the most important, and they were, and are, always vital. But, for Great Britain, trade and supplies had often been of more immediate importance. Threats of invasion, though sometimes the chief preoccupation, were seldom prolonged; and British armies were not usually on such a scale as to make

2

transporting them overseas an unduly hazardous operation. But in the eighteenth century trade, as a moneymaking concern, contributed largely to the warlike power of Great Britain; and in the twentieth century supplies of food and raw materials were essential to the national life and were sometimes almost equally important to the fighting strength of the enemy. It was only natural, therefore, that the unceasing requirements of trade warfare, and particularly of trade defense, often seemed the main preoccupation of the British Navy.

The relative importance of trade and transports, however, did not as a rule concern naval strategists unduly, for it so happened that many of the measures needed for controlling the sea routes were equally applicable to military and commercial traffic. Most of these measures could, in fact, be considered as part of the business of "command of the sea," at one time the phrase most commonly used to describe the principal aim of naval forces. So succinct a phrase could not, of course, be a true description of all that was required; but throughout the history of the English and British navies down to the beginning of the twentieth century the straightforward idea conveyed by this expression was only a slight oversimplification of the state of affairs for which they strove. That this command might often be in dispute between rival navies was admitted, as was also the fact that even the greatest preponderance of naval power could not prevent all attacks on seaborne trade by enemy ships working sporadically. But it was not unreasonable to suppose that a state of affairs might be brought about in which the sea routes throughout the world could be used for the transport of armies, while at the same time the use of these routes could be denied to the enemy.

The underlying facts making this simple conception practicable were the freedom and the secrecy with which warships could move about the oceans. If one combatant was so ill-advised as to disperse all his forces to attack his enemy's trade or transports or to defend his own, they were liable to be defeated piecemeal by a more concentrated fighting force operating secretly. The only way to prevent defeat was to form a concentration superior to anything the enemy was likely to employ, and so to arrange things as to bring his force or forces to action before they could do serious harm to one's own dispersed interests. Fleets were therefore formed and were drilled to fight as a whole, and on the operations of these battle fleets almost everything else depended. The battle fleet did not, except in such early events as the defeat of the Spanish Armada, constitute the whole navy. It contained the bulk of the ships of the line, ships embodying the greatest fighting strength practicable and necessarily of large size; but there were many operations, both offensive and defensive, for which considerable numbers of smaller ships could profitably be dispersed. The risk these smaller and

3

weaker ships ran was reduced to a minimum by the cover provided by the battle fleet; and if, instead of being dispersed, they had been added to the battle fleet the increase of fighting power would have been largely offset by the difficulty of handling so large a number of ships in company.

The central conception of naval strategy, then, was of two battle fleets contending for command of the sea. In particular circumstances the dictates of geography often called for more than one battle fleet in each navy; the Channel and Mediterranean fleets of both England and France, for example, were sometimes of almost equal importance. But even then French strategy was often concerned with concentrating the Brest and Toulon fleets; and it was the well-established British doctrine that if, despite all endeavors, such an amalgamation could not be prevented, all British fleets and battle squadrons must fall back on the mouth of the Channel and concentrate there.

In practice, however, the struggle for command was usually rather one-sided. If both belligerents wished wholeheartedly to gain command, a battle ensued and the issue was decided—at least for the immediate future. But more often the fleet of a nation not vitally dependent on the use of the sea routes preferred to dispute command rather than try to gain it; that is to say, it spent most of its time in harbor out of reach of the enemy's guns and came out only when the weather or some other circumstances made a sortie possible with little risk from the opposing fleet and with some chance of doing damage to the enemy's dispersed forces or shipping. Throughout the sailing-ship era the answer to these attempts to dispute command was blockade, the maintenance of a fleet either directly off the enemy's port so as to keep him in, or so positioned as to ensure bringing him to action if he put to sea.

A fleet of the eighteenth century had little to fear except from the weather or from a superior enemy fleet, but with the invention of torpedo craft, both surface and submarine, a strong battle fleet was seen to be far less invulnerable than hitherto, with the result that it became too hazardous to maintain a blockading position at sea close to the enemy's port. At the same time the higher speeds and decreased dependence on weather conferred by steam propulsion seemed to give a weaker fleet better chances of striking at isolated enemy forces with less risk of being brought to action by its stronger adversary. It would not have been surprising, therefore, if the main ideas of naval strategy had had to be severely modified as a result of the marked changes in ships and weapons of the nineteenth and early twentieth centuries. But it so happened that in the war of 1914–1918 they remained very much what they had been in the days of sail. For this the chief reason was the

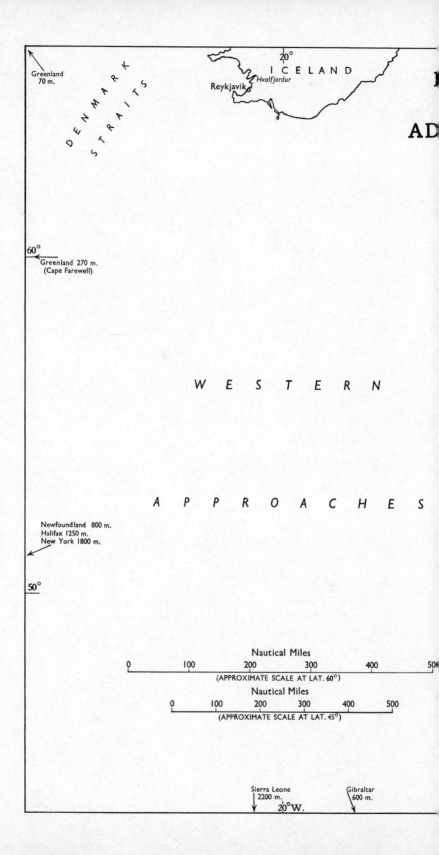

Greenland
70 m.

20°
ICELAND
Hvalfjordur
Reykjavik

D E N M A R K
S T R A I T S

AD

60°
Greenland 270 m.
(Cape Farewell)

W E S T E R N

A P P R O A C H E S

Newfoundland 800 m.
Halifax 1250 m.
New York 1800 m.

50°

Nautical Miles
0   100   200   300   400   500
(APPROXIMATE SCALE AT LAT. 60°)
Nautical Miles
0   100   200   300   400   500
(APPROXIMATE SCALE AT LAT. 45°)

Sierra Leone
2200 m.   Gibraltar
                    600 m.
20°W.

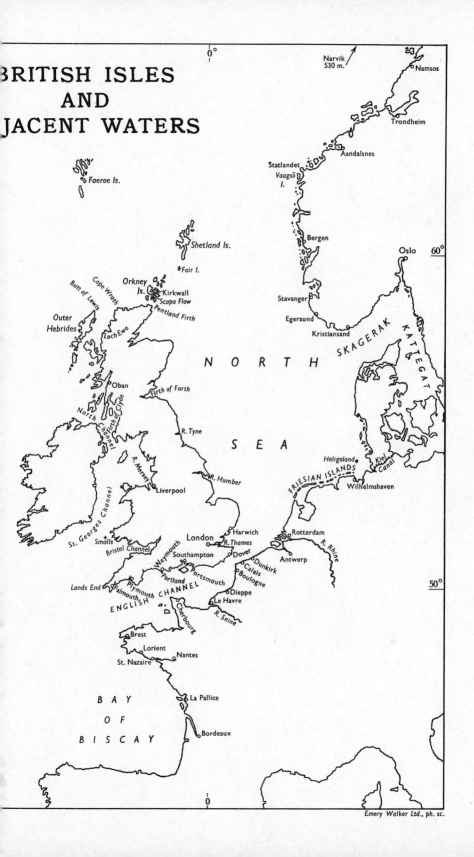

BRITISH ISLES
AND
ADJACENT WATERS

Narvik
530 m.

Namsos

Trondheim

Aandalsnes

Statlandet
Vaagsö
I.

Bergen

Oslo   60°

Stavanger

Egersund

Kristiansand

Faeroe Is.

Shetland Is.

Fair I.

Orkney Is.
Kirkwall
Scapa Flow
Pentland Firth

Cape Wrath
Butt of Lewis

Outer
Hebrides

Loch Ewe

Oban

Firth of Forth

North Channel

Firth of Clyde

R. Tyne

N O R T H

S K A G E R A K

K A T T E G A T

S E A

Heligoland

Kiel
Canal

FRIESIAN ISLANDS

Wilhelmshaven

R. Mersey

Liverpool

R. Humber

St. Georges Channel

Smalls

Bristol Channel

London

Harwich
R. Thames

Rotterdam

R. Rhine

Antwerp

Weymouth
Southampton
Portsmouth

Dover
Dunkirk
Calais
Boulogne

Lands End
Falmouth
Plymouth
Portland

ENGLISH CHANNEL

Cherbourg

Dieppe
Le Havre

R. Seine

Brest

Lorient

St. Nazaire

Nantes

La Pallice

B A Y

O F

B I S C A Y

Bordeaux

decided advantage conferred on Great Britain by her geographical position relative to Germany.

The naval strategy of 1914–1918 was, in fact, very simple. The British Navy's aims were, first, to keep open the trade routes of the British Empire in general and to safeguard the supplies to the British Isles in particular; and, second, to prevent seaborne invasion of Great Britain. The latter object is put second not because of its lesser importance, but because in the circumstances of the time it seemed easier to achieve. There was also the need to prevent the Germans from using their sea power to assist their army in subjugating France and the Low Countries.

All these were defensive aims. Offensively there was little to be done by sea power which could have any immediate effect on Germany. To send a small expeditionary force across the Channel to fight alongside the French was not difficult if the navy was successfully filling its defensive role; and in due course it should be possible to conquer all German overseas possessions, as the enemy would be unable to reinforce them. But neither of these measures would contribute much to Germany's immediate overthrow. Nor could there be much immediate effect from the British Navy's other main offensive effort, the throttling of Germany's seaborne supplies. No doubt, though, there were already those who foresaw the great and perhaps decisive effect the latter might have in the long run if diplomatic difficulties with important neutrals, particularly the United States, could be overcome.

What made the strategy to achieve all these objects, defensive and offensive, a comparatively simple affair was the fact that nearly all the sea routes concerned lay outside the North Sea. Close blockade of the German fleet in the old way was no longer possible, but most of the British aims could be achieved if the enemy's battle fleet could be prevented from passing the Strait of Dover or emerging into the Atlantic north of Scotland.

There might be danger from individual German cruisers that succeeded in breaking out of the North Sea (perhaps armed merchantmen disguised as neutrals), or from those already in foreign waters. But the British cruiser strength was sufficient to deal with this menace in the areas where trade was dense—provided always that the British cruisers could be free from interference by German capital ships. Elsewhere, outside the focal areas of trade, the enemy's harvest could be only a meager one, and even there British cruisers were in some instances able to bring the enemy ships to action.

With a superior battle fleet based on Scapa Flow in the Orkneys, the problem of preventing the German fleet from leaving the North Sea had few complexities. For the Germans to go through the Strait of

5

Dover was clearly so hazardous that the threat posed by mines, submarines, destroyers, and a squadron of old battleships would probably be enough to deter them from making the attempt. And if the more open route to the north of Scotland had been attempted, the danger of interception by the British Grand Fleet would have been high; although it was some years before the Germans realized the fact, this danger was much increased by the use that was made of intercepted German wireless signals.

Almost everything, then, turned as of old on the power of the rival battle fleets. To what extent the North Sea itself could be commanded by either side might be open to dispute. It was fairly certain, however, that the British fleet had sufficient command to prevent an invasion of the British Isles, and perhaps equally certain that unless the German battle fleet could be destroyed it would not be possible to attack the more restricted German coast in force, either in the North Sea or in the Baltic.

The result was that for the first two years of the war naval strategy settled down into almost stable equilibrium. The Germans believed that little could be done unless they could overcome the British battle fleet. If they could do that, there seemed a good probability that the whole fabric of British strategy would crumble and that Britain would quickly admit herself defeated. But the preponderance of force against them was such that they could not hope to achieve this objective with their battle fleet alone. What they did hope to do was to reduce the British fleet by mine and submarine to something like equality with theirs, and then defeat it in battle. But neither of these weapons, though they exerted an important influence on the freedom of movement of the Grand Fleet, and in so doing reduced its chances of coming to grips with the enemy, achieved much material success. The balance of force between the two fleets remained substantially unaltered, and the Battle of Jutland merely confirmed the existing state of affairs.

Two important modifications to the main lines of British strategy, however, were brought about as the war progressed. One was due to the development of the German submarine attack on merchant shipping, and the other arose from the difficulty of defending the Scandinavian trade against raids by the German fleet.

It had always been a cardinal principle of British strategy that sporadic attack on trade, the *guerre de course*, could never be more than a nuisance (though perhaps a serious nuisance) provided proper measures were taken to guard against it. But the use of submarines for attacking merchant ships, sinking them without warning, presented a new, or apparently new, problem of which no immediate solution seemed possible. German submarines could not be prevented from leav-

6

ing the North Sea, and their ability to operate on the Atlantic and Mediterranean trade routes was limited only by their fuel endurance. The answer to this new danger was eventually found in a reversion to the old practice of sailing merchant ships in convoy, a proceeding that had been supposed impracticable with the average steam cargo vessel, but which, when tried, was found both practicable and effective. German submarines at that time had no other thought than to attack singly and submerged (if there was any risk of return fire), and against such tactics even a light escort was fairly effective. Though a submarine might achieve one successful attack on a convoy, she was in considerable danger of counterattack by depth charges, and in view of her low submerged speed she would inevitably drop astern of the convoy and probably lose touch with it.

The convoy system, introduced in the first instance for trial, was gradually extended as the difficulties of organization were overcome and the number of vessels available as escorts (destroyers and sloops) increased. When fully developed it reduced the losses of shipping to a figure that, though still serious, was easily exceeded by new building. Some cargoes were still sent to the bottom, but without decisive effect on the war effort; and of the many thousands of troops transported to Europe from the United States not one man was lost.

The other important strategical problem of the latter part of the war, defense of the Scandinavian trade against attack by heavy German forces, was to a large extent a by-product of the submarine problem. Until the introduction of convoy, the Scandinavian trade had been too scattered to make it worth the German fleet's while to attempt an attack on it, for such an attempt involved serious risk of being engaged by a superior British fleet. But with regular convoys plying to and fro it was a different matter. There was a good chance of a German raiding force making a successful attack and getting away unscathed. This strategy was attempted, successfully, first with two cruisers, then with four destroyers (while another four made an unsuccessful attempt against the east coast route), and then, as the strengths of escorts and covering forces were increased, with the whole German battle fleet, the battle cruisers forming the striking force. The latter attempt failed because of some miscalculations and mishaps, but the problem presented to the defense was a serious one. In view of the number of convoys involved it did not seem practicable to cover each one with the whole British battle fleet, and any weaker covering force risked destruction by the German battle fleet. Had the German fleet maintained an enterprising offensive spirit for the remainder of the war and had the war lasted longer, the only sound solution would have been to increase the size and reduce the number of these convoys to an extent that would have

7

enabled the battle fleet to cover each one. But that would, of course, have reduced the carrying power, already barely adequate, of the shipping available for this important route.

The problem of protecting the Scandinavian convoys in no way changed the traditional view that the battle fleet was the basis of naval strategy, as submarine attack on trade had at one time seemed likely to do. What it did was to show how fortunate Great Britain was as regards her other trade routes because of her geographical position vis-à-vis Germany, and how difficult it might be to assert a general command of the sea in less favorable circumstances against an active enemy fleet, even though it was inferior to the British.

In the years that followed 1918 it was natural for the British Navy to take stock of strategical ideas in the light of experience gained in four years of war, and then to consider what modifications of those ideas might be expected as a result of recent and prospective developments of materiel. Of these the most important was clearly the improvement of aircraft and the weapons they carried. Rapid strides were being made in this field, and there was little conclusive experience to guide speculation, for the war had stopped before flying had had any serious effect on naval operations. Aircraft had assisted in antisubmarine operations near the coast, but had done little to modify battle fleet operations, despite the considerable development of airships for scouting by the Germans.

As already shown, the main plank of traditional naval strategy, the predominance of the battle fleet, had been confirmed by war experience to a degree that seemed remarkable in the face of many prophecies of the battleship's doom. The battleship, with the assistance of destroyers to screen it from submarines and of protector paravanes to ward off mines, had retained sufficient freedom of movement for the British fleet to oppose any attempts of the German fleet to disrupt British use of the sea routes or to make any profitable use of those routes for themselves outside their own coastal waters and the Baltic. Other British forces had therefore been able to stop German seaborne trade with the outside world (so far as relations with neutrals allowed), to prevent invasion, and to protect British trade and overseas expeditions. Protection of trade and transports, which developed for the most part into defense against submarines, required a very large effort in the shape of convoy escorts and other antisubmarine measures, so that it came in time to seem almost more important than the operations of the fleet; but all the antisubmarine measures would have been of little avail had the German fleet been free to attack the forces engaged in them.

Perhaps the most remarkable feature of the battleship's retention of its predominance was the failure of underwater weapons, the torpedo and the mine, to inflict casualties. It was not that hits by these weapons could be disregarded. On the contrary, it was probable that two hits would sink any new battleship and one hit, any old one. What was so notable was that so few hits were made. The moored mine, particularly the contemporary pattern of German moored mine much feared in the early part of the war, was found to be almost innocuous to ships running paravanes. Daylight torpedo attack by surface craft (destroyers and the larger German torpedo boats) failed to achieve anything worthwhile, largely because it seemed suicidal so close to the short ranges by which alone it could be made effectual; and the visibility of approaching torpedo tracks also helped to discount it. Night attack seemed scarcely more effective, mainly because of the difficulty experienced by torpedo craft in finding their quarry—notably the German torpedo craft during the night after the Battle of Jutland, though the British craft on the same occasion made some chance contacts which achieved minor successes. And, finally, submarine attack, very destructive to slow merchant ships, seemed unable to do much against battleships steaming at high speed and zigzagging, screened by destroyers. Torpedo attack by aircraft was still in its infancy and there was as yet no practical experience on which to base an estimate of its effectiveness.

What was clear, then, was that experience had shown a fleet of modern battleships to be capable of sufficient freedom of movement to fulfill its traditional purpose—at all events under the geographical conditions of World War I. The chief threat to its existence, the torpedo, had not come up to the expectations of its backers, and it seemed reasonable to suppose that a battleship's constructional protection against underwater explosions would at least keep pace with the explosive power of underwater weapons.

With confirmation of the ability of the battle fleet still to dominate the scene in its vicinity, two further major questions needed answering: Could the British fleet provide effective cover for minor naval forces if it lacked the geographical advantages of 1914–1918? And would the fleet be able to maintain its predominant position in the face of such air forces as might be developed by the time war again broke out?

The geographical question was a troublesome one containing many uncertainties. The protection of the Scandinavian convoys had shown how difficult it might be to cover trade or transports that had to pass within striking distance of enemy bases; and striking distance might cover a very large area if the enemy bases had comparatively free access to the open oceans. The conclusion reached by the bulk of naval opinion, however, was that the battle fleet could still fulfill its purpose. Improvements in propelling machinery and acceptance of the risks associated with a larger proportion of sea time (which seemed justified by wartime experience) should enable the fleet to be more constantly in a covering position at sea if a suitable harbor position was lacking. It might have to rely more on the deterrent risk to the enemy of being intercepted on return from an operation than on an assurance of meeting him before he could do any harm at all. And there might be the necessity to reduce the number, and increase the size, of bodies of merchant ships and transports, and perhaps to sail them on very roundabout routes, all of which would impose an uneconomical use of none too plentiful shipping. But accepting these disadvantages, there was justification for believing that the fleet could do everything required of it, and a virtual certainty that no other force could be adequate for the purpose in the face of an enemy using heavy ships.

The serious difficulty of keeping in check a hostile fleet based, for example, on the Atlantic coast of France or Spain, would be created mainly by the temptingness of the prizes offered to the enemy in the shape of important Atlantic convoys. If convoy could be dispensed with, as it was from 1914 to 1916, and merchant shipping could be scattered over widely dispersed routes, the opportunities of capturing or sinking a large number of ships before being brought to action would be much reduced. The covering operations of the British fleet would therefore have been concerned mainly with the passage of overseas military expeditions (operations much less frequent and therefore easier to accomplish), and the predominant position of the battle fleet would have been still further enhanced. But the chances of being able to dispense with convoy were not rated high. It might be possible if reliance could be placed on the international agreement that forbade submarines to sink merchant ships without warning—but there was not much faith in that. And whether or not convoy would be needed as a protection against air attack was still unresolved. So it seemed probable that the most challenging responsibility of the fleet must be allowed for: the covering of a large number of convoys, military, supply, and mercantile, against attacks by enemy fleets or squadrons, whatever the geographical circumstances. And it was concluded that, so far as the warfare of seaborne vessels was concerned, there was little doubt that the British fleet could do all that was required, although there might well be anxious and arduous times ahead of it.

The effects of aircraft on naval strategy were far more difficult to assess. Though some useful material data could be obtained (the American trials against the old German battleship *Ostfriesland*, for example), it was not possible to simulate the attacks of aircraft against determined opposition, and it was extremely difficult to arrive at realistic estimates of the strategical setting. It is, in fact, the strategical questions that are always the most troublesome in appraising a new weapon. It may not be too difficult to form some idea of the relative values of different weapons or different types of craft once they are on the scene of action. But it is nearly always very difficult to say whether a new device can be relied on to be where it is wanted at the right time and in the right strength. It was the strategical aspect that had discounted the value of German submarines against British battleships, particularly in the early part of the war when there were still inadequate numbers of destroyers for screening and depth charges were only just being introduced. There seemed little doubt that the submarine was a very deadly weapon if only it could be in the right place at the right time. But in practice it was found that the British battle fleet, in doing all that was required of it, was seldom seriously endangered. Its freedom of movement, even in so comparatively confined an area as the North Sea, when opposed to the virtual immobility of a submerged submarine, called for a far larger number of submarines than Germany possessed if a really deadly menace was to be presented.

As with the submarine before 1914, so with the aircraft after 1918, it was the strategical aspect of the new weapon which was the hardest to assess. But even in the tactical aspects there was much room for discussion, and there was in fact much heated argument between the extreme exponents of rival claims. Setting aside the views of the extremists, however, and accepting, as did the majority of naval officers, that aircraft would be a very important element in naval forces, the main problems that seemed to require solution were: What part would aircraft play in battle fleet strategy? Was it possible that aircraft, perhaps in conjunction with submarines, would succeed, where submarines by themselves had failed, in preventing the use of the sea routes by merchant ships and transports, regardless of anything the opposing fleet and the forces acting under its cover could do?

It was realized that the answer to the first of the above questions must depend in the first instance on the rival power of battleships and aircraft when fighting against each other. If it could be established that a force of aircraft could sink or disable a force of battleships representing an equivalent proportion of national effort, it might then be found that the main concentration of naval force should be composed of aircraft rather than battleships. There would still be a battle fleet under whose cover the control of the sea routes would be effected, but it would be an aerial one, and as such the strategy it would pursue would naturally differ considerably from that of a fleet of surface vessels.

On this main tactical question the evidence prior to 1939 was inconclusive. The aircraft's methods of attack—high-level bombing for penetration, dive-bombing, and torpedo attack—might all inflict serious

11

damage; but the extent to which attack could be warded off by gunfire and by protecting fighters worked from aircraft carriers was impossible to gauge in peacetime. And almost equally difficult to assess was the proportionate number of aircraft to battleships in terms of national effort, though an estimate that forty-three medium bombers (at this time, small twin-engined machines) were the equivalent of one battleship in this respect was made by a committee in 1936; this estimate, accepted by service opinion, gave some basis for discussion. The only general conclusion was that in an action between battleships and aircraft (of roughly equivalent value being always understood) it was by no means certain the latter would have the best of it, and that therefore there were not sufficient grounds for putting one's resources into an aerial battle fleet.

If on tactical grounds the question of battleships versus aircraft seemed in the balance, on strategical grounds there was little doubt that a fleet of battleships would still be needed, at all events by Great Britain. Whoever the enemy, it was almost certain that there would be large areas of sea, some of them embracing important focal points of the sea routes, outside the effective range of shore-based aircraft, either British or the enemy's or both. And apart from the technically effective range, air navigation over the open sea was still very imperfect, and this deficiency, added to the vagaries of weather and visibility, made it by no means certain that aircraft could bring battleships to action where and when they wished to. It was concluded, therefore, that there would be circumstances in which enemy battleships could do untold harm undeterred by anything British aircraft could do, and that this danger could be prevented only by battleships. Equally there would be circumstances in which British forces would be unable to pursue offensive operations, the transport of military expeditions, or an attack on enemy trade in the face of enemy battleships, unless they too possessed ships of that type.

In the light of subsequent events, one factor in the above arguments should be noted: they referred almost entirely to shore-based aircraft. Aircraft carriers were in existence and were considered an important part of any battle fleet both for attack and for defense—as well, of course, as for finding the enemy, which at that time was probably considered their most important function. But carrier-borne aircraft in attack were thought of as auxiliary to the gunfire of the battleships, even though of outstanding value for such matters as slowing down an unwilling enemy to enable him to be brought within gun range. It was assumed that to try to build and maintain carriers and their aircraft in sufficient numbers to dominate a fleet composed mainly of battleships, even supposing that tactical experience showed such dominance to be possible, would be an uneconomical expenditure of effort.

Such were British views on naval strategy in their generalized form. Strategy, however, can never come to life until it envisages a potential enemy and a geographical setting. These were lacking in the fifteen years following the Treaty of Versailles except for the possibility that Japan might one day be an enemy, and even this notion was subject to the "no major war within ten years" rule which continued to be the British government's assumption. But with the rise of Hitler the outlook soon changed, and it became clear that the possibility of war with Germany must be faced once more.

On the other side of the North Sea the strategical views of the renascent German Navy were at first only nebulous. Here all was controlled by Admiral Raeder who had been head of the navy since 1928. Like others of his class in the armed forces, he had adjusted himself to the National Socialist regime, for it had brought with it the enthusiasm of rearmament; and politics, he thought, could be kept out of the navy. Able, experienced, and deeply religious, with firm views on morale and discipline, he was unable at first to believe that war with Britain was a possibility; Hitler had several times told him that it was, in fact, out of the question. Because of this conviction, the original setting assumed for his rebuilding plans was the unlikely one of war against France in isolation. By 1937, however, he realized that war with Britain might have to be faced, however unwelcome, and that he must plan accordingly. For these plans the deadline given by Hitler, who now admitted the possibility, was 1944.

The project adopted by Raeder was to build what he called a balanced fleet, that is, a navy that, though small, had the same proportion as the British in ships of every class, except in submarines where the proportion would be somewhat higher. As Raeder's strategical arguments justifying this proposal were well set out, critics have sometimes concluded that he was a sound strategist; but it seems that he was not so much sound in the German setting as orthodox by British standards. After the war he admitted that, had he foreseen the acceleration of Hitler's ambitions, a strategy that put much stronger emphasis on submarines might have been sounder. But all that remains speculative, for war came when his ambitious shipbuilding program had only just been begun.

13

2

TRADE DEFENSE, I: *The First Seven Months*

I T WAS IN September 1939 that Hitler's invasion of Poland finally provoked Great Britain and France into war, in fulfillment of pledges given six months earlier. At the time there was little offensive action open to these allies which was likely to show any immediate results, and the scope of any such action was soon to be further restricted by Poland's complete defeat. It was essential that the enemy's power should be opposed and overthrown if the world was to be saved from German domination; but how that was to be achieved could hardly be foretold at the time even by the most farseeing. One fact, however, stood out clearly. If Germany was to be defeated, British power to make offensive war must be increased manyfold beyond the ineffectual level at which it then stood, a feat that could be achieved only if the sea routes to the British Isles could be kept open for the importation of essential food and raw materials and such munitions as could be bought abroad. And not only imports, for there must be exports to pay for these things. It was trade defense, then, that was the major concern of the British Navy when war broke out.

With what was British trade threatened? If the experience of World War I was to be the guide, the most serious threat would be from submarine attack. In 1936, however, the German government had voluntarily affirmed its adherence to the international pact that imposed severe restrictions on submarine operations against merchant ships. There were strong doubts as to the value of this German promise, but there was at least the possibility that it would not be broken immediately. The menace from submarines, therefore, might at first be less deadly than it had been in 1917 and 1918; but meanwhile there were evident dangers from surface ships which must be faced at once.

The problem presented here differed considerably from that of

14

twenty-five years earlier. The Germans had only two capital ships in commission, the battle cruisers *Scharnhorst* and *Gneisenau*, and these, though good ships and fast, had lighter armaments than any British capital ships. The British fleet, on the other hand, totaled twelve battleships, three battle cruisers, and four large aircraft carriers.[1] There were in addition seven French capital ships, though five of them were rather too old to be fully effective. So there could be no hope for the Germans, even if the Italians joined them, that they would be able to contest the issue fleet against fleet, unless with the growth of air power the German air arm could make up for the lack of ships. The latter was, perhaps, a possibility; though in fact so dispirited was the German naval command at having to go to war five years earlier than had been planned, and so bad was the cooperation between the navy and the air force, that the danger of this eventuality was far less than might have been supposed. In any event the enemy was unlikely to wait for so doubtful an issue, and meanwhile there was the present fact that the newest and largest German ships, the two battle cruisers, the three so-called pocket battleships, and the three 8-inch-gun cruisers[2] could all, unlike their predecessors of the earlier war, cruise well into the Atlantic; and with an organization for refueling from supply ships in mid-ocean they could keep the sea for long periods. In the more distant waters the most troublesome were likely to be the pocket battleships, which were known to have a very high endurance; though only of 10,000 tons, they carried six 11-inch guns, a seemingly overpowering armament against a British cruiser. But being so heavily gunned they could not be very fast and had little armor, and so were unlikely to risk working for any length of time in areas where they might meet British capital ships. On the vital North Atlantic trade routes, therefore, the faster and more powerful battle cruisers and the 8-inch cruisers were the greatest potential danger. But wherever they intended to operate, any of these German ships that could escape out of the North Sea, either singly or in company, would present a grave problem. It could not be known

[1] Battleships: *Nelson* and *Rodney*, nine 16-inch, 22 knots; *Warspite, Barham, Malaya, Queen Elizabeth,* and *Valiant,* eight 15-inch, 24 knots (the two latter in hand for modernization); *Revenge, Royal Sovereign, Royal Oak, Resolution,* and *Ramillies,* eight 15-inch, 20 knots. Battle cruisers: *Hood,* eight 15-inch; *Repulse* and *Renown,* six 15-inch. Aircraft carriers: *Ark Royal, Glorious, Courageous,* and *Furious.* There were also the carriers *Eagle* and *Hermes,* with considerably smaller aircraft complements.

[2] Only one of the 8-inch cruisers was immediately ready for service, but the other two were expected to be in shape very shortly. Though purporting to comply with the 10,000-ton treaty limitation on this type of ship, they were in fact 14,500 tons standard and 18,500 tons deep load. See p. 53 n. 2, below, for definition of displacements.

that the views of the German naval command on this subject were far from ambitious, with no present intention of risking more than the pocket battleships in commerce warfare.

The danger to British trade from German ships at large in the Atlantic would not have been so serious had it been possible to disregard the submarine threat and disperse shipping over the widest possible variety of tracks. That would have left only the ends of the routes and the passages of narrow waters as areas of grave danger, and these would have been comparatively easy to defend. In the more open spaces the enemy ship's chances of sighting a merchant ship would not have been numerous, and it was hoped that a radio warning from any ship assailed would enable others to be routed clear. But the submarine danger could not be disregarded; convoys might have to be formed for the main Atlantic routes. Outward bound they could be dispersed after passing through the potential submarine danger area, but homeward they must be assembled at ports overseas. If an enemy ship were to sight one of these convoys disaster might well ensue. Despite the preponderance in capital ships, it was not possible to escort each convoy in adequate strength to repel the attack of, say, two of the possible German raiders. Convoys that seemed particularly endangered could be given battleship escort, but the majority had to do without.

This was the strategical setting in which the British Navy had to be handled by Admiral Sir Dudley Pound, first sea lord and chief of the Naval Staff, who had assumed office a few months previously. To wide experience both in command and in staff duties he added abilities that enabled him to keep a clear view of widespread and diverse forces and a sureness of touch in planning their operations. And because knowledge of enemy operations might sometimes be available at the Admiralty in such quantity and at such short notice that it could not well be passed to admirals afloat in time for them to initiate urgently needed action, he had on occasion to direct individual forces as well as plan on a worldwide scale. In addition, he had the by no means easy task of applying his sound judgment of naval affairs in restraint of the impulsiveness of Winston Churchill, now once more, after twenty-four years, first lord of the Admiralty and soon to be prime minister. In this he succeeded admirably, while maintaining their mutual confidence and affection. All these heavy responsibilities he was to bear with steady equability until, four years later, he succumbed to the strain, dying on Trafalgar Day, 1943.

Of the problems now confronting Admiral Pound, the first was to prevent German warships from leaving the North Sea. Should they succeed in doing so, it would then have to be considered what heavy forces could justifiably be detached to bring them to action, or at least

to keep them clear of the areas where merchant ships, whether convoyed or independent, were most numerous. If such operations were
called for, carrier-borne aircraft would be of particular value in searching for the enemy. And perhaps, if he was found, their torpedo aircraft
would succeed in slowing him down. It would also have to be decided
how an inadequate cruiser strength could best be employed: whether in
searching for the enemy in combination with the heavy ships, or in
strengthening convoy escorts, or, in waters beyond the convoy routes,
simply doing what they could to tackle the enemy or keep him at bay
until help arrived.[3]

All these difficulties, however, would be kept within bounds if the
raiders could be met before they reached the open ocean, and this was
the duty that now fell to the Home Fleet under Admiral Sir Charles
Forbes. Of fighting strength the fleet had no lack, but just how that
strength was to be employed presented many problems. Of these the
main were, first, how it was to get news of enemy movements in time,
and, second, what harbors it should use for rest and replenishment.

For getting news of enemy movements the Home Fleet had one
notable advantage over the Grand Fleet of 1914: aircraft could now
fly far enough to stretch right across the North Sea. In 1914 the Grand
Fleet had relied on cruiser patrols in the first instance, but the submarine menace had soon forced these patrols so far back to the northwestward that they were no longer effective as a scouting line for the
fleet. Thereafter the fleet had the great good fortune of being able to
rely on warning of enemy movements being given by the interception
and deciphering of German radio messages. This was one of the main
controlling factors of Grand Fleet strategy until, much later, the enemy
gained an inkling of what was happening and severely restricted his
radio signaling. But by that time, the last year of the war, the failure
of this source of information was to some extent made good by another. British submarines had by then been given radio equipment
powerful enough to reach England from Heligoland Bight. Thus they
could be stationed to watch for and report the enemy's egress, though,
as they were kept at some distance from his ports by minefields, there
could never be complete reliance that he would not slip out unobserved.

In 1939 submarines could again be used for watching enemy waters.
At the outbreak of the war minefields were less troublesome than in
1918, but there were improved antisubmarine devices and weapons

---

[3] Excluding the ships of the Home and Mediterranean fleets and the Northern
Patrol, the following cruisers were available for trade protection in the Atlantic
and Indian oceans at the outbreak of the war, and were based on various ports
overseas for that purpose: five 8-inch, eight-gun; two 8-inch, six gun; four 6-inch,
twelve-gun; five 6-inch, eight-gun; four 6-inch, six-gun; and two 6-inch, five-gun.

to be contended with. What could be done by submarines, therefore, was much the same as before; that is to say, they could be stationed to watch and could remain on their stations in all weathers, and there was some likelihood of their sighting and reporting enemy ships. They might also be able to sink, or at least damage, the enemy with torpedoes and so frustrate his design at the outset. But neither were there enough of them nor were they sufficiently immune from countermeasures to ensure that nothing could put to sea unseen. Since, though very valuable, they could not, therefore, provide all that was required, and since the improved technique of ciphering and German security measures precluded any likelihood of aid from intercepted signals, it was decided to rely on aircraft to provide the main outpost line for the fleet.

Aircraft were not, however, available either in the numbers or in the types that were desired. The Royal Air Force was heavily taxed in building up its strength to meet the Luftwaffe in the expected war of bombing each other's towns, and it could be argued that Fighter Command was its most important commitment and that Bomber Command was almost equally high in priority. The latter, not yet allowed to bomb targets ashore, tried also at first to contribute something to keeping German warships off the trade routes by bombing them in harbor. A gallant and costly attack on Wilhelmshaven Roads and the entrance to the Kiel Canal on September 4 succeeded in hitting the *Admiral Scheer* (at Wilhelmshaven) with four bombs, though without serious effect for they failed to explode. But it was on Coastal Command, the section of the Royal Air Force specifically charged with meeting the requirements of maritime war, that the Admiralty must rely for reconnaissance, and this force was having a hard task in getting up to date. Ansons, of very restricted range, were its main equipment, and though there were some flying boats of longer range they were in very inadequate numbers. Fortunately, however, a supply of American-built Hudsons with a more satisfactory radius was coming forward, and as squadrons were reequipped with these the theoretical possibility of keeping all egress from the North Sea under observation became more nearly an accomplished fact.

The principle on which it was hoped to ensure finding the enemy was to establish a continuous patrol between Scotland and Norway which would sight any ship passing that way by daylight, and to supplement this daytime activity by searching the waters to the southward at dusk and to the northward at dawn. If the areas searched were sufficiently widespread (and that depended on the length of the night), there was a theoretical certainty that any ship trying to run through by night would either be sighted coming up from the southward at dusk or else

18

found in the northern area at dawn. Such patrols were practicable when war broke out in the autumn, but as winter advanced with its longer nights and bad weather (from which the aircraft of those days were by no means immune) the task became harder and the reliability of patrols more doubtful. It was not surprising, therefore, that when, in November, the Germans at last decided to send out the *Scharnhorst* and the *Gneisenau* to feint a raid into the Atlantic, they got clear of the North Sea unobserved. It was not till they reached the waters between the Faeroes and Iceland that contact was made with any British forces. Here they came upon and sank the armed merchant cruiser *Rawalpindi* of the Northern Patrol (see chap. 3). Though they were dimly sighted the same evening by a cruiser, they escaped to the northeastward. Thereafter, despite extensive searches by all ships of the Home Fleet and the aircraft of Coastal Command, the German ships remained undiscovered. Biding their time, they returned through the British search lines in thick weather and reached harbor still unobserved.

If the problem of getting news of the enemy's movements was theoretically a simple one, though with requirements that were difficult to fulfill in practice, the problem of what harbor the Home Fleet should use as its base was at first a very troublesome one indeed. A few years earlier it had been decided that the Firth of Forth should be the main base in a war against Germany, partly from the experience of the previous war (it gave a better chance of intercepting a German fleet that had made a short foray into the North Sea), and partly because the problem of air defense was increasing in importance. The latter was closely bound up with the air defense of Great Britain as a whole, and this in turn with the chain of radar stations that were being installed, in deep secrecy, to give warning of approaching enemy aircraft. It would clearly be an economy if the radar cover and fighter defense of the fleet's main base could be combined to a large extent with the defense of the Scottish industrial areas and of Edinburgh.

But when war was imminent and all the conflicting factors were examined more closely, it was decided that the Firth of Forth had serious disadvantages and that Scapa Flow would be the only satisfactory fleet base. For one thing, Scapa Flow offered much better chances of intercepting enemy ships outward bound for the Atlantic, and, for another, it was believed to be still, at that time, outside the range of German torpedo-carrying aircraft, which were the gravest potential danger the British Fleet had to face, a danger that would have been serious indeed had their range been increased and had Hitler done what he said, five years later and possibly with thoughts of Pearl

19

Harbor, he had wanted to do in 1938. At the end of a conference in July 1943 he described the demonstrations held at the Torpedo Experimental Establishment in 1938, when the navy and the air force, probably the only time they were ever in full agreement, tried to convince him that it would not be advisable to develop an aerial torpedo force. These cleverly executed demonstrations made Hitler abandon his plan to build up a strong aerial torpedo force which could have been used as a surprise measure at the outbreak of war. He would have gone ahead with these plans if the utter uselessness of this undertaking had not been proven to him so expertly at that time by means of "these wretched demonstrations."[4]

Satisfactory defenses for Scapa Flow, however, even against a light-scale air attack, could not be quickly improvised, and to make the anchorage secure required a considerable expenditure of manpower and material and much ingenuity to overcome difficulties and delays. Even the antisubmarine defenses were inadequate. They had been provided only on the scale thought sufficient for a harbor used for occasional refueling, and when it was decided that Scapa Flow should, after all, be the fleet's main base, too much weight was given to the prestige of its security during the earlier war. In consequence, neither the defenses of the main entrance nor the blocking of the unused eastern channels was adequate, and within a few weeks of the outbreak of war a boldly handled German submarine succeeded in entering on the surface by night, passing round the blockships in one of the eastern sounds. She then sank the battleship *Royal Oak* and escaped by the same route, still undetected.

If the antisubmarine security was low, the air defenses were virtually nonexistent. Guns, fighter aircraft, and the means of controlling them were all needed and were gradually supplied, the Fleet Air Arm assisting at the start with its obsolescent fighters. Before a reasonable degree of security was reached there were anxious times to be endured, and during all this time the fleet had to accept the hazards and the wear and tear of keeping to the sea as much as possible. It was, in fact, at sea when, in October, German bombers made their first attack. In this encounter, though it was on only a light scale, they damaged the old battleship *Iron Duke* (the base depot ship) and got away with little loss. After that there was no saying when further and more powerful raids might be made; because of this fear, and the proved inadequacy of the antisubmarine defenses, there was a period in the first winter of the war when it was thought best to move the fleet's base

[4] "Führer Conferences on Naval Affairs" (Admiralty trans., 1947), in *Brassey's Naval Annual, 1948*, p. 346.

farther to the westward. Loch Ewe, on the northern part of the Scottish west coast, was used from time to time in October and November, but the enemy knew that it had been similarly used in 1914, and had sent a submarine to lay some of the first magnetic mines in the entrance. There, in December, the *Nelson* was damaged and had to remain for some weeks much in need of dockyard repairs until, with the then primitive sweeping devices (see p. 30, below), the entrance could be cleared. Thereafter, for the rest of the winter, the Firth of Clyde became the fleet's anchorage, its shortcomings as an intercepting position being accepted so as to give the ships greater security and some much-needed rest. Here, also, some magnetic mines had been laid, but in this instance ineffectively. By March 1940, however, when the defenses of Scapa Flow had been substantially completed, it again became the Home Fleet's main base. Though air raids might still have to be suffered, they could now be opposed with some assurance; and in the event the only damage was one bomb hit on a cruiser (*Norfolk*) toward the end of that month.

Whatever dispositions the Home Fleet adopted, it could not, of course, grapple with enemy ships that were already well outside European waters when war was declared. Such movements had in fact occurred and were likely to result in situations that would cause deep anxiety. In August the two pocket battleships that were ready for service, *Deutschland* and *Graf Spee*, each with a supply ship, had left Germany in anticipation of war, the former for the western North Atlantic and the latter for the South Atlantic. They were ordered to keep off the trade routes during September because of Hitler's hopes of patching things up with the Western powers after the conquest of Poland, but at the end of the month both ships were ordered to start attacking trade.

In this enterprise the *Deutschland* enjoyed little success. Three ships, one British, one Norwegian, and one American, were encountered during the first fortnight of October, the first two being sunk and the American made prize. But that was the *Deutschland's* total harvest, and after further cruising on the northern edge of the Atlantic routes she returned to Germany, north of Iceland, in mid-November.[5]

Meanwhile the *Graf Spee* had fared somewhat better and was likely to be difficult to deal with. After a single capture off Pernambuco she worked for some time on the Cape of Good Hope route, sinking four

[5] After the *Deutschland's* return from this cruise, Hitler insisted that her name be changed (to *Lützow*) before she again set out, for he feared the psychological effect of having "Germany" sunk.

21

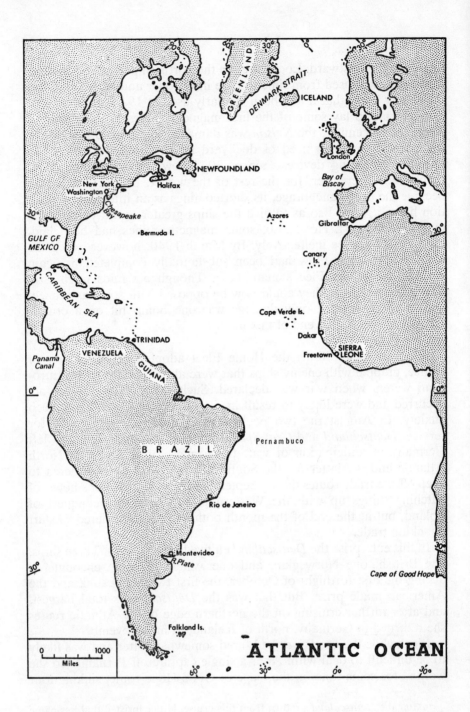

GREENLAND
DENMARK STRAIT
ICELAND
London
Bay of Biscay
NEWFOUNDLAND
New York
Washington
Halifax
Chesapeake Bay
Azores
Gibraltar
GULF OF MEXICO
Bermuda I.
Canary Is.
CARIBBEAN SEA
Cape Verde Is.
Dakar
Freetown
SIERRA LEONE
Panama Canal
TRINIDAD
VENEZUELA
GUIANA
B R A Z I L
Pernambuco
Rio de Janeiro
Montevideo
R. Plate
Cape of Good Hope
Falkland Is.

0   1000
Miles

ATLANTIC OCEAN

ships. Then, so as further to embarrass British strategy, she was ordered into the southern Indian Ocean, where she cruised for ten days south of Madagascar.

British dispositions had, of course, been made at the outset to cope, as adequately as seemed possible, with an enemy warship in southern waters, even before news of the sinking of a merchant ship on September 30 showed that there was in fact a pocket battleship at large. But these dispositions could not be considered fully satisfactory, for a reason that has already been mentioned. They depended necessarily on distributing the available cruiser strength among such focal areas of trade as were likely to be endangered. To cruiser strength was now added a force comprising the aircraft carrier *Ark Royal* and the battle cruiser *Renown*, the combination of searching and striking power most likely to bring a pocket battleship to book once her whereabouts were known. But this force, based on Freetown (Sierra Leone), could not be everywhere. Much must depend on cruisers. And there were grave doubts about the ability of cruisers, however numerous, to prevail against the 11-inch guns of a pocket battleship. If they could not, the only possible action once the enemy had been found would have been to keep him in sight until the *Renown* and the *Ark Royal* could bring him to action. But that might have entailed many days and nights of shadowing and, in those preradar days, many chances that the enemy would manage to break away by night or in thick weather.

These uncertainties, however, were soon to be resolved, for after her short incursion into the Indian Ocean, where she had sunk only one ship, the *Graf Spee* returned to the Cape–Sierra Leone route; and on December 2 she encountered the SS *Doric Star* which succeeded in reporting her by radio before being sunk. Knowing this, and thinking perhaps that his enemies had been thrown sufficiently off the scent, the captain of the *Graf Spee* seems to have decided that the time had come for a more ambitious adventure. This was to raid the waters off the river Plate, one of the most important focal areas of British trade in the outer seas, and one so far from any British base that defense of the shipping there was a task of peculiar difficulty. The British force to protect trade on the South American coast consisted, in fact, only of the 8-inch (six-gun) cruiser *Exeter* and the two 6-inch cruisers *Ajax* and *Achilles*, with the 8-inch cruiser *Cumberland* engaged in a self-refit at the Falkland Islands. As the mouth of the river Plate was presumed to be the point of greatest danger, it was in that vicinity that this squadron was concentrated when the *Doric Star*'s message was received, showing that the enemy was again back in the Atlantic. And when, on December 13, the *Graf Spee* at length appeared it was to meet the *Ajax* (Commodore Harwood), the *Achilles*, and the *Exeter*

23

in company. What followed was an outstanding triumph for British arms and altered considerably the complexion of trade defense in distant seas against the particular menace of the pocket battleship. Though the German 11-inch guns almost disabled the *Exeter*, and the *Ajax* had two of her four turrets put out of action, the *Graf Spee* preferred to seek shelter in neutral Montevideo rather than face her much smaller remaining antagonists and break through to seaward. The only significant damage she sustained was the wrecking of her distilling plant and bakery, both in the unarmored superstructure; but whether the damage occurred before or after she headed for harbor and possible repairs is not known, and it may well be that a more insidious effect on morale can be attributed to the operation orders under which she was working. "Enemy naval forces, even if inferior in strength, should only be attacked if this should be necessary to achieve the main objective [destruction of merchant shipping]."[6] Though this strategy was entirely logical, it cannot have tended to heighten the *Graf Spee*'s fighting spirit. However that may have been, the outstanding fact was that a pocket battleship had been defeated by cruisers alone without the help of heavy ships; and now that it had been done once there was confidence that it could, at need, be done again.

By the time, four days later, that the Uruguayan government compelled the *Graf Spee* to leave harbor or be interned, the *Cumberland* had replaced the damaged *Exeter* and there were rumors that the *Ark Royal* and the *Renown* were near at hand, though in fact they were still a thousand miles away, oiling at Rio de Janeiro. To the *Graf Spee*'s captain the chances of a breakout appeared negligible, and he therefore decided to blow up his ship outside the harbor with all remaining ammunition on board rather than go down fighting, sunk only a few feet in the shallow waters of the Plate with insufficient explosives remaining to prevent his enemies from recovering various secret appliances. Having so written, destroyed his ship, and arranged for the internment of his crew, he shot himself.

As noted earlier, before the outbreak of war there were still uncertainties about the form of submarine attack to be expected against British trade. But such doubts as existed were set at rest when, at the very outset, the passenger ship *Athenia* was torpedoed without warning. This was a mistaken action on the part of the submarine captain, as the German High Command did not intend to start unrestricted submarine warfare until they had greater strength available. But the result

---

[6] Quoted in Friedrick Ruge, *Sea Warfare, 1939–1945: A German Viewpoint*, trans. from German by M. G. Saunders (London: Cassell, 1957), p. 38.

was that it seemed necessary to carry on, so to speak, where things had left off in 1918. Merchant ships would apparently be subjected to much the same risks as in the previous war, and the measures taken to protect them must be those based on the experience of that time, with such modifications and improvements as were called for by technical developments.

The most important defensive measure was to sail ships in convoy through all waters in which intensive submarine attack was probable. All arrangements to implement this policy had already been made, and now they were put in train. Convoys were formed as fast as they could be organized. This could not be done immediately for all shipping, much of which was already at sea, but the process was on the whole a rapid one, and something could be done even for ships not in convoy by ordering them to steer on a variety of tracks outside the regular shipping lanes.

The waters in which shipping was thickest, both convoys and independent ships, were those between the south of Ireland and Ushant. It was here that the homeward-bound convoys converged, those from Halifax (bringing the whole North American trade, since neutral United States ports could not be used for assembly) and from Freetown (the South Atlantic trade), and the Suez Canal and Mediterranean trade from Gibraltar. And it was here that each convoy divided into an east coast and a west coast section, the former being usually the larger because London handled more shipping than any other port. The outward-bound traffic, which was dispersed as soon as the zone of greatest danger had been traversed and could therefore be organized irrespective of destination, was grouped by ports of departure instead of by trade routes.[7] All the outward-bound convoys went out through these same waters to the west of the English Channel, but there was some further dispersal of routes in that some of the independent ships sailing from and to the Mersey and the Clyde were routed north of Ireland.[8]

The general picture, then, was of an area at the mouth of the English Channel and south and southwest of Ireland thickly populated with shipping, mostly in convoy after the first few weeks, with a few ships in the northwestern approaches of the North Channel. It was in these areas, particularly the former, that submarine attack was most to be feared, and it was here in the early months of the war that several

---

[7] Gibraltar convoys needed protection for the whole voyage and were therefore sailed separately from the main outward-bound convoys.

[8] Ships of 15 knots and above, and also ships too slow for convoys, sailed independently.

25

German submarines worked. A factor much to the British advantage was that this area was, by the standards of the time, a long way from German ports. This way would have been much shortened if the submarines had been able to make the passage through the Strait of Dover. To prevent them from doing so, minefields across the strait were laid immediately war was declared. These minefields were, most fortunately, successful in October in sinking three submarines that attempted this route, with the result that it was thereafter prohibited by the German command, and all passages were made northabout, a distance of perhaps 1,500 miles each way. This was the more serious for the enemy because his total submarine force was at that time very small; there were, in fact, seldom as many as ten submarines at sea in the western approaches during the first year of the war.

Forming convoys, arranging that each convoy follow a different track from its predecessors, and if necessary diverting a convoy by radio message to take it clear of any known submarine positions, were steps in trade defense which even by themselves, or rather in conjunction with the arming of merchant ships, could effect much against submarines attacking as they had done in 1917 and 1918, that is, singly and, against convoys, mainly in daylight. The gun armament of the merchant ships was an essential factor if there was no escort; for, failing this protection, a submarine could attack on the surface, where her superior speed would allow her to keep in touch with any convoy until she had done her worst—which she could do most economically with her gun. Every ship was therefore armed as soon as possible with an antisubmarine gun. This gun armament was needed not only to lessen the danger to any convoy that should by some mischance be without escort, but also for the protection of ships sailing independently and those dispersed from convoys which, though through the main danger area, might still be threatened by outlying submarines. There would also inevitably be some ships that straggled from convoys —probably the most dangerous situation of all.

But though grouping ships in convoy might in itself lessen the risks of a voyage, it was only by the provision of strong escorts that real protection would be assured. Here there were serious difficulties. The number of destroyers available, augmented by a mere handful of sloops, was quite inadequate to provide escorts on the scale of eight or ten to a convoy, which had been the rule in 1918. All too few of the destroyers of the earlier war had been retained, though most of those few were to do good service in the six strenuous years ahead of them. And the bulk of the new destroyers were intended for work with the fleet. To offset this difficulty it was hoped, sometimes with exaggerated optimism, that the effectiveness of individual escorts had been much enhanced by their asdic equipment. This device, which detected a submerged submarine by the echo of a supersonic impulse sent out in the form of a beam, had been developed in strict secrecy since 1918; it had great advantages over the hydrophone, the only previous underwater detecting device. It did not depend on any noise being made by the submarine, and it gave accurate ranges and bearings which, it was thought, would allow depth charges to be dropped with deadly accuracy. By dint, then, of using destroyers from the Home Fleet (leaving a bare minimum for fleet duties), by working these destroyers almost to a standstill, and by restricting the zone in which antisubmarine protection was provided to 12° 30' W, escorts on a meager scale were found for each convoy. This limit of the escort zone was a mere 230 miles west of the Scillies and only 80 miles west of Ireland, but it was justified by the experience of 1918 when few convoys had been attacked farther to the westward.

By a combination of circumstances, the escorts proved for the time to be sufficient for their purpose. The effectiveness of asdic in the hands of the highly skilled operators of the first-line flotillas was considerable. Submarines trying to attack convoys were sometimes sunk (sixteen submarines were sunk from all causes during the first six months of the war), and many more must have been badly shaken and at a loss to know how to deal with this new countermeasure. Furthermore, the attack, though vigorous, was not yet *à outrance*, for the enemy realized that his resources were insufficient at the time for his operations to be overwhelming. As already mentioned, he could keep only about ten submarines or less at a time on the profitable cruising grounds, whereas in 1917 and 1918 there had often been as many as thirty operating round the British Isles—and even that strength had proved insufficient. With the prospect of the greatly increased numbers to be provided by an expanded building program, he was feeling his way.

The result, then, of the first few months of submarine attack on trade seemed not unsatisfactory to the defense and had a negligible effect on imports. In September and October, 1939, while the convoy system was getting into its stride, losses were at the rate of about 150,000 tons a month, but thereafter for the next five months (i.e., till the invasion of Norway put an end to the war's first phase) they averaged only 85,000 tons a month, figures that compared well with the average of about 200,000 tons a month in home waters throughout 1918, at a time when it was considered that the submarine campaign was well in hand.

If the destroyer escorts, though apparently successful, were barely adequate for requirements, the situation as regards aircraft was even

27

less satisfactory. Coastal Command, as already noted, were hard put to it to maintain sufficient aircraft for North Sea patrols and searches. There were few available for the western approaches; moreover, the aircraft, unlike the destroyers, had had little training in antisubmarine work. (It was, in fact, two years before they achieved more than a very occasional kill, though thereafter they went from strength to strength, as will be related in due course.) But any aircraft were of value as patrols in the waters ahead of convoys and in the areas where shipping was most concentrated, for a submarine sighting one would almost certainly dive. This would limit drastically the submarine's chances of sighting her quarry and would also prevent her using her high surface speed to get into an attacking position ahead of any ship or convoy she had, in fact, sighted, whereas, with only surface escorts to deal with, she could often get into such a position without being seen herself. So even the few Coastal Command aircraft available must have been of great value, and, to augment their numbers and extend the distance to which shipping could be covered, Fleet Air Arm aircraft flown from carriers were employed to the westward of the mouth of the Channel. The dangers to which a carrier was exposed in such an operation, steering very irregular courses in the open sea in an area where the number of submarines was not high, cannot mathematically have been serious, and such risk as there was seemed well justified. But unfortunately chance here was against the defense. Only a fortnight after war was declared the *Courageous*, one of the few big carriers, was sunk by one of the submarines she was engaged in suppressing.

The Germans, though unable to expect much from the first phase of their submarine campaign, could view their next attack, an attempt to block the approaches of British ports with magnetic mines, in a more favorable light, even though there was little of that wholehearted concentration of effort which is needed for solid achievement and much of the bickering between navy and air force which was to cramp German sea strategy throughout the war. There was not, of course, anything new in the idea of a ground mine actuated by a ship's magnetic field. Such mines had been used by the British off the Belgian coast in 1918. Nor was there anything unexpected in the use of aircraft, in addition to destroyers and submarines, as minelayers. The project of mining the German river mouths in this way had been examined by the Admiralty and the Air Ministry before the war, and suitable mines were being manufactured. But the weapon was undoubtedly a powerful one and by no means easy to counter, for it might take some time after an attack developed to obtain the detailed knowledge needed

28

for the provision of sweeping gear. Its main limitation was that it could be used effectively only in comparatively shallow water, say less than 20 fathoms; but the approaches to most British ports included channels shallower than that, and in these waters it could be very effective indeed.

Magnetic mining by destroyers and submarines in the coastal routes had been in progress throughout the autumn, and several ships had been sunk with no clear indication of the cause. In November these operations were intensified, being extended into the narrow channels of the Thames estuary; and aircraft joined in the attack. On November 21 the first parachute mines were dropped, and thereafter aircraft continued laying them nightly until the initial supply was expended. Their operations were too far to seaward for fighters to do anything effective against them; this circumstance, together with some well-placed fields laid by destroyers, soon made the situation serious. Channel after channel was found to be closed and less and less shipping was able to move. The Downs and Southend Roads became choked with inward- and outward-bound shipping, respectively, and the port of London was almost at a standstill. Though it had always been envisaged that the country might have to be fed and supplied through west coast ports, there could not be an immediate switchover without serious dislocation; and if aircraft mining increased in volume, even the west coast ports would not be immune. Liverpool and the Bristol Channel ports had much shallow water in their approaches, and, apart from a wide distribution over small ports (by transshipment into coasting craft at deepwater anchorages), the Clyde seemed almost the last resource. Even there the use of the docks depended on the narrow channel of the river being kept clear. The outlook was indeed a black one; it seemed that British capacity to import food and raw materials might well be reduced to a disastrously low level.

At the same time everything possible was being done to provide effective sweeping gear. Since the basic principle of sweeping moored mines (cutting the mooring with a towed wire) could have no application, something was needed to explode the mine without injuring the sweeper. Such a device could not be provided until it was known which of the several possible types of firing gear the German mine embodied, knowledge that could only have been obtained slowly by trial and error, probably at the cost of many casualties, but for the fortunate circumstance that one of the first aircraft mines was dropped on Shoeburyness sands where it was dry at low tide. Here, with great courage, Lieutenant Commander Ouvry succeeded in removing the firing mechanism; its secrets were revealed, and the manufacture of sweeping gear could go ahead with confidence. At first the gear was

29

primitive, consisting of an electric coil on a skid towed by a wooden drifter, which also supplied the current from the coil. The magnetic field of the skid exploded any mine it passed over or near; but as it was itself usually destroyed in the explosion, sweeping a heavily mined channel was a lengthy process calling for a large supply of skids. This sweep did, however, succeed in opening sufficient channels for shipping to flow once more, and accumulations of cargo were cleared.[9] The situation had indeed been grave, but thereafter the prospect of actual disaster from this cause never again loomed. The Germans continued to lay these mines off British ports almost to the end of the war, and not without effect. They inflicted some losses, caused delay in getting ships into harbor or away on their outward voyages, and made it necessary to expend much manpower and materiel in keeping channels open and in degaussing all ships, both merchantmen and warships, to cut down their magnetic field and so their susceptibility to mining. But the situation was always in hand. A satisfactory sweep, employing two vessels abreast towing separate electric cables, was soon devised. A further complication, introduced when the Germans included an acoustic device in the firing gear, was also overcome. Fortunately it was not till nearly the end of the war, when their resources were no longer sufficient for an offensive on a large scale, that the Germans produced the so-called oyster mine, actuated by a ship's pressure wave, which would have been very difficult to sweep. By that time, however, the development of night fighter operations would have made it much harder for them to lay mines in effective positions than it had been in 1939.

Though the foregoing chapter has been concerned only with the defense of trade, it is convenient to mention here the British Navy's part in forwarding the war on land in the early months. Fundamentally, defending trade and launching armies overseas are very different aspects of grand strategy. But many of the naval measures required for each operation are similar, particularly in the circumstances of 1939 when the army's overseas route was well covered by the general arrangements for trade defense.

As soon as war was declared, the transportation of a British expeditionary force to France was started. Originally of four divisions, it

[9] In the early struggles against the magnetic mine, help was also given by aircraft mounting a large electric coil which flew close to the water and sometimes succeeded in exploding mines. This method of sweeping, however, was not sufficiently reliable. Another early form of sweeper was a ship that was given so strong a magnetic field that the mines exploded some distance ahead of her—a somewhat alarming arrangement!

was gradually built up to ten. So that they should be as little open as possible to molestation from the air, the main routes of these divisions, their supplies, and their reinforcements ran from Southampton to Havre and Cherbourg and from the Bristol Channel to Brest and Nantes; and the passages were made as much as possible by night. As the enemy did not in fact make any attempt to interfere with these movements from the air, the only danger to which the divisions were exposed was from submarine attack. For fast-moving personnel ships, this danger was very slight, provided the approaches to the ports were made too uncomfortable for submarines to allow them to maintain cruising positions there. Against slower-moving vehicle ships and store-ships the danger was somewhat graver, particularly on clear nights, but it was not outstanding. The risk, then, was not great, but a high degree of security for an army setting out to fight its battles abroad was very desirable. Adequate destroyer escorts were therefore provided for all this shipping, and the whole transportation was effected without loss.

3

THE BLOCKADE OF GERMANY

IN THE YEARS before the war the Nazi leaders had made a strong point of Germany's increased self-sufficiency. "In 1918 we Germans were unable to maintain our fighting strength," so went their story, "because the blockade deprived us of many essential supplies; Germany's economy has now been so modified that this can never happen again." There was much justification for this view, even initially; and with the conquest first of Poland and then of France, German economy was considerably less strained to provide munitions of war and food for the people than was that of the British Isles. By the end of the war, it is true, the whole aspect of affairs had again altered. The destruction of German synthetic oil plants by bombing deprived the enemy, already driven back from the Roumanian oil wells, of the supplies needed to carry on the struggle, and so contributed substantially, perhaps vitally, to the overthrow of his armies. And, had there been no blockade,[1] the Germans might have obtained oil from overseas if there had been neutrals to supply and carry it, though by that time, of course, there were not. But in 1939 there was no prospect that any blockade, however vigorously prosecuted, would tell so severely on Germany as to induce, within measurable time, any serious desire for peace on that account.

Nonetheless, it was clear that there were still many things Germany would like to obtain from overseas if she could, and that to deprive her of these would, at the least, assist the Allies to stand up to her. Lack of some particular products might lower the standard of certain munitions;

[1] The term "blockade" is here used to mean all the measures taken to prevent seaborne supplies from reaching Germany, and not in the older and narrower legal sense implied in a declaration of blockade of a particular coast. This kind of blockade was never imposed on the German coast, in either World War I or World War II.

32

lack of others—rubber, for example—might force on her th
tively uneconomic manufacture of less efficient substitutes.
within reason that could be done to deprive Germany of ov
plies was, therefore, worth doing. From the naval point or view the
supplies that might be intercepted could be classed under two main
headings: those from the Atlantic Ocean and beyond, and those from
the north of Norway—of which more hereafter.

The chief naval concern in this regard was to see that all cargoes that
might find their way to Germany were examined and, if justifiable,
seized. Any German merchant ships intercepted would be captured
and sent in as prizes; but since Germany would not be able to effect
much with her own ships—except perhaps an occasional one with some
special cargo which it might be worthwhile to try to slip through—it
was with cargoes in neutral bottoms that measures were mainly concerned after the first few weeks. Of these, the ships approaching Germany via the North Sea were the most important, including those whose
cargoes were to go in the first place to neutrals adjacent to the enemy.
But there was also the question of supplies reaching Germany via the
Mediterranean through Italian ports, an easy matter to control so far
as the seafaring part was concerned, but of peculiar difficulty from the
diplomatic point of view.

It had been established in World War I that to examine cargoes
thoroughly at sea was impracticable under modern conditions, and that
it was therefore justifiable to send neutral ships in under armed guards
for this purpose. Examination in harbor was the concern of a naval
organization known as Contraband Control Service, and Contraband
Control bases were established at Kirkwall (in the Orkneys), in the
Downs (with subsidiaries at Weymouth and Falmouth in the event that
air attack should make the Downs too unhealthy), at Gibraltar, and
at Port Said.

The problem of making passing ships submit to examination in the
Downs or at Gibraltar or Port Said required very little naval force for
its solution, for each was concerned with a passage through narrow
waters, and a few small war vessels on patrol (assisted in the Strait of
Dover by minefields) were all that was needed. It was in controlling
the passage into the North Sea north of Scotland that the main difficulties had to be faced. The shortest blockade line here would have been
from Scotland to Norway, 240 miles, but this was impracticable because too open to attack by surface ships and aircraft, and also because
it was desired to include the traffic approaching the whole of Norway
in the control. The line that had to be adopted, then, was that between
Scotland and Iceland, 450 miles, with an extension to Denmark Strait
between Iceland and Greenland, or rather to the part of the strait lying

33

between Iceland and the edge of the polar pack ice which fringes the Greenland coast and occasionally extends right across.

To control this line there were employed in the first place some light cruisers that had been in reserve, and later, as soon as they could be got ready for service, between twenty and thirty armed merchant cruisers, known as the Northern Patrol. They were former passenger liners armed with old 6-inch guns, able to carry all the men needed for armed guards and able to keep at sea for two or three weeks at a time and to continue to do so for months on end, with only short intervening spells in harbor for replenishment. As this was before the days of shipborne radar, there could be no expectation of interception at night, and the system of patrol was, therefore, to station ships about 20 miles apart and order them to steer courses at right angles to the line on which they were spread, that is, to steer roughly east and west. If they steered to the eastward during the night at a speed about equal to that of an inward-bound merchantman, they would retain their positions relative to any such ships. And then, turning to the westward at daylight, they would comb a belt of some 200 miles of sea during the day and pick up any approaching merchant ships in it.[2] With this system, little shipping trying to enter the North Sea at normal speeds could slip through, provided visibility by day was not much less than normal; in the depth of winter, however, it was difficult to make the same distance to the westward during the short days as had been steamed to the eastward during the nights.

In this way many neutral ships were sent into Kirkwall for examination, and in the early days many homecoming German merchantmen were intercepted. Not so many of the latter were captured as would have been liked, for they had been given orders to scuttle themselves rather than fall into British hands. And scuttle themselves most of them did, an annoying practice from Britain's point of view, with its need for all ships that could be obtained, but eminently sound from Germany's. The Northern Patrol, then, achieved all that was expected of it, and it was found that within a year the need for keeping large ships on patrol had almost passed. After the first few months the licensing by British consuls overseas of any honest neutral cargoes likely to be affected (on the understanding that the ship would be subjected to the minimum of delay at the Contraband Control base at which she agreed to call)

[2] In addition to asserting belligerent rights in regard to contraband, the British government had also, in November 1939, banned German exports to prevent Germany from securing credits abroad. Whenever, on occasion, it was more important to stop a suspected blockade runner outward than to intercept the inward traffic, the direction of patrol had to be reversed—westward at night and eastward in daylight.

left few probable blockade runners. And shipping intelligence abroad would probably give enough information about any suspects to enable a special watch to be kept for them. Also, of course, within the year the number of adjacent neutrals had been much reduced, and by the autumn of 1940 the Atlantic coast of France offered an easier line of approach for any cargoes specially required by the enemy (as is mentioned in a later chapter). Furthermore, a start was being made in laying a minefield between Scotland and Iceland. This was primarily an antisubmarine measure, but it helped to persuade shipping to follow the routes desired.

After the first year, therefore, it was possible to do nearly all that was required in northern waters with large naval trawlers, though Denmark Strait was still patrolled by armed merchant cruisers. That these changes could be made was fortunate, for the risks to the armed merchant cruisers in the main patrol area were serious and growing. Though out of range of air attack, and to some extent covered by the Home Fleet against attack by surface ships (despite the *Rawalpindi*'s misfortune), they were in waters through which the majority of German submarines passed on their way to their cruising grounds. As was to be expected, they suffered accordingly, and several ships were sunk. In later years, when the number of submarines leaving Germany had much increased, the losses would probably have been such as to make the patrol impracticable in its original form.

We return now to 1939: It has already been noted that the trade to Germany from northern Norway was in a class by itself insofar as blockade measures were concerned. Geographically it could not be covered by the arrangements for stopping the rest of Germany's overseas trade. And it had a special importance of its own, which sprang from the iron mines of northern Sweden. These mines produced a high-grade ore which was essential to Germany both in quality and in quantity, particularly to the munitions industries. During the summer and autumn the ore could be loaded at Lulea at the head of the Gulf of Bothnia and shipped thence down the Baltic, free from molestation by the British Navy. But for four or five months in the year Lulea was closed by ice, and for this reason a railway had been built from the mines across the Norwegian border to Narvik, at the head of the Vest Fjord, which had been developed as an ore port.

The traffic, then, between Narvik and Germany was of great importance, and it was clear that all possible measures must be taken to stop or hamper it, particularly in winter and spring. Unfortunately, the conformation of the Norwegian coasts is such that at only a few places on the 800-mile route between Narvik and the Skagerak did navigational dangers make it advisable to go outside territorial waters, and even then only for brief spells. Much of the route, in fact, was through the inner leads, protected from seaward by chains of islands. The task of intercepting the ore ships with any regularity, therefore, was well-nigh impossible. Occasional destroyer raids in the areas where ships were most likely to be outside territorial waters picked up a few prizes, but in general the situation was unsatisfactory and tantalizing. After prolonged deliberation, the British government accordingly decided to take liberties with Norwegian neutrality to the extent of laying two minefields extending into territorial waters so placed as to force shipping into the open sea for considerable distances and thus expose it to interception by patrols. At the same time troops were held in readiness to garrison Norwegian ports, if invited to do so by the Norwegians as a result of German reactions. On April 8, 1940, one of the minefields was laid and the world was informed. But it was then too late; on April 9 the Germans invaded Norway and the whole aspect of the war changed.

4

THE NORWEGIAN CAMPAIGN

B EFORE 1939 IT HAD BEEN a common boast of German naval officers that, when war came, they would not again be cramped within the North Sea as they had been in World War I. Their High Command, they said, would arrange in one way or another for them to have the use of Norway, and with many good harbors spaced out over a long coastline it would be impossible for the British Navy to prevent their having free access to the Atlantic. But when war with Britain came so much sooner than had been planned, Raeder, commander in chief of the German Navy, shrank from so hazardous a venture. With deep respect for the strength and enterprise of the British Navy and little apparent faith in air power, or at least in the cooperation of the Luft-waffe, he considered the Narvik ore traffic would be more endangered with Norway in German hands than with Norway neutral. But as the months passed there was increasing apprehension that the Norwegians would invite a British occupation, which would cut the Narvik route altogether and perhaps lead to the hostility of Sweden. It was agreed, therefore, that this possibility must be forestalled by a surprise move, despite the risk of grave naval losses. In the early months of 1940 all plans were made, and in April they were put into action.

On April 9, 1940, Denmark and Norway were summoned to submit to occupation by German armed forces, the summons being backed by immediate hostilities wherever there was any sign of resistance. Denmark perforce submitted. Norway resisted to the best of her power. German divisions were poured across the Skagerak into Oslo Fjord (where the 8-inch–gun cruiser *Blücher* was sunk before the defenses were overpowered), and with the help of airborne assaults on neighboring airfields the capital was soon in the enemy's hands. At the same time troops that had been carried to Kristiansand, Bergen, Trondheim, and Narvik in warships captured those ports with the backing of naval gunfire, and airborne troops occupied Stavanger. These things done, the Luftwaffe quickly established itself in Denmark and in southern Norway (round about Oslo and at Stavanger), for it was on the supremacy of his air arm that the enemy relied to overcome British resistance and the counterstrokes by sea and land which he naturally expected. As Raeder had feared, the navy had had to pay for success, for, in addition to the *Blücher*, the light cruiser *Karlsruhe* had been torpedoed and sunk by a submarine off Kristiansand, and the *Königsberg* had been sunk in Bergen by Fleet Air Arm aircraft from Scapa. At the same time British and Polish submarines took toll of the transports crossing the Skagerak to Oslo, and one of the former torpedoed and severely damaged the returning pocket battleship *Lützow*. But nonetheless the position in the south was soon reasonably secure.

The question that then arose for the British was whether Trondheim could be recaptured and the Germans held south of it while the Norwegian forces with British help reestablished themselves in central and northern Norway. If this could be done much would be saved. The German Navy, though it might have the use of Bergen and Stavanger, and thus rather more freedom of access to the Atlantic than hitherto, would not be unmolested there. And the ore traffic through Narvik would be stopped for good. It was to the reestablishment of the position round Trondheim that the main efforts must be bent. Here the problem was a complex one with the range and striking power of the Luftwaffe as the controlling factor (and of this more hereafter).

Meanwhile the extreme north was for the present out of reach of German aircraft, and at Narvik the situation was still a purely naval and military one, the military forces being only the landing parties that had been carried there in ten large German destroyers. The latter had remained temporarily in the port, but intended to leave when refueled. In these waters there had been an early encounter between the forces covering the minelaying (see chap. 3) and the German heavy forces whose movements were designed to draw off the Home Fleet during the invasion: on April 9, the day of the invasion, the *Renown* had engaged the *Scharnhorst* and the *Gneisenau* off the Lofoten Islands. But the German ships had outpaced the British battle cruiser and, despite being hit, had escaped from her. (For northern Norway, see map, p. 198.)

With the situation more fully revealed, further action was needed. During the night of April 9, Captain Warburton-Lee, commanding the 2d Destroyer Flotilla, was given discretion to take action against the Germans in Narvik. Judging that every hour was of importance while the enemy was still engaged in establishing defenses, he decided to take his five ships right into the harbor and engage the enemy destroyers at close range, despite not only their superior numbers[1] but also their superior gunpower, ship for ship, and the probability that at least some fixed defenses were already in place. He would then do what he could to destroy the shipping. In this heroic attempt he sank or disabled three of the enemy destroyers. But with the enemy in even greater strength than he expected the withdrawal was hazardous, and he lost his ship, the *Hardy,* and one other, as well as his own life. Stronger forces were needed to finish the task, and three days later the battleship *Warspite* and nine destroyers under Vice Admiral Whitworth, risking the submarines known to be in the approaches, steamed up the fjord and sank all the remaining German destroyers. The German Navy was still paying heavily for the campaign. Narvik remained for the time in the enemy's hands, but there were no further naval surface forces in these waters to distract attention from the critical situation farther south.

In central Norway success would depend in the first instance on the strength of the land forces that could be sent there and on how soon they could arrive. Unfortunately, with practically all the army's available formations being used to strengthen the position in France, there was no field force that could be sent overseas at a few hours' notice to meet an emergency of this sort. Nor was the navy at that time well equipped to assist the army in amphibious operations. Such a force and such equipment, which should always be ready to give offensive expression to sea power when opportunities arise (as they always have arisen, though seldom foreseen), had had little part in British preparations in the lean years before the war, when it seemed that all resources must be devoted to the primary defensive needs. A force, including some French units, had therefore to be improvised and could not be landed until a week after the German invasion had started.

At that time the Germans were advancing along the two valleys connecting Oslo with Trondheim, with the Norwegian army falling back before them. German reinforcements crossing the Skagerak were being harassed by British submarines, and a substantial toll was taken of them. But here sea power had its limitations. With such powerful enemy air forces so close at hand it was impracticable to keep surface forces constantly in these waters, and troops continued to pour across despite losses. Trondheim could not be reinforced by sea now that the naval situation was in hand on the west coast, but it was within reach of German aircraft and could not be retaken by frontal assault without

---

[1] Warburton-Lee believed there were six German destroyers, but there were in fact ten, as previously noted.

much preparation. Plans for a direct attack were put in train, but meanwhile it was decided to land forces 100 miles on either side, at Namsos to the northeast and Åndalsnes to the southwest, and attempt a converging attack. The southern force should also be able to delay the Germans advancing along the western of the two routes from Oslo to Trondheim.

These landings (they involved only 12,000 men in all) were effected successfully and contact was made with the enemy. But it was not long before it became apparent that the Allied forces were rendered wellnigh impotent by lack of air power. The fighting troops could not stand up indefinitely to heavy and unhampered attacks by dive-bombers; work at the base ports could be done only at night, and then amid the wreckage of continual bombing by day. Much heroic work in antiaircraft defense was done by the ships, particularly some old cruisers converted to antiaircraft ships and a few of the new sloops specially designed for convoy defense against aircraft. But this was not nearly enough. If the situation was to be held something like equality in the air was needed, and if to be recovered some superiority, at least in the immediate area of operations. This could not be provided. The few aircraft carriers, themselves liable to air attack, could not maintain in the air a tithe of the aircraft needed; districts where suitable ground for airfields could be found were nearly all in the hands of the enemy; at that time, also, the Royal Air Force had little strategical mobility. Like the other services it had had to devote itself to the pressing requirements of what seemed its main roles: it had had to concentrate on home airfields, with just sufficient mobile organization for cooperation with the army in France. Beyond that little was available, either materially or in organization. An attempt was made to operate some Gladiator fighters from a frozen lake southeast of Åndalsnes (the Germans had been using frozen lakes extensively), but this effort failed disastrously when the fighters were all destroyed on the ground.

Before long it became clear that the situation was without hope. Even if the direct assault on Trondheim from the sea, originally planned for April 25, had been attempted and had succeeded, or if the converging land attack had been able to capture the port and its adjacent airfield while still delaying the advance of the main German armies from the southward, it would have been impossible to reinforce and hold the place. With only one airfield and such aircraft as could be sent there it would have been impossible to stand up to the overwhelming weight of the Luftwaffe operating from Denmark and southern Norway. It was decided, therefore, about April 26, that withdrawal was the only possible course. Despite continual bombing of the base ports the retreat was effected, and by May 3 all British, French, and Norwegian troops had left central Norway.

During the whole of this campaign the unceasing activities of the Home Fleet and of French cruisers and destroyers associated with it had been directed to escorting and carrying troops and safeguarding their supplies, and to ensuring that the Germans could not transport any more troops to central and northern Norway by sea. In this endeavor, aircraft flown from carriers, as well as some Fleet Air Arm aircraft operating from the Orkneys, played an important part. There were for the present no further clashes between ships, but British forces had to show themselves capable of standing up to air attacks at sea; and there was the added anxiety that their base at Scapa Flow, though now strongly defended, was within much easier range of German bombers. The airfield at Stavanger was the chief thorn in their flesh, and attempts were made to neutralize it, both by Royal Air Force night bombers and by a night bombardment by the 8-inch cruiser *Suffolk*. But neither form of attack achieved anything of value, and the fleet was always in danger of molestation. Fortunately, it came through this period with no more serious loss than two destroyers (one British and one French) and one sloop. On April 9, the day of the invasion, the battleship *Rodney* had been hit amidships by the heaviest type of bomb then in use, but it broke up on her armored deck. The force returning from the bombardment of Stavanger airfield was also heavily assailed: the *Suffolk* was hit and her speed much reduced, but she was not prevented from returning to harbor. The damage to Scapa Flow, too, proved less than might have been expected. In two raids at the outset of these operations (April 8 and 10), fruitless because the fleet was at sea, the defending fighters and guns gave so good an account of themselves as to discourage the Luftwaffe from further attacks.

Though the situation in central Norway was now beyond recovery, the north, including Narvik, was still too far away for intensive attack by German bombers even when working from Trondheim. It was determined, therefore, to transfer the Norwegian government to Tromsö and the base of operations to Harstad, and to prosecute the siege of Narvik with vigor. An airfield was constructed in the vicinity and, pending its completion, fighters could work from an improvised strip. In these circumstances the German garrison could not hold out for long, and on May 28 Narvik was captured by an assault in which new assault landing craft (afterward known as LCA), designed just before the war, were used for the first time.

In these operations around Harstad and in the approaches to Narvik there was, or so it seemed, no opposition from submarines. In fact,

41

strong opposition had been attempted but had failed, resulting in a spell of severe frustration and discouragement for the Germans. In common with other navies they had realized that the effectiveness of a torpedo would be much enhanced if it was made to explode, magnetically, under a ship's keel instead of against her side, and to this might be added the supposition that accurate depth keeping would then be less necessary. There had already been disappointments with magnetic pistols, for torpedoes had several times exploded short of their targets. And now it was found that, when contact pistols were used instead, the torpedoes often ran too deep to hit.

So despairing did the situation seem that its effect on the morale of the submarine captains and crews was a matter of grave concern. But fortunately for the Germans it so happened that, with their subsequent return to trade warfare, these troubles, though not eliminated for two years, diminished in importance. Contact pistols were fairly effective against merchant ships, and deep running was found to be less prevalent. At long last it was found that the latter was due to the high barometric pressure built up in a submarine after many hours under water (when compressed air had either leaked or been admitted to make breathing easier) penetrating into the balance chambers of the torpedoes, thus affecting a mechanism that relied on atmospheric pressure for correct functioning. As submarines working in the Atlantic were not often submerged for long, this trouble, while remaining mysterious, had seldom affected their attacks.

By the time Narvik was taken, however, the situation had again been transformed. Disaster in France was already threatening, and in Norway the enemy had gradually succeeded in extending his power and his airfields northward from Trondheim. It was clear that Narvik and Harstad, already being severely bombed, would soon be untenable unless far heavier British air forces could be brought to the area. This was impracticable. For one thing the battle in France had prior claim, and for another the length of communications to Narvik was such as to engross almost the whole of the available naval forces to keep them open, and even then considerable casualties to warships and transports had to be expected. From Scapa Flow to Narvik was a distance of 800 miles on the direct route, and considerably more when making a detour to keep as far as possible out of range of the Norwegian airfields. Moreover, there were two German battle cruisers and the 8-inch crusiers (still two of these) to be contended with. If they were based on Trondheim, as was probable, the task of guarding communications with the north would be still more arduous.

It was decided, therefore, that the whole of Norway must perforce be abandoned. The King and the government reluctantly left Tromsö, and Narvik was evacuated. Its facilities as an ore port were destroyed, but even this could be little more than a gesture, as the season of Baltic navigation had opened and repairs were in fact effected by the following January. One minor incident in this withdrawal, however, had perhaps more naval significance than was apparent at the time. The commander of the Hurricane squadron that had been operating from the nearby airfield was told that his aircraft could not be packed for reshipment and must be destroyed. But rather than lose them in this way he asked if he might land them on the *Glorious* for passage to Great Britain. This he and his fellow pilots accomplished with complete success, and in so doing disposed of the previous conception that fighters operated from carriers must necessarily be of a type inferior to those flown from airfields. It was not long before the then existing fighters of the Fleet Air Arm were replaced by Sea Hurricanes, and eventually by naval versions of the Spitfire. Though necessarily rather stronger and therefore slightly heavier and slower than contemporary land types, they, and the American-built Wildcats, Corsairs, and Hellcats which joined them later, were never again outclassed as had been the carrier-borne fighters of the past.

The final scene of the campaign was one of disaster. The *Glorious* with Hurricanes on board had been sent south independently of the other returning forces because she was running short of fuel. With her load of fighters she had only five Swordfish aircraft on board, and it appears that they had been very fully employed during the preceding days and none was kept up on reconnaissance. In these circumstances the *Glorious* encountered the *Scharnhorst* and the *Gneisenau* and was disabled before she could fly off her Swordfish with torpedoes. Unable to escape, she sank an hour and a half later. There was, however, one recompense to offset her loss. One of her two escorting destroyers, the *Acasta*, before being herself sunk, succeeded in hitting the *Scharnhorst* with a torpedo. As a result the enemy returned to Trondheim, thus removing what might have been a serious threat to a returning convoy 200 miles to the northeastward which had had to sail without battleship escort.

In connection with the Norwegian campaign there is one further operation, not outstanding at the time but of great subsequent importance, which needs to be mentioned. With the German Navy established in Bergen and Trondheim (particularly the latter, which was outside effective bombing range from Scotland), the task of defending the Atlantic trade routes was clearly going to be harder. If the enemy should succeed in extending his power to Iceland it would be harder still. It would, in fact, in the situation brought about by the fall of France and the consequent diversion of convoy routes to the northward, have been nearly impossible; but this further adversity was still in the future. Since Iceland could not defend itself, the only way of ensuring that the Germans did not get there was to occupy it with British forces. This was done. On May 10, the day the Germans invaded western Europe, a brigade of Royal Marines landed at Reykjavik, and thereafter Great Britain assumed responsibility for the defense of the island. In addition to Reykjavik, Seydisfjordur in the east and Akureyri in the north were occupied and defended. When, later, the Battle of the Atlantic was at its height, the use of Reykjavik (and eventually of Hvalfjordur, in the vicinity) as a fueling base for escorts and the establishment of long-range aircraft on Icelandic airfields were possibly decisive factors in that hard-fought struggle.

5
THE FALL OF FRANCE

T HE INVASION of France and the Low Countries by the Germans on May 10, 1940, had little immediate effect on the naval outlook as a whole. As always when there is work to be done, particularly in times of difficulty and disaster, there was a call for destroyers everywhere and unceasingly. But they were wanted, as a rule, more as emergency transports than as warships, though their guns were often used against enemy troops in last-minute efforts to stem the tide that was overwhelming the Channel and North Sea coasts, and they were constantly in action against aircraft, a task for which, unfortunately, they were not well equipped. Boulogne and Calais saw some gallant work, and the incessant eight-day struggle to evacuate the army from Dunkirk employed not only all available destroyers but everything floating that could be used in those waters and was capable of making the passage. But the only German naval attempt at interference was by a few motor torpedo boats. The fighting was chiefly against aircraft, and, though something was done by the antiaircraft fire of ships, the main burden was borne by the Royal Air Force. In particular, the tireless activities of Fighter Command throughout the operation, though handicapped by the distance from their airfields and radar stations, did much to cut down the weight of bombing to which troops and ships were subjected. Much had to be endured, but without this protection far less could have been accomplished.

The result of this phase was the loss of nine destroyers and the severe temporary depletion of the remaining destroyer forces until such time as heavy damage, mostly from air attack, could be repaired. Twenty-three destroyers were damaged in the Dunkirk operation alone. But it was not till after the further evacuations from Cherbourg and Saint-Nazaire and the final collapse of French resistance on June 22 that the

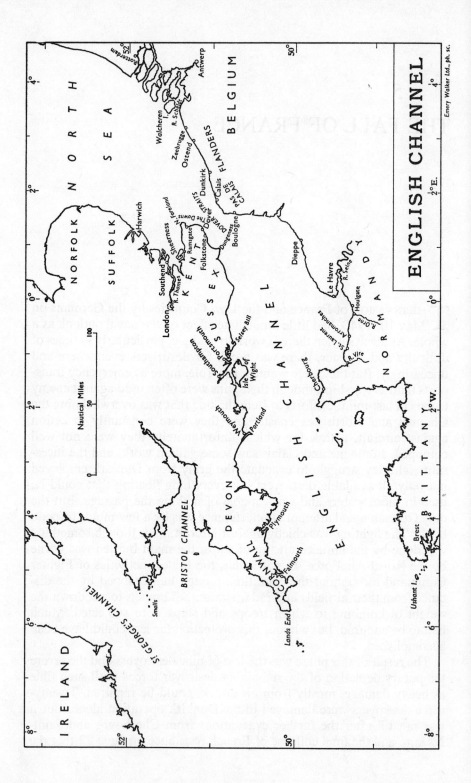

ENGLISH CHANNEL

2° E.

Emery Walker Ltd., ph. sc.

NORTH SEA

NORFOLK

SUFFOLK

Harwich

Southend
London
R. Thames
Sheerness
Foreland
Ramsgate
Folkstone
Dungeness
Boulogne

Rotterdam

Antwerp
Walcheren
R. Schelde
Zeebrugge
Ostend
Dunkirk
Calais
FLANDERS
PAS DE CALAIS
BELGIUM
DOVER STRAITS
Dover
The Downs

KENT
SUSSEX
Selsey Bill
Portsmouth
Southampton
Isle of Wight
Weymouth
Portland

Dieppe

Le Havre
R. Seine
Houlgate
R. Orne
Arromanches
St. Laurent
Cherbourg
R. Vire
NORMANDY

ENGLISH CHANNEL

DEVON
CORNWALL
Plymouth
Falmouth
Lands End

BRISTOL CHANNEL
Smalls

BRITTANY
Brest
Ushant I.

ST GEORGE'S CHANNEL

IRELAND

Nautical Miles
50   100

52°

4°

2°

0°

2°

4°

6°

8°

50°

52°

50°

50°

naval situation was radically altered. Then it was altered very radically indeed.

In the changed situation there were two main aspects, which it will perhaps be best to consider separately: first, the immediate threat of the invasion of England; second, the drastic modifications to strategical geography brought about by German occupation of the French Atlantic and Channel coasts and the entry of Italy into the war (June 10). Coupled with the latter was the change in the balance of capital-ship strength as between the belligerents, with the final balance uncertain while there were still doubts about what line the French Navy would take or have forced upon it.

The threat of invasion was a very real one. It seemed at least as close as in Napoleonic days. Probably it was even closer. Despite all the fears and alarms of the earlier era, St. Vincent, in irascible mood, could tell the House of Lords: "I do not say the enemy cannot come. I only say they cannot come by sea." No one could say that now with such assurance—and now the sea was no longer the only route. Though success in France had been so startlingly rapid and complete that the Germans were by no means prepared for such an adventure, the navy had given the matter some preliminary thought. And it seems that the army, elated by its victories, was prepared to face the risks, perhaps with the valor of ignorance. But when it came to drawing up plans Raeder quailed at the hazards of such an operation with only improvised transport and landing craft, as well he might. He made it clear to Hitler that if the Luftwaffe could completely dominate the Royal Air Force the undertaking might succeed, but that otherwise it was sure to fail. There was therefore a tendency in the High Command to entertain hopes of finishing Britain off by air attack or blockade rather than to take this decisive step. But looked at from the English side of the North Sea and the Channel, there was nothing unlikely in the attempt. It was known that adequate shipping was available to the enemy, and particularly that vast number of barges from the Rhine and other inland waterways could be made to serve many of the purposes required. It was possible that a large number could be fitted with self-propulsion within a measurable period, and so fitted, though not ideal, they could have been used as landing craft on the many suitable beaches between the North Foreland and Selsey Bill and even farther to the westward. East Anglian beaches, too, had to be considered.

Subsequent experiences have made it clear how much planning and training and how much special equipment are needed for a successful invasion against prepared opposition, and these later experiences may seem to show that the hastily devised German plan was hardly practicable. But in 1940 the situation was altogether different. The bulk of the British Expeditionary Force (about 350,000 men) was back in England, but the formations were without equipment and it would be some time before they could be organized in full fighting trim. The army would no doubt have put up a stout resistance behind the beach defenses, which were being installed with all possible speed, and also in local counterattacks; but it is doubtful if any position could have been held against a heavy attack. An invader has most to fear from a heavy counterattack by mobile reserves before he is fully established, and of effective action of this sort the ill-equipped divisions were barely capable. It seemed that the only hope was to stop the enemy at or near the beaches if he got so far, and that, since this could be only a hope, the main concern must be with the efforts of the navy and the air force to prevent his reaching English shores at all in effective numbers.

As early as the beginning of June the possibility of invasion began to affect the British naval dispositions, for at that time Admiral Forbes was told to hold two capital ships in readiness to proceed south at need. This order, which in the light of afterknowledge was clearly premature (for the Germans had hardly the beginning of such an intention at that time), had the unfortunate effect of reducing the cover provided for the returning Narvik expedition, putting one convoy in considerable peril and possibly contributing to the loss of the *Glorious* (mentioned in chap. 4). But it shows how immediately the Admiralty realized the importance of taking all steps to prevent the enemy from crossing the sea in the wake of the retreating army. It was not till August and September, however, after the Germans had established their airfields in France, and were in fact making preparations for a September invasion, that the struggle began.

This struggle never got beyond the air battle. In fact, the planned air operations for invasion were never fully tried, for Hitler allowed Göring to switch to a direct attack on London, and with the Royal Air Force victorious over the Luftwaffe naval measures were never called into action. It had been the enemy's aim in the first place to drive Fighter Command back from its forward airfields. But even this first step was never achieved. Nor could Bomber Command be prevented from taking toll of the assembling transport barges. Some of the Kentish airfields were severely battered, but the fighters were never prevented from operating as far forward as needed. Had they been so prevented the enemy's next step in his original plan would have been to attack all warships at sea or in harbor within reach of the invasion routes. Already Dover was too far in advance to be usable by ships for shelter and replenishments, and the German hope was to extend this state of affairs to Sheerness, Harwich, and Portsmouth. The result, if this step had been successful, can only be a matter of surmise. The British Navy would have had to maintain sufficient strength available for the main fleet to defeat any probable enemy concentration, for without such ascendancy the war could not long be continued, even though the first thrust of invasion was repulsed. But with this proviso all possible warships would have been brought to the area and given such air protection as was still feasible. With or without protection, they would have attacked the invasion flotillas and convoys and would, without doubt, have taken a heavy toll. There would have been no resistance from warships, for the German Navy considered it impracticable to give any protection beyond that provided by minefields to be laid on the flanks of the invasion routes.

In short, then, it can be said that on this occasion, when the enemy's navy was weak and his air force strong, the Royal Air Force was Britain's first line of defense against invasion. That line held. Had it broken or had it been forced back, the Royal Navy would then have been in the forefront and might, despite the enemy's air attacks, have so broken up the invading flotillas as to enable the British Army to drive the invaders back into the sea. There would in addition have been airborne landings, attempting to capture airfields and take the defenses in reverse, and against these the navy could give no help. But they could not have been in large numbers nor heavily equipped, and against them the army, whose main lack was in heavy equipment, would no doubt have prevailed.

Had the enemy attempted invasion without gaining real mastery over Fighter Command, the navy's task would have been the same but under much less arduous conditions and with virtual assurance of success. It was in this light that the problem could be viewed during the next two or three years. At the end of October, with the defeat of the Luftwaffe in the Battle of Britain and the coming of the winter storms, the threat of invasion was virtually over. But although there was then confidence that the enemy would never be so likely in the future to win the air battle as he had been at his first unsuccessful onslaught, the navy had still, in the following summers, to be ready for any attempt to gain a footing on English shores.

With the enemy in possession of the north and west coasts of France, from Dunkirk to the Spanish frontier, the changes in strategical geography as affecting the British Navy's tasks were indeed startling. The basis of British naval strategy against Germany in the four years 1914–1918 and hitherto in World War II had lain in the position of Great Britain athwart the lines of passage of German warships to the Atlantic. For much of World War I the immediate object of the British Expeditionary Force's struggles in France had been to keep the enemy away from the Channel ports. The feeling at that time was that although, after the autumn of 1917, the submarine attack was being held, the balance might well swing the other way if the enemy was able to operate from ports close to the western approaches and the dense stream of traffic in the Channel. The latter was thought to be essential to existence, for it did not seem possible at that time to feed and supply London through the west coast ports, and the route to the Thames down the North Sea was already a particularly hazardous one owing to the activities of small submarines, both torpedo carriers and minelayers, working from Zeebrugge and Ostend.

And now the position previously struggled so hard for was lost. In the first place, the Germans could soon establish bases for their submarines on the Atlantic coast. There they would be within a few hundred miles or less of the main trade routes, instead of the 1,500-mile passage each way they had previously had to contend with. And even with the alteration of routes which soon became necessary the distance was only about 500 miles. A much higher proportion of their time at sea, therefore, would be available for attacking shipping, and in fact the enemy was able immediately to keep several more submarines in the operating area. Second, the enemy could base his heavy ships and cruisers on ports so placed that a British fleet working from Scapa Flow was no longer in a position to intercept them on passage to or return from their operations. Already the situation was difficult with the Germans in possession of harbors in northern Norway, though this danger had been partly counteracted by the occupation of Iceland. But with enemy bases in the Bay of Biscay, practically all hope of interception would be gone once an initial breakout from the North Sea had succeeded. Had British forces had the use of a harbor in southwest Ireland which could have been equipped and defended as a fleet base, the position would have been much less unfavorable both from this point of view and in the war against submarines. But of this, in the then mood of the southern Irish, there was no hope. The one redeeming feature was that the only major dockyard available to the enemy in these waters was at Brest, well within bombing range from England. But there seemed no reason that the Germans should not be able to establish a sufficiently equipped base for their own ships farther south.

A third change derived from German air power. With the Germans in France, not only would trade in the English and Bristol channels be constantly subject to air attack, but the usefulness of the main English dockyards, Portsmouth and Plymouth, was certainly going to be much restricted.

The main immediate effect of these changes was in drastic alterations to the density of shipping on the various routes roundabout the British

Isles and in the western approaches. In the first place, the Channel could no longer be used except for a trickle of coasting trade, and for this two reasons must be added to those already given. One was the presence of motor torpedo boats which the Germans soon brought to these waters; they were fast and effective craft which it was found difficult to contend with and which, attacking by night, were at least as serious a danger as aircraft. The other was the mounting of long-range guns, radar controlled, covering the Strait of Dover. Though radar countermeasures eventually did much to reduce their effectiveness, the passage of the strait was for some time a hazardous one; but it still had to be made by the coasters supplying southern ports with coal.

Not only was the Channel barred to overseas traffic, but the whole area between Ushant and the south of Ireland, through which the bulk of the total trade had previously passed, was also closed to it. With no bases in southern Ireland, it was too hazardous to pass even the South Atlantic and Mediterranean trade through these waters. Here then was a complete change in a bird's-eye view of the shipping which must at all costs be protected. Previously such a view would have shown dense shipping in the English Channel, and somewhat less dense in the Bristol and St. George's channels, coalescing on a broad front (metaphorically speaking, the breadth of front being produced by successive, not simultaneous, convoys) and then fanning out ever more broadly into the Atlantic—all this with ships moving in both directions. There would also have been a thinner stream fanning out from the North Channel. But now all this traffic had to be concentrated in the waters between the north of Ireland and the west of Scotland, where it would be far more dense than it had hitherto been anywhere except, perhaps, in the narrow part of the English Channel. The routes would fan out from there (or converge on it) as widely as circumstances allowed, but far less than had been possible south of Ireland. The Gibraltar and South Atlantic trades would have to make wide detours to the westward and thus add considerably to the length of their voyages, though with the closing of the through Mediterranean route the former was not so important as it had been. There could be no uncertainty then, on the part of an enemy seeking to attack British trade, where his victims were most likely to be found. To offset this difficulty to some extent, defensive measures could be concentrated rather more than formerly; but the balance of advantage still lay with the enemy, for in trade defense it is always better to evade attack by using many routes well spread out than to fight a way through for each convoy.

As previously mentioned in connection with the magnetic mining of the Thames, plans had been made for supplying London through west coast ports. These plans had now to be put partly into effect, for the volume of shipping using the London docks had to be considerably reduced: access to the Thames was more difficult and the docks themselves were the targets for much bombing. But it was by no means intended to give up the use of London altogether. Ships therefore had to come round the north of Scotland, a necessity that gave a new importance to the North Sea route down the east coast. This route was protected to some extent against surface vessels and submarines by defensive minefields which had been laid offshore for almost the whole length of Great Britain. But it had always been vulnerable to air attack and had been subjected to such attack even when it had been concerned only with coasters, the Scandinavian trade, and such ocean trade as had come upchannel bound for the Humber and the Tyne. Now that it was to carry all the trade for the Thames, a far heavier weight of attack must be expected.

The general pattern, then, of British trade routes in home waters in the new situation brought about by the fall of France was the following. There was a dense concentration of routes off the west coast of Scotland, running through the North Channel to the Clyde and the Irish Sea (for Liverpool and the Bristol Channel ports). To seaward of the North Channel the routes ran usually south of the Outer Hebrides but sometimes inside them and round the Butt of Lewis. Loch Ewe and an anchorage off Oban were used as junction ports by the east coast and London trade, separating from or joining the overseas convoys; this trade, formed into separate convoys, went through the Pentland Firth and down the east coast inside the mine barrier. The center of gravity of traffic as a whole, therefore, was shifted much to the northward, and it was because of this shift that a new naval command was established, the Western Approaches, covering everything from the Bristol Channel to Cape Wrath and to the westward, with a commander in chief at Liverpool. On this officer the chief burden of directing the Battle of the Atlantic was to fall.

The further great change in the strategical setting, the war in the Mediterranean, is considered more fully in subsequent chapters. Here it need only be said that the route through the Mediterranean had obviously to be closed to merchant ships for the time being and all the eastern trade sent around the Cape of Good Hope. But with the entry of Italy into the war, not only this situation was altered, but the balance of capital-ship strength. That balance would be further altered, perhaps disastrously, should all the French ships fall into German hands. It is therefore necessary to take stock of the situation as it then was.

In the British Navy there were fourteen capital ships—eleven battleships and three battle cruisers. But of these only three, the battleships

Nelson and *Rodney* and the battle cruiser *Hood*, had been completed
since 1918. The five ships of the *Queen Elizabeth* class had been extensively modernized from time to time, but even those that had been altered most recently could not be considered as good, materially, as
newer ships.[1] In addition, five ships were being built. They were 35,000-
ton battleships of the new type; that is, they had a speed not far short of
30 knots, previously considered the speed of a battle cruiser, but their
protection was that of a battleship. They were armed with 14-inch guns
(ten of them), an apparently retrograde move from the 16-inch guns
of the *Nelson* and the *Rodney* and the 15-inch guns of the older ships;
but it was alleged that their armament with these new guns was in effect
as good as the 15- and 16-inch armaments of new foreign ships. None
of these five ships was as yet in service, but the first two, the *King George
V* and the *Prince of Wales*, were expected to be ready early in 1941, the
Duke of York later in that year, and the *Anson* and the *Howe* in 1942.

The German Navy had the *Scharnhorst* and the *Gneisenau*, already
mentioned, a few thousand tons smaller than most of the British ships
and armed with only 11-inch guns (nine), but faster than any of them
with the possible exception of the *Hood*, and well protected. Two battleships were, however, nearing completion, the *Bismarck* and the *Tirpitz*,
and might for all that was known be ready for service almost immediately. Although these ships purported to be of 35,000 tons (standard),[2]
they were in fact more than 7,000 tons (standard) in excess of that
figure and some 50,000 tons at deep load. They were armed with eight
15-inch guns each, were very well constructed and well protected, as
in fact were all German ships, and were as fast as or faster than the
British battle cruisers. Assuming (given equal skill in design and construction, approximately equal speed, and equal fighting spirit and efficiency) that the power of a ship is proportioned to her tonnage, these
ships were individually more powerful than anything else afloat.

The Italian Navy had two new fast battleships, the *Littorio* and the
Vittorio Veneto, just completing, and four older ships of the *Cavour*
and *Duilio* classes. The latter were certainly much inferior to the battleships of other navies in fighting power, but, having had their speed con-

---

[1] The *Queen Elizabeth* herself, still being modernized, was not ready for service until January 1941.

[2] The Washington Conference of 1922 adopted a displacement that excluded
fuel and reserve feedwater as a standard for purposes of treaty limitations, and
thereafter this rather artificial figure was used by all navies in their published
announcements of the size of ships. The figure is even more artificial for a submarine than for a surface vessel, as the former's fuel tank must always be kept
full, seawater being admitted as the fuel is used. Figures given for submarine
tonnages in this book are true surface displacements.

53

siderably increased, they were still fit for operations. Two more ships of the *Littorio* class were being built.

The capital-ship strength of the French Navy, apart from three old battleships of the *Bretagne* class and two of the *Courbet* class which could be considered as second-line, consisted of the two battle cruisers *Dunkerque* and *Strasbourg*, with eight 13-inch guns each, and two 35,000-ton battleships, the *Jean Bart* and the *Richelieu,* with eight 15-inch guns each, which were nearly ready for service.

Summarizing these figures, as they might shortly be if things were to go wrong with the French Navy and the various enemy ships nearing completion prove to be in advance of the *King George V* and the *Prince of Wales* in coming into service, the fact had to be faced that fourteen British capital ships might be opposed by ten enemy ships (four German, two Italian, and four French), six of which were materially superior to any British ships except perhaps the *Nelson*, the *Rodney*, and the *Hood*. There were also four older Italian ships which might bring the enemy's numbers up to fourteen, and the three old and slow ships of the *Bretagne* class.

It might be thought that these were not in themselves unduly long odds, particularly in view of the difficulties, both geographical and political, of a junction between the German and Italian fleets, and the fact that the fighting efficiency of the Italian ships was not rated very high. But the matter had to be considered in two less favorable lights. The first was that if the enemy, with his freedom of access to the Atlantic from the Bay of Biscay harbors, chose to operate his heavy forces piecemeal against trade and supplies, the British fleet, even if it comprised two or three times his number of capital ships, would have been hard put to it to prevent his doing damage to merchant shipping and to antisubmarine forces. Second, it had always to be considered that, if British luck were out, ships might be sunk by submarine or air attack, or put out of action for long periods from these or accidental causes, in such a way as to make the British fleet inferior to the enemy. Already the *Barham* and the *Nelson* had been put out of action for many months by torpedo and mine, respectively, and if the *Rodney*'s bomb (April 9, 1940) had detonated before breaking up she too would probably have taken some months to repair. In the event of a run of such misfortunes, the outlook would indeed be black. All that had happened so far during the war had done nothing to alter the conviction that ability to keep the sea routes open must be based on a superiority in heavy ships.

These were the circumstances that governed the British view of the situation when France fell. In the final despairing negotiations with the French government, endeavors had been made to ensure that the French fleet should be sailed to British ports before an armistice was concluded

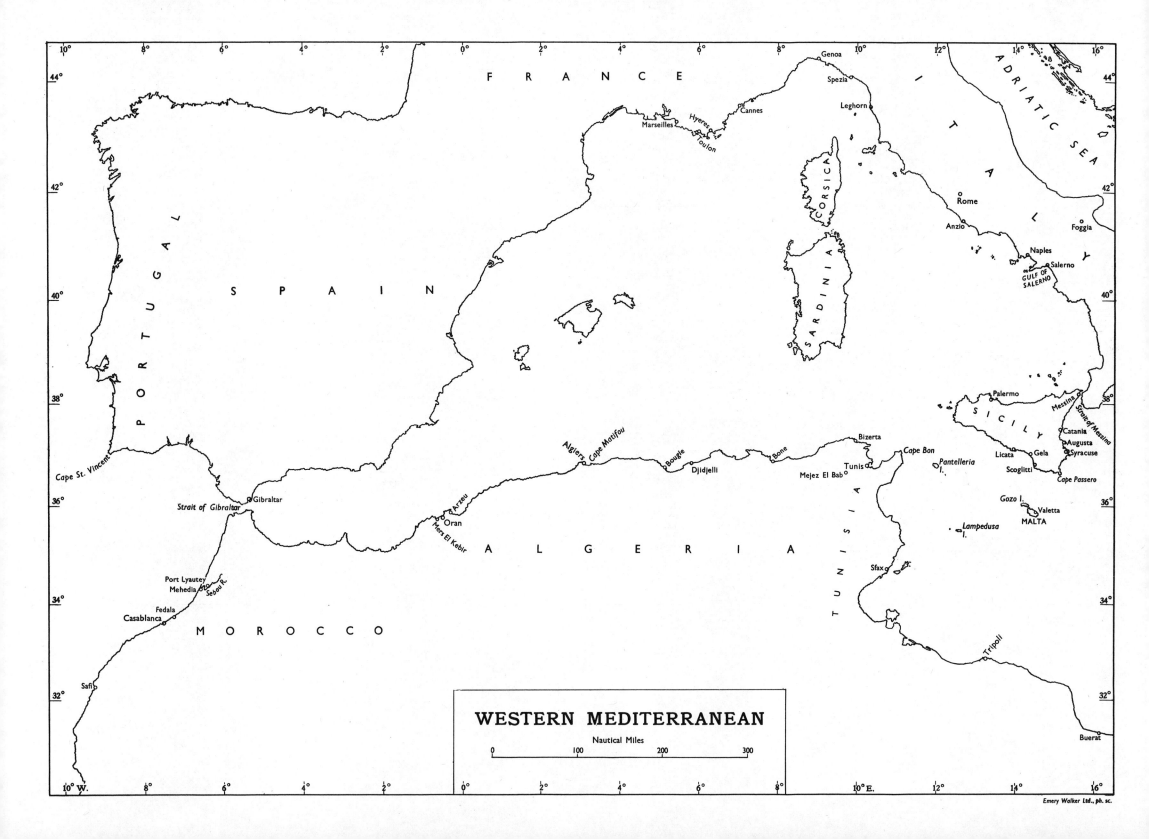

WESTERN MEDITERRANEAN

Nautical Miles

0   100   200   300

with the enemy. But this had not been done, and in fact the armistice terms included a requirement that the French fleet be disarmed under German supervision. This arrangement created no feeling of assurance that the French ships might not eventually be included in the German forces, despite the disclaimers in the armistice terms and the promises received from the French government. All possible action that would prevent the French ships from falling into German hands was therefore called for.

A number of French ships were in British ports. These were put under such restraint as was necessary, and many continued the war alongside their allies. There was also a squadron at Alexandria, including some 8-inch cruisers. These ships were forbidden to sail and eventually agreed to be demobilized under the control of the British Mediterranean Fleet. A more difficult problem was presented by the ships at Mers-el-Kebir, the naval port close to Oran. These included the two battle cruisers and the *Bretagne* class battleships. Clearly they must be prevented from returning to France with the risk of coming under the power of the Germans. On July 3, therefore, a British squadron under Vice Admiral Somerville (*Hood, Valiant, Resolution,* and *Ark Royal,* with cruisers and destroyers) approached Oran and presented to the French admiral several alternatives for the safeguarding of his ships, any of which, it was felt, might have been accepted with honor. But all proposals were refused. Drastic action had therefore to be taken and fire was opened by the British battleships. The *Dunkerque* and two battleships were soon put out of action, but the *Strasbourg* escaped though hit by a torpedo from one of the *Ark Royal*'s aircraft. The British fire was returned but no serious damage was received. For the time being, then, the situation was somewhat less dangerous despite the subsequent return of the remaining French ships to Toulon. And in the outcome the French Navy, though harboring some natural feelings of grievance against the British, prevented its ships from being used to assist the enemy. When "unoccupied France" was invaded in November 1942, all the ships in Toulon were scuttled by their crews.

The French forces in the Mediterranean did not include the two new battleships that were nearing completion. These had already, while France was still fighting, been sent to West African waters where it was hoped they would be out of harm's way—the *Jean Bart* to Casablanca and the *Richelieu,* nearer completion, to Dakar. To ensure that the latter could not be a potential danger, a hazardous exploit was undertaken by the motorboat of the aircraft carrier *Hermes.* On July 8 this boat crept in and dropped depth charges under the *Richelieu*'s stern, so as to distort her propeller shafts. While the motor boat was retiring, torpedo aircraft came in and inflicted further damage, and as a result the

55

Richelieu was immobilized for some time to come. Of the subsequent unsuccessful attempt on September 23 to effect a lodgment of Free French forces at Dakar, which by that time had been reinforced by three 6-inch cruisers from Toulon, it need only be said that it did not in the long run affect the situation, since none of these French ships was used on the German side. But the British forces lost for some time the services of a battleship, the *Resolution*, torpedoed by a French submarine during the operation.

6

TRADE DEFENSE, II: *From the Fall of France to the Entry of America*

WITH THE USE of French ports the enemy's outlook on submarine warfare against trade was very different from what it had been during the first few months of the war. Dönitz, the vigorous and forceful admiral of submarines who had been in charge of this arm ever since its revival in 1935, had not hitherto had sufficient numbers to do more than feel his way. The numbers available for operations were still inadequate and, despite new construction, they did not in fact increase till the following spring; but such as were ready were at once sent to Lorient and later to other ports on the Biscay coast, and Dönitz moved his headquarters into France so as to be both in personal touch with the submarines in harbor and well placed for directing the operations of those at sea. Determined to increase the weight of attack, he took stock of the situation, and to his previously formed views on convoy warfare he could now add the possibility of using aircraft working from France to help the submarines.

It was clear in the first place that the normal method of 1918 against convoys (submerged attack, with submarines working independently in waters where the convoy routes converged) was unlikely to be either decisive or profitable. The British antisubmarine forces using asdic, though few in numbers, had proved far more dangerous than their predecessors of World War I. And the waters round the British Isles and immediately to the westward of Scotland were becoming more and more effectively covered by aircraft. These planes, though not yet deadly, would make life a burden to the submarines in this area, particularly just before the passage of a convoy. If the submarines wished to remain there, they must do most of their patrolling submerged, which severely limited their chances of sighting shipping, unless they took the almost suicidal risks of coming right into such narrow waters

57

as the North Channel. The German aim, then, was to operate outside normal aircraft range of the British Isles. Since they knew, in addition, how short their opponents were of antisubmarine forces, they might hope that their operations would also be beyond the range of surface escorts, or would at all events stretch the latter so severely that the number with each convoy would be much reduced. Their problem was to find the convoys well to the westward, despite the difficulty that in those waters the shipping tracks might be anywhere within a wide zone. Having found a convoy, all available submarines had to be brought to the attack, if possible before the convoy could be succored by antisubmarine forces.

The solution reached had two main factors. Submarines, instead of operating singly, were organized in packs of five or six, an arrangement thought impracticable in 1918. Improvements in radio, however, had transformed the outlook, and pack tactics had already been exercised in the years before the war. In addition, long-range aircraft (Focke-Wulf Kondors) working from Bordeaux would scout for convoys as far to the westward as their range of action allowed.

In clear weather submarines working in packs could achieve much even without the help of aircraft, which were not in fact available till January 1941. In a large convoy there were always some ships making smoke, and although the efforts to cut this down were on the whole remarkably successful, there was nothing unusual in sighting a convoy 20 miles away. A pack of five submarines, therefore, could be spread, say, 20 miles apart on a line across the trade routes, allowing a wide margin for errors and still giving a good chance of sighting any convoy crossing that line by day. They would be covering 100 miles, quite a useful belt of possible convoy tracks even well out in the Atlantic. The pack system necessarily involved the free use of radio and thus gave something away to British direction-finding stations ashore, which were able to plot any submarine that transmitted, though with the high frequencies used the bearings were not very exact. But this disadvantage was accepted by the Germans as inevitable until such time as their technicians could produce better transmitting devices.

The idea, then, was that a pack should be spread out and that the first submarine to sight a convoy should report the position to her consorts, or rather to Dönitz' "control" in France which would pass out whatever orders were required. The remaining submarines would then make for positions ahead of the convoy, which they could usually do without much difficulty, having a seagoing speed of 16 knots against the 8 knots or less of the normal convoy. The original sighter shadowed the convoy from astern as contact keeper so as to give information of its movement in the event it altered course. Sometimes, particularly in the early days, the contact keeper also "homed" the other submarines by radio.

The conventional ideas that had prevailed for most of World War I would then have enjoined that each submarine, as the convoy approached her, should dive and attack. But here a change was made. Night attacks by single submarines had been tried in 1918 but had been found unfruitful on the whole. But the pack system had radically altered the outlook. With a contact keeper to guide them in, the attackers could be sure of finding their quarry; and being small, handy, relatively fast, and difficult to see, these submarines of some 750 tons surface displacement were admirable torpedo craft on the surface at night against slow targets and could be used as such with little risk to themselves, particularly against convoys that, if they were far enough to the westward, might have no antisubmarine escorts. Night attack on the surface was therefore made the rule. So that submarines would not hamper one another unduly, it was at first usual for control to give each submarine an attacking period; but before long it was decided that the greater effectiveness of giving each a free hand justified the risks incurred. There was, in fact, only one fatal collision between attacking submarines during the whole course of the war.

Superimposed on this system, as already noted, was scouting by long-range aircraft, which could be arranged only with difficulty. Relations between the navy and the air force at the higher levels were almost uniformly bad. Incompatibility of temperament between the severely orthodox Raeder and the swashbuckling Göring, who had succeeded in grasping for the Luftwaffe everything that flew except a few seaplanes, engendered constant friction, and the Luftwaffe was disinclined to be guided by naval advice. On this one occasion, however, Hitler was persuaded to accept the naval view and the group of Focke-Wulfs was put under Dönitz' orders. Based on Bordeaux, they could work on the North Atlantic convoy routes out to about 15° W, where they were well out of range of shore-based fighters. And here for a time they were of value in helping submarine packs to get athwart the tracks of convoys. But their usefulness in this respect was limited, and this phase did not in general last long: the main causes were the increase in number and size of submarine packs, so that more lines of approach were covered, and the fact that on the North American routes the submarines were in time forced farther out to the westward, where the aircraft could no longer give sufficient warning of inward-bound convoys. On the Sierra Leone and Gibraltar routes, however, they continued to be of some use to the submarines.

Meanwhile the aircraft themselves had done some attacking and for a time were looked on as a considerable menace. But although they inflicted some damage, it was found by experience that the danger was limited. Their numbers were not great, and having sacrificed protection for radius of action they were comparatively easy to knock down. Even the single antiaircraft guns of merchant ships sometimes achieved this feat; and when arrangements were made for each convoy to include a ship carrying a Hurricane fighter on a catapult, the Focke-Wulf was more reluctant to attack. The Hurricane, of course, could have only one flight and must thereafter "ditch," the hardy pilot hoping to be picked up; but, except with the Gibraltar convoys, which were much of their time within range of Bordeaux, one flight was usually sufficient. When, later, escort aircraft carriers accompanied convoys, the risks to the attacking aircraft became almost prohibitive.

The new methods of submarine attack were first tried in September 1940, and continued with increasing intensity throughout the following winter and spring. They were, during that period, alarmingly successful, and the Battle of the Atlantic could be said to have started in earnest.[1] Fortunately the number of submarines the enemy could keep at sea was still small—about ten to start with, rising to about thirty by May 1941. They could not, therefore, cover all possible convoy tracks, which, coupled with the fact that their radio gave away their rough positions every time they sighted a convoy, often made it possible to divert the majority of convoys clear of danger. But any convoy sighted well to the westward was probably doomed, for at this time the escort situation was deplorable, despite the loan of fifty old destroyers from the United States. The number of antisubmarine craft available was quite inadequate and had been seriously reduced by the casualties of the Dunkirk period. Beyond that, the low fuel endurance of many of the destroyers was a severe handicap. The new corvettes were coming into service in increasing numbers, and in April 1941 the United States lent ten coast guard cutters of high endurance, but there were not yet nearly enough of such craft to meet requirements. Escorts, then, could accompany outward-bound convoys only to about 17° W and there meet those that were homeward bound. But the submarines could and did work farther to the westward, attacking convoys that were still more than twenty-four hours short of their positions for meeting their escorts. The description of these submarine packs as wolf packs was then ter-

---

[1] The Prime Minister had thought it right "to proclaim the Battle of the Atlantic" in March 1941 in order to heighten the importance of the struggle in the minds of all concerned (Prime Minister's speech in the House of Commons, June 25, 1941).

ribly apt, for the convoy was indeed a defenseless flock of sheep, hud-
dled together waiting to be killed by the wolves surrounding it. There
seemed nothing that could be done to alleviate the situation. If the convoy scattered, some ships might in the dark elude the attackers, but
they would then be more difficult to protect when they did eventually
reach the escort zone. If the convoy remained concentrated, it could
expect eventual help from approaching escorts, but by the time the
latter arrived there might be nothing left to help. It is no wonder that
at this time the dividend paid to the enemy in tonnage sunk by each
submarine at sea was higher than at any other period of the war, before
or after. During the year ending June 1941 submarines sank nearly
3 million tons of British, Allied, and neutral shipping.[2] It was indeed
fortunate that the submarines were still so few in number.

Although several such disasters struck unescorted convoys, the picture was not always so black. Some attacks were made in the face of
escorts, and then the submarines suffered. From the autumn of 1940
to the autumn of 1941 the enemy was losing on the average about two
submarines a month. And after a calamitous winter and spring, the summer saw some improvements in the situation. By sending convoys on
tracks well to the northward arrangements could be made for escorts to
refuel in Iceland and so cover a much higher proportion of the route.
Long-range aircraft, working from Iceland and Northern Ireland, gradually extended the area covered by air escorts and searches.[3] By May
1941 the submarines were as far out as 40° W and as far south as the
Sierra Leone area. But by this time there were more antisubmarine craft
available, British and Canadian, and in June the first all-the-way escorts were provided for the Halifax route, the Sierra Leone route following in July. These escorts were at first scanty, but nevertheless the
situation was much improved. Shipborne radar and "snowflake" illuminating rockets, then being fitted, were doing much to enable a small
escort to fight off a night attack. By July, also, the Americans, though
still neutral, had started to "patrol" the convoy routes (virtually to es-

---

[2] During the same period aircraft sank just over 1 million tons: surface ships
(major warships, auxiliary cruisers, and motor torpedo boats), 848,000; and
mines, 300,000. This was by far the worst period of the war for losses by aircraft
and surface ships. "The total tonnage serving us at the outbreak of war can be
variously estimated from twenty-six millions to about twenty-two millions, according to the classes of shipping included" (Prime Minister's speech in the
House of Commons, June 25, 1941).

[3] To ensure full coordination of all antisubmarine forces, operational control
of Coastal Command was transferred in April 1941 from the Air Ministry to the
Admiralty. The long-range aircraft were Sunderland flying boats, increasing
numbers of Catalina flying boats, and, by the end of 1941, some squadrons of
Liberators.

cort some of the convoys) part of the way across, and they had established bases in Iceland.

The effectiveness of aircraft against submarines was also being steadily improved, not only in range but also in the devices with which they were equipped. Airborne radar had been introduced early in 1941, and by the end of the year aircraft were beginning to attack submarines by night as well as by day. Thereafter the numbers of submarines sunk by aircraft rose steadily. More and more as time went on did the waters that could be covered by aircraft become unhealthy for submarines, so that eventually one of the principal problems was how to provide aircraft in the gap between the area covered from European bases and that covered from Newfoundland. But the solution of that problem was still in the future.

By the end of November 1941, then, there had been a marked improvement in the situation and things seemed reasonably well in hand. In fact, the losses for that month were the lowest since the spring of 1940, and almost the lowest up to that time. The decrease was partly owing to a temporary shortage of submarines in the Atlantic, caused by transfers to the Mediterranean and the Arctic. But better defense was the most important factor, and it was at the end of 1941 that Captain Walker fought the first of his many successful battles, while escorting a homeward-bound Gibraltar convoy in the sloop *Stork* with four other escorts. Four submarines were destroyed as well as two Focke-Wulfs, though against that victory had to be set the loss of the *Audacity*, the first of a new type of small aircraft carrier (the escort carriers) converted from a merchant ship. But by this time the situation had again been radically altered. With the entry of America into the war a new and profitable field of action was presented to the submarines. The large quantity of shipping on the American coast and in the Caribbean was virtually without protection, and it was some time before convoy escorts could be provided even with British assistance. It was there that the submarines were to work for the next few months with alarming success. But that story belongs to the next phase of the struggle.

Though it was the battle of the Atlantic that bulked largest in trade defense at this time, a battle in the North Sea was by no means negligible. As already noted, convoys leaving and joining the parent Atlantic convoys traveled to and fro between Loch Ewe and the Thames, by way of the Pentland Firth and the channel inside the east coast mine barrier. On this route submarine attack had been unknown since the early days of the war when the small (250-ton) submarines had worked off the east coast of Scotland against the Scandinavian trade. But air attack was a constant menace, and, as was to be expected, the weight of attack had increased with the growth of importance of this traffic, now that the English Channel was no longer used as a route to London.

These east coast convoys were protected by a miscellaneous collection of escort craft of which some old destroyers converted for antiaircraft work formed an important part. The work of the escorts was not made any easier by the fact that much of the time the convoys were of necessity strung out in length. A small Atlantic convoy of, say, twenty-four ships would cruise in a compact formation, probably in six columns of four ships each. But a similar convoy on the east coast could not navigate the channels inside the shoals south of the Humber on so broad a front. It would have to form in two columns of twelve ships each; and such are the difficulties of keeping a long line closed up that a convoy inevitably covered a great length of water, and an aircraft might well be able to find a line of approach which was not too close to the guns of an escort. Despite this problem, however, the defense was as a rule well maintained, the guns of the merchant ships themselves contributing substantially, and the balloons they towed doing something to hamper close attack. Ships were lost from time to time, but a considerable toll was taken of the attacking aircraft and the flow of trade was not seriously interrupted.

Since these attacks were well within range of the shore some assistance in defense could be given by the Royal Air Force. It was difficult to get warning of particular attacks in time, but whenever conditions made attack probable escorting fighters could be provided. In the north, where the route was sometimes more than 40 miles from the shore, these escorts were the twin-engined fighters of Coastal Command (Blenheims and Beaufighters, which were not numerous and could be provided only in conditions of exceptional danger); but farther south the convoys were well under the "umbrella" of Fighter Command, and the faster and more effective single-seater fighters could be provided. To this end there was a close liaison between the navy and Fighter Command, and the positions of all convoys were kept on the plots at the latter's command and group headquarters.[4]

Besides the east coast traffic, the routes through St. George's Channel and along the south coast of Wales to Bristol Channel ports also needed protection by a similar organization, as they were subject to attack by aircraft working from France and often making use of southern Irish

---

[4] This system of defense for east coast convoys against air attack had been developed in 1939–40, before the Norwegian campaign, when traffic on this route had included shipping bound to and from Scandinavia. But its importance was now enhanced.

territorial waters in their approach. In particular the enemy's practice of attacking ships rounding the Smalls on moonlight nights was difficult to counter, and a few ships suffered. Some coasting trade round Land's End and in the English Channel still had to move mainly by night. But on the whole these routes too were successfully defended.

One other menace to the coastal routes was at times serious and difficult to combat. It was night attack by motor torpedo boats working from Dutch and French ports, an activity to which the German Navy devoted considerable enterprise. As soon as their army had won through to the Channel coast these craft established themselves in French ports, and by the end of June 1940 they had already sunk some ships off Dungeness. Throughout that autumn and winter they gave much trouble, and with the severe shortage of escorts it was difficult to protect even the small amount of shipping (only coasters) now plying in the Channel. There was some improvement as escorting destroyers were gradually equipped with radar, even though the type so far developed could not detect so small a craft till she was close at hand. But throughout the next few years, until he was finally evicted from French ports, the enemy was able to score occasional successes.

It was on the east coast, however, between the Humber and the Thames, that the struggle was most severe. The attack did not start seriously till the winter of 1940–41, but thereafter it was pursued with much vigor by motor torpedo boats working from Dutch ports, and losses on this important route were considerable, averaging about two ships a month in 1941. Gradually the increasing strength and efficiency of the countermeasures prevailed. Destroyers and motor gunboats, additional to the convoy escorts, worked to seaward of the shipping lane, and their operations were much more effective as radar, both shipborne and from shore stations, increased in efficiency. A sharp engagement during the night of March 14–15, 1942, in particular, discouraged the enemy. Though it cost the Briitsh forces a destroyer, the attackers were severely handled and their damaged craft were chased and attacked by motor gunboats and aircraft the next morning. In all, the Germans lost five motor torpedo boats in this operation, and there was little more trouble that year from torpedo attack, though there was still activity in the less hazardous business of minelaying. But vigilance could never be relaxed, and occasional attacks, in which the defenses were sometimes pierced, continued right up to March 1945.

Though attacks on merchant ships by submarines, aircraft, and motor torpedo boats were, apart from the Mediterranean war, the most constant anxiety during the period covered by this chapter, it was at this time, between the autumn of 1940 and the beginning of the Russian war in June 1941, that attempts by the German Navy to disrupt Britain's Atlantic communications with heavy ships rose steadily to their climax in the sortie of the *Bismarck*. Thereafter, with the *Bismarck* sunk and the *Scharnhorst* and the *Gneisenau* substantially disabled, the enemy lacked the means to continue the attack in force; and when, later on, such means were again available in the *Tirpitz* and the repaired *Scharnhorst*, it was not to the Atlantic trade but to the more easily accessible North Russian convoys that the enemy turned his attention. But in the early months of 1941 it was only with difficulty that a grip was kept on the Atlantic situation.

The first cruise of this period was that of the *Admiral Scheer*, which left Germany in October 1940 to work on the North Atlantic routes. On November 5, about halfway between Newfoundland and Ireland, she encountered a homeward-bound convoy escorted by an armed merchant cruiser. The latter, the *Jervis Bay*, engaged her adversary as effectively as was possible for an unarmored ship carrying old 6-inch guns. She was still firing short when her fire control was put out of action, but her occupying the *Admiral Scheer*'s attention for a while before her inevitable end helped the ships of the convoy to scatter and make smoke before the enemy was free to attack them. As darkness was falling by this time, many of them escaped, but five out of the convoy of thirty-eight were sunk.

The *Admiral Scheer* then worked in the lower latitudes of the Atlantic and eventually in the Indian Ocean, sinking eight more ships and sending in two prizes in a further four months of cruising.

That the *Jervis Bay*'s fight, in conjunction with the late hour of the day, helped to save several merchant ships does not alter the fact that her loss was to be deplored, and this raises the question whether the policy of escorting Atlantic convoys with armed merchant cruisers was justified. The policy had had its origin in World War I, when, after the end of 1914, the only raiders likely to be at large were of merchant-ship type. An armed merchant cruiser should have been able to deal with such a raider, though 6-inch guns and mountings more than thirty years old, and fire control of the most primitive description were hardly a match for a ship that, within the limits imposed by merchant-ship design and disguise, was likely to have the most up-to-date equipment and a picked crew. But the chances that such raiders would attack convoys in the North Atlantic were now negligible, whereas attack by regular warships was not merely possible but probable. Against the latter an armed merchant cruiser could do little except report the enemy (which the merchant ships of the convoy could do just as well) and perhaps delay him for a short time before being sunk; she would have no real chance of inflicting serious damage. The probability, then, was that this policy would involve throwing away a ship and a ship's company without any sufficient countervailing advantage.

It has often been said that a convoy inadequately protected is worse than no convoy at all. That these convoys were inadequately protected there is no doubt. But the problem was a very difficult one. As mentioned earlier, ships had to sail together from the far side of the Atlantic so that they could be in convoy by the time they could be given antisubmarine protection. That, until then, they were vulnerable both to submarine and to surface attack seems to have been inevitable. The submarine danger was eventually reduced by the provision of all-the-way antisubmarine escorts. But the surface danger was not appreciably reduced by having an armed merchant cruiser in company. Had regular cruisers been used, with speed sufficient to shadow any assailant they were not powerful enough to engage effectively, so enabling other forces to be brought to bear, something would have been achieved; but, as always throughout British history, there were not enough cruisers to go round and shipping suffered accordingly.

The next ship to give trouble was the 8-inch cruiser *Admiral Hipper*, which came out in December 1940 and worked mainly on the Sierra Leone and South American routes. On Christmas Day, about 300 miles northeast of the Azores, she made contact with a military supply convoy, bound for Suez via the Cape, which in view of its importance had been given the 8-inch cruiser *Berwick* and the light cruiser *Bonaventure* as escorts. Attacking against opposition was not a raider's role, and the Germans cleared off after a brush with the British cruisers in poor visibility. Unfortunately contact with the *Admiral Hipper* was then lost. After returning to Brest to replenish she essayed another short cruise, but she was not seen again by any forces capable of attacking or shadowing her until aircraft reported her in Brest on her second visit there in late February. Meanwhile, on February 12, she had encountered an unescorted Sierra Leone slow convoy of nineteen ships east of the Azores and had sunk seven of them, low visibility enabling the rest to escape. This was a substantial haul; but apart from a single ship on Christmas Day (sunk soon after the *Hipper*'s encounter with the *Berwick*) and a straggler from a Gibraltar convoy on February 11, it was the only profit she could claim for her two cruises. From Brest she returned to Germany northabout in March for a dockyard refit of her main turbines.

The danger from these surface raiders was not only to convoys and outward-bound shipping dispersed from convoys,[5] but also to ships sailing independently. This risk, though not mathematically large, was one that little could be done to alleviate. Although the convoy system covered all the North Atlantic routes, ships of 15 knots or more were still sailing independently so as to gain the substantial increase in available tonnage given by their quicker passages and the elimination of delays waiting for convoys to form. And, in fact, in the then conditions of submarine warfare (i.e., with submarines working in mid-ocean rather than in focal areas) they probably ran less risk than if they had been in convoy. The chances of encountering a submarine so nearly ahead that she would be able to attack submerged were mathematically remote; attack on the surface could be beaten off with a gun; and a submarine had not sufficient speed to work round out of sight to a position ahead from which she could attack by night. The faster the ship, the less the danger, and in fact casualties to these fast ships from submarine attack in the North Atlantic were rare. Throughout the later years of the war the mammoth passenger ships *Queen Mary* and *Queen Elizabeth* plied to and fro independently with great frequency between New York and the Clyde carrying up to 15,000 troops each, a seemingly breathtaking risk despite their high speed; but there was no resulting mishap. But with fast surface raiders it was another matter. Safety lay solely in the merchant ships being few and far between and their routes well spread out. Because of this only very few ships were likely to pass through the raider's relatively small circle of visibility, even if increased by the use of aircraft; but such as did were almost inevitably doomed if the raider saw fit to attack.

None of these fast independent sailings were actually intercepted by raiders in the North Atlantic, partly because the German cruisers and battle cruisers trying to intercept convoys were disinclined to approach single ships which might report them before being silenced. But beyond the convoy routes there were more ships sailing independently, slow as well as fast, and it was on the principle of reaping a fairly steady though small harvest, and also in hope of disturbing British strategy, that the enemy thought it worthwhile to send out auxiliary cruisers of merchant-ship type, with very high endurance, to supplement the pocket battle-ships in those waters and to work even farther afield. Six were out at

[5] Until all-the-way antisubmarine escorts could be provided (not until the summer of 1941; see p. 61, above), outward-bound convoys, except those carrying troops and medical supplies, were dispersed as soon as the antisubmarine escorts left them. It seems that they did not always thereafter spread out on sufficiently diverse tracks, for example, those encountered by the *Gneisenau* and the *Scharnhorst* on February 22 and March 15–16 (see pp. 68, 69, below).

this time, two in the South Atlantic, two in the Pacific, one in the Indian Ocean, and one in the Antarctic, the latter to break up the whale fishery. Some damage was done, inconsiderable compared with that wreaked by submarine attacks—but still troublesome—and with the annoyance that it was impossible to eliminate the danger completely. The hope that something could be done by the British armed merchant cruisers proved an illusion, as already suggested, because of the antiquity and inadequacy of their armament and fire control. The raider *Thor* in the South Atlantic made good her escape from the *Alcantara* and the *Carnarvon Castle* in July and December 1940, respectively, after disabling her adversary each time. In April 1941 the same ship sank the *Voltaire* while the latter was on passage from Trinidad to Freetown. Occasionally, however, a raider was encountered by a regular cruiser and sunk. The *Pinguin* was so disposed of in the Indian Ocean by the *Cornwall* in May 1941; the *Atlantis*, in the South Atlantic by the *Devonshire* in November; and the *Kormoran*, off the west coast of Australia by the Australian cruiser *Sydney* in November, though unfortunately at the cost of the latter ship which succumbed to a fire started during the action. And from time to time the supply ships on which the raiders had eventually to rely were swept up by British searches. But they continued to be an annoyance up to the end of 1942 and occasionally even later.

Before the *Admiral Hipper* had finished her second cruise in February 1941, a stronger force was at large. The *Gneisenau* and the *Scharnhorst* had been turned back from a first attempt to break out by making contact with a British cruiser squadron south of Iceland; early in February, however, they succeeded in getting away, avoiding a patrolling armed merchant cruiser during their night passage through Denmark Strait by the use of radar. Four days later (February 8) they intercepted a homeward-bound Halifax convoy, only to find that it was escorted by the *Ramillies*. As it had been determined that in no circumstances would they risk action with a British battleship, they hauled off, hoping to find a later convoy less strongly escorted. In this hope they were disappointed. Nothing more came their way until February 22, when they sank five ships that had been dispersed from an outward-bound convoy, four of them in ballast.

Thereafter the *Gneisenau* and the *Scharnhorst* shifted their cruising ground to the waters between the Canaries and the Cape Verde Islands, and there, a fortnight later (March 7–8) they made contact with and shadowed a homeward-bound Sierra Leone convoy. But as it, too, was escorted by a battleship, the *Malaya*, they dared not close. Three submarines working in these waters were directed to the convoy and one of them sank five ships in a night attack. This event made matters no better for the German battle cruisers, and next day they sheered off to look for shipping less heavily protected.

A week later (March 15–16), once more in mid–North Atlantic, the two battle cruisers came across many ships dispersed, but not sufficiently dispersed, from an outward-bound convoy, and they sank or captured sixteen of them. On the evening of the second day, just as they were finishing their work of destruction, they were disturbed by the *Rodney* which had received distress signals from the first ships encountered and had hastened to the scene, leaving the homeward-bound convoy she was escorting to the *Royal Sovereign*, which was on passage in the vicinity. On the *Rodney*'s appearance the German ships at once made off, shifting their cruising ground to the southeastward.

The haul of March 15–16 was the last success of the *Gneisenau* and the *Scharnhorst*. Considering the strength employed, a total of twenty-two ships (a Greek had been sunk on March 9), most of them in ballast, in a six weeks' cruise could not be considered an outstanding achievement. But it was serious enough, and these German ships had eluded all efforts to bring them to action. Now, at the end of March, they put into Brest for needed dockyard repairs, which it was hoped could be effected in time for the two ships to join the *Bismarck* and the *Prinz Eugen*, then preparing to leave Germany for an Atlantic cruise. But the enemy miscalculated. Thenceforward the battle cruisers were the targets of frequent and heavy attacks by the Royal Air Force. Soon after they arrived the *Gneisenau* was torpedoed by an aircraft of Coastal Command, shot down at the moment of success; and Bomber Command attacked with strong forces on every suitable night. In July the *Scharnhorst* succeeded, despite the night attacks, in moving to La Pallice, some 200 miles to the southward, intending to operate from there. Fortunately this move was at once detected by aerial photographs. Despite the additional distance, bombers reached the *Scharnhorst* in strength, and in a series of attacks inflicted such damage as forced her to return to Brest. There both ships remained, battling with bomb damage successfully enough to keep afloat but unable to renew Atlantic operations until finally they escaped upchannel in the following February (see chap. 11).

From the course of events up to April 1941 it is clear that the hopes entertained of covering the Atlantic trade with a fleet operating to the north of Scotland had not been fulfilled. Except for the slight delay imposed on the *Gneisenau* and the *Scharnhorst*, no ship had been prevented from entering the Atlantic or from returning to Germany northabout. The hopes with which the Admiralty had started the war had, of course, been much diminished by the German occupation of Norway.

Patrols on the relatively short Scotland–Norway line were no longer of use, and the best that could be expected against ships sailing from Norwegian harbors was to make contact with them on the much longer Scotland–Iceland–Greenland line and to intercept them as close to the southwestward of that line as could be managed. Chances of interception, supposing reconnaissance to be adequate, were increased by the establishment of an advanced base for the Home Fleet in Hvalfjordur near Reykjavik, since the natural tendency of enemy ships was to keep well to the northward, a tendency increased by the published intention of laying a mine barrier between Scotland and Iceland.

Mining these waters in the hope of taking toll of submarines was started in the autumn of 1940, despite the almost impracticable depth of water, and was continued throughout 1941, the work being done by a squadron of converted merchant ships with a combined capacity of about 2,000 mines for each lay. In fact, the technical shortcomings of the mines made them entirely ineffective for this purpose, and as a large proportion exploded soon after being laid the resulting barrier was so much an openwork one as to be of negligible danger even to a surface vessel if she passed through at right angles, protected by paravanes. But the details and shortcomings of the fields were, of course, unknown to the enemy; and there is no doubt that minefields once marked on charts, usually in all the impressiveness of heavy red ink, have a strong psychological effect on strategy, an effect that is often much in excess of their material effectiveness. And so it seems to have been on this occasion. In consequence the enemy was given a bias toward the use of Denmark Strait.

Yet, as suggested earlier, it seemed impossible to make contact with any of the enemy ships outward bound, at all events under winter conditions with long nights and bad weather. British aircraft, hard pressed by the requirements of antisubmarine operations, were insufficient in numbers and equipment for the task. A year or two later, with more aircraft and the great strides made in the development and reliability of airborne and shipborne radar (which eliminated many, though not all, of the handicaps of night and low visibility), such a campaign might have been possible, though the escape of the *Gneisenau* and the *Scharnhorst* from Brest in February 1942 showed how fallible air patrols using radar could still be at that time (see chap. 11). But as things were, it had been necessary to fall back on the far less satisfactory strategy of dealing with ships that were already in mid-Atlantic.

This ocean strategy comprised the protection of convoys by a combination of escort and cover, a complicated and difficult business despite a preponderance in heavy ships, now less than it had been because of the requirements of a Mediterranean war. Direct protection

70

could not be afforded continually, but whenever an enemy ship was known to be at large—probably after she had already inflicted some damage—the convoys most immediately threatened could be given escort by the older battleships; and, as already related, the *Ramillies* and the *Malaya* had saved their respective convoys from attack by the German battle cruisers. The remaining battleships of the Home Fleet (which at the beginning of 1941 included the *King George V* and later the *Prince of Wales*), the three battle cruisers, and the aircraft carriers (the *Ark Royal* and the newly completed *Victorious*) were available for covering operations; the *Ark Royal* and a battle cruiser were based on Gibraltar as Force H. The nature of the covering operations necessarily depended from day to day on the positions of the various convoys and the most recent news of the enemy. At all times a strong natural tendency for such an operation to develop into a wild-goose chase had to be resisted. The desire in these circumstances to eliminate all danger by sinking the enemy is rightly very strong and should be given all reasonable scope. But it should not go beyond that, and the tendency to fruitless searching can be countered only by a full realization of how quickly news of a fast-moving enemy becomes uselessly stale and what a small proportion of the broad Atlantic Ocean can be searched in a given time even with a large number of ships and aircraft.

As already recounted, these protecting operations were partly successful. The enemy was sometimes deterred from attack, and many of his successes were against outward-bound ships in ballast, less valuable than laden ships. But in this there had been at least a fair share of good fortune. And such were the losses already being suffered from submarine attack that the standards of safety at this time were not high. It cannot be said that the British forces had done all that could be desired, and in no case had the enemy been brought to action. Without more aircraft carriers and a greater preponderance in heavy ships, however, complete security against surface attack could have been achieved only by more intensive and better-equipped air patrols on the Scotland–Iceland–Greenland line than were then available.

In the final episode of this campaign, fortune was kinder and the strategy of intercepting enemy ships outward bound at last justified itself, albeit by a slender margin. Some of the success achieved was owing to the summer season with its virtual absence of night in high latitudes, and some also to the photographic reconnaissance of enemy harbors, now developed by the Royal Air Force to a high pitch of efficiency. In a general way visual reconnaissance from the air was of little value for this purpose, for it is always difficult and often impossible to distinguish between different types of ships except at the hazard of flying low. By

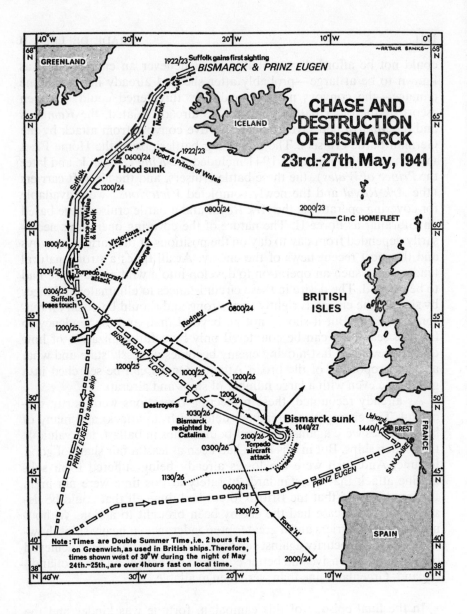

CHASE AND
DESTRUCTION
OF BISMARCK
23rd-27th. May, 1941

~ARTHUR BANKS~

GREENLAND

ICELAND

BRITISH
ISLES

FRANCE

SPAIN

1922/23 Suffolk gains first sighting
BISMARCK & PRINZ EUGEN

0600/24
Hood & Prince of Wales
1922/23
Hood sunk

Norfolk

Suffolk

1200/24

1800/24 Prince of Wales & Norfolk

Victorious

0001/25 Torpedo aircraft attack

0306/25
Suffolk loses touch

1200/25

BISMARCK LOST

K.George

0800/24

2000/23
C in C HOME FLEET

0800/24
Rodney

1200/25

1000/25

1200/26

PRINZ EUGEN to supply ship

Destroyers

1030/26
Bismarck re-sighted by Catalina

0300/26

1200/26

Bismarck sunk
1040/27

2100/26
Torpedo aircraft attack

Dorsetshire

Ushant
1440/1
BREST

ST. NAZAIRE

1130/26

0600/31

PRINZ EUGEN

1300/25

Force 'H'

2000/24

Note: Times are Double Summer Time, i.e. 2 hours fast
on Greenwich, as used in British ships. Therefore,
times shown west of 30°W during the night of May
24th.-25th., are over 4 hours fast on local time.

expert examination and measurement of photographs, however, all the information wanted could be obtained provided the sky was sufficiently free of cloud.

On May 21 photographic reconnaissance revealed the presence of the *Bismarck* and an 8-inch cruiser (afterward known to have been the *Prinz Eugen*) in a fjord near Bergen. The following day a daring reconnaissance in low cloud by a Fleet Air Arm aircraft showed that the ships had sailed and apparently had not returned to Germany. On the assumption that they were outward bound, the Home Fleet was disposed for intercepting them. On May 23, in the evening, the cruisers *Norfolk* and *Suffolk*, patrolling Denmark Strait, sighted both enemy ships steaming at high speed to the southwestward. As visibility was poor and variable, shadowing was difficult, despite the absence of darkness in this latitude. With the help of radar, however, touch was maintained, and by early the following morning the *Hood* and the *Prince of Wales* had been brought to a position barring the enemy's path.

The action that followed was brief and disastrous. The *Hood*, the biggest ship in the British Navy (about (42,000 tons standard displacement) and generally believed to embody all the lessons of the Battle of Jutland, was in fact inadequately armored. Hit at a range of 23,000 yards by a shell or shells which probably penetrated the 3-inch armor over her after magazine, she blew up and sank. Shortly afterward the *Prince of Wales*'s bridge was wrecked by a 15-inch shell; by this time also there had been several breakdowns in her turrets which were of new, unproven design and had been in the hands of their crews for only a few weeks. Action was therefore broken off. The *Bismarck*, hit three times by the *Prince of Wales*, was reported by a Coastal Command aircraft which had now joined to be leaving an oil track. In fact, she had lost 1,000 tons or more of fuel, and because of this damage had slightly reduced her speed. The *Norfolk*, the *Suffolk*, and the *Prince of Wales* continued in contact throughout the day, and in the afternoon, when the *Bismarck* turned toward the British ships for a while to screen the breakaway of the *Prinz Eugen*, ordered to a mid-Atlantic refueling position, the *Prince of Wales* fired a few more salvos at her. No hits were scored, however, the *Bismarck* quickly turning away again and shortly afterward resuming her southerly course.

Meanwhile the commander in chief, Admiral Tovey, was approaching in the *King George V*, having sent on the *Victorious*[6] to do what she

---

[6] The newly commissioned *Victorious* was not fully fit for service, and had only nine Swordfish and six Fulmars on board. These aircraft had been embarked only a few days before, and most of the pilots had had little experience in deck landing.

could with her aircraft. A strike of torpedo planes, sent off as soon as the carrier was within range, reached the *Bismarck* in the evening. She was hit by one torpedo, but it had no appreciable effect on her and she continued on her way to the southward with the cruisers shadowing.

By this time a lower latitude had been reached, and for a few hours darkness set in. The *Suffolk*, the only ship with effective radar, continued to shadow from the port quarter. Despite the darkness she continued, also, to zigzag, a procedure that at night only slightly reduced the danger of submarine attack, and in this instance jeopardized unjustifiably her paramount duty of keeping in touch with the enemy, for at the end of each port leg of the zigzag she broke radar contact. For a time, as she swung in again, contact was regained with such regularity that all seemed plain sailing; but at length, for some reason still unexplained, the expected time of regaining contact showed nothing on the radar screen. This was the calamitous situation that faced the *Suffolk* at about 3 A.M.[7] It was then supposed that the *Bismarck* must have taken avoiding action, and search was made to cover what seemed her most likely courses. But all was unavailing. Thereafter there was no clue to the enemy's movements except surmise; and surmise was not enough to enable the *Suffolk* and her consorts to regain touch with a high-speed enemy at large in the Atlantic.[8] The *Bismarck* was, in fact, almost as far south as the line between Newfoundland and Scotland, somewhat nearer the former than the latter. Once again British forces had failed to prevent an enemy ship from reaching the trade routes.

It has sometimes been said that the two most important principles of action in naval warfare are "never lose time" and "never lose touch." On this occasion no time had been lost. But the supreme importance of keeping touch does not seem to have been given the place it deserved. Had it been, it would not have been hazarded for the slight additional safety from submarine attack which, at night, is all that zigzagging can achieve. In that event, continuous radar contact would have been maintained and the subsequent period of uncertainty and acute anxiety would have been avoided.

As it was, the operations had virtually to begin again. But they began with one substantial advantage on the British side. The *Bismarck* had

---

[7] The 3 A.M. was British double summer time, as kept by the British ships. As the *Suffolk* was more than two hours west of Greenwich, however, in reality the time was about 11 P.M.

[8] It was assumed at the time, and for several years afterward, that, while the *Suffolk* was out of contact on her port zigzag leg, the *Bismarck* had hauled to the westward and then to the northward and eastward, crossing the wakes of the British cruisers. In fact, however, she made no drastic alteration of course, and was unaware that her pursuers had lost touch.

74

been forced to steam at high speed for so long a time that she had used a considerable proportion of her fuel before reaching the trade routes, and her shortage of oil was accentuated by the shell hit that had resulted in leaking tanks. She could be assumed to have an oiler waiting for her not far away, but on the whole it was unlikely that she would hazard the comparatively slow and vulnerable process of fueling at sea. Damaged as well as short of fuel, she was more likely to make for harbor. But what harbor? Would she make for Brest or Saint-Nazaire, the nearest ports available, risking the bombing to which the *Scharnhorst* and the *Gneisenau* were being subjected? Or would she attempt to break back to Germany where, in the Baltic, her damage could be repaired without molestation? These were the main alternatives for which British dispositions had to attempt to provide, with the balance thrown toward a French port as the most probable objective.

It was in fact for Saint-Nazaire that the *Bismarck* had decided to make, and she was steering to the southeastward at the best speed her remaining fuel would allow. On this course she was unmolested for more than thirty hours. Then, at 10:30 A.M. on May 26, while still nearly 600 miles from France, she was sighted by a searching Catalina flying boat of Coastal Command. Unfortunately, in difficult cloud conditions and as a result of the *Bismarck*'s fire, the aircraft failed to keep touch, but the fact that the enemy was making for France had been established. The *King George V* was coming down from the northward with the *Rodney*, which had previously been on passage to America to refit, steering to join her; and, from the direction of Gibraltar, Force H under Admiral Somerville, comprising the *Renown*, the *Ark Royal*, and the *Sheffield*, was approaching at high speed. At the time of the Catalina's discovery the *Ark Royal*'s aircraft were already beginning to search the same area, and three-quarters of an hour later one of them regained the lost contact.

The situation was still one of grave anxiety lest the *Bismarck* succeed in reaching harbor. This at her present speed she might well do, for the battleships to the northward would probably be unable to bar her path, and in addition they were themselves beginning to feel a shortage of fuel after much full-speed steaming. The *Renown*, with her comparatively light armor, was in no sense a match for the enemy. Everything depended, therefore, on forcing the *Bismarck* to slow down. Here hope lay, first with the *Ark Royal*'s aircraft, and, second, with four destroyers of the Tribal class and a Polish destroyer, under Captain Vian of the *Cossack*, approaching at high speed from the northward despite the difficulties of a heavy following sea.

About 4 P.M., in rough weather and poor visibility, the first strike of the *Ark Royal*'s torpedo aircraft found and attacked what they believed to be the *Bismarck*. But in fact it was the *Sheffield* which, unknown to the aircraft, had been sent ahead to make contact. Fortunately all torpedoes missed.[9] At 7:15 P.M. a second striking force was sent off. Aided by homing signals from the *Sheffield*, which was now in touch with the enemy, this attack was successful despite the extremely bad weather. Two torpedoes hit the *Bismarck*, one amidships and one right aft which jammed the rudders. It was the latter that was the decisive stroke of the operation, for, despite all efforts to free it, the starboard rudder remained jammed well over, and thereafter the *Bismarck* was unable to steam at anything but slow speed, and even at that could not hold the course for Saint-Nazaire. During the night Captain Vian's destroyers came up and attacked with torpedoes, though unsuccessfully; the next morning (May 27), in difficult visibility, the *King George V* and the *Rodney* arrived and engaged with gunfire. Before long the enemy was silenced, but she remained afloat until finally further torpedo hits from the cruiser *Dorsetshire* sent her to the bottom, being then about 400 miles west of Ushant.

Thus ended the enemy's most serious attempt to attack the Atlantic trade routes with heavy ships. In the next few days five supply ships were rounded up, and the consequent inability of the *Prinz Eugen* to refuel made her cut short her operations. Within a week she had returned to Brest after a fruitless cruise, and the whole episode was at an end.

Such were the difficulties and setbacks faced by the British forces in this operation, including the disastrous loss of the *Hood*, that it is of interest to consider what might have been done by the Germans had they had the patience to wait until the *Tirpitz* was ready for service and then launched a concerted attack, either fully concentrated or somewhat dispersed, with two battleships and two battle cruisers. This policy had in fact been considered by the German Naval Staff, but the battle cruisers were no longer fit for such service, and the idea of waiting another six months or so for the *Tirpitz* had been turned down by Raeder on the grounds that by that time conditions, including perhaps American entry into the war, might be even more discouraging than they were. A piecemeal attack had therefore been accepted. This operation failed and so, one hopes, would a concentrated attack have failed. But had chance favored the German ships, a heavier attack might well have inflicted grave damage on trade and perhaps also on the warships opposed to them. There were, however, two factors, neither foreseen

---

[9] Several torpedoes exploded soon after entering the water, owing to the imperfections of their magnetic pistols. Aircraft thereafter used the old-pattern contact pistol until the magnetic pistol could be made more reliable.

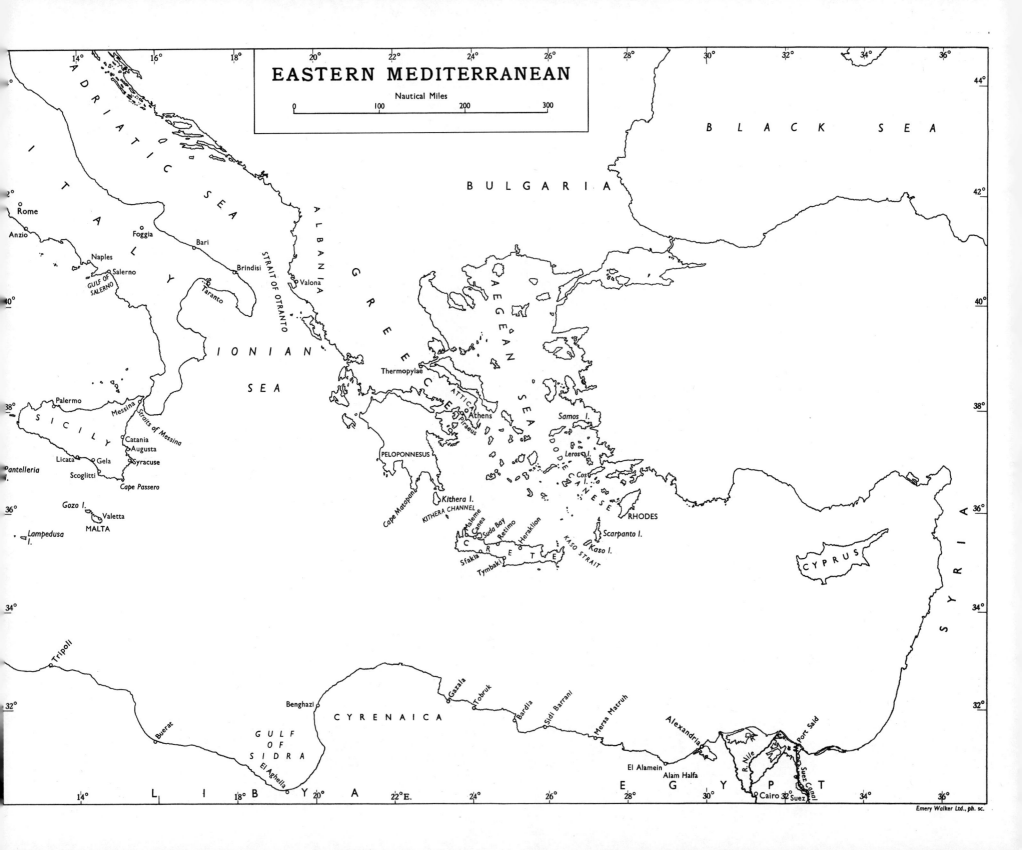

EASTERN MEDITERRANEAN

Nautical Miles

0   100   200   300

BLACK SEA

ADRIATIC SEA

ITALY

Rome

Anzio

Naples
Salerno
GULF OF SALERNO

Foggia

Bari

Brindisi

Taranto

STRAIT OF OTRANTO

ALBANIA

Valona

GREECE

BULGARIA

IONIAN SEA

AEGEAN SEA

Thermopylae

ATTICA

Athens
Piraeus

Samos I.

Palermo

SICILY

Messina
Straits of Messina

Catania
Augusta

Licata   Gela
Scoglitti   Syracuse

Cape Passero

Pantelleria

PELOPONNESUS

DODECANESE

Leros I.

Cos I.

Gozo I.

Valetta

MALTA

Lampedusa I.

Cape Matapan

Kithera I.

KITHERA CHANNEL

Maleme
Canea
Suda Bay
Retimo
Heraklion

RHODES

Scarpanto I.

CRETE

Sfakia
Tymbaki

KASO STRAIT

Kaso I.

CYPRUS

SYRIA

Tripoli

Buerat

GULF OF SIDRA

El Aghella

Benghazi

CYRENAICA

Gazala
Tobruk
Bardia
Sidi Barrani

Mersa Matruh

Alexandria

Port Said

El Alamein
Alam Halfa

R. Nile

Suez Canal

Cairo   Suez

LIBYA

14°   16°   18°   20°   22°E.   24°   26°   28°   30°   E G Y P T 32°   34°   36°

Emery Walker Ltd., ph. sc.

by Raeder, which would probably in any event have prevented such an enterprise, if postponed beyond the end of 1941, from being launched. From early in 1942 onward Hitler was obsessed by the fear that Norway might be invaded, and that such an invasion would be a grave blow. He therefore insisted that the heavy ships be kept in northern waters for defense. Second, in March 1942, a raid on Saint-Nazaire using an old destroyer as an explosive ship had crippled the only dry dock on the French Atlantic coast which might have been able to take the *Tirpitz* and the *Bismarck*.

7

THE MEDITERRANEAN, I: *From June 1940 to March 1941*

IN MANY OF ITS underlying motives, naval strategy in the Mediterranean in 1940 and subsequent years differed markedly from the strategy pursued elsewhere. The chief concern of the British Navy was, as always, the control of sea routes; but the balance of importance and urgency between the use of those routes and their denial to the enemy was very different from that in home waters and the Atlantic. When Italy joined her German ally, declaring war on June 10, 1940, it was evident that the use of the Mediterranean as a through trade route to the East, its main importance to Great Britain in peace, could no longer be sustained. All traffic to India, the Far East, and Australasia must now go round the Cape of Good Hope, a longer passage and therefore absorbing more tonnage, but without insurmountable difficulties. The resulting heavier proportionate loss in getting oil from Persia and Irak and merchandise from Egypt, because of the immensely longer haul, had perforce to be accepted.

If, then, the trade route through the Mediterranean could not be kept open, why need British forces concern themselves with the command of that sea? For what fundamental purpose was so large a proportion of none too ample naval resources to be employed in hard and sometimes costly fighting against sea and air forces that were in sum far more numerous?

Underlying everything was undoubtedly the view that Britain's position in the Mediterranean meant much to her standing in the world and hence to her chance of survival in the desperate situation she now faced. This view was firmly based on tradition, and held perhaps by no one more strongly than by Winston Churchill. Speaking on the navy estimates in March 1939, in the days when he was still a lone voice, he said: "Now, there is a school of thought which favours what is called 'sealing up both ends of Mediterranean' and leaving it as a closed sea. This policy will, I hope, be rejected by the Admiralty—I hope particularly by the present First Lord of the Admiralty [Earl Stanhope] who, in a matter like this, may hear the promptings of ancestral voices. To gain and hold command of the Mediterranean in time of war is a high duty of the fleet. Once that is achieved, all European land forces on the shores of North Africa will be decisively affected. Those that have command of the Mediterranean behind them can be reinforced to any extent and supplied to any extent. Those that have no such command will be like cut flowers in a vase."

Little more than a year later Churchill was prime minister, bearing full responsibility, and the policy he had outlined then was to be pursued to the utmost extent of Britain's power, despite the withdrawal of France which, in 1939, had been envisaged as an ally in a Mediterranean war. Everything possible was to be done to prevent the Italians from reinforcing their army in Libya, and offensive action against the Italian Navy was to be pressed to such an extent as might even permit the reinforcement of the army in Egypt by the direct route past the enemy's very threshold.

The immediate danger was to the position in Egypt. It may be that even then the Prime Minister, with his foresight and buoyant courage, looked forward to a success in the Mediterranean which would eventually permit an attack somewhere on "the soft underbelly of the Axis." But that would be a long way ahead, and in the meanwhile all efforts must be directed to maintaining the position in the region where Africa joins Asia, and thus preventing an advance of the enemy to the Indian Ocean and perhaps down the length of Africa.

The decision to hold on in the eastern Mediterranean, not only with an army assisted by air and light naval forces, but with a fleet prepared to face anything Italy could send against it, was one of greater boldness and courage than is easily realized in the light of after events. At that time no one knew how much might be achieved by enemy aircraft, working from Rhodes, in blocking the Suez Canal and in damaging the fleet's inadequately defended base at Alexandria, which had only a floating dock for the repair of big ships. It might well be that ships damaged in these waters would be bottled up there, unable to regain fighting trim and unable to withdraw because, with Tunisian harbors and airfields no longer in friendly hands, passage past Sicily would be too dangerous for a damaged ship. But these risks were accepted. Because of increasing Italian truculence during the German advance in France, the Mediterranean Fleet, virtually disbanded the autumn before, had recently been reconstituted. Four battleships—*Warspite, Malaya, Royal Sovereign,* and *Ramillies*—and some cruisers and destroyers had been sent eastward, and the aircraft carrier *Eagle* and some additional cruisers and destroyers had joined from the East Indies, bringing the total light forces to seven 6-inch cruisers and eighteen destroyers. Now, despite the uncertainties of the situation elsewhere, and even while the fate of the French fleet was still unknown, it was determined that the position on the eastern Mediterranean should be maintained.

The opposition to be faced at sea was an Italian navy whose main purpose was to put life into Mussolini's boast of the Mediterranean as *Mare Nostrum*, but which had in fact no strategical aim other than defense of the lines of communication between Italy and Libya. Its battleship strength consisted of two new and four old (12.6-inch) ships, though the former and two of the latter which were being reconstructed were not ready until a few weeks after the declaration of war. That the British fleet could face these ships with assurance there was no doubt, but in other types the enemy had a preponderance of about three to one, a superiority that might well hamper operations not in the immediate vicinity of the battle fleet. Seven 8-inch and twelve 6-inch cruisers, with thirty-six modern and nineteen older destroyers, amounted to a force that should have been formidable, even though it lacked aircraft carriers. The navy had wanted them but they had been vetoed by Mussolini on the grounds that, with Italy's central position and her airfields in the Dodecanese Islands, all that was needed could be done from the shore; and for this purpose the air force was equipped with a sizable body of aircraft trained in sea warfare, against which the *Eagle*'s handful of fighters could do nothing effectual. Cooperation between aircraft and ships, however, had in every instance to be organized through their respective headquarters in Rome, a cumbrous arrangement that did not make for effectiveness in battle.

On these material factors the war in the Mediterranean was to be based, but they were perhaps of less importance than the personality of the British commander in chief. Admiral Sir Andrew Cunningham's career had been an unusual one for an officer in high command at this time. As a lieutenant he had not specialized, as had most of his distinguished contemporaries, and his only Admiralty service had been for a few months just before the war. His junior service had included seven years in command of the destroyer *Scorpion*, a continuity unprecedented in modern times, which almost equaled the famous eight-year command of the *Foudroyant* a century and a half earlier by John Jervis, afterward Earl of St. Vincent. Cunningham had in fact not a little in common with his great predecessor. Both were inflexible in demanding the highest standards of discipline and battleworthiness, though in each there was a deep humanity underlying his outward sternness. And both were unshakable in resolution. When hard times came to Cunningham's fleet, as they were to come before long, no ship would be allowed to plead that damage or defects prevented her putting to sea if it was physically possible for her to go. But those times were not yet, and now, with his zest for action, Cunningham at once set about establishing a moral ascendancy over the enemy which was for a time to override his numerical inferiority in ships and aircraft.

In the operations of the next eighteen months there were several clearly marked phases. Of these the first covered the period from June 1940 till the appearance of German aircraft on the scene on January 10, 1941. During this phase Admiral Cunningham had only Italian forces opposed to him and could shape his course accordingly.

Despite his readiness to meet the Italian fleet in battle, however, he could not by any means do all he wanted to in regard to cutting the enemy's communications with Libya. As already indicated, the fleet had to be based on Alexandria. Malta, though ideally situated close to the routes from Italy to North Africa, was almost bare of defenses with which to meet air attacks from nearby Sicily, and so could not be used for the present by anything except submarines (of which there were only six at the start) and a few flying boats. Its fighter defenses, in fact, totaled four Gladiators flown by flying-boat pilots, and it was two months before they were reinforced by some Hurricanes flown in from a carrier in the western Mediterranean. With the main British forces based 900 miles away in Egypt, then, the situation in the central Mediterranean was rather a paradoxical one. Usually it is more practicable to deny particular sea routes to the enemy, or at least to hamper his use of them, than it is to use routes in the same area oneself. In the Atlantic, for example, British forces could prevent any regular flow of enemy shipping, though they were hard put to it to defend their own. But here, though the passage from Italy to Africa was so short and so close to the enemy's main strength that he could keep it in use at this time with little danger, Admiral Cunningham's activities were so aggressive and the enemy's opposition by sea and air so ineffectual that the route to Malta from Alexandria could continue in use at will, and (as mentioned later) it was also found possible, at need, to pass military convoys through from the west.

It was in connection with convoy operations that the first brush between the fleets came about. On July 9 the British fleet (less the *Ramillies* and two cruisers), while on its way to cover some convoys from Malta to Alexandria, nearly succeeded in barring the path of an Italian squadron consisting of two battleships of the *Cavour* class and a strong force of cruisers and destroyers which was on its return from escorting a convoy to Benghazi. The enemy battleships, reported by a submarine early on the 8th when steering to the southward, were later found by a flying boat from Malta, by which time they were heading back for Taranto. Admiral Cunningham steered to intercept them, and on the afternoon of the 9th action was joined at long range. The *Warspite* hit an Italian battleship before the latter was screened by smoke, but thereafter the range could not be closed any further. With his way to Taranto barred, the enemy made for the Strait of Messina. The hope that he might be slowed down by the *Eagle*'s few torpedo aircraft was not realized; and, with the Italian coast and its airfields only 25 miles away and no ground having been gained, the chase had to be called off. The British fleet then closed Malta and covered the passage of two convoys to Alexandria without mishap.

This demonstration of the fleet's ability to do much as it liked in the central Mediterranean was not achieved without interference from the Italian air force. Throughout July 8 and 9, and again on the return passage, the ships were constantly attacked by considerable numbers of high-level bombers, and against these there was no adequate defense. Gunfire was a slight deterrent, but the *Eagle*'s few fighters could do little to help, for she had no means of directing them. In fact, at this time the value of the small numbers of fighters in aircraft carriers was seriously in question as far as the defense of a fleet was concerned. Despite the lack of opposition, however, the bombers scored only one hit, on the bridge of the cruiser *Gloucester* (July 8), and it was clear that unless their aim was much improved they could not prevent Admiral Cunningham from doing as he wished. That their one hit should have achieved far more than material damage by killing the captain of the *Gloucester*, thought by many to be one of the most able and promising officers of his rank in the service, was a result disproportionate to their accuracy.

Ten days later the fleet's fighting superiority over the Italians was again displayed when, in the Aegean, the Australian 6-inch cruiser *Sydney* and five destroyers sank an Italian 6-inch cruiser and routed her consort, an action that showed how insecure were the Italian lines of communication to the Dodecanese Islands and to the Black Sea.

Six weeks later important reinforcements were sent from Great Britain both to the army in Egypt and to the fleet in the eastern Mediterranean. So great was the Italian preponderance of numbers in Libya that the strengthening of the British forces, particularly with armor, was essential if the enemy was to be prevented from reaching the delta of the Nile. Should he gain a firm foothold there it might well be impossible to maintain the position in Egypt and the Levant. So dire was the need, therefore, that it was decided, despite the imminent possibility of invasion, to send out the only three armored regiments in England which could be made ready for service overseas. It has sometimes been said that of all the weighty and courageous decisions made by the Prime Minister during the war, this one was outstanding. Not only was he resolved that these 150 precious tanks should go, but he strongly urged that they should be sent through the Mediterranean with the naval reinforcements.

To this latter proposal the First Sea Lord would not agree. The hazards of the passage past the Italian naval bases and close to the airfields of Sardinia and Sicily, though they could be faced by fast and relatively well-protected warships, were as yet too untested to be accepted for merchant ships, even the so-called fast motor transport ships of 15 knots. Such ships might well be slowed down by torpedo or bomb hits and perhaps, therefore, have to be abandoned; for high speed seemed essential to success. With the proviso that the risk would nevertheless be accepted if at the last moment the military need in Egypt was clearly urgent, the Admiralty ordered the transports to be convoyed to Suez round the Cape.

These reinforcements sailed at the end of August, and since the situation was then quiescent enough, they proceeded as planned. While the transports steamed into the South Atlantic, Admiral Somerville's Force H, which included the *Hood* and the *Ark Royal* and was based on Gibraltar, advanced eastward into the Mediterranean with the naval reinforcements in company. These were the battleship *Valiant*, the new aircraft carrier *Illustrious*, and two antiaircraft cruisers. Simultaneously Admiral Cunningham's fleet escorted a convoy from Alexandria to Malta.

The whole operation was a remarkable success, presenting notably less difficulty than had been expected. It did not offer the opportunity for fighting the Italian fleet which had perhaps been hoped for. Though Italian battleships were sighted by the *Eagle*'s aircraft, they kept out of harm's way. But the reinforcing warships came through the Sicilian narrows without incident, the *Valiant* and the cruisers landed some guns and ammunition at Malta, and all then joined Admiral Cunningham to the eastward on September 3 for the passage to Alexandria. The only casualty throughout was slight bomb damage to one ship in the Alexandria–Malta convoy.

The arrival of the *Illustrious* altered considerably the aspect of future fleet operations and the protection of convoys with which those operations were usually concerned. Not only had she more and better fighters than the *Eagle*, but being equipped with radar she could direct them against approaching enemy aircraft. The appliances for this were primitive in comparison with the fighter-direction equipment and organization in use in aircraft carriers at the end of the war; but they were sufficient soon to prove their worth against the Italians. Not only could approaching bombers be engaged and shot down or scattered before they reached their dropping positions, but shadowing aircraft could often be shot down before they had had more than a fleeting glimpse of the British ships. This new effectiveness much reduced the chances of the bombers' finding the fleet at all, and also denied important information to the enemy surface forces should they dare to take a hand in the operations.

Soon afterward the Italians made two moves on land, both important but both singularly unsuccessful. On September 13 the Libyan army advanced through a part of the desert which was Egyptian territory. But it got no farther than Sidi Barrani, only 50 miles across the frontier and still 200 miles short of the Nile Delta. There it was halted and there it remained for the next three months. On October 28 Mussolini made an unprovoked attack on Greece, to the annoyance of his German ally who had not been consulted. Here also the Italian army failed signally, being held by the Greeks at nearly all points. For the British Navy, however, the situation was considerably altered. Obligations to Greece extended naval commitments, but at the same time the fleet was at liberty to use Greek harbors, and in particular Suda Bay in Crete where an advanced fueling base was at once established. Thus a virtual stop could be put to any trade between Italy and the Black Sea, and it also became difficult for the Italians to send any reinforcements to the Dodecanese.

The additional commitments of the Greek situation made more important than ever the next step that had been planned for asserting still further Admiral Cunningham's ascendancy over the Italian fleet. This was to be an attack by carrier-borne torpedo aircraft on the fleet in Taranto Harbor. Success in this endeavor might have, in addition to its general benefits, the further merit of enabling help to be given to the Greeks on their west coast as well as in the Aegean.

The intention was to launch the attack with the full strength of both aircraft carriers; but as the *Eagle*'s gasoline tanks were leaking as a result of near misses by bombs in a previous operation, the task had to be undertaken by the *Illustrious* alone, though with five Swordfish from the *Eagle* to strengthen her striking force. On the night of November 11 the attacking aircraft were sent in, in two waves three-quarters of an hour apart, from a position about 180 miles southeast of Taranto. The attack was remarkably successful for so small a force against ships in a heavily defended harbor. Twenty aircraft went in. Of the six Italian battleships in harbor three were torpedoed: the *Littorio* with three hits sank in shallow water (though she was afterward docked) and two of the *Cavour* class settled down after one hit each, one of them being severely damaged. All but two of the aircraft returned. The strength in which the Italians could have tried conclusions with Admiral Cunningham, had they been so minded, had been drastically reduced for some time to come; and, adding still further to the British fleet's liberty of action, the Italians, lest worse should befall them, transferred their main base to Naples.

Simultaneously with this operation, a force of cruisers and destroyers raided the Brindisi–Valona route in the Strait of Otranto, the main Italian supply line to their armies in Greece. A returning convoy was encountered and most of it destroyed.

While these offensive operations were keeping the enemy well occupied, the opportunity was taken to pass a convoy from Alexandria to Malta under cover of the battle fleet, and for the latter to be reinforced by the *Barham* and two cruisers from England. All these movements were effected without molestation, except from aircraft, and without damage.

Experience in these operations made it clear that a convoy could be sent past Sicily without undue risk, and a fortnight later this was done. Protected by Force H (in which the *Renown* had replaced the *Hood*), the convoy of three fast motor transport ships advanced through the western Mediterranean. With it, in addition to the *Sheffield* of Force H, were two other cruisers, *Manchester* and *Southampton*, each carrying 700 Royal Air Force reinforcements for Egypt. Until the longitude of Sardinia was reached no enemy was encountered; but there, on November 27, the convoy faced for some hours the possibility of attack by Italian forces which included two battleships, one of them modern, and six cruisers. The enemy ships were sighted to the northward at a time when the *Ramillies*, two cruisers (*Newcastle* and *Berwick*), and a destroyer screen, sent by Admiral Cunningham for passage to Gibraltar with the returning Force H, were already through the Sicilian narrows and about to join Admiral Somerville. The subsequent advance of Admiral Somerville's combined force toward the enemy, however, which resulted in a long-range action with the Italian cruisers, was sufficient to deter the battleships from coming any closer. As torpedo aircraft from the *Ark Royal* failed to slow down the retreating enemy, Admiral Somerville had then to break off an action that he could not press and rejoin the convoy, which had been diverted to the southward. A bombing attack en route failed to damage any of his ships, and he continued in company with the convoy till dusk. Then he returned toward Gibraltar, and the convoy with its close escort and the eastbound cruisers passed south of Sicily unscathed. It was met next morning by a strong force of the Mediterranean Fleet off Malta, to which two of the transports were bound, and thence the third transport and the warships proceeded to Alexandria without further incident.

At this time and during the next six weeks the British position in the Mediterranean was more clearly dominant and freer from menace than it was to be again for two years to come. It was still impossible to do more than harass the enemy's lines of supply to Africa and to Greece; and Malta was still too much in the front line to be a suitable base for strong naval forces. But there was no difficulty in keeping Malta provisioned by convoy from Egypt, and the passage of military supply convoys to Malta and Egypt through the Sicilian narrows had been effected with negligible damage.

Though it was impossible to prevent the enemy from building up his land forces, this seemed to be amply counterbalanced by the success of the British and Greek armies. In Greece not only were the Italians firmly held, but at some points they had been driven back into Albania. And in Libya, on December 7, General Wavell's attack at Sidi Barrani started a victorious advance which was to take him forward in two months to Benghazi and beyond. It was for this purpose that he had been steadily reinforced by the Red Sea route, particularly by Australian troops, as well as, for urgent equipment, by a transport through the Mediterranean, as already mentioned. Even the Red Sea route had at one time been potentially dangerous, for the Italians had had destroyers and submarines at Massawa, in Eritrea, which had not yet fallen to the land forces.[1] But though these enemy ships stretched still further the escort resources, the convoys from the south were uninterrupted, and by the end of August all the submarines but one had been sunk.[2]

To both the defense of Greece and the advance in Libya, the navy, with its dominant position and liberty of action, was able to contribute. To the former it contributed only fleetingly, on December 18, by a battleship night bombardment of Valona, the Italian base in Albania, accompanied by a cruiser raid into the Adriatic. But in the Libyan campaign naval cooperation was continuous, both in keeping the forward troops supplied by sea and in providing fire support from the seaward flank. Monitors and gunboats were constantly in action despite enemy aircraft, and on January 3 the battleships lent the weight of their 15-inch gunfire to an attack that drove the enemy from Bardia.

[1] Massawa was captured by the army four months later, on April 8, 1941.
[2] The one submarine that escaped destruction successfully circumnavigated Africa and returned to Italy.

It was on January 10, 1941, that the first cloud came over the horizon, portending the coming storm of German attack. So badly were things going with the Italians that Hitler decided he must do something to rectify the position. A campaign through Bulgaria against Greece was planned for the spring, to be followed by the capture of Crete, and perhaps thereafter by a thrust at Irak through Syria. In Africa the Italians were to be strengthened as soon as possible with German armored formations. This assistance would greatly increase the striking power of the enemy's army, and in conjunction with the threat from the northward might well be able to outmatch General Wavell's straitened resources and thrust him back into the Nile Delta and beyond. Meanwhile, as immediate succor and to prepare the way for these blows, a strong force of the Luftwaffe, mostly dive-bombers, was sent to Sicily to challenge the British fleet's liberty of action in the central Mediterranean.

By this time the passage of a through convoy had become a well-accepted operation, and early in January further supplies for Malta and Greece (where there was a small contingent of the Royal Air Force with some attached troops) were sent out by this route. The convoy, protected in the western Mediterranean as before by Force H, was taken on through the narrows by a small escort of cruisers. Early in the morning of January 10, this escort swept aside some Italian destroyers that had stumbled upon it, sinking one. There was nothing unusual or untoward in this, nor in the few desultory bombing attacks that followed. Shortly afterward the main body of the Mediterranean Fleet, including the *Illustrious*, came into touch with the convoy, which was then about halfway between the Tunisian coast and Malta, steering to the southeastward.

About midday, however, the situation was drastically transformed. Some shadowing aircraft had been shot down by the *Illustrious'* fighters, and some unsuccessful Italian torpedo aircraft were chased away. But while most of the available fighters were so employed and more were being flown off, a large force of Ju 87's and Ju 88's came on the scene; the defense was heavily outnumbered and a strong dive-bombing attack was made on the fleet with the *Illustrious* as the principal target. The latter, though severely crippled, managed to make good her damage sufficiently to enable her to reach Malta. There she remained for nearly a fortnight, the constant target of bombing attacks; but despite the great difficulty of repairing under such conditions, she was away again on January 23 and succeeded in reaching Alexandria without further damage.

Meanwhile the convoy, with the fleet covering it, had reached its destination, though not without more casualties. Some of the cruisers had been heavily attacked on January 11, and the *Southampton* was so badly damaged that she had to be sunk.

The outcome of this operation was to make it clear that the British fleet could no longer trail its coat in the waters of the central Mediterranean. German dive-bombers in the numbers now established there could swamp any fighter defense the fleet could put up, even if the seriously damaged *Illustrious* was replaced. And dive-bombing with German determination and apparent disregard of losses had shown itself effective against ships. Fortunately, the area in which these aircraft could operate was not for the present very extensive. They were of comparatively short range, particularly the Ju 87's, which were the more numerous type. They were confined to working from Sicily and Tripoli, for General Wavell's victorious advance still continued, and by February 7 Benghazi had been captured and all Cyrenaica was in his hands. That British forces still had liberty of movement in the western Mediterranean, too, was being shown by Admiral Somerville with Force H. The *Ark Royal*'s aircraft attacked targets in Sardinia on February 1, and on the 9th Genoa was bombarded by a battleship and a battle cruiser while aircraft bombed Leghorn.

Unfortunately the replacement of the *Illustrious*, so as to give Admiral Cunningham's fleet some measure of fighter protection, could not be effected immediately. The passage past Sicily seemed for the present too hazardous for such a purpose, and the enemy had at last succeeded in blocking the Suez Canal, at least temporarily. Aircraft from Rhodes were able to sow magnetic-acoustic mines too thickly for the local sweepers to keep the passage clear, and reinforcements equipped with gear able to deal with the new type of mine had therefore to be sent from South Africa. It was not until the middle of March that the canal was again open. Then, as soon as passage was feasible, the *Illustrious* passed south, bound for a United States navy yard where several British warships were now being refitted under lend-lease arrangements. At the same time the *Formidable* came through to the northward to relieve her.

Then began a time of great adversity for British arms in the Mediterranean by sea, land, and air, with only the victory off Cape Matapan to lighten for a moment the gathering gloom. Thereafter, though British forces throughout displayed great heroism and endurance, and though much was achieved locally with slender resources, the stream set strongly against them with only a temporary slackening at the end of the year when the army again advanced in Libya. It was not till the battle of El Alamein and the landings in Algeria and Morocco, still

eighteen months ahead, that the possibility of dominating the Mediterranean theater again came in sight.

In February it had been decided that substantial help must be given
to the Greeks in face of the German attack that was clearly imminent.
Arrangements were made, therefore, to send more than half of General
Wavell's forces—British, Australian, and New Zealand—to Greece,
leaving only a slender, but it was hoped sufficient, force to hold
Cyrenaica. Intelligence about German reinforcement of the Italian
African army was very meager, but it was thought that there was little
likelihood of an enemy offensive for some months, by which time further
troops would be available for service in the field. The immediate concern of the navy, therefore, was to safeguard the transport of an army
comprising an armored brigade and three infantry divisions to Greece,
an operation it was estimated would take two months. The armored
brigade was the first to go, and on March 7 it landed at Piraeus.

A particularly sharp eye had to be kept on the Italian Navy lest it
be tempted to interfere with the convoys of transports passing between
Egypt and the Aegean. To cover one of these convoys, Admiral Cunningham's fleet put to sea on March 27 in its full available strength:
three battleships, the newly arrived *Formidable* and nine destroyers
from Alexandria, and four 6-inch cruisers and four destroyers from
Piraeus. The immediate information on which this move was decided
was an air report of three enemy cruisers in the Ionian Sea steering
to the southeastward. A convoy, due to pass between Crete and Cape
Matapan on the 28th, was therefore turned back to the eastward for a
time, while Admiral Cunningham shaped course for a position halfway
between Crete and Cyrenaica and ordered the cruisers to join him there.

Next morning, March 28, scouting aircraft from the *Formidable* reported a force of three cruisers and four destroyers south of the west
end of Crete steering southeastward. It seemed at first as if this might
have been an erroneous report of the British cruisers that were in that
vicinity on their way to join the Commander in Chief. But this doubt
was soon dispelled when Vice Admiral Pridham-Wippell, commanding
the cruisers, sighted a force of three 8-inch cruisers to the northward
of him. The British cruisers (*Orion, Ajax, Perth,* and *Gloucester*), out-
gunned, outranged, and of slower speed, could only retire toward the
battleships, hoping to escape serious damage until help was at hand and
the tables could be turned.

An hour later, at 9 A.M., the enemy cruisers turned away, having
been ordered by their commander in chief, approaching in the *Vittorio
Veneto,* to lure the British toward him. Admiral Pridham-Wippell
turned to follow them, and not long afterward a force of torpedo aircraft was sent off from the *Formidable* to attack the enemy cruisers

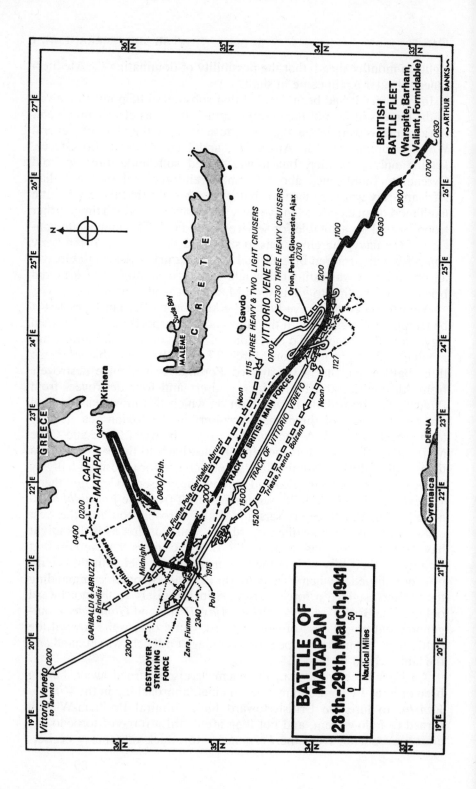

BATTLE OF
MATAPAN
28th.-29th. March,1941

BRITISH
BATTLE FLEET
(Warspite, Barham,
Valiant, Formidable)

ARTHUR BANKS

GREECE

CAPE
MATAPAN

Kithera

CRETE

MALEME
Suda Bay

Gavdo

THREE HEAVY & TWO LIGHT CRUISERS

0730 THREE HEAVY CRUISERS

Orion, Perth, Gloucester, Ajax
0730

VITTORIO VENETO

TRACK OF BRITISH MAIN FORCES

TRACK OF VITTORIO VENETO

Trieste, Trento, Bolzano

Zara, Fiume, Pola, Garibaldi, Abruzzi

GARIBALDI & ABRUZZI
to Brindisi

British Cruisers

DESTROYER
STRIKING
FORCE

Zara, Fiume

Pola

Vittorio Veneto
to Taranto

DERNA

Cyrenaica

Nautical Miles

in the hope of slowing them down. The chase continued, with the enemy sometimes drawing out of sight and sometimes being regained to view, until 11 A.M., when the situation was once more transformed. At that time the British cruisers sighted the *Vittorio Veneto* to the northward and had again to retire toward the main body. They were soon under 15-inch gunfire and were being overhauled by the faster enemy, but they made much smoke and no damage was sustained.

Half an hour later there was another change of scene. The *Formidable*'s aircraft, sent off to attack the enemy cruisers, had sighted the *Vittorio Veneto*. Rightly recognizing her as a far more important target, the commander of the striking force changed his objective and concentrated his force on her, though unsuccessfully. For the Italian admiral this was the first indication that an aircraft carrier was opposed to him. He had no defending aircraft and, though the first blow had failed and he still knew nothing of the British battleships, he was disinclined to risk advancing farther. He therefore abandoned the attack on the cruisers and turned for home.

The operation now became a direct chase, and the main question was whether the *Vittorio Veneto*'s speed could be reduced sufficiently for Admiral Cunningham to overhaul her before she reached waters dominated by German dive-bombers. The British battleships were at this time 55 miles astern of their quarry, steaming at their full speed of 23 knots. But the enemy battleship was steaming at 25 knots or more, and the only hope lay in a drastic reduction of her speed by further air attacks.

In addition to the *Formidable*'s aircraft, there were three Swordfish available at Maleme airfield in Crete. They also had taken part in the morning's operations, but had struck at the cruisers before the battleship appeared. Royal Air Force bombers from Greece, twenty-three in all, also attacked some of the enemy cruisers during the course of the afternoon, but without hitting. About 3:15 P.M., however, another strike from the *Formidable* scored a hit that seriously damaged the *Vittorio Veneto* and slowed her down. But it was not long before she was able to increase speed again, for a time attaining as much as 19 knots, and the remaining hope lay in a third strike planned for evening twilight. At 7:30 P.M. all available aircraft attacked—eight from the *Formidable* and two from Maleme. The target was heavily hit and appeared thereafter to be stopped; and all aircraft returned safely to Maleme. It seemed then that the hoped-for success was within Admiral Cunningham's grasp. But it was not to be. In the bad light there had been a mistake in identification of the target; the ship attacked was not, in fact, the *Vittorio Veneto*, but the *Pola*, one of a group of three 8-inch cruisers which had previously been to the northward and had just joined the enemy's main body.

Believing he had a good prospect of overtaking the enemy during the night while still being clear of the dive-bombers in the morning, Admiral Cunningham stood on in chase, determined to accept the hazards of a night action with its possible confusions and dangers to the big ships from torpedoes, rather than let the enemy escape. At the time these hazards must have seemed even more formidable than they really were, for the various reports from scouting aircraft suggested that there were two more battleships in the group, which in fact comprised only the *Pola* and her consorts.

Hoping to inflict still heavier damage on the enemy before his battleships delivered the *coup de grâce*, at 8:40 P.M. the Commander in Chief sent eight destroyers ahead, giving them the enemy's estimated position, course, and speed and ordering them to attack with torpedoes. But this information was not sufficient to put them in touch with the enemy. With air reconnaissance only by day, so long a period had to elapse between the last air report of the enemy and the time when a destroyer force, starting a chase from 35 miles astern, could reach its objective that any prediction of the enemy's position would almost certainly be widely in error. Had the cruisers been spread for searching, the chances of finding the enemy would have been the best achievable; but Admiral Pridham-Wippell, though chasing ahead at his best speed, had kept his squadron concentrated, the better to fight the superior number of enemy cruisers that might at any moment have been encountered. Though intending to spread as soon as circumstances permitted, various considerations prevented his doing so, and in the event neither cruisers nor destroyers found the enemy's main force.

The destroyers, however, might have missed the enemy's main body even if the cruisers had found it. For the latter did find an enemy which they believed to be the *Vittorio Veneto*. At 8:30 P.M. the *Ajax* detected by radar (still primitive in those days) a large ship lying stopped, and a signal to this effect reached the Commander in Chief soon afterward. The signal, however, was not received by the destroyers, and presumably they might have missed other reports of the enemy had such been made. Admiral Pridham-Wippell then turned his force northward in the hope of encountering more enemy ships, but in this effort he was unsuccessful.

The British battleships—*Warspite*, *Valiant*, and *Barham*—stood on for the immobilized enemy, which was in fact the *Pola*, and at 10 P.M. gained contact with her on the port bow and altered course together to close. While closing, however, two other large ships were sighted to the westward steering an east-southeasterly course. Admiral Cunningham at once turned his battleships to a west-northwesterly course, bringing the strangers on to his port bow. Searchlights showed the enemy to be two 8-inch cruisers and some destroyers, evidently returning to the assistance of their damaged consort. In a matter of seconds the 15-inch broadsides of the three battleships were poured into them, and fire was continued for three or four minutes. By that time the two cruisers *Zara* and *Fiume* were stopped and burning. A brief and brilliant display of tactics and gunnery was completed by a sharp turn away to avoid the torpedoes that might be expected from enemy destroyers following the cruisers. Admiral Cunningham then retired from the scene, leaving his screening destroyers to engage the enemy destroyers and finish off the crippled ships. After a time of some confusion, these five destroyers were joined by the striking force returning from its unsuccessful quest. The *Fiume* had sunk about 11 P.M. At 2:30 A.M. the striking force finished off the burning *Zara*, and soon after 4 A.M. the *Pola* was sunk, after her crew had been taken off. In the morning all destroyers rejoined the Commander in Chief and the fleet returned to Alexandria.

So ended the battle of Matapan. Three Italian 8-inch cruisers had been sunk and one of their newest battleships damaged, set against the loss of the aircraft that had torpedoed the *Vittorio Veneto*, the only British casualty throughout the operation. In the grave times immediately ahead this outcome somewhat relieved the burden on the Mediterranean Fleet by making it far less probable that any serious interference need be feared from the Italian Navy. To the Germans it must have been equally clear that anything they hoped to do in the Mediterranean could be done only by virtue of an overwhelming strength in the air, the bulk of which they would have to contribute themselves, and that, though they might well be able to command waters within range of such airfields as they could establish and equip with dive-bombers, beyond that range they could not hope to go. One of their principal aims, therefore, had to be to push their airfields ever farther forward, hoping that they might so diminish the area in which British ships could operate as finally to command the whole expanse of the Mediterranean Sea by means of air power. Only if the British could bring a comparable air power, whether shipborne or shore-based, against them could the balance be held or reversed, and of this possibility there was at present no sign.

8

THE MEDITERRANEAN, II: *From April to December 1941*

N O SOONER HAD Admiral Cunningham's victorious fleet returned to Alexandria than the blow fell in Cyrenaica. Already the situation there had been made difficult by the constant bombing of Benghazi, which had forced the army to stop using it as a supply port and to use Tobruk, more than 200 miles farther back, instead. In addition, far earlier than expected, the Germans had a light armored division ready for service in conjunction with two Italian divisions, the whole virtually under the command of Rommel. On March 31 the enemy attacked at El Agheila (150 miles south of Benghazi) and drove back General Wavell's scanty forces without difficulty. On April 3 Benghazi was evacuated, and by the 11th the army had been forced back to the Egyptian frontier, leaving only Tobruk, occupied by an Australian division, holding out behind the enemy's lines. This occupation, denying the port to the enemy, was a symbol of determination to return one day to the attack; but meanwhile the area of sea that could be dominated by German dive-bombers had been much increased, and the passage westward from Egypt between Cyrenaica and Crete was seriously menaced.

The menace was not immediate, however, and while the enemy was still establishing himself the navy did what was possible to damage his communications afloat and ashore. Four destroyers under the command of Captain Mack of the *Jervis* were sent to work from Malta against the supply convoys from Italy, and on the night of April 15–16 they annihilated an outward-bound convoy off Sfax, sinking five merchantmen and three destroyers for the loss of the destroyer *Mohawk*. In the early hours of April 21 the battle fleet bombarded Tripoli by the light of flares dropped by the *Formidable*'s aircraft, sinking ships in the harbor and damaging installations ashore. The British forces withdrew unscathed before daylight; their only casualty throughout the operation was the loss of one of the *Formidable*'s fighters.

While their advance in Cyrenaica was still in progress, the Germans attacked Greece. Their invasion from Bulgaria started on April 6, and within a few days it became clear that the Greek army and the British imperial forces fighting with them were inadequate to hold the enemy back. As in every German attack in the early part of the war, the Luftwaffe dominated the air and virtually prohibited the movement of troops by day. And bombing soon made Piraeus unusable as a supply port. The army consisted only of an armored brigade (whose tanks were quickly wearing out), the New Zealand division, and part of an Australian division, but it was impossible to reinforce them; with the Greek army disintegrating for lack of modern equipment, it soon became evident that to hold even the Thermopylae line, to which they were withdrawing, would be of no avail. On April 19, therefore, it was decided that evacuation from Greece was imperative, and so quickly was the situation deteriorating that embarkation had to begin on the night of April 24–25.

From then on, for the next five nights, the navy was concerned with taking the army off, partly in transports and partly in warships. As Piraeus had been put out of action by air attack, the embarkations had to be from beaches, three in Attica and three in the Peloponnesus. As the last twelve Hurricane fighters in Greece, which might have helped to protect the convoys, had been destroyed on the ground by enemy attack on April 23, there was no air cover except such as could be provided by a handful of long-range fighters working from Crete. Everything, therefore, had to be done by night and the ships got as far as possible to seaward, away from the German dive-bombers, by the morning.

As was to be expected under such difficult conditions, there were some inevitable delays and failures in the arrangements. Ships were not always far enough to the southward when daylight came, and two transports and two destroyers were lost by dive-bombing. But 43,000 of the 57,000 men who had been taken to Greece were reembarked, and of these all but 500, who were in one of the bombed transports, were safely landed. Twenty-seven thousand were landed in Crete, partly to reinforce it and partly to economize shipping by using the shortest passage until evacuation was complete; the other 16,000 were taken direct to Egypt under cover of the battle fleet.

There followed a breathing space while the Germans were establishing themselves, and particularly their airfields, in Grece. This momentary cessation of activity, with the providential help of a fog, enabled one more convoy from home to be brought through—the last through convoy for two years to come. Five merchant ships carried 200 tanks and other vehicles for reequipping an armored division, and with them came the battleship *Queen Elizabeth* and two cruisers to reinforce Admiral Cunningham. As far as Sardinia the convoy was, as before, accompanied by Force H, and before it parted company with its escort some air attacks were sustained. Thanks to the *Ark Royal*'s fighters and the ships' gunfire no hits were received; but during the following night, when just past Cape Bon, one of the merchant ships, carrying more than a quarter of the tanks, was sunk by a mine. Further desultory air attacks came that night and the next day, when a junction was made with the Mediterranean Fleet near Malta. But no damage was received, and a misty day was followed by a night of fog, unusual in the Mediterranean. By the next morning the most dangerous waters had been cleared, and the remaining three days of the passage, until arrival at Alexandria on May 12, were disturbed only by occasional aircraft, all driven off by the *Formidable*'s fighters.

Three weeks after they had expelled the British forces from Greece, the Germans were ready for their next venture, an airborne and seaborne attack on Crete. Maleme airfield, 20 miles west of Suda Bay, was the key position, with Suda Bay itself and the airfields at Retimo and Heraklion, 30 and 60 miles to the eastward, respectively, also of importance to the defense. It was in these four areas (later three, when the Maleme and Suda Bay commands were amalgamated) that the defending forces were concentrated. They comprised 27,500 troops, of which a large proportion were still disorganized after the evacuation of Greece. The only aircraft assisting in the defense were two Hurricanes which arrived three days after the attack started, the few others previously there having been withdrawn owing to the virtual impossibility of preventing their being destroyed on the ground. Largely in consequence of the lack of aircraft, it had been found impossible to strengthen the defenses with guns and supplies from Egypt, for the enemy's air attacks on shipping were constantly increasing in intensity, and several of the ships that were sent with supplies were sunk by dive-bombing.

The attack opened soon after dawn on May 20. Simultaneously with a bombing attack on Maleme airfield, a number of troop-carrying gliders landed in a nearby riverbed and, augmented by parachutists, captured the airfield. With the airfield in his hands, and with air support always on call to drive back every attempt at recapture, the enemy was able to build up his force by air transport. The troop-carrying aircraft suffered at first from artillery fire, but as the defenders were driven back the enemy's rate of reinforcement increased. By the fourth day enemy air landings could no longer be molested. In addition, parachute troops were dropped near Canea, near Suda Bay, at Retimo, and at Heraklion. Before being disposed of, they helped to disrupt communications and confuse the situation.

Though the main weight of the initial attack was airborne, it was apparent to the Germans that seaborne transport was needed in addition if their operations were to be quickly decisive. Here the defense was, for a few days, more successful. All British ships in these waters were in constant and grave danger from bombing aircraft, and air cover was entirely lacking. Even the *Formidable*'s few fighters could not help for a few days, until the wear and tear of recent operations had been made good. Nonetheless, all available naval forces were employed in preventing the enemy from crossing to Crete by sea.

Two months had elapsed since the battle of Cape Matapan, and now, if ever, it seemed possible that a major force of the Italian Navy, with the ever-present help of strong German air forces, might risk interference. To prevent this the British battle fleet cruised in a covering position to the west of Crete. For several days before the invasion this position had been occupied by the battleships *Queen Elizabeth* and *Barham*, with light forces which were frequently detached for night sweeps into the Aegean. On May 20 they were relieved by the *Warspite* and the *Valiant*, and this force was to maintain its ground during the critical time ahead. No interference by the Italian fleet was, however, attempted, and it was only within the Aegean that British warships found any surface targets to engage.

On the night of May 20–21, the night following the invasion, the only encounter was an indecisive action between a cruiser and destroyer force under Rear Admiral King and some Italian motor torpedo boats working from the Dodecanese, which were met in Kasos Strait, to the eastward of Crete. But the next night and the following morning two groups met and frustrated the first attempts at seaborne invasion. Of these the first, three cruisers and four destroyers under Rear Admiral Glennie, sweeping in from the westward through the Kithira Channel, met and scattered an invasion convoy of miscellaneous coasting craft about 20 miles north of Canea, shortly before midnight. Ten ships were sunk and for two hours Admiral Glennie's ships scoured the vicinity till it was clear that none of the convoy had got through to Crete. The remainder had in fact taken refuge on the Grecian coast. After a further search to the eastward, Admiral Glennie retired before daylight to join the covering force of battleships under Rear Admiral Rawlings.

Meanwhile the eastern force under Admiral King—two cruisers, two antiaircraft cruisers, and three destroyers—had entered by Kasos Strait, as on the preceding night, with the intention of sweeping through the Aegean about 60 miles north of Crete and then retiring to the westward. Nothing was met during the night, but next morning another convoy of small craft, carrying troops and guns, was sighted. Two were sunk while the remainder retired to the northward under cover of smoke made by an Italian destroyer escort. By now, however, air attack was becoming continuous and heavy, and antiaircraft ammunition was running dangerously low. It seemed to Admiral King that further pursuit of the enemy could not be justified. The force therefore retired to the southwestward, and so heavily was it attacked from the air that Admiral Rawlings was asked for help. Steaming in at full speed from the westward the battleships met Admiral King's force soon after midday in the Kithira Channel, and all then retired. But the day's casualties were severe. Both battleships and two of the Admiral King's cruisers had been damaged, and a destroyer had been sunk. And worse was to follow. Two cruisers, the *Gloucester* and the *Fiji*, which had been working off Cape Matapan and had then joined Admiral Rawlings, were almost out of antiaircraft ammunition. Before the day was over both were sunk by bombing, the *Gloucester* in the Kithira Channel and the *Fiji* just before dark while retiring round the southwest of Crete.

When stock was taken of the situation that night, it was clear that operations to prevent the invasion of Crete by sea must soon come to an end. So overwhelming had been the enemy's success in airborne attack on the island that by this means alone he would have been able eventually to overcome the defending forces. Further prevention of his sea passage could do no more than postpone defeat, and there was no doubt that the cost of such measures would be the destruction or crippling of the remaining warships. Furthermore, though Crete might be lost, the North African situation was still in the balance and still vital to the whole position in the Middle East; and with it went both the importance and the fate of Malta. If the situation was to be saved, and particularly if Malta was to be kept supplied, strong naval forces would still be needed. Admiral Cunningham, therefore, was firmly of the opinion that to sacrifice everything in a delaying action could not be justified, and to this opinion he adhered despite some peremptory urging from the Chiefs of Staff in London which only the most resolute mind could have resisted. Once more destroyers swept by night into the Aegean and along the north coast of Crete, and one more coaster carrying invasion troops was sunk. But the next day, May 23, all forces were withdrawn to Alexandria.[1]

A year earlier, in the Norwegian campaign, it had been shown that the great benefits inherent in amphibious operations would no longer accrue if the amphibious force could not be supported from the air, both in the fighting line and over its bases and lines of communication. For this task no mobile air force had been available. In the Cretan campaign the need for a mobile air force was equally apparent, for without such help warships alone could no longer assert a command of the sea of which they would otherwise have been capable, and which would in all probability still have dominated the situation. It is true that, as already noted, airborne attack alone might have subdued the forces in Crete. But for this the reason was that command of the sea routes had been so jeopardized by air attack on shipping, unopposed in the air, as to make it impossible to reinforce the island with guns and vehicles, and particularly the guns to protect airfields from which defending aircraft could work.

Had Britain rearmed fully in the years before the war, the air power needed might perhaps have been provided by aircraft carriers, as later the Americans were to provide it in the Pacific by a tremendous achievement of construction and training. Or possibly it might have been provided more economically in the comparatively restricted theaters of the European war by strong units of shore-based aircraft trained and equipped to move about the world, making and defending their airfields where needed. But, as already noted in connection with the Norwegian campaign, there had been little development of or planning for such a force. The Royal Air Force had been, perhaps necessarily, so engrossed in the tasks of defending Great Britain and preparing to counterattack German industries that little had been left to help British warships assert their power in waters within range of enemy airfields. With warships and aircraft in cooperation, command of the sea could have been exercised just as strongly as in the past and with the same paramount effect. But, without the aircraft, sea power, Britain's most potent asset, could not be sustained.

Although the situation in Crete was desperate, the time had not yet come to throw up the sponge. There was still some justification for

---

[1] The immediate occasion of Admiral Cunningham's signal to withdraw (timed 4:08 A.M. on May 23) was an error in a signal received by him which seemed to show that the battleships had run out of pom-pom ammunition, whereas in fact they still had plenty. It is almost certain, however, that in any event the ships would have been withdrawn that day.

holding on, if only to ensure that an eventual withdrawal might be
orderly. To this end the fighting ashore was stubborn, and, by bringing some final reinforcements and ammunition, the navy was still able
to help. But help could be brought only in fast warships by night,
and only infantry could be carried. In all, five battalions were landed,
some at Suda Bay and some for Heraklion, the latter being landed at
Tymbaki on the south coast and marched across.

On May 25 the navy tried to assist further by a bombardment by
the *Formidable*'s aircraft of Scarpanto airfield in the Dodecanese, from
which many hostile aircraft were operating. The scale of attack was too
small, however, for appreciable results, and the *Formidable* was seriously damaged by bombing during the withdrawal. In fact, nothing
else could be done to save the situation ashore, and on May 27 the
decision was taken to evacuate. The defense of the Suda Bay area had
virtually collapsed, and at Heraklion the situation was one of imminent
danger. The enemy, using sea transport, had landed tanks, and no defensive position could be held for more than a few days.

Evacuation from Heraklion was direct, a cruiser and destroyer force
under Admiral Rawlings reaching there during the night of May 28–
29. All troops were embarked except those too badly wounded to be
moved, and by daylight the force was away. But it could not get far
enough away to escape air attack, and heavy bombing had to be endured during the forenoon. Two destroyers were lost (one as a result
of damage on the preceding day) and the *Orion*, Admiral Rawlings'
flagship, was severely crippled. The Admiral himself was wounded and
his flag captain killed.

For what remained of the force that had been defending Suda Bay
no direct embarkation was possible, and a difficult march had to be
made across the island to Sfakia on the south coast. From this town,
for four nights, May 28–29 to May 31–June 1, cruisers and destroyers
under Admiral King brought away all they could. But despite their
utmost endeavors some troops had to be left behind. Although no
more ships were lost, cruisers and destroyers were constantly being
damaged by bombs and many were crippled.[2] The Royal Air Force
did everything possible to protect returning ships with fighters from
Egypt, but the small numbers available and the difficulties of making
contact prevented their help from being more than an alleviation. On
the last night one cruiser, three destroyers, and a fast minelayer were
all that could be mustered for the final lift. The strain on the navy had

[2] The antiaircraft cruiser *Calcutta* was sunk by bombing on June 1, while on
her way to join the last evacuation force on its return passage. The latter, however, had the good fortune to escape the enemy's attentions.

been exhausting almost to breaking point, but all that ships and men could do had been done. Of the 27,500 troops in the island when the attack started, 14,500 were brought back to Egypt.

The loss of Crete marked the end of a phase in the Mediterranean and brought about changes in the strategical setting which were to last almost till the end of the war. For one thing, it would no longer be possible to interfere with supplies to the Dodecanese except with submarines. Nor, with the same exception, could enemy shipping be prevented from plying between southern Europe and the Black Sea. Thus the enemy position in southeastern Europe was firmly consolidated and the status of Turkey as a potential friend of Britain made even more delicate than formerly. But of more immediate importance was the fact that the northern shore of the 200-mile-wide passage between Crete and Africa was now in enemy hands; and, if the Germans chose to build up their air strength in Crete and Cyrenaica, supply convoys from Egypt to Malta would be exposed to grave, perhaps prohibitive, risks. If Malta could not be kept supplied it would no longer be possible to attack the sea route between Italy and Africa with surface forces or aircraft, and even what could be done by submarines would be decreased. From now on, therefore, an advance into Cyrenaica was of dual importance; it was not merely a driving back of the enemy from the frontiers of Egypt but also an important step in reducing the hazards of running supplies to Malta, which in turn would help to prevent the enemy from building up the forces that were threatening Egypt.

If the German occupation of Crete increased British difficulties, it also marked the end of the enemy's thrust in this quarter. How much this was due to his future preoccupation with the attack on Russia, which opened in June, and how much to the casualties inflicted on his airborne forces by the defenders of Crete, it is impossible to say with assurance. In such decisions there are always many crosscurrents, and in all German decisions Hitler's moods and whims played an important and often decisive part. Much must also have been due to the failure of the revolts engendered by German intrigues in Irak and Syria. But, whatever the reason, the encirclement of the British position in the Middle East by an attack through Cyprus and Syria was never to be attempted. From now on, until the invasion of Sicily, all land fighting was to be along the African shore.

From June to October 1941 was a time of comparative quiet in the eastern Mediterranean. There were constant, hazardous, and gallant activities by minor forces, but no well-defined landmarks. In Libya, an attempted advance by the army on June 15 had been brought to a halt after three days' fighting, and the situation had once more been stabilized. In consequence, the navy's main concern in these waters continued to be the transport of supplies to besieged Tobruk, a task successfully achieved by an inshore squadron comprising every sort of vessel from destroyer and river gunboat to landing craft, and including many small merchant ships. Casualties and losses of ships were severe, for the last 70 miles of the run was past an enemy-held coast, and Tobruk itself was subject to constant air raids. But supplies were maintained and Tobruk held out.

In the central Mediterranean, Malta was not yet being subjected to the savage attacks it was destined to withstand later. The island's position was clearly one of serious danger, but for the present it was adequately provisioned and was proving its importance as a base for attacks on the enemy's supply lines to Africa. So heavy, however, had been the toll taken by the Cretan campaign that there were as yet no surface forces available for this duty. Everything had to be done by submarines and aircraft—the Fleet Air Arm cooperating with the Royal Air Force. And done it was with great effectiveness.

It was perhaps at this time that the constant vigilance and gallantry of British submarines had their most pronounced effect on the course of a campaign. There were on the average only ten or twelve submarines working from Malta, but they reaped a rich harvest in transports, tankers, and other supply ships sunk and damaged. No escorts were able to deter them from attacking convoys, and during the second half of 1941 these submarines and about an equal number working from Alexandria in the less fertile waters of the eastern Mediterranean sank some fifty transports and other vessels, aggregating 200,000 tons.[3] Their bold tactics necessarily entailed casualties, eight submarines being lost from May 1941 to the end of the year; but there was no relaxation of effort. Preeminent at this time, and perhaps contributing more than any other individual to the enemy's discomfiture, was Lieutenant Commander Wanklyn of the *Upholder*. In a year of persistent audacity and brilliant achievement, ending in April 1942, when the *Upholder* was lost with all hands off Tripoli, he sank three large liners carrying troops and ten other ships (tankers and store carriers), all heavily escorted.

During the same period, from June 1941 until hampered by the bad weather of winter, Malta's aircraft were equally persistent in their

---

[3] In the same six-month period British submarines also sank one destroyer, two torpedo boats, and one submarine, and damaged one battleship, two 8-inch cruisers, and one 6-inch cruiser.

attacks, both by day and by night. Blenheims bombed convoys at low altitude by day despite the hazards of this form of attack, and Swordfish attacked with torpedoes at night, while the longer-ranged Wellingtons bombed the ports. So heavy were the losses and the damage inflicted on the enemy by submarines and aircraft that not only was the available tonnage sharply diminished, but the Italians were so discouraged that they failed to make full use even of what remained, despite the urgings of their German allies. So few ships crossed that the volume of supplies reaching the African shore was barely enough to maintain Rommel's army at its existing strength. Throughout these months, therefore, while the Eighth Army was being reinforced via the Red Sea, the prospects for a British advance in Libya were steadily improving.

All this activity, however, called for Malta to be kept well supplied. Until the enemy could be evicted from Cyrenaica convoys from the east were too hazardous, and once more it seemed worthwhile to attempt the run from the westward, despite the dangers of the passage past Sardinia and Sicily. Force H was again available in the western Mediterranean after playing its decisive part in the destruction of the *Bismarck*; and the *Ark Royal*'s fighters could do much to keep off enemy aircraft, at least as far as the waters south of Sardinia. Malta itself, too, had been considerably reinforced with Hurricane fighters, flown in on two occasions in April from the *Ark Royal* working in the waters north of Algeria; consequently effective air cover could now be given to a convoy nearing its destination. In July, therefore, the attempt was made and its success was outstanding. For two days, July 23 and 24, convoy and escort were subjected to attacks by aircraft, and during the night of the 23d–24th by motor torpedo boats; although one ship was damaged, all succeeded in reaching Malta. Of the escort, a destroyer was sunk by an aircraft torpedo, and the cruiser *Manchester* was torpedoed but succeeded in returning to Gibraltar for repairs.

The main weight of these attacks was borne by Italian torpedo aircraft which, being handled with greater skill and boldness than formerly, were now a serious menace. They were not, however, so grave a danger as the massed attacks of German dive-bombers had been, and it was to the reduction of German air strength in this region that success must to some extent be attributed. While almost the whole weight of German arms was being devoted to the attempt to knock Russia out before winter, the task of supplying Malta from the westward was somewhat lightened.

The arrival of the July convoy was followed, three days later, by an Italian attempt to attack the ships that were unloading in harbor. Three motor torpedo boats escorted nine explosive boats and two midget submarines which tried to penetrate the boom defenses at dawn. They were everywhere repulsed. No damage was done to shipping, and all the enemy craft were sunk.

Two months later another convoy was passed through to Malta with the loss of one ship. Italian torpedo aircraft were again the chief opposition encountered, and in one of several attacks on the afternoon of September 27 the *Nelson*, wearing Admiral Somerville's flag, was torpedoed; but she was able to continue in company and then return to Gibraltar without difficulty. Again the operation had been a remarkable success, considering the dangers that must be run by a comparatively slow convoy in a passage past enemy territory. For 400 miles the merchant ships were within easy range of Sardinian or Sicilian airfields, and much of this distance had to be traversed in daylight. Yet only one was lost. On September 28 the other eight ships arrived undamaged, and once more Malta was supplied with the fuel and stores needed to maintain its own defense and to nourish the forces attacking the enemy's supply lines.

By the beginning of November 1941 affairs in North Africa were reaching a new climax. The Eighth Army was nearly ready to attack. Rommel's Africa Korps and its Italian allies were being maintained only with difficulty. To increase the enemy's embarrassments during the crucial period, a surface force was sent to Malta to harass still further the cross-Mediterranean shipping, attacking such convoys as might elude, or be too strongly escorted for, attack by submarines and aircraft. This was Force K, under Captain Agnew, comprising the cruisers *Aurora* and *Penelope* and two destroyers. On November 8 it scored a resounding initial success by destroying all ten of a Brindisi–Benghazi convoy and sinking two of the four escorting destroyers. At dawn the next morning the submarine *Upholder*, which had closed the position during the night, sank another destroyer.

Further successes were achieved on November 23 and December 1. On the latter occasion the force, strengthened by the *Ajax* and the *Neptune* and two more destroyers, was led by Admiral Rawlings. The utmost effort that Malta could support was now being put forward, for on November 18 the army had started its advance in Libya, and everything that the navy could do by boldness and energy to sink enemy supplies had to be done. After severe fighting the siege of Tobruk was raised on December 1; a fierce counterattack by Rommel from December 13 to 15, about 60 miles west of Tobruk, was met and defeated; and on December 24 the Eighth Army again occupied Benghazi.

Meanwhile the strain put on Malta's resources by the high level of

offensive activity—surface, submarine, and air—was being increasingly felt. The cruisers and destroyers working from Malta were all or
more than the island could continue to sustain, and additional supplies
were urgently needed. The problem of providing the latter was, however, somewhat eased by the fact that the enemy had been dispossessed
of the Cyrenaican airfields. Steps were taken, therefore, to send a fast
supply ship, the *Breconshire*, from Alexandria, escorted by the 15th
Cruiser Squadron (5.25-inch cruisers) under Rear Admiral Vian for
the first half of the passage and thereafter by Force K. Not only were
air attacks encountered (as was to be expected despite the improved
situation), but on December 17, just as the two cruiser forces reached
their rendezvous, an Italian force composed of battleships of the *Cavour*
class and 8-inch cruisers was encountered to the northward. All Admiral Vian's skill and audacity were needed to cover the *Breconshire*
and bluff the enemy, one of whose forces had a convoy in company,
into beating a retreat. But this he did. Force K regained its base at
Malta bringing the *Breconshire* with it, and the 15th Cruiser Squadron
returned to Alexandria undamaged.

The brilliance of these operations in November and December 1941
did much to bear up Britain's fortunes in the deeply adverse circumstances surrounding Mediterranean strategy. And of the same type,
displaying a pronounced ascendancy over the Italian Navy, was the
brief night encounter on December 13, under Cape Bon, of three
British and one Dutch destroyer on passage from Gibraltar to Malta
(under Commander Stokes of the *Sikh*) with two Italian 6-inch cruisers.
Both enemy ships were sunk without damage to the Allied force.

Circumstances, however, were gradually becoming too strong for
the British forces. That it had been possible to achieve so much must
be attributed, at least in part, to German preoccupation in Russia. With
the return of strong forces of the Luftwaffe to the Mediterranean, the
tide of battle was soon to set the other way once more, until (as recounted in a later chapter) the outlook became darker than ever. And
already, while the army was advancing victoriously and all seemed to
be going well, the navy was suffering severe losses in heavy ships. German submarines, starting a new phase of activity in the Mediterranean,
had had some remarkable initial achievements. On November 13 the
Ark Royal, of Force H, was torpedoed while operating west of Sardinia,
and she sank the next day; on November 25 the *Barham* was torpedoed
and sunk near Alexandria. So also was the cruiser *Galatea* on December
2. Perhaps spurred on by this, the Italian Navy then achieved one of
the rare but brilliant successes of which it has shown itself capable from
time to time. In the early morning of December 12 Italian human torpedoes succeeded in penetrating the defenses of Alexandria harbor and

fixing their explosives onto the bottoms of the *Queen Elizabeth* and the *Valiant*. Both battleships were seriously damaged, and, though subsequently repaired, they were out of action for many months to come.

It was just at the year's end too, that Force K, now led by Captain O'Conor in the *Neptune*, suffered disaster. About 20 miles off Tripoli the *Neptune*, the *Aurora*, and the *Penelope*, with their destroyers, ran into a minefield in waters whose depth seemed to make mining unlikely. The *Neptune* was lost with all hands, a destroyer also was lost, and both the other cruisers were damaged by mines that had been exploded by their paravanes. The exploits of Force K were at an end.

At this time, then, when the entry of Japan and the United States into the war imported many new problems of strategy and, until American strength could be built up, loaded Britain with new and heavy burdens, the situation in the Mediterranean was precarious. While the army held Cyrenaica, Admiral Vian's force of small cruisers and destroyers based on Alexandria could just enable Malta to be kept supplied from Egypt; but even this would have been impossible save for a prowess and fighting spirit which enabled them to outface strong Italian forces of far heavier gunpower. In the west Force H was still on guard at Gibraltar, lest the *Scharnhorst* and the *Gneisenau* break out of Brest and make for Italian ports; but the navy was so short of aircraft carriers, cruisers, and destroyers that for the present there could be no further exploits toward Malta. The position was still in hand, but there was nothing to spare.

9

JAPAN AND AMERICA ENTER THE WAR

In the years of Hitler's rise to power in Germany a hardly less serious menace to peace was evident in the Far East. For many years Japan had looked to the domination of China as her manifest destiny and had been steadily strengthening her armed forces, steps that helped to alleviate the problems of industrialization and a rapidly increasing population. The occupation of Manchuria in 1931 had been followed by various forms of penetration into northern China, and by 1937 the stage of open hostilities had been reached. Thereafter war was continuous, though spoken of by the Japanese merely as "the China affair."

During these years Japan occupied and controlled practically all parts of China which had hitherto been accessible to foreign traders. But of any benefit derived from her "Greater East Asia Co-Prosperity Sphere" there was little sign. Even after the fall of Nanking and the establishment there of a puppet Chinese government, Chiang Kai-shek and the Kuomintang party continued to rule much of the country from Chungking—in somewhat uneasy alliance with the Communists of the northwest. The pot of Japan's warlike economy was kept boiling, but little nourishment was derived from it either in martial glory or in material wealth. It was clearly of importance to Japan to be finished with the China affair as soon as might be, and to switch her energies to some other direction.

The outbreak of war in Europe eased the situation somewhat. Though Japan had no real love for Germany, it was her obvious course to align herself diplomatically with the Axis and reap what she could from the discomfiture of France and the peril of the British Isles. So hard pressed was Britain at this time that in the summer of 1940 she had to accept the humiliation of closing the Burma Road, China's remaining supply line, at the behest of the Japanese. At the same time the Vichy government of France, encouraged by Germany and powerless to do otherwise, agreed to allow Japanese troops to enter Indochina. Neither of these measures was sufficient to finish the China affair. They helped to stabilize the situation, and a footing in Indochina was a useful step to the southward. But a new venture was called for.

In Japan the army bulked larger in the national life than the navy, both numerically and in political power. It was also more hotheaded. The larger part of the army, despite the China affair, was in Manchuria, with Russia as its potential enemy. But here there seemed little to be gained by aggression, and the results of local clashes on the frontier in 1938 had not been to the Japanese taste. Even the invasion of Russia by the Germans did not induce Japan to risk burning her fingers for so inadequate a prize as eastern Siberia, or for the satisfaction of thrusting communism somewhat farther back from the confines of China. Expansion must therefore be to the southward, and here the navy must lead the way. The limitations of shipping would prevent more than a comparatively small part of the army from being employed, but that small part would probably be larger than, and in Japanese eyes certainly a match for, anything their opponents were likely to be able to bring to the scene. The advantages of expansion to the southward were manifest: the oil, rubber, and tin of the East Indies and Malaya, and beyond that perhaps domination of India and occupation of Australia.

Of the eventual wisdom of this policy the more farseeing officers of the Japanese Navy seem to have had their doubts. They had, as a rule, a wider knowledge of world affairs and a more sober view of possibilities than their military colleagues, and they probably realized how strong were the latent forces pitted against them. The gathering momentum of an aggressive economy, however, was inescapable, and it received fresh impetus from the oil embargo by which, in July 1941, America, Britain, and the Netherlands sought to counter Japanese expansion into southern Indochina. It was clear that oil would have to be obtained by force. The navy, therefore, was ready to cooperate wholeheartedly with the army in conquering Southeast Asia and the Eastern Archipelago, or perishing in the attempt. It also had a justifiable pride in the fighting strength of a fleet that, though not the largest in the world, was by no means outclassed by its potential enemies.

In battleship strength the Japanese were inferior to both the British and the Americans, and they were slightly behindhand in building the new fast type that was beginning to supersede the older ships. In November 1941 their best ships were still the *Mutsu* and the *Nagato*, completed twenty years earlier, which, with eight 16-inch guns each, were of about the same stamp as the *Nelson* and the *Rodney*. Four older

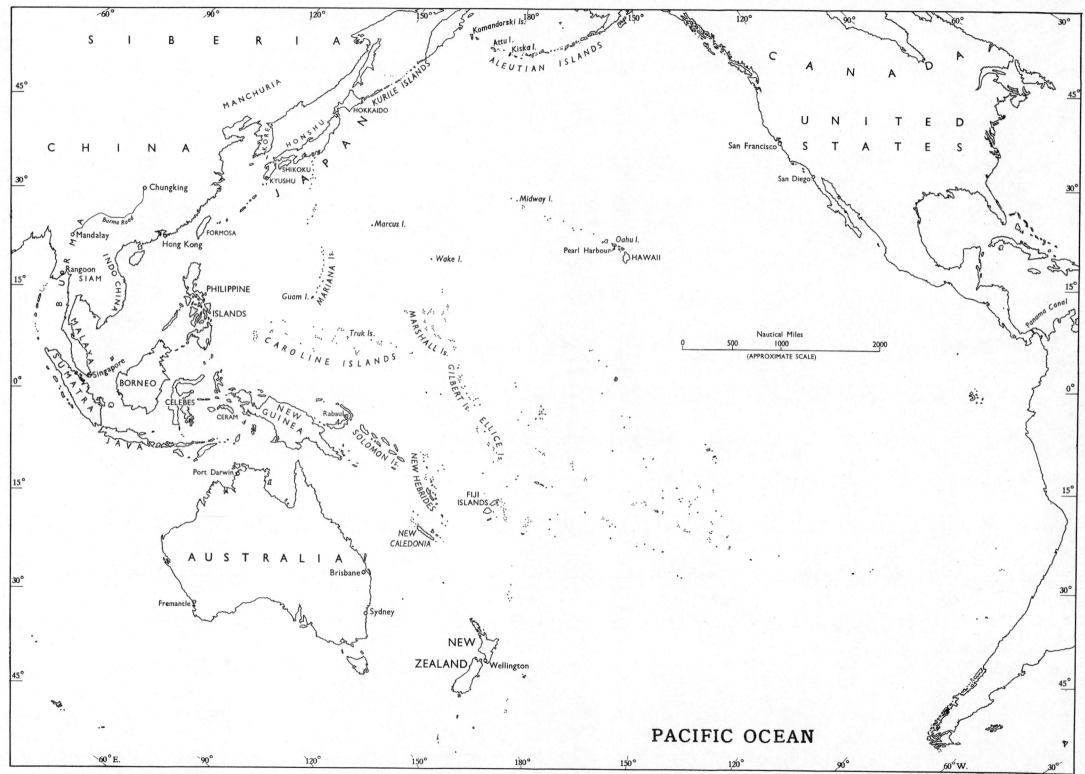

PACIFIC OCEAN

ships (*Ise, Hyuga, Fuso,* and *Yamashiro*) mounted twelve 14-inch guns each, and four more older still (*Kongo, Hiyei, Haruna,* and *Kirishima*) had eight 14-inch guns. These latter, with a speed of 26 knots, were originally classed as battle cruisers; but although they had been extensively modernized and were capable of at least their original speed, they were slower than the modern British and American type. Two ships on the point of completion, however, outclassed all rivals. The *Yamato* and the *Musashi,* the largest warships ever built, had a deep-load displacement of 73,000 tons (as against the 52,000 of the *Iowa* class, which would not be ready for another year or more), an armament of nine 18-inch guns, and a speed of 28 knots, particulars that had been kept profoundly secret.

But if, despite these two Goliaths, the Japanese were in general somewhat lacking in battleship strength, their navy had been the first to realize that the striking power of carrier-borne aircraft might in many circumstances be at least as important as the hitting power of big guns. To this idea full scope had been given. For several years the Japanese, realizing that aircraft carriers might share with battleships the functions of capital ships, had given priority to naval air training and the development of strike aircraft. In particular they had accorded an important place to torpedo aircraft, rightly believing that a combination of torpedoing and bombing was the most effective way of attacking ships. The United States Navy also had been paying close attention to aviation, and particularly to dive-bombing, but it had lagged in the development of aircraft torpedoes and attack technique. The British Navy had always believed in the torpedo as the major aircraft weapon against ships, having particularly in view the need to slow an enemy down to enable a superior battle fleet to overtake him. But the unfortunate division of responsibility for development between the Admiralty and the Air Ministry in the years before the war had resulted in the navy's being sadly behindhand in aircraft types. It was the Japanese, therefore, with their need to redress an adverse balance in battleship strength, who had made the most progress in preparing for a new type of contest, a contest in which a main fleet might assert its ascendancy over its opponent, with all that that implied, without the ships ever having sighted one another.

To make good their policy, the Japanese had in commission the largest fleet of aircraft carriers afloat. There were six classed as fleet carriers (*Zuikaku* and *Shokaku, Soryu* and *Hiryu, Kaga* and *Akagi*), two regular light fleet carriers (*Ryujo* and *Hosho*), and two light fleet carriers converted from merchant ships (*Zuiho* and *Shoho*). In addition, five new big carriers were being built (*Taiho, Shinano, Unryu, Katsuragi,* and *Amagi*), and two large passenger ships (*Hitakai* and

Hayataka) were being converted and would shortly be commissioned as the *Hiyo* and the *Junyo*.

In cruisers and destroyers the Japanese were scarcely behind the British and the Americans. Eighteen heavy (8-inch) and twenty light cruisers put the Japanese Navy on a rough equality with the United States Navy. Unlike the Americans, however, the Japanese had few new cruisers building. With ninety-eight destroyers in commission they were inferior to their rivals; but here, as with aircraft, they had sought to redress the adverse balance of battleship strength by giving great weight, both figuratively and literally, to the torpedo armament. A large torpedo with strong explosive effect and long range had been developed, and each destroyer mounted more tubes than an equivalent British or American ship. For each tube there was also a second torpedo, and handling arrangements were excellent; in any normal weather all tubes could be reloaded in twenty minutes.

In the development of submarines the Japanese lagged somewhat behind other navies. There were, however, sixty-one in commission, and some of these were to prove their worth for a time in one campaign, the fighting round the Solomon Islands.

In Japanese minds there could be no doubt that expansion to the southward would involve war with America. Even had the Philippines not been scheduled for conquest, it seemed certain that the United States, increasingly restive about the China affair, would resist attack on British or Dutch possessions. The United States Navy, therefore, loomed as a major obstacle to success.

The Americans had, at this time, a considerably more powerful fleet of battleships than the Japanese. The Pacific Fleet had three 16-inch ships (*Maryland, Colorado,* and *West Virginia*) against the Japanese two, and eleven 14-inch ships against Japanese eight. Moreover, two of the new 16-inch, 29-knot ships (*Washington* and *North Carolina*) were in commission, though not yet fully ready for war, and two more (*Indiana* and *South Dakota*) were soon to be commissioned. Looking farther ahead, another two of this class, and four larger and still faster ships of the *Iowa* class, were being built, but these need not enter into immediate calculations.

In aircraft carriers, however, the United States Navy was weaker than the Japanese. All the American carriers were large, and all carried large numbers of aircraft for their size. But there were only seven in all: the old *Lexington* and *Saratoga*, originally built as battle cruisers; the *Ranger*, the *Enterprise*, and the *Yorktown*, which had been in commission several years; and the *Wasp* and the *Hornet*, commissioned recently. Only three of the carriers were at this time in service with the

Pacific Fleet. A large number of ships of the new *Essex* class were being built (seventeen were in commission by the end of the war), but none of them was likely to be in service for at least a year. The American light fleet carriers (nine of them) and the large force of escort carriers (seventy-eight) were also in the still unpredictable future.

Mention has already been made of the rough equality between Americans and Japanese in number of cruisers. That the Americans would commission an additional thirteen heavy and thirty-three light cruisers within the next four years was not a matter of immediate moment.

Of destroyers the Americans had 171 in commission, nearly double the number the Japanese possessed. But when American commitments in the Atlantic against German submarines were considered (and Germany had promised to back Japan), the call on these destroyers was evidently going to be very heavy.

Last, the American submarine force was 112 strong. This force, with more submarines being built, was going to be more of a thorn in their flesh than perhaps the Japanese foresaw. But for the moment it was unlikely to deter them from their plans of conquest.

The Japanese, then, had to launch their offensive operations in the face of an American navy that might of itself be more than a match for them and must be presumed to have the help of some British and Dutch forces. Despite British commitments in the Atlantic and the Mediterranean, some ships might be spared for the Far East. In fact, the British Prime Minister had already (on November 10) made it known that heavy ships were on their way; when the *Prince of Wales* arrived at the Cape en route the news had been allowed to leak out. But here the facts of geography entered largely into the picture. A fleet could not exercise its power irrespective of the distance from its base. And the distances between American fleet bases and the intended area of Japanese operations were immense, while the Japanese, with smaller distances to go, had every opportunity for establishing advanced bases on the China Coast and in Indochina.

The United States had, indeed, a fully equipped fleet base well out into the Pacific; Pearl Harbor in Oahu, one of the Hawaiian Islands, was more than 2,000 miles from the Californian coast. But even 2,000 miles was only a short step toward the threatened area. A fleet in Pearl Harbor was still 3,300 miles from Japan, and the distances to the Philippines and the Dutch East Indies were even greater—4,500 miles to San Bernardino Strait in the eastern wall of the Philippines, another 300 miles on to Manila, and about 5,500 miles to Java. To join hands with a British force at Singapore, the only first-class naval base in these waters, the American fleet would have to steam at least 6,000 miles.

111

There were, of course, minor American bases in the Philippines, in Manila Bay and the nearby Subic Bay. But they were not equipped to support a large fleet, nor were their defenses against air attack on a sufficient scale. As already noted, they were nearly 5,000 miles from Pearl Harbor; and such stepping-stones as there were on the way were quite inadequate to afford the help needed for a forward policy. Wake Island, 2,000 miles from Pearl Harbor, was only a coral atoll with an airfield. Guam, about halfway between Wake and Manila, was in the process of being developed as a naval base, but it had no adequate natural harbor and little had been done so far in either harbor works or defenses. Also it was close to the Japanese-held Mariana Islands, and as these were only 1,300 miles from Japan, with Iwo Jima as a halfway house, they were easily reinforceable by air. Guam, therefore, could be tenable as a base only if its defenses were of a very high order.

These were the conditions of geography on which, in part, Japan's strategy had to be based. Even if it were granted that the American fleet might be superior to the Japanese, the chances of the former interfering in the Philippines or the East Indies direct from Pearl Harbor were remote, and it would be a long time before it could make a step-by-step advance, say via Australia which is 4,000 miles from Pearl Harbor. Everything possible had therefore to be done to oppose and postpone such a movement.

On the American side of the Pacific, though there was no doubt that war might come one day, little could be done in the way of strategical planning beyond arranging for the defense of American waters in the unlikely event of a Japanese attack, and giving some training for the amphibious assaults that might well have to play their part in this island-studded ocean. On one occasion it had been proposed that the annual maneuvers should include the transfer of the fleet and its supply ships from Pearl Harbor to Manila, but this project had been vetoed by the State Department for fear of irritating the Japanese and had been abandoned.

It was in this setting that the Japanese Navy had to plan. Chief among the planners, in effect if not in name, was Admiral Yamamoto, whose title was commander in chief of the Combined Fleet. Individual, numbered fleets were organized on a basis of types, so that the Combined Fleet was in fact everything that floated. But Yamamoto's authority went even further than that. Trusted throughout the navy and the nation as the ideal commander, his views carried so much weight with the Chief of the Naval General Staff, his official superior, that they could be sure of acceptance.

By Yamamoto and the Japanese Navy the doctrine that the main fleet is a dominant factor in strategy was as firmly held as by the British and Americans. If, therefore, it was argued, the first act of hostilities could be to cripple the American fleet, not only could the invasions in Southeast Asia go ahead with little risk, but there was also every possibility of maintaining a strong position in the western Pacific for a long time to come. It was in this way that the Japanese had dealt with the situation in 1904, when the Russian Asiatic Fleet, lying in Port Arthur, had been severely damaged by Japanese torpedo boats before the formal declaration of war. Why not bring this simple conception up to date and use the powerful carrier striking forces for a surprise attack on the American Pacific Fleet, known to be based on Pearl Harbor?

This was the bold step the Japanese decided on. The question having been decided, secrecy was the first essential, not only to ensure the effectiveness that comes from a surprise blow, but to safeguard the attacking force from the possibility of a severe defeat. To take all their big aircraft carriers within 300 miles of the enemy's main base, and more than 3,000 miles from their own nearest harbor, was an enterprise of exceptional daring. It is true that the carriers and the two battleships that would accompany them to protect them from cruisers were faster than the American battle fleet, and this circumstance should enable them to refuse action if the Americans were aroused to activity too soon. But against this benefit had to be set, first, the restrictions on speed imposed by fuel limitations when more than 3,000 miles from one's base, even with oilers accompanying the fleet; and, second, the danger of damage by American torpedo aircraft which might slow down some of the ships. Viewed from any angle the operation involved grave risks.

To preserve secrecy, the Japanese Foreign Office put up a smoke screen as inpenetrable as their skill could devise. They could not be entirely successful, for the Japanese ciphers had been broken and the American President and his cabinet knew that the Japanese forces were poised to strike in Southeast Asia, and realized before the blow fell that Japan would soon join Germany and Italy in war against Britain and the Netherlands. But the consciousness of danger from surprise attack on American forces had not penetrated sufficiently to the naval and military commands at Pearl Harbor. The commanders there had been told to take precautions, but the mental atmosphere was not so tense as to make them fear an air attack so far from Japan without some further warning. All information suggested that any Japanese thrust would be to the southward. That the Pearl Harbor defenses were surprised, therefore, must be ascribed in the main, not to diplomatic deception, but to the audacity that launched this bold venture of the

113

aircraft carrier fleet simultaneously with full-scale attacks on Malaya and the Philippines.

On November 26 Vice Admiral Nagumo with a fleet of two battleships, six aircraft carriers, three cruisers, and nine destroyers, with several oilers in company, sailed from an out-of-the-way anchorage in the Kurile Islands. The submarines that were to take part in the attack, being slower, had sailed some days earlier. For eleven days the fleet steamed eastward, fueling en route, until by the early morning of December 7 (Hawaiian time; it was already December 8 in Tokyo) it had arrived in position 275 miles north of Pearl Harbor. From this position its air striking force was launched. As it was Sunday morning, there was full confidence that the American fleet would be in harbor.

Just before 8 A.M. the blow fell. No warning had been received by the defenses. Soon after 7 A.M. a noncommissioned officer who was instructing a private in the use of the army's new radar set had detected a large number of aircraft 130 miles to the northward. But the officer to whom he reported, assuming that the aircraft were Flying Fortresses which were due from the mainland, took no action. Neither did the fact that an unidentified submarine had been detected and sunk off the harbor mouth shortly before 7 A.M. cause the naval command to take additional precautions. The usual dawn patrol of aircraft had gone out, but had sighted nothing. When the attack came, therefore, both fleet and army were entirely unready.

The first Japanese aircraft to bomb the airfields and attack the fleet with torpedoes and bombs were free to do so with little interference, and the effect was tremendous. The second wave, an hour later, had to endure vigorous gunfire which accounted for about thirty aircraft, but it was able to add substantially to the damage. When all was over the American Pacific Fleet had been wrecked.

The Japanese had also attacked with midget submarines which, having been carried to the scene of action strapped to large submarines, were given the duty of sinking any emerging battleship in the harbor mouth. With these craft the Japanese had been unlucky, and all five midgets had been sunk. But the aircraft had done all that was needed.

Only two of the eight battleships in the harbor (*Arizona* and *Oklahoma*) had been sunk so as to be irreparable, but all had been severely damaged; of the two 16-inch ships present, the *West Virginia* had virtually to be rebuilt. As it was more than a year before the majority were again ready for service, the Japanese could feel that they were free to go ahead in Asia without fear of serious interference from America for a long time to come. They had done all they could have hoped to do. Or nearly all—for on one count fortune had eluded them. None of the American aircraft carriers was in Pearl Harbor at the time of the attack. The *Saratoga* was refitting at San Diego, the *Lexington* was exercising near Midway Island, and the *Enterprise* had just been taking fighters to Wake Island, and her return had been delayed by bad weather. The remaining four were in the Atlantic. Nor were any of the new battleships present. Though the United States battle fleet could not for the present dispute command of the sea with the Japanese, the Americans still had the means to build up a fast striking force of aircraft carriers, with heavy cruiser and fast battleship support, with which to hamper their enemies if they again thrust far from their base.

There was one other item that the Japanese had to put on the loss side of their account. It can hardly be doubted that a Japanese invasion of Malaya and the Dutch East Indies would eventually have roused the United States to war. But there is little doubt, also, that this successful attack without warning stung the American nation into a fury of activity which might otherwise have been lacking. The sense of shame, too, in the navy and the army at being caught unawares, in exactly the same way as the much-criticized Russians at Port Arthur in 1904, heightened the urgency with which they set about their tremendous expansion in ships, aircraft, and men. In these respects the Japanese had in the end to reap where they had sown. But there was no doubt that they had won the first round. America had to rebuild and expand her navy while keeping the enemy at bay as best she could with depleted resources.

This heavy task devolved largely on Fleet Admiral Ernest King who, as commander in chief of the United States fleet and chief of naval operations, had reached the summit of his career. For this position he had trained himself throughout his service, seeking experience in every branch, even to the extent of qualifying in aviation at the mature age of forty-eight so that he might command a carrier. Enjoying his reputation as a taut seaman, always sure of himself, and sometimes irked by the preference given to the European theater, he was at times likely to be as aggressive in conference as in campaign. But he was a loyal and proud member of the Combined (British and American) Chiefs of Staff Committee, and bowed to majority opinion when hard enough pressed. As to his success in expanding the navy and the soundness of his views on the strategy of the Pacific war there was never any doubt.

No less successful than the raid on Pearl Harbor, and of more enduring value to the enemy, was the simultaneous attack on Malaya. Here the Japanese had bases comparatively near at hand in Hainan

MALAY ARCHIPELAGO

Nautical Miles

0   100   200   300   400   500
(SCALE AT LAT. 10°)

100°

120°

20°

20°

FORMOSA

Canton

Hong Kong

HAINAN I.

SOUTH

Lingayen Gulf

LUZON

Manila

Atimonan

SIAM

INDO

CHINA

CHINA

Subic Bay

Legaspi

Bernardino Str.

CHINA

Camranh Bay

SEA

Saigon

Singora

Patani

MINDANAO

Kota Bahru

Jolo

Davao

Penang

MALAYA

Brunel Bay

Miri

Kuantan

Endau

Tarakan

Str. of JOHORE

MOLUCCA PASSAGE

Malacca

Singapore

Menado

SUMATRA

BORNEO

0°

0°

Lingga I.

Balik Papan

CELEBES

Kendari

Palembang

Banka Strait

MACASSAR STRAITS

Amboina 100 m.

JAVA SEA

Sunda Straits

Batavia

Macassar

Surabaya

J A V A

Bali I.

TIMOR

Tjilatjap

P. Darwin 300 m.

100°

120°

Emery Walker Ltd., ph. sc.

Island off the South China coast and in southern Indochina, and there was little doubt that the blow would fall before long, possibly in such strength as would strain British resources to the utmost. About 2 A.M. on December 8 (local time), just as bombs were falling on Pearl Harbor, a small force landed at Kota Bahru, the northernmost airfield in Malaya, and two hours later the main Japanese forces started landing at Singora and Patani in Siamese territory, 40 miles north of the Malayan frontier. From there they advanced down the Malay Peninsula. Though opposed by British and Indian troops, they made steady progress.

Mention has already been made of the passage of the *Prince of Wales* to the East, where she had been joined by the *Repulse*. It had been the original intention to send an aircraft carrier with them, and a force so composed would have been a serious menace to Japanese seaborne expeditions. With fighter aircraft to defend it against air attack, strong hitting power, and sufficient speed to refuse action with a superior force of battleships, the force might have done much to dislocate Japanese plans, hampering their raids on Allied communications and making it necessary for them to escort their convoys with battleships. But it was at this time that the British fleet had the grave misfortune to lose the *Ark Royal* (see p. 105, above). Of the carriers that could have met the requirements of this force, only the *Victorious* remained in service,[1] and it was adjudged that the needs of home waters, where the *Tirpitz* would soon be ready for action, would not permit of sending her to the Far East.

Nevertheless, the decision to send the *Prince of Wales* and the *Repulse* had been adhered to, and by this time they had arrived at Singapore. It was thought that much might still be accomplished with no more than justifiable risk, either with the help of Royal Air Force fighters from neighboring airfields or when there was low cloud, for the Japanese air striking forces were not yet equipped with radar. Furthermore, Admiral Phillips, who was in command of this force and had formerly been vice-chief of the Naval Staff, was of the school that believed the air menace should not be overrated; that in many circumstances the chances of aircraft finding ships were not great, and that battleships should be able to beat off aircraft if only in small numbers. An officer of high courage, great intellectual energy, and

---

[1] The *Indomitable* had recently been commissioned but was under repair, having run aground while working up. The *Illustrious* and the *Formidable* were still making good their Mediterranean damage in United States yards. The *Furious* was too old and worn for service so far from home. The *Eagle* and the *Hermes* were too slow, and had too few aircraft, to qualify for a striking force.

firm determination, he was averse to holding back the heavy ships from striking what might be decisive blows merely because it was impossible to have a carrier with them. To hold them back would be a tacit admission that they were of little use; in that event why not risk them?

The danger of air attack near the enemy's landing operations was, of course, realized; but here it seemed that too much credit was given to what could be done by the Royal Air Force in providing defense. Even more than in other outlying theaters, there were not nearly enough aircraft for requirements. Britain was so hard pressed everywhere else that the needs of Malaya, threatened but not until now at war, had received little satisfaction. The only fighters there were Brewster Buffaloes, which, though outdated, might have made some showing against a Japanese striking force if they had met one—certainly if the latter was without a fighter escort. But for the Royal Air Force to protect ships—that is, to meet the attacking force before it arrived—required more than that. If a battleship was to direct shore-based fighters effectively, a degree of experience in cooperation, which here was lacking, was called for.

Despite these difficulties and shortcomings, Admiral Phillips set out with his squadron on the afternoon of December 8 for Singora and Patani. He was promised all the protection the Royal Air Force could give, but was warned while en route that such protection could not cover his movements during the morning of December 10 in the neighborhood of the landings. On December 9, however, which proved to be a day of low cloud and drizzle, with the squadron standing to the northward well away from the coast, the Admiral decided that, with his movements covered by the weather, he would go on and strike at the enemy's transports and their escorts at dawn, accepting the risk of attack during his withdrawal. Before sunset, however, the sky cleared and Japanese scouting aircraft were sighted. Reluctantly the decision was taken to abandon the attack, and the ships were turned for home.

But here fortune failed Admiral Phillips. Before dawn the next morning (December 10) the squadron was sighted by a Japanese submarine. As soon as her report was received a strong force of shore-based long-range aircraft was sent off from an airfield in Indochina. The submarine's report of the British squadron's course as south was in error, for at that time it was steering southwest to close Kuantan, a bomber airfield on the east coast of Malaya, 160 miles north of Singapore, where a further landing had been reported—mistakenly. This error caused the aircraft to miss their mark on the outward flight. On their return, however, more spread out, the British ships, now standing to seaward again and about 50 miles from the land, were sighted by a scouting aircraft. At 11:15 A.M. the first blow fell, a force of high-level bombers scoring a hit on the *Repulse*. Half an hour later torpedo aircraft attacked in two waves of nine each. Though some planes were shot down, two of their torpedoes got home on the *Prince of Wales*. Half an hour later again two more torpedo attacks and a bombing attack followed. Both ships were now lying stopped. At 12:30 the *Repulse* capsized and sank. Fifty minutes later the *Prince of Wales* followed, taking Admiral Phillips with her. Survivors were picked up by the three escorting destroyers and taken back to Singapore.

It was only when the last Japanese aircraft were disappearing that some British fighters arrived, summoned too late to be of any help, and questions raised subsequently suggest that the Admiral should have asked sooner for fighter protection. This would have been out of the question on his original route, 150 miles from land. But on approaching the coast he would not have been too far to seaward, and, in fact, eleven fighters were standing by at Singapore to answer any calls from the ships. If these planes had used Kuantan for refueling, they could presumably have maintained an umbrella of five or six guarding the fleet until it was again too far to seaward. Why Admiral Phillips did not call for help can never be known. Perhaps he thought that if Kuantan was in fact being attacked there would already be fighters there, and that if the enemy was not there it was best to keep radio silence. Nor is it known what track he intended to follow in returning to Singapore. Whether this small force of fighters could have saved the ships in face of the enemy attacks can only be a matter of speculation. But the lesson of this tragic episode was too clear to need underlining. Thereafter it was well understood that battleships should not operate in waters where they would be open to attack by air striking forces as efficient in sea warfare as were those of the Japanese Navy, unless they could be given strong and well-directed fighter protection. It was also clear that the range from enemy airfields to which such waters extended far outdistanced those that had been menaced by Germans and Italians. Wherever Allied ships might try to interfere, even when 500 miles from Japanese airfields, they would be liable to heavy and well-handled attacks.

10

THE PERIOD OF JAPANESE EXPANSION

SIMULTANEOUSLY WITH THEIR attacks on Pearl Harbor and Malaya, in December 1941, the Japanese struck at Wake Island, Guam, and Hong Kong. The result in each instance was a foregone conclusion, however heroic the defense; the only question was how long each place could hold out. And to hold out at all was to uphold the national prestige rather than to have any material effect on operations. Guam, virtually defenseless, lasted four days. Wake, which was so small as to make landing difficult, held out for a fortnight before the Japanese, after losing two destroyers and suffering severe casualties, could get a footing and overwhelm what remained of the garrison of 500 United States Marines. At Hong Kong it was two days more before, on Christmas Day, the last resistance was crushed.

Whether Hong Kong should have been defended at all is a question difficult to answer satisfactorily. There was only one airfield, which was on the mainland, and it was so inadequate that all aircraft had already been withdrawn. Also, it was well understood that the colony could not hold out for long against the large Japanese forces in neighboring Chinese territory, with ample airfields at their back. Furthermore, the problems, as well as the ethics, of defense were complicated by the large and crowded Chinese population of a first-class commercial port. And yet there was retained in Hong Kong a garrison of six battalions (two British, two Canadian, and two Indian) with the normal fortress complement of artillery and engineers. To have withdrawn the garrison while there still seemed hope that the Japanese threat would not materialize, might, perhaps, have appeared as a pusillanimous move inviting aggression. But there is no doubt that to have withdrawn in November or earlier, or to have left only a token force, would in no way have affected Japanese plans. And it should already have been as

120

clear as anything can be that, in a war against Japan, Hong Kong could have been of no use as a naval base, even on the most minor scale, during the time for which it might hold out. So it seems that a withdrawal to Malaya would have been the sounder strategy. If at the same time the inevitability of war had had been faced and it had been possible, despite the immense difficulties, to send to Malaya enough aircraft, armored formations, and infantry divisions to put the forces there in good fighting posture, there would, of course, have been less temptation to put up the desperate bluff that forbids withdrawal any-where lest the whole fabric collapse. But so overwhelming were the difficulties elsewhere that the faint hopes of averting a Japanese war had of necessity to be clung to. Britain could only hold on as best she might, and this general determination was made to include Hong Kong.[1]

Insofar as their effect by naval action on the Japanese advance was concerned, the Philippines were in somewhat the same situation as Hong Kong. Though airfields were available, it was well understood that the scale of air defense was insufficient to allow the naval bases in Manila and Subic bays (Cavite and Olongapo) to be kept in operation. Even the scale of attack from Formosa would be too large; and if, as was probable, the enemy gained a footing in Luzon, conditions would be even more difficult.

Had there been any lingering doubts on this point, they would have been dispelled by the heavy air raids with which the war opened. On December 8 all the airfields in Luzon were attacked in force, and two days later Cavite Navy Yard was virtually wiped out. But in fact the situation had been foreseen, and in November the United States Asiatic Fleet of three cruisers and a dozen destroyers had gone south to the Dutch East Indies, leaving only the submarines to operate against Japa-nese invading forces and some motor torpedo boats for local defense.

As to the defense of the land itself, and particularly of Luzon, how-ever, the situation differed radically from that at Hong Kong. Here there was an American-Filipino army of 60,000 men, of which three-quarters were Filipinos trained by the Americans. The honor of both nations was involved in resistance to an invader. Though the air com-ponent of this army was inadequate, there seemed hope that, under the inspiring leadership of General Douglas MacArthur, the defense might at least be so prolonged as to prevent the enemy from gaining much

---

[1] Additional infantry divisions were, in fact, already on their way to, or under orders for, Malaya when the Japanese attacked. It would have needed several months' prescience to strengthen the position there at all adequately.

benefit from such conquests as he could make. It might also embarrass and delay his future plans.

The forces in Luzon were not sufficient to oppose landings in the extreme north of the island, where, on December 8 and 9, and also at Legaspi in the southeast, the Japanese gained their first footings and established airfields. Thereafter they had virtual command of the sea. A handful of aircraft did their best to dispute these and subsequent landings, but there were not enough of them. More might have been expected from the twenty-six submarines that were available, but hardly anything was achieved. When the main force approached its landing place in the Lingayen Gulf, 150 miles north of Manila, on December 22, the seventy or so transports were heavily escorted, and before they were attacked they had reached an anchorage in waters so shallow as to make submarine operations particularly hazardous. In addition, the Americans discovered the serious shortcomings of their torpedoes, defects remarkably similar to those that had had so discouraging an effect on the German Navy two years earlier. Their magnetic exploders proved quite unreliable (as had also the British ones), and, though many of the submarines in this fleet carried an older pattern of torpedo with a contact exploder, these exploders also failed through faulty depth keeping which took them under their targets. In fact only one transport was sunk. As with the Germans, it was more than a year before these things were put right, and severe disappointments were to be suffered by American submarines in their ever-expanding operations against Japanese trade.

The Lingayen Gulf landings, though opposed by such troops as could be brought to the scene in time, could not be prevented, and the defenders were gradually forced south through the central plain of Luzon. A few days later the enemy landed at Antimonan on the east coast, 75 miles southeast of Manila. With heavy pressure from both directions, it was clear that the capital could not be defended, and on December 26 General MacArthur withdrew his forces to the Bataan Peninsula on the west side of Manila Bay.

In Bataan the army maintained a heroic defense for more than three months, the exhausted remnant capitulating on April 9. Corregidor Island, south of the peninsula, held out for nearly a month longer. General MacArthur himself had left Bataan early in March by order of President Roosevelt, to take up supreme command of the Allied forces in the southwest Pacific. It was a hazardous journey by motor torpedo boat to a secret airfield in Mindanao, and thence by Flying Fortress to Australia. Though MacArthur had had to leave with the tragic end of a chapter plainly in view, he was firmly resolved that at long last a new chapter in Philippine history would open with his triumphant return. At the time there must have been many who found it difficult to share his well-grounded faith.

So well equipped were the Japanese for amphibious operations that they had not even waited for the launching of their main attack on Luzon before thrusting farther south. On December 14 the oil fields at Miri, in northern Sarawak, were occupied. On December 20 the Japanese seized Davao, in Mindanao, and started to establish their air forces there. And a few days later Jolo in the neighboring Sulu Archipelago was occupied. These conquests on the latitude of the southern Philippines and northern Borneo were rounded off on January 5, 1942, by the occupation of Brunei Bay, a fine natural harbor the Japanese started to develop as a fleet anchorage.

Having reached thus far south, the Japanese took the next step as soon as their air strength at Davao and Jolo was sufficiently built up. On January 10 amphibious forces struck at the Tarakan oil fields on the east coast of Borneo and at Menado in the extreme north of Celebes. Resistance, necessarily meager, was soon overcome, and at Menado the Japanese had another airfield at their disposal.

The enemy's main drive in this area was for Java, by far the richest and most populous island in the Dutch East Indies. Here the best approach, at least till Malaya was conquered, was through Macassar Strait, between Borneo and Celebes. An additional advantage for the Japanese in coming from this direction was that they could take en route the rich oil fields of Balikpapan on the Borneo side of the strait. The occupation of Menado, however, was aimed more at furthering a southeasterly thrust through the nearby Molucca Passage to Amboina. From there it would be only 500 miles to Port Darwin in Australia; and on this line the Allies could at present offer no serious resistance. Such naval resources as there were had to be devoted to hampering the main attack on Java.

With the enemy advancing through Macassar Strait, the time had come to use American surface forces in an attempt to stem the current. On the night of January 24, therefore, four destroyers attacked the amphibious force that was assaulting Balikpapan and sank four transports. But the Japanese operations were not seriously affected. Though fighting continued ashore round Balikpapan, and American and Dutch aircraft delivered such attacks on shipping as they were able to, the enemy were soon firmly established. The Japanese also occupied Macassar on the Celebes side of the strait. By the end of January they were in full control of Macassar Strait and only 500 miles from Java.

The Japanese southeasterly thrust, too, had gone well ahead. Kendari, in southeast Celebes, had been occupied on January 24, and a week later Amboina, the chief Dutch station in the Moluccas, was as-

123

saulted and overpowered, its airfield being captured after three days' fighting. And this was not the only attack to the eastward. Though to conquer Australia might not be within their immediate plans, the Japanese were determined to thrust in that direction to what seemed the safe limit of their resources. If fortune did not favor them to the extent of permitting an invasion of Australia itself, they would at least be drawing Allied forces in that direction and establishing a bastion to their position in the Eastern Archipelago from which to resist American attempts at reconquest. They could have had no illusions about the eventual growth of American fighting strength. Everything depended on consolidating their conquest while there was time. With these ideas in mind, therefore, eastern New Guinea and the islands to the eastward of it (Bismarck Archipelago and the Solomon Islands) were clearly of importance. This region was 1,600 miles to the eastward of their other operations, but they had a convenient jumping-off place at Truk, in the Carolines, only 700 miles to the northward, which had been a fleet base for some years past. From there they struck at Rabaul, the capital of New Britain, on January 23, overpowering the Australian garrison by an amphibious operation supported by carrier-borne aircraft; from there also they established a footing in Bougainville, the northernmost of the Solomons, without resistance.

During all this time the campaign in Malaya had been going ill for the British. Reinforcements had been arriving at Singapore in considerable numbers, escorted across the Indian Ocean and up from Sunda Strait by British, Australian, and Dutch cruisers and destroyers. But neither aircraft, nor armor, nor time was available to enable the mass to be shaped into a fighting entity; and the enervating hothouse climate told strongly against endeavors at improvisation. By the end of December the Japanese were about halfway down the peninsula. On both flanks they could use sea transport to help them move forward, their own shipping on the east coast and captured local craft in the Strait of Malacca. Little naval opposition was within Allied resources, though on January 26 a gallant action against superior forces was fought by an Australian and a British destroyer in which the latter was sunk. This was off Endau, about 80 miles north of the Strait of Singapore, where the Japanese were landing strong forces in a successful attempt to outflank and cut off a part of the defending army and to consolidate their position in Johore, the southernmost of the Malay States. A few days later they reached Johore Strait, separating Singapore Island from the mainland, and on February 8 they crossed the strait and invaded the island. On February 15 Singapore could no longer be held, and the army surrendered.

With the exception of the precariously held harbors of Java, the Allies now had no naval base nearer than Ceylon, 1,600 miles to the westward. To the eastward was Port Darwin, 1,200 miles east of Java. But it was inadequate for such a purpose and had little hope of defending itself against Japanese aircraft. In fact, on February 19 it suffered a devastating raid launched partly from Amboina and partly from Admiral Nagumo's carrier fleet which had just appeared in these waters. After February 20 Port Darwin was even more closely threatened by the Japanese occupation of Timor.

As soon as the fall of Singapore was clearly in sight, the Japanese were able to exploit the western route to the Dutch East Indies. On February 14 a combined seaborne and airborne attack, based partly on airfields in western Borneo, occupied previously, captured Palembang in south Sumatra, the center of important oil fields. Ten days later Japanese troops had reached the west side of Sunda Strait.

Java was now threatened from east and west, and the time was approaching for a last attempt by Allied naval forces to stave off invasion. Surabaya, the naval base in eastern Java, had already been much damaged by air attack, and the naval headquarters had been moved to Tjilatjap on the south coast. During a sortie against the enemy's advance on Sumatra, an American-Dutch force under Rear Admiral Doorman of the Netherlands Navy had been heavily bombed. The light cruiser *Marblehead* had been forced to retire to the south coast for repairs, and the heavy cruiser *Houston* had had one turret put permanently out of action. And then, on February 19, the Japanese landed in Bali, just east of Java. An attack the following night by Allied destroyers and a cruiser on the transport anchorage did not succeed in upsetting the enemy's plans, and resulted in the loss of a Dutch destroyer.

In this desperate situation Vice Admiral Helfrich, the Dutch admiral who was now Allied naval commander in chief, sent all available forces into the Java Sea to attack the invasion convoys that must soon be expected. Now that Malaya had fallen, the Dutch squadron, under command of Rear Admiral Doorman, had been joined by British and Australian ships. So reinforced it comprised the 8-inch cruisers *Houston* (U.S.) and *Exeter* (British), the 6-inch cruisers *De Ruyter* and *Java* (Dutch) and *Perth* (Australian), and nine destroyers.

On the afternoon of February 27, soon after leaving Surabaya, Admiral Doorman's squadron encountered a similar Japanese force which was covering an invasion convoy. An action followed in which the Japanese at first wasted many torpedoes by firing them at a range that, though within their running capabilities, was too long to give them any chance of hitting. On closing, however, gunfire and torpedo fire both had more effect, and hits were inflicted on the Allies. The *Exeter*, her

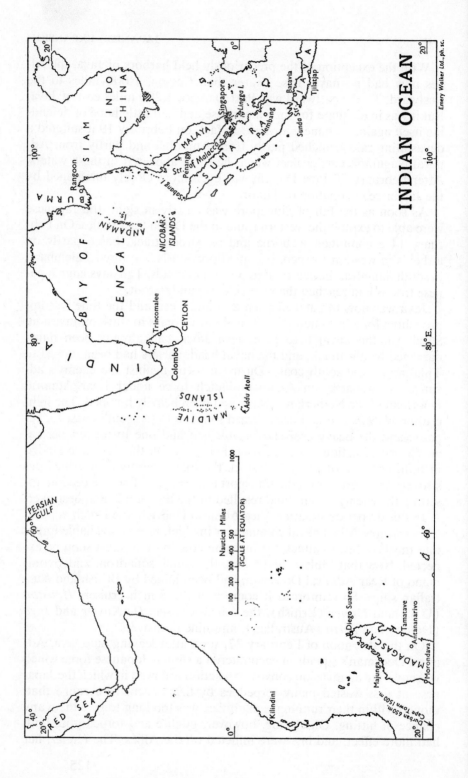

INDIAN OCEAN

Emery Walker Ltd., ph. sc.

speed reduced by a shell in her boiler room, had to part company with the squadron; and two destroyers (one Dutch and one British) were sunk, the former by torpedo and the latter by gunfire. The Japanese eventually turned away, breaking off action; later the Allied forces withdrew toward the Java coast to try to intercept the convoy.

During the ensuing night there were two more encounters with enemy ships, in which the *De Ruyter* and the *Java* were sunk by torpedoes and another British destroyer was lost. The Allied force was now a mere remnant. The *Houston* and the *Perth* succeeded in reaching Tanjong Priok (the port of Batavia), and the *Exeter* got to Surabaya, but attempts to escape through Sunda Strait during the next two days resulted in all these ships running into Japanese cruiser squadrons. The squadron met by the *Houston* and the *Perth* during the night of February 28–March 1 had been escorting an invasion convoy, and, encountering the anchored transports first, the Allied cruisers succeeded in sinking one and driving three others ashore before being themselves overwhelmed after an hour's fighting. The *Exeter* and the two destroyers with her were sunk by another Japanese force twelve hours later. Of the whole force that Admiral Doorman had taken into the Java Sea, only four American destroyers escaped. The remaining naval forces in Java, which had been at Tjilatjap on the south coast, were evacuated to Australia, several ships being sunk by Japanese forces before they could get clear to the southward.

On February 28 the Japanese army landed in Java. A week later all organized resistance was at an end. The enemy had gained control of the whole Eastern Archipelago, more than 3,000 miles east to west from the Solomons to Sumatra, and 1,500 miles north to south from the Philippines to Java and Timor.

Before the flood of Japanese conquest was to be checked, and then, after further blows given and taken, gradually pressed back, two more main thrusts were to be made. One, to the westward through Burma, threatening India, was supported at first by a naval raid into the Bay of Bengal and the waters round Ceylon. The other was to the southeastward, aimed at southern New Guinea and its flank guard in the Solomons, Guadalcanal.

Burma was invaded from Siam in January 1942. Rangoon fell in March. The scanty British and Indian forces were pressed northward in a stubborn fighting retreat, and by the end of May the whole country was occupied. This land action did not in itself have any notable effect on the naval situation, but it was clearly to the advantage of the Japanese to exploit their sea power in threatening India and its sea communications. In this way they might force the British to disperse their

resources and so lighten the task of a land invasion from Burma with
sea transport on its flank.

For all that could be done to prevent them, the Japanese might
achieve much more than that. With no serious threat from the American Navy, they were able to bring heavy forces into the Indian Ocean
and to establish advanced bases, for air reconnaissance and for fueling
destroyers, in the Andaman Islands. On the British side there were
neither the ships nor the aircraft to challenge Japanese command of
these seas. The Eastern Fleet was being formed under command of Admiral Somerville, but it comprised only the *Warspite* and four battleships of the *Revenge* class, the *Formidable*, the *Indomitable*, and the
Hermes, and a few cruisers and destroyers. Nor was the base situation
satisfactory. Ceylon, with its harbors of Trincomalee on the east coast
and Colombo on the west, was too exposed and as yet too ill defended
for the fleet's purpose; a base was therefore being made at Addu Atoll
in the Maldive Islands, 450 miles farther west. This position was too far
away even to attempt to control communications in the Bay of Bengal.
If the British fleet could maintain itself in being in this area, it might
prevent the enemy's interfering with the routes to western India; but
that, for the time being, was the best that could be expected.

The immediate anxiety, in fact, was not for the use of Ceylon as a
naval base, but to prevent its falling into the hands of the enemy. To
this end all possible reinforcements of troops and aircraft were sent
there, including three squadrons of Hurricanes, a notable accession of
fighter strength for this theater of war. But even then, with the recent
examples of Malaya and Java in mind, it was doubtful whether the navy
could do much to prevent a landing. It was true that the enemy had no
airfields within reach. But his carrier strength was impressive. And if
he should conquer Ceylon, virtually all British communications with
India might be broken, and the danger extended even to the sea routes
up the east coast of Africa to Egypt and the Persian Gulf.

The conquest of Ceylon, however, was not the Japanese plan. Realizing that before long he would have to defend his eastern conquests
against growing American strength, the enemy had decided to limit his
western venture to a raid in force, to break up communications in the
Bay of Bengal, draw the opposing troops and aircraft as far as possible
to the southward and away from Burma, and generally damage British
prestige in India.[2] To this end a fleet comprising four battleships of the
Kongo class and five aircraft carriers, with cruisers and destroyers in

---

[2] Two months earlier the Japanese had told their allies that they intended to
establish bases in Ceylon and possibly in Madagascar; the prospect of thus sever-
ing British communications with Egypt and the Persian Gulf had been hailed

company, steamed westward under Vice Admiral Nagumo. On April 5 a striking force of ninety-one aircraft attacked Colombo, bombing the harbor and the airfield. Though the Hurricanes took some toll of the attackers, an armed merchant cruiser and a destroyer were sunk and some aircraft were destroyed on the ground. Meanwhile Admiral Somerville was advancing from Addu Atoll, intending at first that his carriers should launch night attacks on Nagumo with their torpedo aircraft. The 8-inch cruisers *Dorsetshire* and *Cornwall*, however, steering for Colombo to join him, were caught by Japanese aircraft and sunk; this disaster, and some apprehension that the enemy might get between him and Addu Atoll and subject him to air attack, decided him to keep clear. After holding on long enough to pick up the cruisers' survivors, therefore, Admiral Somerville reluctantly retired to the westward.

During the next few days Japanese cruisers, destroyers, and aircraft swept the Bay of Bengal, capturing or sinking some 100,000 tons of shipping. Then, on April 9, came an attack on Trincomalee, and again the raid was followed by a naval disaster. The aircraft carrier *Hermes*, which had sailed from Trincomalee without her aircraft in the hope of evading the expected attack, was caught by an air striking force and sunk. On this occasion the enemy fleet, located by the British air search, was attacked by a squadron of Blenheims, the sole striking force of the Royal Air Force in the Eastern theater of war. This squadron, however, was virtually wiped out without achieving any success. The whole Japanese exploit had been an ample demonstration of the power of a fleet wielding strong air striking forces.

Despite its success this attack was the last blow by Japanese surface and air forces in the Indian Ocean. In time British trade was able to use again the routes off the east coast of India; and before long Trincomalee became the base of a useful force of submarines which attacked Japanese shipping taking supplies to Burma by sea. But at first there could be no certainty of not having again to face strong naval thrusts, perhaps going beyond Ceylon. And it would obviously be to the advantage of the enemy (or at least to his Axis allies) to develop a heavy submarine attack on trade and transports moving up and down the east coast of Africa. The Japanese had done very well for themselves in the use of French Indochina, and it seemed probable that they would exploit their relations with the Vichy government to gain a base in Madagascar.

---

with enthusiasm by the German High Command. But a detailed consideration of ways and means, perhaps influenced by the nascent activity of American aircraft carriers in the Pacific, seems to have persuaded the Japanese that this undertaking would be stretching their commitments beyond the limits of prudence.

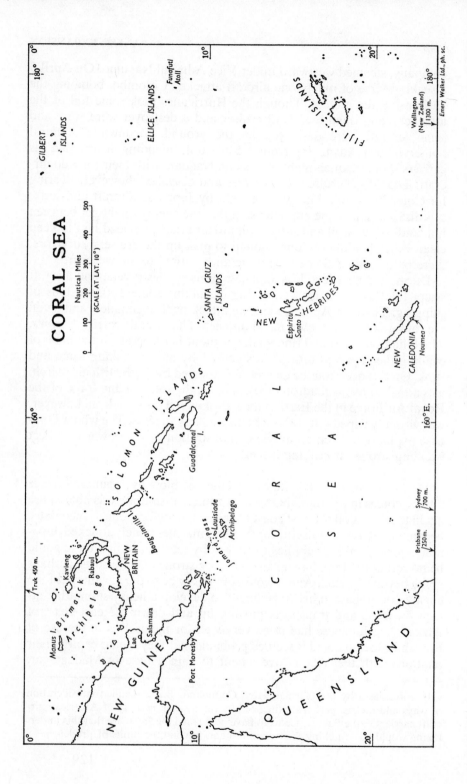

CORAL SEA

Nautical Miles
0   100   200   300   400   500
(SCALE AT LAT. 10°)

GILBERT
ISLANDS

ELLICE ISLANDS

Funafuti
Atoll

FIJI ISLANDS

Wellington
(New Zealand)
1300 m.

Emery Walker Ltd., ph. sc.

SANTA CRUZ
ISLANDS

NEW HEBRIDES

Espiritu
Santo I.

NEW
CALEDONIA

Noumea

SOLOMON ISLANDS

Guadalcanal I.

Bougainville

Truk 450 m.

Manus I.

Kavieng

Bismarck Archipelago

Rabaul

NEW BRITAIN

Lae

Salamaua

NEW GUINEA

Port Moresby

Louisiade Archipelago

China Strait Pass

C O R A L   S E A

QUEENSLAND

Brisbane
250 m.

Sydney
700 m.

160° E.

So seriously would such a base threaten Allied communications with Egypt, the Persian Gulf, and India that it could not be risked. The occupation of Madagascar by British forces was therefore determined on.

The initial objective was Diégo-Suarez, the fine harbor and naval base at the northern end of Madagascar. It was hoped that there would be little opposition, despite the known hostility of the governor of the island; but to ensure that any resistance could be overcome, an infantry division was assigned to the task. The expedition was escorted by a squadron under Rear Admiral Syfret which included two aircraft carriers, the *Illustrious* and the *Indomitable*. These ships provided all the air support that was needed to overcome local air resistance and assist the troops in their advance, the first use of the British naval air arm for such a purpose.

On May 5 the troops were landed in Courier Bay on the west coast, to march some 15 miles across a peninsula and capture Antsirane, on Diégo-Suarez Bay, the headquarters of the district. After an initial advance without much difficulty, stubborn resistance was met in the approaches to the town, and it looked as if there might be some heavy and much to be lamented bloodshed before it could be occupied. The Gordian knot was cut, however, by the bold exploit of a destroyer, the *Anthony*, which despite the serious risk of opposition from the defenses, steamed into Diégo-Suarez Bay by night, berthed alongside a quay in Antsirane, and landed a party of Royal Marines who seized the artillery headquarters. With a hostile force thus established in the center of the position, the heart was taken out of the defense. The garrison surrendered, and on May 7 Admiral Syfret's squadron came in and anchored.

The main harbor of the island had thus been effectively denied to the enemy, and the British had a base from which there should be little difficulty in preventing the use of other Madagascan harbors. As, however, the Vichy governor in the capital, Antananarivo, continued in defiance, and might thus be in a mood to succor the enemy, the situation was not entirely satisfactory. Four months later, therefore, on September 10, hostilities were reopened, this time against the central part of the island. Landings were effected at Majunga and Morondava on the west coast, and later at Tamatave on the east. The expeditions advanced against some resistance, but fortunately with few casualties on either side. On September 23 Antananarivo was occupied and the campaign was virtually at an end.

Even before the first Madagascar operation, the center of gravity of the Eastern war had shifted from the Indian Ocean to the southwest Pacific. Here the dominant factor was the threat to Australia, which clearly could not be faced by the Australians alone. However keenly the Americans desired to strike at Japan by the shortest line practicable when their strength should be great enough, their immediate strategy was dictated by this threat. With good management of available forces, the danger of Australia's being invaded need not be serious; but a spearhead that had already reached Rabaul and showed every sign of thrusting farther must be parried and countered. The American Chiefs of Staff, therefore, made this the first charge on their resources. Troops and aircraft were sent to Australia, and in March, as already noted, General MacArthur assumed duty as supreme Allied commander in the Southwest Pacific Area.

Both to protect the sea routes between the United States and Australia and to parry and counter Japanese thrusts, ships, aircraft, and bases were needed. The Fiji Islands, nearly on a line from Pearl Harbor to Sydney (2,700 miles from the former and 1,700 miles from the latter), were well placed for providing an intermediate base and staging point, and no time was lost in sending there the equipment needed. But for the use of the forces most likely to come to grips with the enemy, a position was needed nearer the scene of Japanese activities. A well-placed harbor was found in Espiritu Santo (New Hebrides), which lies between the Fijis and the Solomons, about 700 miles from the center of each group. Here was built up what was to be an important advanced base of the United State Navy for many months to come. At the same time shore-based naval air forces were established in New Caledonia, 300 miles to the southward, and here also (at Nouméa) was another naval base which was to become the headquarters of the naval commander in chief, South Pacific Area.

As regards the ships to be employed in these waters and the Central Pacific, Admiral King had not as yet sufficient forces at his disposal to challenge the Japanese main fleet to battle. As already recounted, he must postpone decisive action until the many new ships building could be brought into service and those damaged at Pearl Harbor repaired. But there was good reason to suppose that much could be done by aircraft carriers with cruiser protection. In the early months of 1942 three, and later four, aircraft carriers were available for service in the Pacific, and as early as the end of January forces under Vice Admiral Halsey (the *Enterprise* with three cruisers and six destroyers) and Rear Admiral Fletcher (the *Yorktown* with two cruisers and four destroyers) started a series of raids on Japanese airfields and anchorages in the Marshall and Gilbert Islands. A few weeks later (February 20) the *Lexington*, with cruisers and destroyers, attempted a raid on Rabaul, which the Japanese were making into an important base. While approaching the launching position this force was assailed by Japanese shore-based aircraft, and a considerable air battle ensued in which the enemy were routed with the loss of sixteen aircraft; but since the plan had depended on surprise the raid was then abandoned and the *Lexington* withdrew to refuel.

To the northward Admiral Halsey was again active. On February 24 he took the *Enterprise* with two cruisers and seven destroyers to shell and bomb Wake Island; and a week later the *Enterprise*'s aircraft bombed Marcus Island, 800 miles farther west and only 1,000 miles from Japan.

In these exploits much experience was gained in the technique of replenishing with fuel oil and aviation gasoline from accompanying oilers—the fleet train. They also brought out the strategical and tactical problems of keeping the fleet train, necessarily slower than the fighting ships, safe from enemy attack. These techniques were to be developed later to such a pitch as to give a huge fleet, ten times the size of Admiral Halsey's original force, an enduring mobility unknown since the days of sail.

There was one other carrier operation in the Central Pacific during this period. In April the *Enterprise*, joined by the *Hornet* and accompanied by a cruiser escort, steamed toward Japan. On April 18, when about 650 miles from Tokyo, the *Hornet* launched a force of sixteen medium bombers of the Army Air Force commanded by Lieutenant Colonel Doolittle. The *Enterprise* provided fighter cover for the operation. Colonel Doolittle's force bombed Tokyo and then went on to land (or parachute) in China. Though the carrier force had been sighted by Japanese patrols, air forces could not reach it before it withdrew from the danger zone and the ships returned to Pearl Harbor without further event.

The Tokyo raid has taken us ahead of the story of events in the south and the growing Japanese menace to New Guinea and Australia. In these waters the *Lexington* had recently been joined by the *Yorktown*, and to the five heavy cruisers and twelve destroyers working with these carriers were added an Australian squadron of three cruisers, two heavy and one light. This was the force that was to oppose any further Japanese advance.

The first Japanese move after equipping their base at Rabaul was to send an expedition from there to occupy Lae and Salamaua in Huon Gulf on the northeast coast of New Guinea, both of which had airfields. This was done on March 7. Three days later the *Lexington* and the *Yorktown*, with escorting cruisers and destroyers, were taken into the waters south of New Guinea, whence their aircraft, flying over the mountain ranges, attacked the Japanese shipping engaged in landing troops and supplies for consolidating these new conquests. But this attack had no appreciable effect on the enemy, who steadily built up his forces in the area.

For some weeks afterward there was much cross-raiding by the shore-based aircraft of both sides, the chief Japanese target being Port Moresby, on the south coast, which looked across 300 miles of sea to Cape York Peninsula of northern Queensland. Port Moresby was in fact the next enemy objective. If the Japanese could establish themselves there they would deprive the Allies of an important airfield, and at the same time a step to the mainland would begin to look possible. Although that part of Queensland is somewhat barren, a step-by-step, or airfield-by-airfield, advance down the coast might become practicable strategy. To prevent the Japanese from reaching the south coast of New Guinea, therefore, was a matter of prime importance.

From Salamaua to Port Moresby is only 160 miles across the peninsula of eastern New Guinea, but high mountains and thick jungle intervene. The Japanese, therefore, deciding to attack Port Moresby by sea, assembled an amphibious expedition for the purpose. At the same time they sent a small expedition to establish a seaplane base at Tulagi, an islet off Florida Island, which lies north of Guadalcanal.

It was not long before the Americans had an idea of the general trend of these plans, for at this time they had one notable advantage over their enemies. The Japanese had not advanced so far in the science of ciphering as had most other nations. The Germans, with their painful experiences of 1914–1918 behind them, had taken scrupulous care to make their ciphers unbreakable. And no doubt the British and Americans were equally aware of the high importance of this matter. But in this respect Japanese awareness and ingenuity seem to have fallen short, and for at least the first eighteen months of the war[3] the American services were able to decipher many of the enemy's radio messages, a tremendous advantage, particularly while they were building up their strength.

The expedition to Tulagi arrived on May 3. As soon as the news was received, a force of the ships nearest the scene was sent to interfere. This force, under Rear Admiral Fletcher, comprised the *Yorktown*, three heavy cruisers, and six destroyers. It arrived about 100 miles southwest of Guadalcanal on the morning of May 4, and from there the *Yorktown*'s aircraft struck at the shipping in Tulagi Harbor, sinking a destroyer and inflicting some other damage but having little lasting effect on the situation.

[3] In May 1943 American fighters were enabled to shoot down a plane carrying Admiral Yamamoto, the Japanese commander in chief, by the deciphering of a message that gave details of his itinerary.

The signs of Japanese activity in the New Britain area, reported by air reconnaissance, called for all available forces. On May 5, therefore, Admiral Fletcher was joined by the *Lexington*, three more American cruisers, two Australian cruisers, and five more destroyers. By the afternoon of May 6 the Japanese expedition had sailed. The convoy and its covering force, which included the small (converted) carrier *Shoho*, were routed for the Jomard Passage, the only practicable channel through the Louisiade Archipelago which extends for 200 miles from the southeast point of New Guinea. But knowing that American forces had been working near the Solomons, the Japanese sent their main covering force in that direction, hoping to make contact with their opponents before the latter could do any harm to the expedition. This force consisted of the fleet carriers *Shokaku* and *Zuikaku*, two heavy cruisers, and six destroyers. It had sailed from Truk, the fleet base in the Carolines, and had shaped course to the eastward of the Solomons. In this way the Japanese hoped to elude Allied shore-based search and to come on the American forces from an unexpected direction, should any such forces try to interfere with the convoy.

The general trend of these dispositions, though not the course being followed by the big carriers, had been indicated to Admiral Fletcher by intercepted radio messages and shore-based reconnaissance. To counter them he sent a force of three cruisers and five destroyers, under Rear Admiral Crace of the Australian squadron, to the southward of the Jomard Passage to bar the convoy's path in the event it had not been turned back sooner. This force, though repeatedly attacked by shore-based aircraft (including some misguided American Army Air Force bombers), suffered no damage. With the remainder of his force (two carriers, five cruisers, and eight destroyers), Admiral Fletcher steered for a position about 100 miles southeast of the Louisiades.

The American dawn search on May 7 found two cruisers north of the Louisiades and erroneously reported them as carriers. The same search, however, missed the *Shokaku* and the *Zuikaku* which, though well within range to the eastward, were concealed in an area of bad weather. The full American striking force was therefore sent against the imagined carriers to the northwest. By chance it found the *Shoho* off the northern approach to the Jomard Passage, and promptly sank her.

Meanwhile the searches from the big Japanese carriers had missed Admiral Fletcher's force, which was also covered by bad weather, but they had sighted his oiler and her escorting destroyer 150 miles to the southward of the Japanese ships. On a first false report of a carrier the striking force was sent in this direction. Since on arrival they could find nothing else, they attacked the oiler and her escort and sank them.

135

Later in the day the two main forces approached nearer to each other. Some returning Japanese aircraft mistook the American carriers for their own and, after they had been disillusioned, there were some fights above the clouds. This action enabled the Americans to track the Japanese aircraft by radar back to their carriers, and so gave them a good idea of the enemy's position, which was in fact only 30 miles away. Admiral Fletcher decided not to attempt a night attack with his cruisers and destroyers, but to keep his force concentrated. So as to open the range for the intended air battle of the next day, he steered to the south-eastward during the night, while the Japanese, wishing to close their convoy which was now marking time and had no carrier protection, steered to the northward. In this move the Americans were unlucky, for they came out into clear weather while the Japanese still had partial cloud cover.

Next morning, May 8, the positions of the two forces, about 170 miles apart, were revealed to each other by their respective air searches. Both sent off their full striking forces, and at about 11 A.M. each force struck at its enemy's carriers. The American attack was hampered by cloud and rain squalls and some aircraft never found their target, but the *Shokaku* was heavily assailed and, though all torpedoes missed, she was badly damaged by bombs and had to haul off for Rabaul. The Japanese attacked in full strength and hit both the *Yorktown* and the *Lexington*, the latter with torpedoes as well as bombs. The striking forces of both sides suffered severe casualties from gunfire and defending fighters, the Japanese losing more than half their aircraft and the Americans about one-third of theirs. When the surviving Japanese aircraft drew off, neither of the American carriers appeared to be vitally damaged, and fires were got under control. But a few hours later there was an explosion of gasoline in the *Lexington*; bad fires followed, and before the day ended the ship had to be abandoned and sunk.

Though in this dingdong battle the Japanese had not been heavily defeated, they had been deprived for the time being of two of their big aircraft carriers, a factor that was to have an important, perhaps a decisive, effect in the next battle.[4] And they had been persuaded to modify their plans. The show of American strength in the Coral Sea, which included the persistent but so far unsuccessful operations of the Army Air Force, was enough to deter the Japanese from their project of an amphibious attack on Port Moresby. Their convoy, which had already turned back when American forces were first discovered, therefore returned to Rabaul. They were not prepared to extend their efforts

---

[4] Although the *Zuikaku* had not been hit, her air squadrons had been so badly knocked about that she was rendered inoperative for several weeks.

beyond what seemed prudent, and to attempt an invasion through seas the command of which was seriously disputed was not, in their view, a justifiable operation. A check had for the first time been imposed on the enemy's continuous expansion, and though the Japanese still contemplated an advance southeastward to the Fijis, the prospect of bringing them to a halt and driving them back seemed at last to be in view.

11

THE BATTLE OF THE ATLANTIC AT ITS
HEIGHT: *From the Entry of America to May 1943*

BEFORE RECOUNTING THE story of the submarine war at its height in 1942 and 1943, mention must be made of an episode that derived from the surface operations of the preceding year. This was the escape of the *Gneisenau*, the *Scharnhorst*, and the *Prinz Eugen* from Brest in February 1942.

It will be remembered that the *Gneisenau* and the *Scharnhorst* had been in Brest since March 1941, and the *Prinz Eugen* since June. All three ships had been the constant targets of Bomber Command, and, though none had been put permanently out of action, they had all been prevented from attaining full seagoing and fighting efficiency.[1] At the beginning of 1942 it was decided to try to get them back into the North Sea, whatever the risk. The decision was made by Hitler himself, who insisted that it was better to make the attempt than to let the ships die gradually where they were. At this time and during the next year he was obsessed by the idea of an Allied attack on northern Norway, and considered that his big ships, which so far had been singularly unsuccessful in whatever they had attempted, might be of value in repelling such an invasion. A return route up the English Channel was decided on. The advantages of this plan were (1) that the German ships would be able to avoid the Home Fleet and (2) that fighter defense could be provided (though the Luftwaffe officer responsible declared that his forces were too weak for what was needed). Moreover, Hitler believed that the British authorities would be surprised by so

---

[1] The torpedo hit on the *Gneisenau* by an aircraft of Coastal Command (see p. 69, above) had made an important contribution to this immobilization of the three German ships.

apparently hazardous a plan, and would not react with sufficient speed to do anything effective before the ships were through the danger zone.

The idea that the British would be altogether surprised by a break upchannel was erroneous. A plan to counter such an action had been agreed upon between the Admiralty and the Air Ministry as far back as April 1941. Therefore, when all three ships appeared to be ready for sea, and the arrival of destroyers at Brest seemed to presage an operation, the Admiralty were again of the opinion that a dash upchannel was the most likely move. On February 3 the agreed precautionary measures were put in train by the naval and air commands concerned. The probability seemed that, with the long nights available, the ships would leave Brest just before dark and steam at such high speed as would get them through the Strait of Dover before dawn. The German plan, which was to leave after dark and pass through the strait in daylight, was to that extent a surprise.

The forces available to stop the German ships were, in most respects, scanty. It was not considered justifiable to keep battleships in these waters, where they would be exposed to air attack and the hazards of minefields, to meet so uncertain an event. The only surface forces available, in fact, were six destroyers at Harwich and eight motor torpedo boats at Dover and Ramsgate. There were also six torpedo Swordfish at a Kentish airfield and thirty-six torpedo Beauforts divided among Norfolk, Sussex, and Cornwall. The one element that might be able to attack in great numerical strength was provided by the aircraft of Bomber Command; but, for their high-level bombing to be effective, daylight and a clear sky were needed, and even in such conditions they were without experience in attacking ships steaming at high speed. The success of any attacks, air or surface, if they were to be delivered by day, must, of course, depend in large measure on the extent to which British fighter squadrons would be able to defeat German fighters, which would obviously be used at full strength to defend their ships. For this purpose Fighter Command had in all about 500 aircraft available, against about 250 available to the enemy.

From the start almost everything went wrong for the British. The German squadron left Brest at 10:45 P.M. on February 11. It had then to pass close to two aircraft patrol lines established by Coastal Command—one directly off Brest and one parallel to the north coast of Brittany. But during the critical period both these aircraft were absent; in both the radar had broken down and they had returned to their base. The one off Brest was eventually replaced, but by that time the enemy had passed. The one off the north coast was not replaced. Thus the enemy was first sighted by fighter patrols in the eastern Chan-

nel on the following morning (February 12), and it was not until nearly
11:30 A.M., when the Germans were off Boulogne, that all commands
were apprised of their presence. Thereafter there was some precipita-
tion in the way British forces were thrown into battle, for haste seemed
essential to ensure interception. The six Swordfish attacked at 12:45
P.M. without waiting for their full fighter escort and all were shot down.
Only four Beauforts were immediately available, and after some initial failures to find the enemy they attacked piecemeal during the afternoon. Most of the rest were in Cornwall where they had been stationed
to attack the German ships if they went out into the Atlantic, and
others had just arrived in Norfolk from Scotland. Nine of these latter
and three latecomers from Sussex also attacked during the afternoon.
But no torpedo hits were scored by any of these aircraft.

Meanwhile, at 12:30 P.M. (i.e., before the Swordfish attack), four
motor torpedo boats from Dover had attacked the *Gneisenau* and the
Scharnhorst, but a screen of German motor torpedo boats had forced
them to fire at long range and they had missed. Then, at 3:45 P.M.,
when the enemy were off the Dutch coast, five of the Harwich destroyers attacked, pressing in to 3,000 yards, but with no more notable
success.

Throughout the afternoon the clouds were getting thicker and lower,
and the visibility was growing less. Coordination of aircraft operations,
therefore, became increasingly difficult. Owing to the weather, and to
avoid delay, the idea of separate escorts had to be abandoned, and
Fighter Command put in its most intensive effort as a general covering operation between 2 P.M. and 3 P.M., when the attacks by Bomber
Command and the torpedo Beauforts seemed most likely to take place.
But in fact it was not till later that the bulk of the heavy bombers were
operating. There were 242 of these all told, but the conditions were
so difficult that only 39 of them were able to find the enemy and attack. None scored a hit.

The news that two German battle cruisers had succeeded in breaking through the Strait of Dover and reaching their home ports was received in England with dismay. It had been accepted that these narrow
waters were unsuitable for sustained operations by the big ships of
either side, and hence that there could not be a British battle squadron
there to hold the strait; and it had perhaps also been assumed from this
that the enemy could not pass. It seemed, then, that the Germans had
given British forces a chance to sink two of their three capital ships,
an object always of great importance, and of this chance advantage
had not been taken.

The fact was that the forces in the Channel and in southern England
were not sufficient to bar the passage of the strait to heavy ships. In

the absence of British battleships, such a force could best have been provided by torpedo aircraft with, by day, a strong fighter escort practiced in working with them. A valuable supplement to the aircraft, particularly by night, would have been several flotillas of motor torpedo boats, with motor gunboat support to enable them to fight their way through the enemy's screen. On this occasion, though, the situation was far otherwise. The six Swordfish that had attacked so gallantly were so slow that their fighter escort, unused to working with them, had great difficulty in keeping in company and in fact failed to protect them. More might have been done if the Swordfish had waited for their full escort, but it is doubtful if the difference would have been significant. Of the thirty-six torpedo Beauforts in home waters, only four were immediately available, with another twenty-four joining in the operation somewhat later. But of these latter, only twelve succeeded in finding the enemy, and it seems that the standard of training in torpedo attack was not high. Of the thirteen torpedoes dropped in all by the Beauforts, none hit. Neither, apparently, were the torpedo aircraft well practiced in working with fighter escorts. In fact, they attacked without them, but in the low cloud and poor visibility this was of less importance than it would otherwise have been. Of motor torpedo boats there were only eight. One of these broke down, and a division of three from Ramsgate failed to find the enemy.

Even if all the existing forces had been fully available and a clear sky had enabled British fighter squadrons to dominate the air in strength, it is doubtful if the enemy would have been stopped and sunk. At the time it may have seemed natural to put some confidence in the great numerical strength of Bomber Command. German dive-bombers had shown that they could be effective against ships if used in large numbers in good weather. But in fact it was unlikely that more than one or two hits would have been scored by each hundred heavy bombers, even under good conditions, and the chance that Bomber Command would be able to stop the enemy was remote.

It must be accepted, therefore, that there was not a sufficiency of force to stop the enemy ships. But, though they got through, both battle cruisers were damaged in the air-laid minefields of the Frisian Islands (see chap. 17); the *Gneisenau*, docked in consequence, was so severely crippled by an aircraft bomb a few days later that she was never used again. The *Scharnhorst* and the *Prinz Eugen*, though subsequently a threat to the Russian convoys, did not in fact inflict any damage in those waters; but had they been employed with vigor in conjunction with the *Tirpitz* they might have caused far more trouble than they did. It is fair to conclude, then, that there ought to have been stronger forces guarding the strait than were in fact available. To keep those forces so strong as to make quite certain of stopping the enemy would, in this time of stringency, have been unjustifiably lavish. But to maintain a considerable force of aircraft and motor torpedo boats well trained in striking at fast warships would have detracted little from other operations and would have been fully worthwhile. A special force for this service was certainly essential, for events had shown that aircraft, however numerous, cannot be diverted effectively from their normal tasks to one for which they are not well suited and in which they are virtually untrained.

In an earlier chapter the story of the submarine attack in the Atlantic was taken to the end of 1941, when the situation seemed not unfavorable for the defense. By November 1941 the average dividend paid in tonnage sunk by each German submarine at sea had fallen from the 400 tons a day of the earlier part of the year to less than 100 tons. Now that the increase in British air strength was driving the submarines farther into the Atlantic, the convoys were harder to find, and when found they were better protected. Though 1941 had seen a marked increase in the number of submarines at sea, this development had been offset in the Atlantic by the diversion of substantial numbers to the Mediterranean in September (see pp. 62, 105, above). The overall efficiency of the submarine campaign, therefore, was not very satisfactory for the Germans.

In this situation the tremendous increase in the number of vulnerable targets, resulting from Germany's declaration of war on America four days after the Pearl Harbor attack, came to the German Submarine Command as a welcome relief. Up and down the east coast of the United States, from Florida to New England, there was an endless stream of shipping which was virtually without protection. Much of it, too, was shipping of peculiar importance to the Allied cause. The industrial life of northeastern United States was dependent in many respects on the supply of gasoline and fuel oil brought from the Gulf of Mexico and up the east coast in tankers; and though work was at once started on overland pipelines which would reduce the need of seaborne supplies, many months would be required to complete them. Up the American coast, too, came the tankers bringing oil from Venezuela on their way to Halifax where they would join convoys for Great Britain. In addition to all these tankers, there was a large volume of general traffic, which included vital supplies of bauxite (aluminum ore) from Brazil and the Guianas. The enemy could hardly ask for anything more promising, and to these waters he now transferred his main effort.

There was, of course, some inevitable delay, for the distance to be traversed was 3,000 miles and more, and just at first Dönitz was unlucky in having few submarines to send, partly because of the large force still maintained in the Mediterranean. But the numbers soon mounted, and once across the Atlantic the Germans had reached El-dorado. Their only concern was how large a profit they could derive from their outfits of torpedoes, and to what extent they could supplement this activity by sinking ships by gunfire.

In these circumstances Allied shipping losses from submarine attack mounted rapidly. From September to December, 1941, they had averaged 135,000 tons a month in all theaters, but from February to May, 1942, the average sinkings rose to 400,000 tons in the western Atlantic alone, and in June to 500,000. During all this time the Americans were striving to put their defense in order, but at the start they were so grievously lacking both in resources and in experience that much time was needed. Even so small a contribution to their strength as the loan of ten corvettes and twenty-four trawlers from the British Navy was very welcome; as for experience, Dönitz could report to Hitler in May that the American patrol vessels and aircraft were not yet a serious threat to the submarines. At that time only one submarine had been sunk off the American coast since the campaign had started.

Both numbers and experience, however, were growing. The Germans had already found it advisable to send some of the larger (1,100-ton) submarines to attack tankers in the Caribbean and the Gulf of Mexico, where there was even less defense than on the eastern American coast, and to the waters east of Trinidad where they could assail American supplies to Egypt and the Persian Gulf (for Russia), as well as the Brazil and Guiana trade. Finally, in May, the Americans found it possible to start a few coastal convoys. At first these covered so small a proportion of the shipping routes that they resulted only in more submarines being sent to the southern areas. Sinkings continued to mount. But in July the system of convoys was almost complete. This was what the Germans had been expecting. An efficient convoy system in comparatively shallow water with plenty of airfields close at hand would cut down the profits and increase the cost of attack so sharply as to make it no longer worthwhile to employ the bulk of their forces at a distance of 3,000 miles from home. The 1,100-tonners continued to pay good dividends in the West Indies where they could now remain for longer cruises, refueled by the first tanker submarines to be commissioned, which had just reached these waters. But all the medium-sized submarines working off the United States coast were withdrawn (with some minelaying in the mouth of Chesapeake Bay as a Parthian shaft), and, no doubt refreshed and with confidence enhanced by this period of almost unhampered slaughter, they returned to the grimmer task of convoy attack in mid-Atlantic.

143

The Battle of the Atlantic was now nearing its climax. The Germans had at this time some 140 operational submarines, at sea or in harbor. An additional 120 new submarines were in the Baltic in various stages of working up, a process that usually required from four to six months. Submarines were leaving the builders' yards at a rate of more than 20 a month, increasing to 30 by the early autumn, and during the first six months of 1942 only 21 had been lost, all told. The number available for operations, therefore, was rising steadily. In fact it reached its peak figure of more than 200 early in 1943.

Of the operational submarines, about 100 were in the Atlantic, 20 in northern Norwegian waters, and 20 in the Mediterranean. Of those in the Atlantic about two-thirds were usually at sea (either operating or on passage), and the remainder were in the Bay of Biscay ports. Of those at sea, a few worked in the waters off Sierra Leone, Trinidad, Brazil, and the Cape of Good Hope, where, supplied by tanker submarines, they earned a steady dividend—off the Cape a spectacular one for some weeks on their first appearance. The remainder concentrated against the North Atlantic convoys. In addition to the Germans, a few Italian submarines worked individually in the Atlantic, and some half-dozen Japanese operated in the western Indian Ocean.

The shipping that the North Atlantic submarines sought to attack at this time comprised about fifteen inward-bound convoys a month. A usual convoy was about thirty ships, but many were much larger (sixty ships or more), particularly on the northern route; and as the battle intensified a policy of larger and fewer convoys with bigger escorts, though a more wasteful use of shipping, was found to reduce losses. All these ships had, of course, to sail again for America, the South Atlantic, or Gibraltar, also in convoys. In all, perhaps 2.5 million tons of shipping entered and left British ports each month. If submarines took as heavy a toll of these as they had of the traffic along the American coast in the preceding six months, the situation would be serious indeed. In that time they had sunk, there and elsewhere, more than 3 million tons, including a tanker tonnage of nearly 1 million. It is true that the immense American shipbuilding program, just getting into its stride, forecast a production of 7 million tons a year and perhaps more later.[2] But the loss of merchant-ship crews was becoming a serious factor; and, moreover, it was essential that the Allies do

[2] United States yards built more than 5 million tons in 1942, more than 12 million in 1943, and just below 12 million in 1944. In addition, British yards were producing about 2 million tons a year. These figures are in deadweight tons, and are therefore perhaps 30 percent higher than the gross tonnage measurement used in this book in statements of losses.

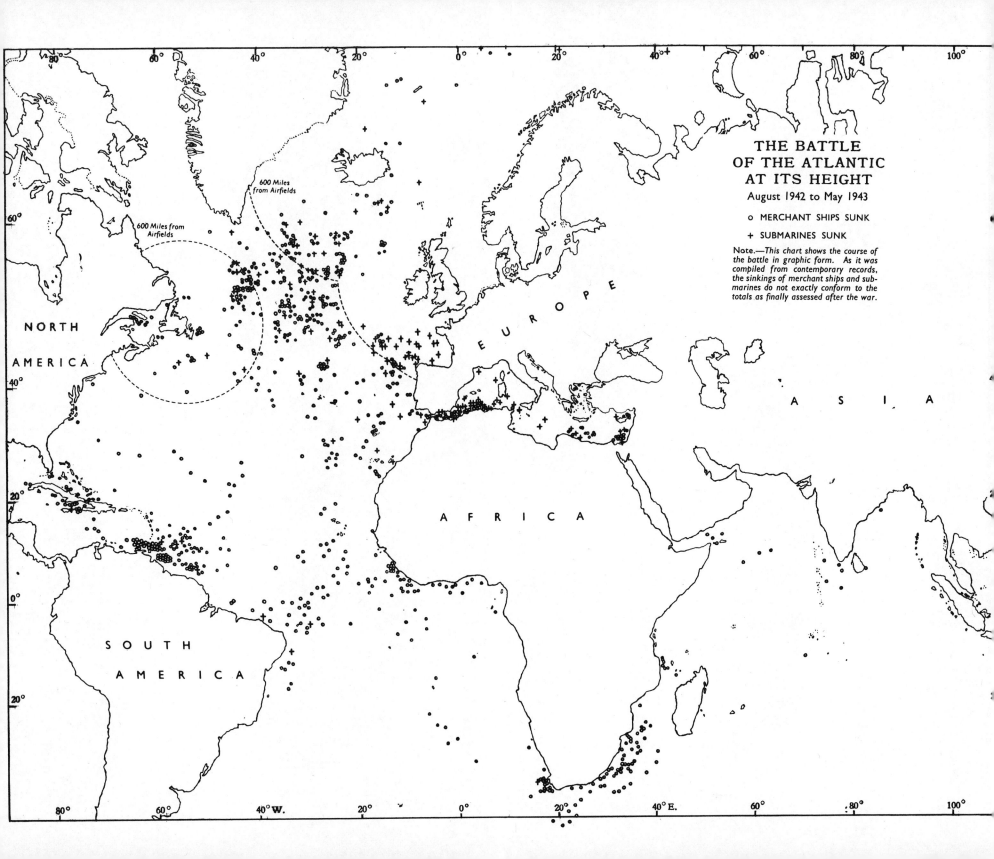

THE BATTLE
OF THE ATLANTIC
AT ITS HEIGHT
August 1942 to May 1943

o MERCHANT SHIPS SUNK

+ SUBMARINES SUNK

Note.—This chart shows the course of
the battle in graphic form. As it was
compiled from contemporary records,
the sinkings of merchant ships and submarines do not exactly conform to the
totals as finally assessed after the war.

600 Miles
from Airfields

600 Miles from
Airfields

NORTH

AMERICA

EUROPE

ASIA

AFRICA

SOUTH

AMERICA

far more than replace lost tonnage. If the rapidly growing American army and air force were to be used offensively in Europe and Asia to the full extent of their powers, a sharp increase of shipping was needed, and it could be obtained only if the present effectiveness of submarine warfare could be drastically reduced.

This, then, was the setting for the great convoy battles that started in August 1942. Since the battles of the preceding year, the defense had gained considerable strength, and convoys could be more strongly escorted. Antisubmarine weapons and technique had also improved. In particular, direction-finding sets were coming into service which could take bearings of the high-frequency radio signals made by submarines in the initial stages of a pack attack. Ahead-throwing weapons, too, were gradually being introduced, and these gave an attack on a submerged submarine a higher probability of success than could be attained with dropped depth charges. The strength of the air forces— British, Canadian, and American—engaged in the battle had also been much increased, and in particular the number of aircraft that could work at long distances from their bases had grown. But here still lay the weak link in the system of defense. Convoys with good surface escorts could be considered reasonably safe when there were adequate aircraft to range the seas round them and keep the submarines down. But when everything possible had been done by aircraft from the British Isles, from Iceland, and from Newfoundland there was still a belt in mid-Atlantic some 500 miles broad where no adequate help from shore-based aircraft could be expected.

From August to November heavy attacks on convoys were almost continuous. Some convoys were constantly assailed for as much as four days and nights. Sometimes a convoy lost nearly half its ships. During these four months more than 2 million tons of shipping were sunk, and in fact there was no diminution in the rate of loss as compared with that in the almost unopposed attacks of the earlier period. Submarine tactics were those of the wolf packs described in an earlier chapter, and they were pursued with great boldness and determination. In mid-ocean the escorts could put up a vigorous defense, but they could neither prevent all casualties nor beat off all their assailants. Only when convoys again reached waters where they could be succored by aircraft could they begin to shake themselves free.

But if there was little difference in rate of loss between these convoy battles and the attacks in American coastal waters of the earlier part of the year, there was a notable difference in the casualties inflicted on the submarines. In the first six months, as already noted, twenty-one submarines were sunk; in the second six months, sixty-four were sunk, of which the large majority were in the North Atlantic. It seemed possible that the Allies might eventually reduce the weight of attack by sinking submarines faster than they were coming into service. But there was still a compelling need to reduce the rate of shipping losses in the meanwhile.

During this period a great body of Allied shipping was used for the invasion of North Africa (as mentioned in a later chapter). That all convoys of the original expedition sailed many thousand miles through and across the Atlantic unassailed by submarines was marvelously fortunate: only one transport in the assault convoys was torpedoed in the Mediterranean, and she did not sink. The Germans knew that something was afoot, but they had assumed that Dakar was the objective and had disposed their submarines accordingly. When the true situation was finally revealed, however, they could take advantage of the concentration of shipping in the western Mediterranean and its approaches and also of the reduced strength of North Atlantic convoy escorts, imposed by the heavy demands of the African operation. This they did to great effect, with the result that the November losses of more than 700,000 tons were the highest for the whole war. The bold venture of launching such an expedition when the submarine campaign was at its height of necessity carried a high price, but it was justified by the success achieved.

After that there was a lull for two months. The bad weather of December 1942 and January 1943, particularly in the latter month, brought the sinkings for these two months to lower figures than any for the past year—337,000 tons and 203,000 tons, respectively. But in February losses started to mount again, and in March both the number of submarines attacking and the number of convoyed ships sunk reached their peak. In all waters during the month 108 ships of 627,000 tons were sunk, and no less than 85 of these were in, or had straggled from, convoys, a larger proportion than ever before. In April and May, however, the rate of loss fell to about half that of March. Though the fury of the attacks was unabated and the losses were still considerable, the battle had in fact been won. It had been won not only because the sinkings were so much less but because the Germans were losing submarines at a rate such as no navy could long sustain. From February to April the average monthly loss had been 18, almost equal to the rate of building. In May the losses leaped to the terrific figure of 41, about one third of all the submarines at sea. Of these, 24 had been sunk on the North Atlantic convoy routes and 7 by aircraft working on the submarines' passage routes through the Bay of Biscay. Dismayed by these losses, the German command withdrew all submarines from the North Atlantic convoy routes. Before the Germans could again undertake anything more than attacks in the outlying areas (the Azores, Sierra Leone,

146

Brazil, the Cape, and the Indian Ocean), they had to lick their wounds and take stock of the situation.

This great and decisive victory, for such it was despite the enemy's later return to the fray, cannot be credited to any one cause. The antecedent factors alone, human and material, were legion, varying in nature from the priority accorded at the top by the Anti-U-Boat Committee (presided over by Winston Churchill) and by the Washington Atlantic Conference of March 1943, to the individual and group training of ships and aircraft and the supply of the numberless weapons and devices they needed.

The basis of victory was, of course, a sufficiency of ships and aircraft. The main burden of organizing and directing these forces was borne by the commander in chief, Western Approaches, the air officer commanding-in-chief, Coastal Command, and the commander in chief, United States Atlantic Fleet.[3] Admiral Noble had played the chief part in building up the Western Approaches command and carried the responsibility there for nearly two years. In November 1942 he was succeeded by Admiral Horton, an outstanding submarine captain of World War I, whose ingrained knowledge of how things looked from the submarines' side, added to a relentless drive, contributed greatly to the success of the convoy battle at its climax. In directing the British air effort Air Marshal Slessor had succeeded Air Chief Marshal Joubert in February 1943. Throughout this period Admiral Ingersoll commanded the United States Atlantic Fleet, which included a large number of shore-based aircraft and an increasing number of aircraft carriers. In the actual fighting the chief responsibility fell on the commanders of escort and support groups, the captains of escort carriers, and the commanding officers of individual aircraft.

Among the immediate causes of victory one of the most important was a mainly technical one concerned with radar. By the autumn of 1942 most escort craft were equipped with a radar set that would detect surfaced submarines at considerable ranges, and early in 1943 sets of similar characteristics were fitted in aircraft. Aircraft had, as already

---

[3] Western Approaches and Coastal Command were not commands of the same type. The latter included all British shore-based aircraft concerned in antisubmarine warfare, and also the air forces attacking German shipping on the coasts of Europe, whereas the commander in chief, Western Approaches, with a group of Coastal Command working under his direction, was responsible for the operations of ships and aircraft in a defined area, bounded on the west by the U.S. Atlantic Fleet Command and on the east by the west coast of Great Britain. But it is fair to say that the commanders in chief, Western Approaches and Coastal Command, were the two officers who bore the main burden of antisubmarine warfare on the eastern side of the Atlantic.

mentioned, been carrying radar for two years, but the type then fitted, though useful, was not of very high efficiency and had been easily detected by the submarines by means of a simple search receiver. A submarine had therefore had notice that an aircraft was searching, probably before the aircraft gained contact. Surprise was avoided and the submarine could escape attack by diving. But against the new radar sets a submarine no longer had warning of the enemy's approach. It could be surprised by surface craft at night and in fog, and by aircraft under almost any conditions. The aircraft, too, were now attacking very effectively by night, using radar for the approach and a searchlight for the final stage of the attack.

The Germans soon realized that something was wrong, but they were at their wits' end to put it right. They suspected the trouble was an improvement in radar, but they were not sure even of that and chased many other hares. In the course of their investigations they discovered that the search receiver they had been using, successfully, to detect the old type of radar was guilty of radiations that might be picked up by ships and aircraft without these assailants having to give themselves away by transmitting. This fact was never used by or even known to the Allies, but it so impressed the German authorities that they forbade the use of any search receiver that was not entirely free from radiations, and this stringent requirement, combined with the difficulty of finding out what radar wavelengths their enemies were using, prevented any effective instrument from being produced until it was too late. The submarines, therefore, had to accept the fact that whenever they were on the surface they could be detected at a considerable range, and in many circumstances might be attacked before they were aware of danger. This fact was an immense asset to the Allies.

If full use was to be made of this, a main requirement was to have aircraft in that mid-Atlantic gap where hitherto the surface forces had had to fight the battle alone. The achievement of this objective at this time—partly by working aircraft at even longer distances than before from their bases in the British Isles, Iceland, and Newfoundland, and partly by including small aircraft carriers, British or American, in the convoy escorts—contributed substantially to the victory. The Swordfish carried by the British ships, though old-fashioned and slow, could tackle a surfaced submarine very effectively with rocket projectiles, though they sometimes needed the support of fighters' cannon to keep down the submarine's antiaircraft fire if surprise had been lost. In operating these aircraft, direction by the carriers through their radar system was of great help, and this direction could also be given to any shore-based aircraft that might be cooperating.

By this time the submarines were trying to fight off, not only the virtually defenseless Swordfish, but also the large aircraft that were attacking them in increasing strength on their lines of passage through the Bay of Biscay. Unable to prevent surprise by night, they could no longer rely on darkness for making good their distance run. They must therefore make distance in the daytime. So instead of diving on the approach of an aircraft, and perhaps getting sunk by a depth charge in the process, they were ordered to remain on the surface and fight it out with the multiple close-range weapons they now mounted. This policy cost the Allies many aircraft, and their aircraft had also at times to contend with German long-range fighters. Nevertheless, these aircraft operations, sustained with vigor and amounting in effect to a blockade of the submarine bases, were significant both in the delay imposed on the submarines' passages and in the damage inflicted. As already noted, seven submarines were sunk in this way in May.

One other important factor in the defeat of the wolf packs must be mentioned. There were now enough antisubmarine vessels to allow the formation of support groups comprising destroyers, sloops, and frigates, which could be sent wherever they were most needed to help the escort groups fight off attacks, to break up incipient concentrations of submarines reported by aircraft, or to act as an extended screen which would make it harder for any submarine to sight and report a convoy. These support groups, of from four to six ships each, were trained to fight as a unit, as were also the escort groups of similar size but composed mainly of corvettes, and this training derived much assistance from a tactical school established at Liverpool. The exigencies imposed by damage and breakdowns did not always allow the groups to be maintained intact, but whenever they could be their effectiveness was much increased. A convoy with a close escort, a support group on an extended screen outside it, and aircraft from an escort carrier ranging the waters still farther out, was so well protected as to be able to pass through a submarine patrol line with little fear of damage. The boldest wolf pack that tried conclusions with such a force was almost certain to be broken up and to suffer severe casualties.

Finally, something must be said of the German side of the picture. There is no doubt that the German submarine service had stood up to a severe hammering with little sign of flinching. Conditions had got so bad that the submarines had been withdrawn; but they were to be put into the battle again later and were to continue to accept high casualties to the end, despite the fact that their hopes of eventual success could be kept up only by somewhat hollow encouragements. A principal factor in any calculation of defense must always be an estimate of the rate of casualties the enemy will put up with in the long run, for it is hardly conceivable that any service will fight to the last man in attack. It was perhaps on this count that an earlier victory in the Battle of the Atlantic had been hoped for by those who put faith in the proved effectiveness of asdic and the casualties that, in conjunction with depth charges, it would be able to inflict. These hopes were falsified because the enemy adopted night attacks on the surface, which largely defeated the asdic, and also because the submarine crews showed a staunchness that excelled the performance of their predecessors of 1917–18. This staunchness, insofar as it exceeded the generally high standard of the German forces, derived partly from the privileged position accorded to the submarine service, and partly from the efficiency with which that service was organized, trained, and commanded by Admiral Dönitz. Against any less resolute body victory would have been gained sooner and at less expense.

12

THE MEDITERRANEAN, III: *From January 1942 to the Conquest of Tunisia*

IN THE MEDITERRANEAN, it will be remembered, the strain had been slightly eased by the recapture of Benghazi on December 24, 1941. Early in January, aided by bad weather and low visibility, a small convoy was slipped through to Malta. But it was not long before the position again deteriorated. On January 21, 1942, Rommel, who had been forced back to El Agheila, once more attacked, and once more the Eighth Army was swept back to the eastward. Benghazi was evacuated on January 28, and all northern Cyrenaica was lost. The Axis forces, however, were not as yet capable of much further effort. Early in February they were held on a line running south from Gazala, about 40 miles west of Tobruk, and there they remained for several months.

It had become clear to the enemy that if he was to achieve anything decisive in Africa he had to eliminate Malta as a base for forces that could attack his communications. With the Russian campaign in the grip of winter, more aircraft were available for the Mediterranean. Thither they were sent and the real pounding of Malta commenced. During the next few months the buildings round Grand Harbour were pulverized, and work in the dockyard became more and more difficult.

So intense was the activity demanded of the defending fighters and guns that the need for supplies, particularly gasoline and ammunition, was more urgent than ever. In February another small convoy set out from Alexandria, but met such severe air opposition that it had to turn back. A major difficulty in all such operations was the slow speed of the merchant ships, so depressing a feature when running the gauntlet. Warships steaming at high speed could still get through from both ends of the Mediterranean with comparatively little risk; and in February the *Cleopatra* had called there on her way through from Gibraltar to join the 15th Cruiser Squadron at Alexandria. But even a so-called fast

151

convoy usually could not steam more than 14 knots, and with such ships as were available for supplying Malta 12 knots was more common.

Another attempt, however, had to be made. A service of large submarines did much to keep the fighters going, but more than that was needed.[1] On March 20, therefore, a convoy of four ships sailed from Alexandria escorted by Admiral Vian in the *Cleopatra* (his previous flagship, the *Naiad*, had recently been sunk by a submarine), with the *Euryalus*, the *Dido*, the antiaircraft cruiser *Carlisle*, and ten destroyers.

All went well until the morning of the 22d. At that time the escort was reinforced by the *Penelope* and one destroyer from Malta; but at that time, too, air attacks started. From then on, the convoy was not only heavily assailed by aircraft, but was also threatened by strong surface forces. From the latter it was preserved, as had been the *Breconshire* in December, by the gallant bearing, audacity, and skill of Admiral Vian's ships. The first Italian ships to make contact, one 6-inch and two 8-inch cruisers and some destroyers, were ridden off with comparative ease; but it was not long before they were back again in company with the battleship *Littorio* and a total of ten destroyers. That Admiral Vian's weak force was able to keep the convoy out of harm's way and drive the enemy back was beyond all reasonable expectation; but such was the event. Fortunately he was to windward with a stiff breeze blowing, and by skillful use of smoke, under cover of which destroyers and cruisers attacked with torpedoes and guns, he so impressed the Italian admiral with the dangers of breaking through the smoke screen that the enemy dared not attempt it. The *Littorio* was slightly damaged by gunfire, and without more ado the Italian squadron drew off. Two British cruisers and three destroyers had been damaged by gunfire, but they were still in fighting trim.

Admiral Vian had protected the convoy for just long enough; he had done as much as he could do. As there was not enough oil at Malta to refuel his ships, he had to return to Alexandria. Against air attack the four ships of the convoy had been successfully protected by the *Carlisle* and some destroyers of the Hunt class;[2] at dark they scattered, each proceeding at its best speed and hoping to arrive at Malta at daybreak. The

[1] In all, some 1,300 tons of aviation fuel were carried by these submarines, as well as a considerable quantity of other supplies. The submarines made twenty-two trips in 1941 and sixteen in 1942.

[2] Destroyers of the Hunt class, named from packs of foxhounds, were small ships specially designed for convoy and antisubmarine duties. They were therefore similar in function to the American destroyer escorts which came into service from 1943 onward, though the latter carried three torpedoes in addition to their antisubmarine and antiaircraft equipment.

152

Penelope, the *Carlisle*, and her destroyers also went to Malta.[3] The next morning one merchant ship, still too far short of the island, was sunk by bombing. The *Breconshire*, veteran of this run, was also hit before she could reach her destination. She eventually sank close to the shore, and a little of her cargo was saved. The other two ships reached harbor, but both were sunk soon afterward with most of their cargo still on board.

Though success in this operation had seemed within grasp, Malta's eagerly awaited blood transfusion had amounted to only a few drops, and the patient was still weakening. The air onslaught was at its height, and it had to be admitted that the island was no longer an effective base for attacking Axis supply lines. A few Wellingtons, Swordfish, and Albacores could still be allowed some gasoline for taking off from the cratered runways and attacking enemy shipping. But they were too few to achieve anything substantial, despite the remarkable success of the night torpedo attacks on such ships as were encountered. For surface forces the position was too hazardous, and adequate maintenance was no longer possible. All that remained, therefore, were sailed. The *Carlisle* and four destroyers went to Alexandria, the *Aurora* and a destroyer went to Gibraltar, and later the sorely battered *Penelope*, constantly damaged in dry dock, was at last got clear. She also made a safe passage to Gibraltar. For a few more weeks submarine patrols were maintained, the only remaining serious obstruction to Rommel's reinforcement; but as submarines in harbor had to submerge by day, it was becoming more and more difficult to keep them efficient.

In April the island defenses were reinforced by forty-seven Spitfires flown in from the *Eagle* and the United States carrier *Wasp*, operating in the western Mediterranean, and it seemed that conditions might improve. But in fact so strong was the enemy reaction that in a few days nearly all these Spitfires had been destroyed. Once more the defense had had to rely mainly on guns—guns, moreover, that were strictly rationed as to ammunition. So severe was the bombing, and so intensive, also, was the minelaying (by aircraft and motor torpedo boats), that even the submarines could no longer be operated. The minesweepers that remained in action could not keep the approach channels clear, and at the end of April there was no option but to withdraw the remaining submarines to Alexandria. Three had been sunk by bombs during air raids, and another, the last to leave, was sunk by a mine off the harbor mouth.

Early in May a further reinforcement of Spitfires arrived, again via the *Wasp* and the *Eagle*, and so also did some ammunition brought by

[3] Two destroyers of the Hunt class were lost during this operation, one torpedoed by a submarine and the other mined off Malta.

the 35-knot minelayer *Welshman* from the west. This time the defense was more successful. After fierce air battles on May 9 and 10 there was something of a lull. The enemy, having suffered severe casualties, considered that Malta had been so battered into uselessness as to need only harassing raids to prevent its resuscitation. Plans were made for taking the island by assault, but the time for that endeavor had not yet come.

Despite the partial lull, the supply situation was again becoming desperate. An attempt at simultaneous replenishment from east and west was therefore determined on, and every available warship was mustered for the task. The Eastern Fleet contributed to the eastern escort, and a force from the Home Fleet was sent to Gibraltar for the western attempt. Ten merchant ships were ready at Alexandria, and six were at Gibraltar. On June 11 both convoys sailed.

The eastern convoy was escorted by eight cruisers and twenty-seven destroyers under Admiral Vian. Occasional air attacks were suffered from June 12 onward, but it was not till the 14th that the situation began to look serious. During that afternoon the air attacks were heavier and one merchant ship was sunk; and in the evening news was received that an Italian squadron of two battleships of the *Littorio* class, eight cruisers, and many destroyers had been seen leaving Taranto and steering to intercept. Admiral Harwood, who had relieved Admiral Cunningham as commander in chief and was directing the operation from Egypt, then ordered the convoy to turn to the eastward until it was seen what could be done by Allied aircraft. Some American Army Air Force bombers attacked the Italian squadron from Egypt, as did also some torpedo Beauforts from Malta. The 8-inch cruiser *Trento* was hit and was afterward sunk by a submarine.

During this same night, while the convoy was retiring, an attack by motor torpedo boats damaged the cruiser *Newcastle*, but was without other result. In the morning, as the Italians did not seem to have advanced very far, the convoy was again turned to a course for Malta, but not for long. The enemy squadron was found to be only 100 miles away, and the expedition had again to retire while another attempt was made to drive the enemy off by air attack. Meanwhile, throughout the day, convoy and escort were bombed heavily and continuously. The cruiser *Arethusa* was damaged and two destroyers were sunk. By the evening, however, the enemy squadron, somewhat damaged by air attack and perhaps fearing more, had at last started to haul off, and the question arose whether one further attempt could be made to get through. But it was now too late. All ships were short of ammunition and the escort could not continue much farther; with no fuel in Malta they must keep enough in hand for their return. The convoy could not, therefore, be escorted far enough, and Admiral Harwood had to order the attempt abandoned. On the return passage the *Hermione* was sunk by a submarine.

The western convoy had fared somewhat better. This operation was under the command of Vice Admiral Curteis with his flag in the *Kenya*, and he had with him the *Malaya*, the *Eagle*, and the old carrier *Argus*, normally used only as an aircraft transport. There were two other cruisers (besides the *Kenya*) and eight destroyers with this force, and in addition the antiaircraft cruiser *Cairo*, nine destroyers, and some minesweepers which would accompany the convoy the whole way to Malta.

During the afternoon of June 14, by which time the expedition was south of Sardinia, German dive-bombers and Italian torpedo aircraft attacked in strength, but they were for the most part driven off by fighters from the *Eagle* and the *Argus* and the guns of the fleet. One ship of the convoy was sunk and the *Liverpool* was torpedoed, but the latter succeeded in getting back to Gibraltar.

By that night the time had come for the covering force to turn for home while the convoy and its escort stood on. It was an uneventful night, but the convoy's prospects for the next day were not encouraging. Two Italian 8-inch cruisers and four destroyers had been reported leaving Palermo, and the chances of eluding them seemed remote. And, to fight a way through, there were only five fleet destroyers to stand up to the enemy, for the rest of the escort, the *Cairo* and four destroyers of the Hunt class, had no torpedoes and would in any event have their work cut out as antiaircraft escorts. Nevertheless the task was accomplished. Though twice during the day the Italian squadron approached to attack, it was driven off by the five destroyers led by the *Bedouin* (herself severely damaged by gunfire and later sunk by torpedo aircraft), and it was further discouraged by the torpedo attacks of a few Albacores and Beauforts from Malta. The convoy, after some evasive maneuvering, was able to stand on. But it was all the time being heavily bombed, and three of the remaining five ships were sunk. Two struggled on and that night both entered harbor, though not without further trouble. As already noted, minelaying by motor torpedo boats and aircraft was adding substantially to the many hazards of approaching Malta, and in the darkness, with no lights to mark the swept channels, one merchant ship struck a mine before being got in. So also did several of the escort, one being sunk. But something had been achieved. Two ships of the sixteen that had sailed (ten from Alexandria and six from Gibraltar) had arrived, and a few days earlier the *Welshman* had come in again with more ammunition. The island was still holding out, however straitened its circumstances. Despite heavy casualties in warships sunk and out of action being incurred to succor it, that succor must still be afforded.

It was just at this time that, with Malta unable to do more than defend itself, Rommel had built up his forces sufficiently to attack once more. On May 27 battle was joined. By June 17 the Eighth Army had been beaten and was in retreat. On June 20 the defenses of Tobruk were overrun and the port, for so long during the preceding year a symbol of British determination to endure, became the most important link in Rommel's communications. Falling back farther than ever before, the Eighth Army passed through Sidi Barrani and Mersa Matruh until, on June 30, when only 60 miles from Alexandria, it took its stand at El Alamein. There, on July 5, after five days of fierce fighting, Rommel was brought to a halt. Intermittent fighting continued till the end of the month, but the position was now firmly held.

So encouraging did the prospect seem to the enemy at this time that Hitler postponed the projected assault on Malta. With Rommel's supplies coming in through Tobruk, the island was of less importance as a menace to his communications even if it were to recover from its pounding. And if he could once get a footing in the well-watered Nile Delta and have Alexandria as a port, the whole situation would be transformed. Malta would be a tough nut to crack even in its weakened state; and to capture it forces would have to be expended, particularly aircraft, which Rommel badly needed. The decision, therefore, was that Malta should, as before, be kept quiescent by harassing raids. As yet the outlook for the enemy was not so gloomy as to make him foresee the part to be played next year by Malta-based forces in the fall of Tunisia and the invasion of Sicily. In the event, however, the island was not even kept quiescent. More minesweepers were available in July, and by the end of the month the submarines had returned and were once more patrolling the central Mediterranean.

Though Malta was to be spared the ordeal of defense against invasion and was once more a base for striking at enemy communications, more supplies must be received before long if the island was not to starve. With the enemy at El Alamein, relief from the east was manifestly impossible, and the warships that remained in these waters had to operate from Levant ports and the Suez Canal zone. Everything, therefore, had to be staked on a convoy from the westward, and in August the shipping and naval forces for this operation were assembled, this time under command of Vice Admiral Syfret with his flag in the *Nelson*.

During the night of August 9–10 the convoy, fourteen fast merchant ships, passed through the Strait of Gibraltar. Four cruisers and eleven destroyers under Rear Admiral Burrough in the *Nigeria* were to take it through to within reach of its destination. The remainder of the force, two battleships, three carriers (*Indomitable*, *Victorious*, and *Eagle*), three cruisers, and fourteen destroyers, would cover the operation as far as the Sardinian channel and then turn back. With Admiral Syfret was also the *Furious*, carrying Spitfire reinforcements to be flown to Malta.

The battle started on the afternoon of August 11 when, while the *Furious*' Spitfires were being flown off, the *Eagle* was torpedoed by a submarine and sunk. Air attacks followed in the evening but no further damage was done. The next morning there were more attacks, and throughout the day the air battle was almost continuous; but the defense by fighters and guns was powerful and comparatively few hits were received. By the late afternoon, when it was time for the covering force to turn back, the *Indomitable* had been badly damaged by bombs, one merchant ship had been hit, and a destroyer had been torpedoed and had later to be sunk; but, considering the great weight of air and submarine opposition thrown against it, the convoy could be said so far to have prospered.

From then on, however, the convoy and Admiral Burrough's force were subjected to attack after attack, and casualties mounted. In the evening the *Nigeria* was torpedoed by a submarine and forced to retire to Gibraltar, Admiral Burrough transferring his flag to a destroyer. About the same time the *Cairo* was sunk and two merchant ships were damaged. At dusk there were more waves of air attacks, and two merchant ships were destroyed; a little later the *Kenya* was torpedoed by a submarine, though she was able to continue with the force. Worse was to come. It was soon after midnight, when the convoy was rounding Cape Bon, that the most serious damage was received. A heavy attack by motor torpedo boats from Pantelleria sank the cruiser *Manchester* and four merchant ships, and another merchant ship was damaged.

With more than 100 miles to be steamed next day, the outlook was grim. As yet, however, the Italians gave no sign that they were going to send battleships or cruisers to try conclusions with the remnant of Admiral Burrough's force; and the convoy had steered well to the southward after passing Cape Bon so as to keep as good an offing as possible from the Sicilian airfields. By 8 A.M., however, when the convoy was about 35 miles north of Lampedusa, aircraft had again found and attacked it, and thereafter attacks were continuous until, late in the afternoon, it came under the effective protection of the Malta fighters. Then at last the convoy, or what remained of it, was through its troubles, and Admiral Burrough could turn it over to local escort and retire. An Italian cruiser squadron had been sighted coming south but had not pressed on. It was discouraged by a small strike of torpedo aircraft from Malta, and on its way back to Naples one of the cruisers was torpedoed by a British submarine. But of the original fourteen merchant ships only three remained, two of them damaged. Two more damaged ships, which had escaped by steering down the Tunisian coast, crawled in next day. When all was over Malta had been given a replenishment that at least was more substantial than anything received since the preceding September. Rations, which had been within a week of exhaustion, could be maintained for another four months. The cost of this help in warships had been one aircraft carrier, one cruiser, one antiaircraft cruiser, and one destroyer sunk, and one aircraft carrier and two cruisers badly damaged.

In looking back over the heroic efforts and severe losses entailed in keeping Malta supplied, it is natural to wonder whether all this need have been. In the circumstances, not only were the efforts necessary, but their success was a factor of great importance in the future course of the war. But there seems here an outstanding example of the price that must be paid for parsimony in time of peace. It should always have been clear that in a war with Italy, even with France as an ally, Malta might be isolated for long periods and would certainly be heavily assailed from the air. Had steps been taken before the war at comparatively trifling cost to accumulate provisions and supplies, as well as to provide effective air defense, much might have been saved. Rock shelters for submarines and minesweepers, not difficult to build there, would have much enhanced Malta's offensive value.[4] But in the belated rearmament of the prewar years such things were too easily swamped by urgent needs nearer home, and Malta had been left ill defended and unprepared for its ordeal. For this neglect the Fates had exacted a heavy toll in warships, merchant ships, and lives.

For the next two months there was a comparative lull in the Mediterranean except for the incessant activities of British submarines on the enemy's supply lines, some of which now ran via Greece and Crete to Tobruk. In these activities long-range bombers from Egypt, British and American, could help by bombing departure and staging ports, and occasionally ships in passage. But the submarines were still the sharpest thorn in Rommel's flesh, and from July to September inclusive their sinkings totaled 80,000 tons of the diminished Axis shipping. Rommel was just able to mount one more offensive, but it was to be the last. At the beginning of September he attacked at Alam Halfa and was defeated, and his attempts to reach the Nile Delta were at an end.

At Malta there was another flare-up in mid-October, when the island again suffered a period of heavy air bombardment. But this, too, was the

---

[4] The building of rock shelters had been proposed from 1935 onward by the three officers successively in command of the Mediterranean Submarine Flotilla. The estimated cost was only £300,000, mainly in local labor, but the project was never undertaken.

last fling. Thenceforward the enemy would need everything for defense, and the island's ordeal was nearly over.

By the third week in October the Eighth Army (now under General Montgomery who had already won the battle of Alam Halfa) had been substantially reinforced and reequipped via the Cape and Suez, particularly with American tanks. On the night of October 23–24 it attacked at El Alamein. Eleven nights and days of maneuvering and hard fighting followed. By nightfall on November 3 what remained of Rommel's army was in full retreat, and one of the decisive battles of history had been won. The pursuit was pressed with deliberate vigor. On November 20 the Eighth Army once more entered Benghazi, and the whole of Cyrenaica was in its hands.

Simultaneously no time was lost in reprovisioning Malta. On November 20 four storeships arrived from Alexandria; since the island's long siege had virtually been raised, surface forces could once more be based there. By the end of the month the 15th Cruiser Squadron, now under Rear Admiral Power, and two destroyer flotillas, transferred from Egyptian waters, were making more and more difficult the enemy's task of succoring his hard-pressed army.

It was at this time that the war's main turning point was reached. Though in the Battle of the Atlantic the crisis was still to come, the change from defense to sustained attack had already been firmly marked in the Libyan desert. It was being marked at Stalingrad, from which the flood of German conquest was beginning to recede, and at Guadalcanal, whence the Japanese were soon to be evicted. And now it was to be not less evident in western North Africa, where the largest Anglo-American forces yet to take the field had just landed and were beginning to move eastward.

Soon after America's entry into the war and the formation of the Combined Chiefs of Staff Committee to direct the Allied forces, the British and American governments had made the key decision that the war against Germany was to have priority over the conquest of Japan. To the German war, therefore, the bulk of America's fast-growing army was assigned. The eventual objective could be nothing less than the continent of Europe and Germany itself. Planning for an invasion was therefore started, and a command to direct it was set up.

As to the latter, the Chiefs of Staff agreed to accept the doctrine that an amphibious operation should be directed by a supreme commander, a doctrine that, though opposed to the traditional practice of joint responsibility, had for several years found advocates in both Britain and America. Since, in an assault on Europe, the ground forces would have to strike the main blow and would, in addition, be by far the most numerous and the most complex, and would probably suffer the heaviest casualties, it was decided that the supreme commander should be a soldier. And, because the American armies would in the end far outnumber the British, he should be an American soldier. For this post of transcendent importance, General Marshall, who expected in the final act to fill it himself, chose in the meanwhile Lieutenant General Eisenhower. No more inspired choice could have been made.

As yet, however, the Allied forces were not strong enough in men to launch an assault on northern Europe, nor were there yet available the large number of special craft that would be needed for a landing against severe opposition. The Allied air forces, too, had still to assert the overwhelming superiority that would be needed for success. Some venture more immediately within Allied resources must be looked for, and in this respect an invasion of French North Africa had eminent advantages. If the ground was well prepared by Allied sympathizers and the show of force was sufficient to allow for surrender without dishonor, little opposition need be expected; such landings against opposition as might prove necessary would afford valuable experience for the future. And beyond that lay an important strategic prize. If the Allies could achieve the occupation of all French North Africa, while at the same time evicting the Axis forces from Libya and Tripoli, supply lines to the East could once again run through the Mediterranean. The resulting economy would in effect add several million tons to the shipping available to the Allies, thus increasing the pace at which the new American armies could be deployed against Germany, and later against Japan. In addition, North Africa could provide a line of approach to Sardinia or Sicily, Italy or the Balkans, if, later, the course of the war made such indirect blows at the Axis worthwhile. To the rapid achievement of the success needed there might be one major bar: a strong German reaction that would occupy Tunisia in greater force than could be overthrown immediately, preventing still the passage of the central narrows. The opening moves, therefore, had to include a rapid advance eastward, while accepting the need for large-scale land operations should the first dash be unsuccessful.

Briefly the Allied plan included three expeditions, one against the Atlantic coast of Morocco which would seize Casablanca, one aimed at Oran, and one directed at Algiers. The Casablanca operation was needed, despite the serious difficulties to be apprehended from the surf which swells from the Atlantic storms so often raised on this coast, because it would gain a bridgehead in North Africa whatever might be the turn of affairs in the Mediterranean, and particularly in the Strait of Gibraltar. German intervention in Spain could by no means be ruled out, and in addition to possible resulting difficulties in the passage of the strait, the Mediterranean plan hung on one slender thread—the intensive use of a single landing strip on the North Front of Gibraltar from which the aircraft, particularly the fighters, needed in Algeria would be dispatched. The landings at Oran and Algiers were by no means as far east as could have been wished, and further jumps to Bougie and Bône were intended if circumstances permitted. But the crucial factor was the Axis strength in Sardinia, little more than 200 miles from Bougie. Until Allied air forces could be established in North Africa, Algiers was the most easterly port on which reliance could be placed.

The landing in Morocco was assigned to an all-American force (the Western Task Force) under Rear Admiral Hewett and Major General Patton which would make a direct passage from the United States. Inside the Mediterranean, American forces would be landed at Oran and the British First Army at Algiers by the Central Task Force (Commodore Troubridge) and the Eastern Task Force (Vice Admiral Burrough), respectively. Subject to the supreme command of General Eisenhower, all these naval forces were under the orders of Admiral Sir Andrew Cunningham. Since French antagonism was less likely to be aroused by American soldiers than by British, the spearheads of the First Army were provided by American contingents. Everything possible was done to damp down the possibility of French opposition, including a hazardous meeting in Algeria between Allied sympathizers and responsible American officers, carried there in a British submarine. November 8 was chosen as the day for the landings.

Though it was hoped to establish the army ashore with little opposition from the French, the sea passage of so large a force was obviously going to be one of great danger. German submarine strength in the Atlantic was at its zenith, and Allied escorting forces were strained to the utmost. Some losses on passage, therefore, seemed inevitable. That the launching of a great armament overseas was in preparation could not be entirely concealed. Fortunately, however, the Germans were deceived insofar as they considered Dakar as the most probable objective, and some of their submarines were disposed accordingly. But there were still many submarine packs in mid-Atlantic which could be avoided only by great good fortune. The Western Task Force had a long passage to make from the Chesapeake, and the Central and Eastern Task forces had much the same distance to steam, for they must go well out into the Atlantic in their passage from the Clyde so as to avoid German long-range aircraft from Bordeaux.

On October 23 and 24 the Western Task Force sailed from Chesapeake Bay, the two sections making rendezvous at sea on the 26th, and being joined there by the heavy warships. The force comprised twenty-eight personnel and vehicle transports carrying 37,000 troops. To protect the transports and give support to the landing there were the new battleship *Massachusetts*, the old battleships *New York* and *Texas*, the aircraft carrier *Ranger*, four escort carriers, seven crusiers, and numerous destroyers, minesweepers, and auxiliaries. Taking a route well to the southward of the Azores, the force was undetected by the enemy; by the night of November 7–8 it was nearing the Moroccan coast.

Meanwhile the remaining forces needed for the first stage of the operations (though only a fraction of the land forces needed for the advance into Tunisia) had sailed from the Clyde. Here a more complex organization was needed than the concentrated voyage of the Western Task Force, for so grave were the dangers of the passage that it would not have been justifiable to sail the troop transports in company with the slower storeships and motor transport ships; nor need the warships not required for escort reduce their pace to that of the convoys. The first to sail was, therefore, a slow convoy on October 22, followed five days later by a fast convoy carrying the troops—some 72,000 in all, of which 49,000 were American.

The voyages of both these convoys were mercifully uneventful, owing in part to the fact that many submarines that might have sighted them as they came in from the westward had been drawn off to attack a northbound convoy from Sierra Leone which had crossed ahead a few days earlier. As the Strait of Gibraltar was approached, intricate maneuvering and timing were needed. Fast and slow convoys each had to split into Algiers and Oran divisions; each division and the warships of the supporting and covering forces had to pass through the strait by night and in the right order, so that all could maintain their speeds and yet arrive at their destinations simultaneously; and many of the escorting vessels had to refuel at Gibraltar by night and rejoin their charges in the morning. All this was successfully accomplished. On November 6 the Eastern Task Force and the warships of the covering force (Force H under Vice Admiral Syfret) were within the Mediterranean, and thus far there had been no casualties. That afternoon a transport was torpedoed by a submarine, though not sunk, and that day too one of the convoys was sighted by German air reconnaissance. Air attacks followed the next afternoon (November 7) but there were no hits, and the enemy were still in ignorance of the magnitude and the objective of the operation, interpreting it merely as another attempt to replenish Malta. By the night of November 7–8 all was in order, and between 1 A.M. and 3 A.M. on the 8th landings were made on all the intended stretches of coast.

The Eastern Task Force made three landings, two to the westward and one to the eastward of Algiers. As there was no appreciable opposition, before long the assault forces were advancing on the town. By 8 A.M. the airfield at Maison-Blanche, on which much depended, was in Allied hands, and two hours later aircraft from Gibraltar were landing there.

At sea the situation was by no means so satisfactory. Only a fraction of the forces and equipment carried in the sixteen troop transports and sixteen motor transport ships had so far been landed—in the assault, personnel, and mechanized landing craft (LCA, LCP, and LCM) which these ships carried. To land everything in this way would have been too slow even if the weather had remained favorable; and as the day advanced it began to deteriorate, with increasing surf on the beaches. Not only did these ships have to be berthed in sheltered water, unloaded, and returned for reinforcements, but the large number of ships carrying the main body of the First Army, many of them already in convoys on passage from the Clyde, had also to be unloaded without delay on arrival if the advance into Tunisia was to succeed. In the meanwhile the safety of this large body of shipping from Axis attack must be assured, a problem obviously causing increasing anxiety. With a strong covering squadron in the offing, not much danger need be apprehended from the Italian fleet; and the fighter protection afforded from the carriers *Victorious* and *Formidable* of that squadron could be relied on to break up any daylight raids of enemy bombers, which would be too far from their airfields to have fighter escort. But there could be no doubt that before long German submarines would reach the area in increasing numbers, and, although Admiral Burrough's force included thirteen destroyers, three sloops, seven corvettes, and eight trawlers, there would probably be casualties of shipping lying off the open coast however vigorous the antisubmarine defense.

Early entry into Algiers was, therefore, essential to the fulfillment of Allied hopes, and here there were more serious difficulties than those that had confronted the landings. The French Army was not ill disposed toward the Americans and had been virtually won over before the event. But the French Navy still harbored a heavy grudge against the British, and it was the French Navy that controlled the port and manned most of the forts defending it.

In an attempt to solve this crucial problem two destroyers had been ordered to break into the harbor before daylight. It was hoped that surprise might be effected and that, once they were inside, the *fait accompli* might be accepted by the French and sabotage prevented. But the forts detected their approach and resisted. One destroyer was hit and forced to withdraw. The other broke the boom and berthed alongside; but she soon found herself in a perilous position, and she too had to withdraw, to sink some hours later from the damage sustained. The attempt had failed, and had it been necessary to rely on overcoming the French Navy's opposition by force the situation would have remained one of deep anxiety. The fort on Cape Matifou, the eastern point of Algiers Bay, continued to engage any ships within range and had to be neutralized by a bombardment from the cruiser *Bermuda*; and the batteries immediately defending the harbor were still manned. Fortunately, however, the negotiations ashore were effecting all that was needed. By the evening of November 8 a truce had been signed, and American troops had occupied the town. At daylight next morning Admiral Burrough entered the harbor in his flagship, the headquarters ship *Bulolo*, and at 8 A.M. all the transports were ordered to join him. Those to the eastward had had a noisy night of air raids during which one American transport had been sunk and a destroyer hit. But soon all were assembled, the harbor taking as many as could be berthed and the rest anchoring close outside. With the help of local labor, unloading was soon in progress and thereafter proceeded according to plan, with emptied ships leaving and fresh ones arriving in a prearranged order. Night air raids had still to be suffered, but the defense provided by ships, particularly three antiaircraft ships of Admiral Burrough's force, was soon augmented by shore-based fighters, and the casualties suffered were not heavy.

Meanwhile the Central Task Force had been having a rather more difficult time. As at Algiers, the troops had been landed at three points, two west and one east of the town, the latter near the small port of Arzeu. And, as at Algiers, there was virtually no opposition to the landings, and Arzeu was soon seized. But the attempts to open Oran harbor with two cutters (formerly U.S. Coast Guard cutters) were an equally complete and far more bloody failure. Both ships were sunk and nearly all members of their crews and of the special landing parties they carried were killed. The antagonism of the French Navy had in fact been fanned into full blaze, and it was soon clear that vigorous action by all ships and aircraft of the Central Task Force would be needed to help the army capture the town, while at the same time protecting the shipping (twenty troop transports and twenty-three motor transport ships) that was continuing to unload the United States 1st Division. These naval forces under Commodore Troubridge's orders included the battleship *Rodney*, the carrier *Furious*, two escort carriers, the cruisers *Aurora* and *Jamaica*, thirteen destroyers, and numerous smaller ships. The chief opposition came from a fort above Mers-el-Kebir (the naval base just west of Oran) which had frequently to be engaged by the *Rodney*, and there was potential danger from two airfields which were kept under attack by the shipborne aircraft until captured by the army. Five

French destroyers, too, came out at various times, but all were either sunk or driven ashore by British cruisers and destroyers before they could do any damage to the transports. Throughout November 8 and 9 hostilities continued. The army advanced from east and west and unloading was carried on despite increasingly difficult weather. An assault on the town with full support from ships and aircraft (shipborne and from a captured airfield) was planned for November 10, but on that day the French at last decided to submit to *force majeure.* A truce was signed and the town and harbor were occupied. The threat to the route between Gibraltar and Algiers, which would have resulted from an Oran in unfriendly hands, had been finally removed, and a base had been obtained (at Mers-el-Kebir) from which British heavy forces could operate against the Italian fleet should it make any move to interfere.

The problems that confronted the Western Task Force on the Atlantic coast differed in two important respects from those of the forces within the Mediterranean. First, there was the strong probability that surf would make it difficult to land on open beaches; and, second, there were considerable naval forces in Casablanca whose hostility must be allowed for. The new battleship *Jean Bart,* though not ready for sea, could fire some of her guns, and there were two cruisers, three flotilla leaders, six destroyers, and twelve submarines that must be considered ready for action. It was largely for these reasons that the landings of General Patton's forces were widely spread. Casablanca was their final objective, but the occupation of small harbors might be necessary before sufficient troops could be landed to force its surrender. The main landing, therefore, was to be at Fedala, 12 miles north of Casablanca, but there were to be important secondary landings at the Sebou River, 65 miles to the north (with Mehdia at its mouth and the airfield of Port Lyautey 9 miles up the river), and at Safi, 125 miles to the southward. For gaining access to these harbors there was to be no half-and-half mixture of persuasion and force such as was planned for Algiers and Oran. Any resistance that showed itself was to be opposed with the full strength of American arms. There was not, however, to be any attempt at a direct entry into Casablanca harbor, for it was clear that any resistance there would be too strong to be overcome by such means.

This policy was conspicuously successful at Safi, where a footing was gained in the harbor in the early hours of November 8. Before long the opposition had been subdued sufficiently to allow transports to enter and start unloading at the quays. Destroyers had done the close work, and heavy fire from the battleship *Texas* and the cruiser *Philadelphia* had crushed the resistance of such batteries as remained in action. The force of some 6,000 men and 100 tanks carried in the transports could therefore be landed with little delay, and by November 10 it had started its march up the coast with the navy cooperating on the seaward flank.

The other secondary landing, at the mouth of the Sebou River, had been more hotly contested. Despite the support provided by the battleship *Texas*, the cruiser *Savannah*, and some destroyers, it was not till the morning of November 10 that the defenses of Mehdia were sufficiently mastered for a destroyer to enter the river carrying a party of troops to seize the airfield at Port Lyautey. Even then resistance at Mehdia continued and was not finally overcome till that afternoon.

Meanwhile, the main landing at Fedala had met with some opposition, and French aircraft and the ships in Casablanca Harbor were putting up a fight. Fortunately the weather remained fine, and, with no serious surf to hamper the assault, Fedala was captured by 2:30 P.M. on the 8th. But it required a bombardment by the *Massachusetts* and two cruisers to keep down the fire of the *Jean Bart* and the Casablanca batteries; during the forenoon the cruiser *Primaguet*, two flotilla leaders, and five destroyers came out to give battle. They were opposed by the bombarding ships reinforced by two more cruisers, and all were sunk, driven ashore, or forced back into the harbor. But the French refused to capitulate, and for the next two days General Patton continued to disembark his division at Fedala. On November 10 another attack on the *Jean Bart*, this time by dive-bombers from the *Ranger*, scored two hits, but she still had a 15-inch turret in action. Preparations were therefore made for a land assault on the 11th; but by that time word had come through that Admiral Darlan had been accepted by General Eisenhower as the responsible authority in French North Africa, and that Darlan had agreed that all resistance should end and that he would cooperate with the Allies. A truce was therefore concluded and Casablanca was occupied without further bloodshed.

This outcome did not, however, end the peril at sea. German submarines were gathering, and, as there was some delay in getting the transports into harbor, losses were suffered. Four ships were sunk (fortunately they had already landed their troops), and two more and a destroyer were torpedoed but survived. Against this loss could be set one submarine sunk by American destroyers.

An important part of the plans for an advance into Tunisia lay in the landing of troops as far to the eastward as practicable, so as to ease the burden on the inadequte Algerian roads and railways. With the successful occupation of Algiers on November 8, this further expedition could be launched, and on November 10 a slow convoy of four motor transport ships followed by a fast convoy of three troop transports sailed from Algiers for Bougie, 100 miles farther east. Rear Admiral Harcourt was in charge of this operation with his flag in the cruiser *Sheffield*, and he had with him a 15-inch monitor (*Roberts*), an antiaircraft ship, and some destroyers, minesweepers, frigates, corvettes, and trawlers to provide fire support and antisubmarine protection. Fortunately fire support against the shore proved unnecessary, for on its arrival on November 11 the force was welcomed by the local authorities and all ships were berthed in or close to the harbor. But it had yet to be shown that the port was not too near the Sardinian airfields to be of real value. At the start the plans for air defense went awry. They were based on the occupation of Djidjelli airfield, 35 miles farther east, by Allied fighters. To this the French had agreed, but attempts to land gasoline there were frustrated by surf, and there was some delay before supplies could be sent from Bougie. In the meantime heavy attacks had been suffered. Two troop transports, a storeship, and the antiaircraft ship had been sunk, and several others had been hit; another large troopship was sunk in the approaches a few days later. Once the fighters were established at Djidjelli conditions improved, but the use of this port remained hazardous.

Another 130 miles farther east, Bône and its airfield had been occupied on November 12 by a commando group carried in two destroyers. As it was only 130 miles from Sardinia, the menace of air attack was too severe at first for the unloading of vehicles or bulky supplies, but Bône was used for landing men, carried there in fast ferry steamers to relieve the strain on communications inland. For this purpose it proved its worth, and it was used eventually for stores and vehicles as well.

Despite all efforts the first thrust at Tunisia failed. With no further opposition from the French in Algeria, troops could be sent eastward at their best speed; but such was the state of communications that only a single division could be maintained beyond the Tunisian border, 300 miles east of Algiers; and here, at Mejez-el-Bab, 60 miles across the border and 40 miles short of Tunis, the advance was halted. Ever since the Allied landings, Axis troops had been poured into Tunisia by sea and air, a movement to which the French admiral commanding at Bizerta had given his help. Allied forces could do little to interfere with this operation. Though British surface forces were just returning to Malta and a force under Admiral Harcourt was working from much-raided Bône, the passage was too short for effectual interception in face of the enemy's local air superiority. During the night of December 1–2 the *Aurora*, the *Sirius*, the *Argonaut*, and two destroyers, working from Bône, annihilated a small convoy; but one such isolated exploit could not effect substantial improvement. Nor could submarines do enough to prevent reinforcements by so short a route where the enemy's air and surface forces were still unhindered, though three British submarines were lost in the attempt. By the end of December, therefore, it was clear that the conquest of Tunisia must await the spring, and that large-scale concerted operations by the First and Eighth armies would then be needed.

But if the First Army was now held up, the Eighth, with its partner the Desert Air Force, was advancing at a remarkable speed, considering the difficulties and risks involved in keeping the forward troops supplied. Benghazi was rapidly being rehabilitated (by the beginning of January its capacity was 3,000 tons a day), and with this port at his back General Montgomery was able to turn Rommel out of the El Agheila position on December 15. A severe gale at Benghazi on January 4 and 5 which breached the breakwater had a calamitous effect on the working of so patched-up a port, and for a time its capacity was much reduced. Nevertheless, the army's further advance was made to adhere to its time-table. Rommel was defeated at Buerat on January 15 and on the 23d the victorious army entered Tripoli. Much demolition had been done in the port, and the entrance had been blocked; but in five days naval clearance parties cut a passage sufficient for the entrance of small craft which were used to discharge ships anchored outside, and by February 3 storeships could enter the port and unload at quays. By February 10, 2,000 tons a day were being discharged, a rate that was soon to be doubled. The position was now assured, and the attack on Tunisia could be built up from the firm bases of Tripoli and Algiers.

The transport of supplies and reinforcements to Algiers was proceeding with smoothness and safety. As was to be expected, the supply lines through the western Mediterranean had been much assailed by Axis submarines. In the first few days of the operation, when urgency and lack of escorts had made it necessary to send emptied ships back unescorted, casualties had resulted. But since then losses had been few, whereas the attackers had suffered considerably. From the start till the end of December, five German and four Italian submarines had been sunk in these waters by ships and aircraft, and many more had been damaged.

It was in May 1943 that the end came in Tunisia with victorious advances from west and south. By that time the Allied air forces had been so strengthened that, in conjunction with submarines from Malta and Algiers, they were able to cut down supplies and reinforcements for the defenders to a mere trickle. Submarines alone had sunk about 150,000 tons during the first four months of the year, though they had paid heavily, eight (about one-third of the number operating) being lost. When, on May 12, the Axis resistance was finally overcome (Tunis

168

and Bizerta had been occupied on the 7th), there could be no thought of evacuation by sea. Some 248,000 troops (three-fifths of them German) laid down their arms and the campaign was over.

On May 17 a through Mediterranean convoy, the first since 1941, sailed from Gibraltar. Its passage was unmolested, and nine days later it arrived in Alexandria. The first aim of the North African operations had been achieved.

13

THE TIDE TURNS IN THE PACIFIC:
Midway, the Aleutians, and the Solomons

WITHIN A FEW DAYS of the Battle of Coral Sea (May 8, 1942; see chap. 10), intercepted Japanese radio messages indicated that the enemy's next thrust would be against Midway Island, 1,200 miles west-northwest of Pearl Harbor. For the time being, therefore, the situation in the southwest Pacific must be left to take care of itself so far as American naval forces were concerned; everything available must be ranged against this new threat. The *Enterprise* and the *Hornet*, which had been sent south after the Tokyo raid but had arrived too late for the Coral Sea battle, were hurried back to Pearl Harbor, as also was the damaged *Yorktown*, to be repaired at utmost speed. By the end of May forces comprising three aircraft carriers, eight cruisers, and fourteen destroyers were at sea and steaming toward Midway, Rear Admiral Spruance with the *Enterprise* and the *Hornet* being two days in advance of Rear Admiral Fletcher in the *Yorktown*. On June 2, however, the two forces joined and were then under Admiral Fletcher's command, though still operating tactically as distinct units. There were also fourteen submarines disposed west and north of Midway. General directions for the whole operation were given by Admiral Nimitz, commander in chief of the Pacific Fleet, at Pearl Harbor.

The American surmise of a Japanese attempt against Midway Island was in fact correct. The commander in chief of the Combined Fleet,[1]

---

[1] The Japanese organization was one of numbered fleets, several of which were brought under a single command as the Combined Fleet. The most important of the numbered fleets were the Second Fleet, comprising the majority of the battleships, and the Third Fleet, consisting of the big aircraft carriers. There were also a number of air fleets (i.e., shore-based aircraft), some of which were included in the Combined Fleet. The Commander in Chief, Combined Fleet, was normally afloat, but in his influence on major strategy he seems to have

170

Admiral Yamamoto, had persuaded his government that the capture of Midway, and at the same time of some of the Aleutian Islands, would fend off still further any American threat to Japan. He hoped also that it would bring about a successful fleet action in Hawaiian waters against what remained of American naval strength and thus postpone, perhaps indefinitely, any serious offensive in southern waters or through the Marshalls and Carolines. The value of Midway itself to the Japanese would not have been high, for it contained only a small airfield and a shallow harbor which could be used only for fueling destroyers and submarines. But in Japanese hands it would certainly have given trouble, and the Americans would have been deprived of a base, 1,200 miles in advance of Pearl Harbor, from which their submarines were already beginning to have an appreciable effect on Japanese supply lines. So that he might have ample strength both to capture the island and to deal a crushing blow to any American forces that dared oppose him, Admiral Yamamoto came to sea with the strongest force he could muster—eleven battleships, including the new *Yamato* flying his flag, and four aircraft carriers,[2] with a large number of cruisers and destroyers, and transports carrying 5,000 troops.

As already noted, it was no part of American strategy at this time to meet the Japanese with an inferior fleet of battleships. The latter must be held back until, by repairs and new building, they had attained the superiority that was inevitable in time if they were not frittered away. Meanwhile, the aircraft carriers and cruisers must do the best they could to hold the line, a defensive role of many hazards but one in which there seemed hope that the carriers, with their power of striking at long range, might be able to achieve more than a materially weaker fleet had usually been able to do in earlier wars. To this end the American carrier forces took up a position some 200 miles north-northeast of Midway on June 3.

At this time the Japanese forces were approaching in three bodies. To the northward under Vice Admiral Nagumo were the carriers, *Kaga*, *Akagi*, *Hiryu*, and *Soryu*, with two battleships and some cruisers and destroyers. Their task was to overcome Midway's aircraft and any opposition that might be put up by carrier-borne aircraft, should there be

---

approximated more to the British Chief of the Naval Staff and the American Chief of Naval Operations (who was also commander in chief of the United States fleet) than any of the Allied naval commanders in chief of individual fleets or stations.

[2] It will be remembered that the *Shokaku* had been damaged in the Battle of the Coral Sea and that the *Zuikaku* was training new air squadrons. As neither of them could be ready in time for this operation, Yamamoto's strength in carrier-borne aircraft was one-third less than had been intended.

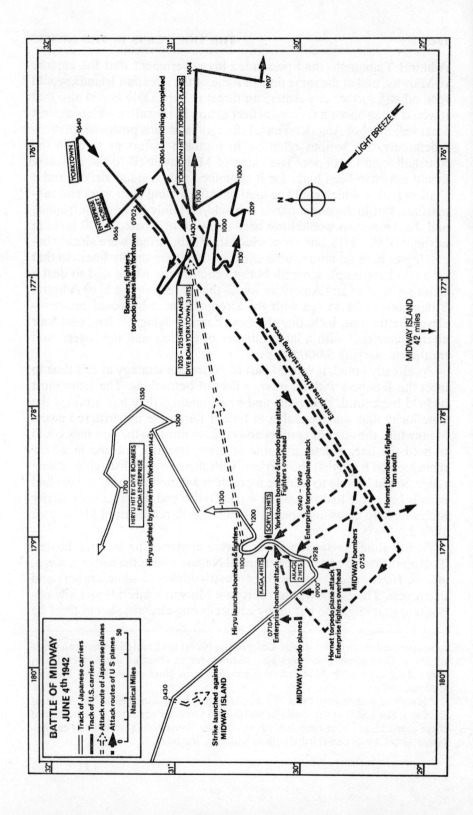

BATTLE OF MIDWAY
JUNE 4th 1942

Track of Japanese carriers
Track of U.S. carriers
Attack route of Japanese planes
Attack routes of U S planes

Nautical Miles
0   50

Strike launched against
MIDWAY ISLAND

0430

0710 Enterprise torpedo planes
Hiryu launches bombers & fighters
MIDWAY torpedo planes
Hornet torpedo plane attack
Enterprise fighters overhead
0900
0755 MIDWAY bombers
0928
AKAGI 2 HITS
KAGA 4 HITS
SORYU 3 HITS
0940 - 0949 Enterprise torpedoplane attack
Yorktown bomber & torpedo plane attack
Fighters overhead
Hornet bombers & fighters turn south

Hiryu sighted by plane from Yorktown 1445
HIRYU HIT BY DIVE BOMBERS FROM ENTERPRISE
1700
1550
1500
1300
1200
1100

Enterprise hit by forces

1205 - 1215 HIRYU PLANES DIVE BOMB YORKTOWN, 3 HITS

Bombers, fighters, torpedo planes leave Yorktown

0806 Launching completed
YORKTOWN HIT BY TORPEDO PLANES
1604
1907

LIGHT BREEZE

N

ENTERPRISE HORNET
0656
0902
YORKTOWN
0940

1430
1530
1300
1209
1000
1130

MIDWAY ISLAND
42 miles

any in the neighborhood, though presumably they hoped for sufficient surprise to make immediate interference by the latter an unlikely contingency. From the west-southwest came the transport and supply convoy, which had sailed from the Marianas, with its escorting warships, ready to assault and occupy Midway as soon as air opposition had been overcome. From the northwestward, some 350 miles west of the carrier force, came Admiral Yamamoto's battle fleet in general support, ready to oppose any subsequent interference by American surface forces and to exploit such situations as might arise. The Japanese submarines in these waters were spread on a north–south line west of Pearl Harbor to report any approaching American forces.

At first fortune seemed to be favoring the Japanese. The carrier force to the northward was in an area of low cloud and so seemed to have every chance of escaping detection by Catalina flying boats (not yet equipped with the high-efficiency radar of later years) which were scouting to a distance of 700 miles from Midway. One Catalina did, however, succeed in sighting the assault convoy, which was under clear skies, at 9 A.M. on June 3, and as soon as the report was received nine Flying Fortresses were sent from Midway to attack. All bombs missed, however, and a subsequent night attack by four torpedo-carrying Catalinas scored only the minor success of one hit on an oiler. The Japanese now knew that their enemies were warned, but they could still hope to reach their objective without encountering the opposition of more than local forces.

At dawn next morning, June 4, the Japanese carriers had reached a position 200 miles northwest of Midway; from there they launched their first striking force, about a hundred bombers escorted by fifty fighters. The American carriers were at this time about 200 miles east-northeast of the Japanese, and each force was in ignorance of the other. Soon afterward, however, Midway patrols sighted first the approaching Japanese aircraft and then their carriers, and the situation began to take shape.

The first American reaction was from Midway. Fifteen Flying Fortresses which had been sent to attack the assault force were diverted to bomb the carriers. All Midway aircraft were flown off, the fighters to meet the approaching Japanese striking force, the torpedo aircraft and dive-bombers to attack the carriers. All suffered severe casualties. The marine fighters brought down some of the enemy aircraft, but not enough to prevent all installations on Midway from being well bombed; the dive-bombers and torpedo aircraft attacked the carriers with great gallantry, but they had no fighter protection and were virtually annihilated with nothing achieved. About the same time the Flying Fortresses came in at 20,000 feet, with little opposition, and dropped more than a hundred bombs, but without scoring a hit. The situation still seemed favorable to the Japanese.

It was at this time, however, that the Japanese were at last apprised of the existence of the American carrier force, which had just been discovered by one of their scouting aircraft. Nagumo therefore took steps to give it battle, altering course to the northeastward to close the enemy, while refueling and rearming the aircraft just returned from Midway. Had Nagumo been better served by his scouting aircraft, he would have received news of Amercan carriers in time to launch a striking force that had been kept in reserve for this purpose, possibly with marked effect on the result of the battle. But by now he was committed to the recovery of his Midway force.

Meanwhile the American carriers, on receipt of Midway's information about the Japanese, had been closing in, and at 8 A.M., as soon as they were within striking range, the *Enterprise* and the *Hornet* sent off a force of about a hundred aircraft, the *Yorktown*'s aircraft being held in reserve until the situation developed further.

The story of this first striking force is a checkered one, and its operations were lacking in cohesion. As there were no aircraft shadowing the enemy, it was assumed that the latter was standing on toward Midway, and the course of the attackers was shaped accordingly; the Japanese carriers, however, as already noted, had in fact altered course about 90 degrees to port. At 9:20 A.M., therefore, when the supposed position of the enemy had been reached, nothing was in sight. The coordination of the striking force was insufficient to deal with this situation, and each component proceeded to act independently. The *Hornet*'s dive-bombers and fighters turned south, found nothing, and either reached Midway or ran out of fuel short of it. The *Hornet*'s torpedo aircraft, which had become separated from the remainder soon after leaving their carrier, found the enemy by chance, attacked at once, unsuccessfully, and all fifteen were shot down either by fighters or by gunfire. The *Enterprise*'s dive bombers continued to the westward and then made a sweep to the northward, where they eventually found the enemy. Meanwhile the *Enterprise*'s torpedo aircraft and fighters, though out of touch with each other, had turned more directly to the northward; the former had found and attacked the Japanese carriers, losing ten of the fourteen planes without scoring a hit. The fighters also found the enemy and patrolled high overhead for half an hour, waiting for their dive-bombers until shortage of fuel forced them to return. When, therefore, the *Enterprise*'s dive-bombers approached from the westward about 10 A.M., they would have been without any fighter protection had it not been for the chance that brought the whole of the *Yorktown*'s striking force, launched about an hour later than the others and now coming in from the southeastward, to the same position at the same time.

At this time, therefore, when the Japanese carriers were engaged in refueling and rearming the aircraft returned from Midway, they were about to be attacked by the *Yorktown* torpedo aircraft and the *Enterprise* and *Yorktown* dive-bombers, all acting independently, with the *Yorktown* fighters overhead. As the Japanese ships had as yet no radar for fighter direction, their fighters were sent mainly against the torpedo aircraft as being both the most dangerous and the most readily attackable at short notice. Despite anything the *Yorktown*'s fighters could do, ten of the twelve torpedo planes were shot down and no torpedoes hit. But in the resulting melee the approach of the dive-bombers, fifty-four in all, was unopposed, and it was the blows they now delivered which virtually won the battle. The *Kaga* was hit by four bombs, the *Soryu* by three, and the *Akagi* by two. Uncontrollable fires broke out in all three ships, there were ammunition explosions, and eventually all of them lay stopped. At dusk the *Soryu* went down, to be followed shortly afterward by the *Kaga*; and early next morning the *Akagi*, still afloat but derelict, was put down by one of her own destroyers. But that takes us ahead of events still to be related.[3]

The devastating American attacks had come just too soon for the Japanese to launch their striking forces. But at 11 A.M. the *Hiryu*, so far unmolested, got hers away, and soon after noon it arrived, fighters and dive-bombers, making for the *Yorktown*. Interception by American fighters accounted for some of the bombers, but three bomb hits were scored before the remaining ones were destroyed. Though damage was severe, the worst effects were soon righted, and two hours later the ship could steam at 19 knots. But soon afterward she was attacked again, this time by the *Hiryu*'s torpedo aircraft. Again the approaching enemy was intercepted and the majority of the force destroyed, but four aircraft came on and dropped their torpedoes before being shot down by gunfire, and two of the torpedoes hit. The *Yorktown* was now a derelict.

By this time aircraft from the *Yorktown* had found and were shad-

---

[3] For some years after the war it was supposed that the destruction of the *Soryu* was partly due to three torpedo hits from an American submarine (see Samuel Eliot Morison, *History of United States Naval Operations in World War II* [15 vols.; Boston: Little, Brown, 1947–1962], IV, 129); but it now seems clear that there was only one submarine hit, on the *Kaga*, and that the torpedo did not explode (see Wilfred J. Holmes, *Undersea Victory: The Influence of Submarine Operations on the War in the Pacific* [Garden City, N. Y.: Doubleday, 1966], p. 143).

owing the *Hiryu*, which had continued on a northeasterly course after the disaster to her consorts, and had later turned to the northwest. Dive-bombers from the *Enterprise* (some of them refugees from the *Yorktown*) were therefore sent off to attack. There were no fighters to go with them but it was judged correctly that the enemy would not have enough fighters left to put up an effective defense. At 6 P.M. these bombers attacked and scored four hits on the *Hiryu*, stopping her and setting her on fire, to sink the following morning.

Though the last shot of the battle had not yet been fired, a great victory had already been won. It was a victory that not only put an end to Japanese hopes of postponing the day of reckoning by expanding their area of conquest in the North Pacific, but also cost the Japanese Navy two-thirds of its big aircraft carriers, ships that now and for the rest of the war had at least as much right as battleships to the title of capital ship. History can show no other instance of a fleet so strong and of so high a fighting spirit as the Japanese being so gravely defeated by a numerically inferior enemy.

In this victory important parts were played by American foreknowledge of Japanese plans and by inferior Japanese scouting, factors that combined to enable the American carriers to get their own blows in first and at a time when their opponents were most vulnerable. Luck in the fortuitous combination of torpedo aircraft and dive-bombers at a critical time was also an important element. But it is to the dash and energy of the American carrier-borne aircraft, and particularly to the skill of the dive-bombers in retrieving an initially adverse situation, that must be ascribed eventual credit for the spectacular result.

During the night Admiral Yamamoto reluctantly realized the extent of the disaster that had cost him his whole carrier strength, and about 3 A.M. he canceled instructions for a night attack and ordered a general retirement. Shortly afterward the heavy cruisers *Mogami* and *Mikuma*, part of a squadron that had previously been ordered to bombard Midway, collided while trying to avoid an American submarine. Both were seriously damaged, the *Mogami* leaving a conspicuous trail of oil.

During the same night (June 4–5) Admiral Spruance, who had succeeded to the active command now that the *Yorktown* was out of action, kept to the eastward, for he was still much inferior in surface forces and did not know that the enemy was about to retire. Nor could he yet realize how overwhelming had been his victory against long odds, for at the start his role had been so clearly a defensive one. But early next morning he turned to the westward and pursued at high speed. That day, June 5, nothing could be made of the situation from reports of scattered Japanese formations, which were all his scouting aircraft could give him; but next day the *Mogami* and the *Mikuma* were found and were severely hammered by aircraft from the *Enterprise* and the *Hornet*. The *Mikuma* was sunk, but the *Mogami*, though apparently a wreck, managed eventually to struggle back to Truk, 2,000 miles to leeward. The American force, nearing the limit of its fuel endurance, turned back for Pearl Harbor.

On the same day, June 6, the *Yorktown*, still struggling to right herself sufficiently for towing back to harbor, was torpedoed by a Japanese submarine. The following morning she sank.

It will be remembered that a minor part of the Japanese plan was an operation in the Aleutian Islands. In this action the Japanese were more successful. Attu, at the western end of the chain, and Kiska, 150 miles east of it, were occupied on June 7. Little was gained thereby, for, after the defeat at Midway, forces in the Aleutians were no longer of value as a diversionary thrust or flank guard for an advance in the Central Pacific. Nor were these barren islands of any real use in the defense of Japan. Though they were on the shortest (great circle) route between America and Japan, their foggy and inhospitable climate made them of little value as stepping-stones. Some trouble was caused, nevertheless, for it seemed unwise to allow the Japanese to remain unmolested, and American and Canadian forces were employed in attacking their communications and eventually in evicting them.

These operations resulted the next year (1943) in a cruiser battle off the Komandorskie Islands, which lie 150 miles west-northwest of Attu. On March 27 an American force of two cruisers and four destroyers had located a small Japanese convoy and had begun to engage the escort with gunfire when it was found that the latter was of far greater strength, with four cruisers and five destroyers. By that time the enemy ships were to the eastward of the Americans, who were therefore hard put to it to disengage. Both sides sustained damage, one of the American cruisers being stopped for a time. But by the use of smoke she was shielded from further harm; and shortly afterward the Japanese, fearing an air attack and being short of ammunition after a three-hour battle, drew off to the westward and ordered the convoy also to retire. The Japanese had failed in their mission, therefore, despite locally superior strength. Thereafter they found it increasingly difficult to keep their island garrisons supplied.

By May 1943 the time had come to turn the Japanese out; Attu, as the least strongly held island, was tackled first. A landing on May 10 was successful, but fierce fighting followed and it was not till June 2 that the garrison of 2,000 or more had been exterminated, at a cost of some 500 American killed and 1,100 wounded.

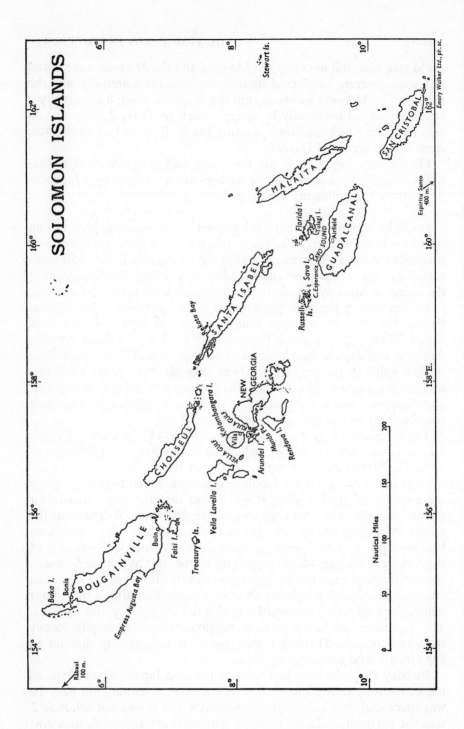

SOLOMON ISLANDS

Stewart Is.

SAN CRISTOBAL

MALAITA

Florida I.
Tulagi I.
SAVO SOUND
C. Esperance
Savo I.
Russell
Is.
GUADALCANAL
Airfield

Espiritu Santo
400 m.

Kieta Bay

SANTA ISABEL

NEW
GEORGIA

Kolombangara I.
Vila
Arundel I.
KULA GULF
Munda
VELLA GULF
Rendova I.

CHOISEUL

Vella Lavella I.

Treasury Is.

Faisi I.

Buin

BOUGAINVILLE

Empress Augusta Bay

Bonis

Buka I.

Rabaul
100 m.

Nautical Miles

0   50   100   150   200

Emery Walker Ltd., ph. sc.

6°   8°   10°   162°   160°   158° E.   156°   154°   6°   8°   10°

177

During the following months the Japanese made several attempts to withdraw troops from the now isolated and useless Kiska, employing both submarines and surface vessels and suffering losses and setbacks in the process. But at length, on July 28, covered by the almost incessant fog, they succeeded in taking off the remaining 6,000 men in cruisers and destroyers. The withdrawal was unknown to their opponents, who continued preparations for an assault with ample strength. On August 15 an American-Canadian force of a hundred ships and 34,000 men arrived. The troops were landed as planned under cover of a heavy bombardment, but, to their wonderment, found that there was no one to fight. The campaign of the Aleutians was at an end.

We must now return to the summer of 1942.

Frustrated at the battle of Midway Island, and with no prospect of gaining any substantial advantage from their captures in the Aleutians, the Japanese turned to strengthening the southeastern bastion of their position. The main feature was to be an airfield on the north coast of Guadalcanal, an island some 90 miles long by 30 broad in the southeast part of the Solomon group, lying about 600 miles from the Japanese base at Rabaul and a little less from the American advanced base in Espiritu Santo. The Americans had already decided to oppose their enemies in this area where, at Tulagi, the Japanese had established a seaplane base. And when, in July, the Americans discovered work in progress on the Guadalcanal airfield, they recognized both a danger to be countered and a profitable opportunity for offensive action on such a scale as they could at present afford, still a modest one when provision was made for the impending invasion of North Africa. It was important psychologically, however, that the fight against Japan should not be allowed to lull. The threat of a further advance to the southeastward was perhaps no longer a serious one, but the danger of a Japanese occupation of the Solomons so firm as to defy eviction was real. At this time, though the idea of cutting the enemy's communications by an advance through the islands north of the equator was beginning to take shape in American strategy, there were not yet nearly enough resources for that purpose. It still seemed important, therefore, that the Japanese should be driven back step by step in the south along much of the route by which they had come.

The opportunity for offensive action was a more pressing one than would have been freely chosen for it was clear that an attack made before the Guadalcanal airfield was finished would be far less difficult than later. It was decided, therefore, that the island must be seized early in August with such forces as were available and as much planning and preparation as time permitted. The time for planning, in particu-

179

lar, was so short as to involve serious risk of disorganization in the event. All landing plans had to be prepared at sea and distributed by destroyers, and there was only one subsequent opportunity for a meeting of senior officers. Nor was there time for the orthodox approach of securing command of the sea either before or immediately after the invasion. The result was a four months' campaign of tremendous intensity, Homeric in the crashing blows given and received and in the swift changes of fortune. Throughout this time command of the sea was constantly in dispute until, eventually, the American forces asserted their supremacy. Thereafter they not only made Guadalcanal safe, but by degrees evicted the enemy from other islands of the Solomon group.

The invading force comprised some 19,000 United States Marines under Major General Vandegrift carried in twenty-three transports, protected by five American cruisers (four heavy and one light), three Australian cruisers (two heavy and one light), and fifteen destroyers, the whole under Rear Admiral Turner. To cover the invasion there was a force under Rear Admiral Noyes of three aircraft carriers, *Saratoga*, *Enterprise*, and *Wasp*, the new battleship *North Carolina*, five heavy cruisers, a light cruiser, and some destroyers. These two forces, invasion force and covering force, were controlled by Vice Admiral Fletcher, and the whole operation, which included shore-based air forces, was directed by Vice Admiral Ghormley, commanding the South Pacific Force.

The invasion convoy sailed from New Zealand and a junction was made to the south of the Fiji Islands with the covering force, which had sailed partly from Pearl Harbor and partly from San Diego. After the landing was rehearsed on a beach in the Fijis, the expedition stood to the westward and thence north, approaching Guadalcanal from the southwest. For much of the passage it had the good fortune to be covered from air observation by low cloud. At dawn on August 7 it entered Savo Sound, a sheet of water some 20 miles broad between Guadalcanal and Florida, with Savo Island in its western approach. Here, close to the embryo airfield, the bulk of the marines were landed, as were also some construction battalions—the Seabees. These were organizations under naval discipline, equipped with small arms against emergencies, which had been trained in every task needed for establishing a forward base, including particularly the rapid construction of airfields. From this time on they were to play an ever-valuable part in the advance across the Pacific.

Simultaneously with the Guadalcanal landing another force of marines seized Tulagi. These assaults were made under cover of bombardment by escorting warships and attacks by carrier aircraft on the Japanese defensive positions and seaplanes at Tulagi.

The enemy were completely surprised. As they had few troops on Guadalcanal, there was virtually no opposition to the attackers. Japanese air attacks from Rabaul followed that afternoon and the next morning; they were partially intercepted by aircraft of the carrier covering force, and aircraft on both sides were shot down. One transport was destroyed, but unloading continued. By the afternoon of August 8 the marines had captured the airfield and seemed well on the way to being firmly established, despite some rather serious disorganization in the landing of equipment and stores. On Tulagi and two adjacent islets there had been some hard fighting, but these too were soon in American hands.

The Japanese Navy, however, reacted in such strength as it could muster: five heavy cruisers, two light cruisers, and a destroyer from Rabaul which were sent to do what they could in a night attack. On their approach through the central Solomons they were sighted by Australian aircraft; but erroneous reports of their course and composition made it appear that they were seaplane tenders and other reinforcements for the Japanese seaplane base at Rekata Bay in Santa Isabel Island, 120 miles northwest of Guadalcanal. There were no carrier-borne aircraft for further investigation, for by this time shortage of fuel and growing apprehension of submarine and air attack were causing Admiral Fletcher temporarily to withdraw the covering force. The positions assumed for the night of August 8–9, therefore, by the Allied escorting forces under Rear Admiral Crutchley of the Australian squadron, were those that seemed advisable as a general protection, without there being any particular danger to be apprehended. In view of the withdrawal of the American carriers and the increased threat of seaplane attack, Admiral Turner decided that the transports must leave next morning, by which time General Vandegrift would have unloaded enough stores to hold on for a time. Provided the anchorage could be protected till then, therefore, the situation, though continuing to be dangerous, would be in hand.

To afford this general protection Admiral Crutchley formed his ships into three divisions. The *Australia*, the *Canberra*, and the *Chicago* with two destroyers patrolled on an east–west line inside the channel south of Savo Island; the *Vincennes*, the *Astoria*, and the *Quincy* guarded similarly the approach north of the island, but having a broader channel could patrol round a square; and the *San Juan* and the *Hobart*, with two destroyers, watched the eastern entrance to Savo Sound, where an attack seemed less likely. The latter force was at the same time near enough to the transport anchorages to be able to add to their defense at need if attack came from the west. Such a disposition of ships whose crews had been wearied by thirty-six hours of action stations in a tropical climate could not, of course, have been effective against unexpected attack without some warning of the enemy's approach. The attacker, keyed up for the moment of contact, has on such occasions an immense advantage over a patrol whose duty is both continuous and unexhilarating. Nowadays such warning could be afforded by radar. But at that time no great reliability could be expected of this device, especially where side shadows from the land much affected the sets then fitted; to clear them the ships would have to have been farther to seaward and in a less favorable position for defense. For warning of an enemy's approach from the westward, therefore, reliance was placed on two destroyers to seaward, one watching the approach to the south channel and one to the north. The lookout from these ships was assisted by radar whose range, though limited, should have been sufficient for the purpose.

Soon after midnight seaplanes from the approaching Japanese squadron reconnoitered the area and correctly reported the Allied dispositions. Then, as the cruisers approached, their seaplanes were again sent ahead, this time to illuminate the Allied forces with parachute flares as soon as the ships were within effective range. About 1 A.M., as the Japanese neared Savo Island, both the American lookout destroyers were sighted, but there was no reaction from them and the cruisers passed between them and entered the south channel. They had been neither detected nor seen, despite having the southern destroyer in full view as they crossed her wake.

The surprise effected on the Allied cruisers, therefore, was complete, and the resulting Battle of Savo Island was a holocaust. The *Australia*, of the southern patrol, was absent in the transport anchorage for a conference between Admiral Crutchley and Admiral Turner about next day's withdrawal, leaving the *Canberra* to lead the line. It was this ship that took the first blow, and she was quickly disabled, while the *Chicago* was torpedoed and in the ensuing confusion took no effective part in the battle. The enemy then turned to port and within a few minutes had knocked out the three cruisers of the northern patrol. More than that the Japanese admiral was not prepared to do. Being somewhat disorganized and delayed by the action and not wishing to court air attack at dawn, he withdrew to the westward without attempting to penetrate to the transport anchorage. He had left the transports afloat and thus failed to attain an objective well within his grasp which might have led to decisive victory. But he had dealt terrific blows. The *Quincy* and the *Vincennes* had sunk almost at once; the *Astoria* remained afloat till noon the next day when she too went down; and the *Canberra*, which was still afloat in the morning, had to be sunk, as there was no ship available to tow her away. The Allies had lost four heavy cruisers, with another torpedoed, and in return had made only five or six shell hits on the enemy. It was only a partial recompense that the heavy cruiser *Kako* was sunk a day later by an American submarine while she was approaching Kavieng, in New Ireland, the enemy base subsidiary to Rabaul.

The future situation of the marines on Guadalcanal was more uncertain and hazardous than before. Unloading, which had been suspended during the Japanese attack, had to be continued during the next day so as to land enough stores for the time being, and the planned withdrawal of transports was thus delayed. There was no untoward outcome of this delay, but so heavy had been the American cruiser losses that subsequent reinforcement of the island in face of the victorious Japanese surface forces was going to be more difficult than ever. For some time the position was one of suspense. The Americans could not attempt a full command of the waters round Guadalcanal, but the Japanese, not realizing how overwhelming had been their victory and knowing that there was still a strong American carrier force somewhere in the vicinity, were not immediately ready to attempt recapture of the island. When, ten days later, they took a first step, they had seriously underestimated the strength of the marines and so landed only some 1,000 men from destroyers by night, east of the American position. Admiral Ghormley, warned of the impending enemy move, had already arranged to risk some destroyer transports with food and ammunition for the garrison; they arrived on August 20, as did also some aircraft for the now completed airfield. When the Japanese troops attacked, therefore, they were met in strength and with vigor and were virtually annihilated.

A few days later the enemy attempted reinforcement in greater strength under cover of a powerful carrier force. Four transports with a destroyer escort approached from the northward supported by the small carrier *Ryujo*, whose aircraft were to neutralize those on Guadalcanal. Farther to the eastward were the large carriers, *Shokaku* and *Zuikaku*, with two battleships and some cruisers and destroyers, prepared to counter any move by American warships. The defeat on August 21 of the first attempt to dislodge the marines had somewhat checked the operations of these forces; but by August 24 they were again advancing and were about 250 miles north of Guadalcanal.

Admiral Fletcher, with some general ideas as to what the enemy was doing but without detailed information, was at sea with his carrier forces to the east of the Solomons. On the evening of August 23 he had had to send the *Wasp* south to refuel, but by noon the next day his air searches had found the enemy transports and the *Ryujo*. A striking force from the *Saratoga* then attacked the latter, putting her out of action with bombs and torpedoes (she sank the following night), while the *Ryujo*'s planes were attacking Guadalcanal and being heavily hammered by the defending fighters. But the main event of this battle —known as the Battle of the Eastern Solomons—was an attack on the American carrier force. The Japanese had already located the Americans, and about 3 P.M. a striking force was sent from the *Shokaku* and the *Zuikaku*. Somewhat earlier the enemy carriers were found by a search from the *Enterprise*, but no striking force had been sent against them. The American carriers were thus left with more than fifty fighters as a combat air patrol, and the Japanese force of some eighty planes was roughly handled during its approach. The enemy concentrated against the *Enterprise*, which was hit by three bombs despite all that could be done by the defense, including heavy antiaircraft fire from the *North Carolina*. But no torpedo aircraft penetrated this defense, and soon afterward the *Enterprise* was able to steam as much as 24 knots and operate aircraft again. Very few of the Japanese aircraft regained their carriers. At this time a second Japanese striking force was on its way, but it failed to find the American carriers.

The Americans then withdrew to the southward to protect the *Enterprise* on her return to Espiritu Santo, while the refueled *Wasp* stood to the northward, closing Guadalcanal. The Japanese continued to advance. But the next day, August 25, bombers from Guadalcanal attacked the convoy, sinking a transport and severely damaging the light cruiser *Jintsu*. Later some Flying Fortresses from Espiritu Santo sank a destroyer of this force. These losses, added to that of the *Ryujo*, persuaded the Japanese that to fight a convoy through to Guadalcanal by daylight was too expensive an operation to be advisable, particularly with the further handicap of shortage of fuel which they were then suffering. They therefore withdrew. Though the Americans had not achieved anything against the main Japanese force, they had done something to rectify the position resulting from the Battle of Savo Island, and as they were shortly to be reinforced by the *Hornet* they could hope to give more effective backing to Guadalcanal in the future.

In the next few weeks, however, while there was a lull in the fighting, the Japanese showed themselves more resourceful than their opponents. They realized that the Americans would not risk maintaining strong naval forces continuously in the waters round and to the westward of Guadalcanal, and they therefore developed an organization of fast supply ships and troop-carrying destroyers working from their advanced bases at Buin and Faisi, in and to the south of Bougainville Island (about 250 miles away). These ships brought nightly reinforcements and landed them on both sides of the American position, escorting destroyers using gunfire at the same time to harass the marines and any American vessels present. So successful was this policy that the Japanese built up their army to nearly 30,000 men during the next six weeks (though these troops necessarily lacked heavy equipment), and they also made Savo Sound so unhealthy by night that American ships were allowed there only in daylight, when they could be protected by the local aircraft.

By comparison, the American operations were hesitant. No heavy reinforcements of marines or army troops were immediately at hand, and Japanese submarines were adding seriously to the dangers of the passage to Guadalcanal for such supplies and reinforcements as were available. At the end of August the *Saratoga* was torpedoed and had to return to America for repairs. In mid-September a force including the *Wasp*, the *Hornet*, and the *North Carolina*, which was covering a convoy carrying 4,000 men and important supplies, was attacked with serious effect. The *Wasp* was hit with three torpedoes and had eventually to be sunk in consequence of the resulting gasoline fires and explosions; the *North Carolina*, hit by one torpedo, was out of action for some months. The convoy, however, reached its destination and was unloaded in safety.

Further efforts at reinforcement were made early in October. With 3,000 fresh troops available, steps were taken to hamper the nightly Japanese operations prior to passing in a new convoy. There resulted, during the night of October 11–12, the Battle of Cape Esperance (the northwestern point of Guadalcanal), in which a force of two heavy and two light cruisers and five destroyers, under Rear Admiral Scott, routed three Japanese heavy cruisers and two destroyers which were approaching to bombard. In this encounter the Americans were much helped by radar and by an idea in the minds of the Japanese that they were being fired on by their own forces. The *Furataka* and a destroyer were sunk, the *Aoba* was badly damaged with the Japanese admiral killed, and the *Kinugasa* also was hit. On the American side a destroyer was sunk, and the light cruiser *Boise* was so badly damaged that she only just remained afloat and had to return to America for extensive repairs.

On October 13 the American convoy arrived, and the ships were successfully unloaded during the day. But that night Japanese pressure was renewed. Further reinforcements were sent, and two battleships, one cruiser, and eight destroyers bombarded the airfield with such severity that nearly all the aircraft were destroyed.

A week later an assault on the American position was started in earnest, and by the evening of October 25 the marines were being heavily attacked from the southward. Meanwhile a Japanese fleet was

185

cruising to the northward waiting to fly in aircraft and send in a convoy
of supplies and reinforcements as soon as the airfield should be captured. This fleet was in two divisions, the first being composed of the
Shokaku and the *Zuikaku* and the small carrier *Zuiho* with two battleships, four cruisers, and twelve destroyers. The second division comprised the carrier *Junyo*, two battleships, six cruisers, and twelve destroyers.

In this critical situation, indicated by deciphered radio messages,
the Americans had to act in whatever force they could muster. Two
new battleships had joined, the *Washington* and the *South Dakota*,
but there were only two carriers, the *Hornet* and the patched-up *Enterprise*, and a force of cruisers and destroyers weaker than the enemy's.
The *Washington*, with some cruisers and destroyers, closed Guadalcanal, while the two carriers with the *South Dakota*, six cruisers, and
fourteen destroyers, under command of Rear Admiral Kinkaid, were
sent to the area north of the Santa Cruz Islands, some 350 miles to
the eastward.

About 8 A.M. on October 26 air searches from the opposing fleets
sighted their enemies, search aircraft from the *Enterprise* hitting the
Zuiho with two medium bombs in the process. (It should be remembered that the Japanese still had no radar in most of their ships.) Cross
attacks by air striking forces followed, two of the opposing attack
waves meeting head on and fighting a battle en route. In this encounter both sides suffered losses, and the American force (from the
Enterprise) was somewhat disorganized and failed to find the enemy
carriers. It attacked some battleships instead, but unsuccessfully. The
Hornet's attack, however, was more fruitful. The enemy's main carrier
force was found and the *Shokaku* was hit with six heavy bombs. Although she did not sink, she was out of action for many months to
come. A second wave from the *Hornet* made three hits on the heavy
cruiser *Chikuma*.

Meanwhile the enemy's first striking force had arrived and had
found the *Hornet*, which was operating at some distance from the
Enterprise and the *South Dakota*. A plane crashed into her and started
a bad fire; two torpedo hits followed and then three bomb hits and
another crash. Fires were extinguished, however, and later the ship
was taken in tow by a cruiser. About 11 A.M., an hour or so after the
attack on the *Hornet*, another enemy force of dive-bombers found the
Enterprise and the *South Dakota*. The *Enterprise* was hit by three
bombs and the *South Dakota* and the light cruiser *San Juan*, by one
each. At the same time a destroyer was torpedoed and sunk by a submarine.

The American forces then retired to the southeastward, the *Hornet*

limping along in tow of the *Northampton*. The Japanese followed.
During the afternoon the *Junyo*'s aircraft found the *Hornet* and she
was again severely hammered, this time suffering two bomb hits and
one torpedo. She had then to be abandoned, to sink during the night
in sight of the Japanese. The latter then retired to the northward.

In this battle of the Santa Cruz Islands, which left the Americans
with no carriers in action, the Japanese had shown themselves superior
at sea for the time being, and they were well on their way to evicting
their enemies from the Solomons. But in this objective they were foiled
by stubborn fighting ashore. The tenacity of the United States Marines
under Major General Vandegrift resisted all attempts to drive them
into the sea. The enemy fought hard to gain possession of the airfield,
but in a fierce action on October 26 they were repulsed. Once again the
Japanese were prevented from sending in the aircraft and equipment
they wished to establish there.

During the next fortnight both sides were preparing for what was to
be the decisive struggle. Though weakened in their main naval forces,
the Americans under Vice Admiral Halsey (who had succeeded Vice
Admiral Ghormley in command of the South Pacific Force) had strong
reinforcements of army troops at hand. They had also an increasing
number of motor torpedo boats, based in Tulagi Harbor, and with
these and the aircraft that had been reestablished in Guadalcanal they
developed a policy of vigorous attacks on the nightly stream of Japanese
reinforcements. The Japanese, on the other hand, with an urgent need
for heavy equipment, prepared once more for reinforcements on a large
scale. Strong forces including battleships were to be employed both to
cover the transports and to provide heavy bombarding support for
attacks ashore.

The operations that are known comprehensively as the Battle of
Guadalcanal started on November 11. On that day American transports
with cruiser escort unloaded and withdrew; the next day more transports arrived with a reinforcement of warships (the whole under Admiral Turner), and they too were discharged, to the accompaniment
of a local air battle of some intensity. The same day American air
searches discovered strong Japanese forces approaching from the northwest. These forces included the battleships *Hiyei* and *Kirishima*.

The American heavy forces, the *Washington*, the *South Dakota*,
and the war-hardened *Enterprise* (once more repaired and ready for
action), were still some distance to the southeastward. Admiral Turner
therefore withdrew his forces clear of the land, sending back Rear
Admiral Callaghan with five cruisers and eight destroyers to fend off
the enemy as best he could until support arrived.

Admiral Callaghan's force reentered Savo Sound from the eastward soon after midnight (November 12–13). Not long afterward the Japanese battleships came in from the west, intent on bombarding the airfield. The two forces, therefore, were meeting almost head on. The Americans should have had the advantage of getting early warning, but the radar in the flagship, the *San Francisco*, had been put out of action by a suicide aircraft the afternoon before, and though other ships picked up the enemy the use of radiotelephony was so undisciplined that sufficient information did not reach the admiral in time. The Japanese, who were of necessity highly trained in night lookout, were therefore the first to sight and open fire, using searchlights. Then everyone began firing, and there followed half an hour of the fiercest and most confused fighting of the war. Much of the shooting was indiscriminate, and there seems little doubt that at times ships on both sides assailed their friends. Admiral Callaghan was killed, probably by fire from the *Hiyei*, which became the main target for American cruisers and destroyers and had to limp away to the westward, steering with difficulty. Meanwhile the *Portland* had been battered to a standstill, the *Juneau* had retired to the eastward with several torpedo hits, and the *Atlanta* was badly on fire with Admiral Scott dead. She had to be scuttled the next day. Four American destroyers also went down during the battle or on the following day. The remnant of the American force drew off.

Next day the *Portland* managed to follow them, after sinking a crippled Japanese destroyer; but the *Juneau*, which had got clear to the eastward during the preceding night, was sunk by a submarine while on passage to Espiritu Santo. Meanwhile the *Hiyei*, lying stopped not far off Savo Island, became the target for repeated air attacks. After aircraft from the *Enterprise* hit her with three torpedoes, she was scuttled that evening.

Despite the damage on both sides, the battle was by no means ended. Enemy transports bound for Guadalcanal had drawn off for the time being, but three cruisers and four destroyers entered the sound the following night and bombarded the airfield for an hour. They were opposed only by motor torpedo boats which attacked them with vigor but without scoring any hits.

By the next day (November 14) the Japanese were again advancing. They were discovered off New Georgia, 150 miles to the westward, by air searches, and soon afterward an attack from the *Enterprise* sank the heavy cruiser *Kinugasa*. Recent Japanese air losses had been so heavy that their convoy had only light air cover, and, when further attacks from Guadalcanal followed, seven of the eleven transports were sunk or gutted. But the remnant continued to advance, as did also a Japanese bombardment group, including the *Kirishima*, which had been holding off to the northward.

The latter group had also been sighted by air search, and that afternoon Admiral Halsey ordered Rear Admiral Lee with the *Washington* and the *South Dakota* to oppose the enemy in Savo Sound. After dark, therefore, the battleships came up from the southward, passed outside Savo Island, and then entered the north channel, to sweep round the sound and out south of the island. While the Americans were passing north of the island the Japanese were approaching in two groups, the bombarding ships from the northeast and the remnant of the reinforcing convoy from the northwest. Neither group was detected by Admiral Lee's force, but the American battleships had in fact been sighted by the bombardment group, and a light cruiser and two destroyers shadowed them into the sound.

When the Americans turned to the westward to leave Savo Sound, the shadowers were detected by radar and driven off. But meanwhile the rest of the bombarding force—the *Kirishima*, two cruisers, and a number of destroyers—were coming down outside Savo Island where they were screened from radar detection; at the same time the American battleships, still well inside Savo Island, were unseen by the Japanese destroyers which had been sent ahead to attack. The latter found the American destroyers, however, which were some way ahead of the battleships, and in a few minutes three of the four American destroyers were out of action and sinking.

Ten minutes later, when both main forces were clear of the land, contact between them was at last made, and the Americans prepared to engage by radar. Unfortunately the *South Dakota*'s radar failed; she lost touch with the *Washington* and inadvertently closed to within 6,000 yards of the enemy, where she was received with heavy fire and had one of her three 16-inch turrets put out of action. The *Washington* then joined in and the Japanese were driven off, the *Kirishima* being so badly damaged that she had to be scuttled. Thereafter the American battleships turned to the southward, the *Washington* coming in contact with the Japanese reinforcing group, which fired torpedoes, without hitting, and turned away under smoke. Admiral Lee then withdrew. He had defeated the Japanese intention to bombard, and the operation was almost at an end. The four remaining transports succeeded in beaching themselves, but at dawn they were battered to pieces by American coastal guns and aircraft, and little of value was landed. The attempted reinforcement had been a costly and virtually complete failure.

Before the Japanese gave up hope, Savo Sound was to be the scene of one more fierce night action. This was a fortnight later (November

30) and was named the Battle of Tassafaronga from a place on the north shore of Guadalcanal halfway between the airfield and Cape Esperance. In it a Japanese force of troop-carrying destroyers with other destroyers escorting them, eight in all, inflicted heavy damage on the American cruisers sent to put a stop to these still too frequent reinforcements. The American force of five cruisers and six destroyers came in from the eastward about 10 P.M., but, despite early radar contact and a torpedo attack by the four American van destroyers, damage was inflicted on only one of the enemy, which had wrongly opened fire with guns and was promptly sunk. Meanwhile the Japanese had fired their torpedoes with startling success. The *Minneapolis* (two torpedoes), the *New Orleans*, and the *Pensacola* were hit at once, and ten minutes later the *Northampton* suffered two hits. The enemy then withdrew, leaving the American force in such confusion that some cruisers fired on their own destroyers. The *Northampton* sank three hours later.

Despite this final success by Japanese destroyers, Guadalcanal had in fact seen the last of its naval battles. Japanese reinforcements continued to trickle in by night during the next two months, but meanwhile the American position ashore was becoming more and more firmly established, and the battle-worn marines were relieved by fresh army troops. Early in February 1943 the Japanese at last gave up hope and withdrew their remaining men by night in destroyers. The campaign of Guadalcanal was at an end.

In this bitterly contested campaign the Americans had won through by the staunchness of the marines and the hard fighting of ships and aircraft, an achievement due in large measure to the forceful and inspiriting leadership of Admiral Halsey. With the help of cruiser, destroyer, and shore-based aircraft reinforcements (but for the present there were no more carriers), determined fighting had counteracted heavy losses.[4] In these operations the United States Navy had not yet developed that steady confidence and sureness of touch which were to characterize many of its later exploits; but it may well have been the heavy blooding received in four months of battle, in conjunction with a background awareness of steadily and vastly increasing strength, which laid the foundations for the overwhelming successes of later campaigns.

Although the American offensive subsequent to the evacuation of Guadalcanal coincided with the opening of a parallel campaign in New

---

[4] Seven new light cruisers and ninety destroyers had been commissioned by the United States between June 1942 and March 1943, inclusive.

Guinea, to be recounted later, it is convenient to complete here the narrative of events in the central Solomon Islands.

With Guadalcanal secure American air power was much enhanced, and late in February 1943 the air forces were given wider scope by construction of an airfield in the Russell Islands, 60 miles nearer the enemy. Admiral Halsey's Third Fleet, too, was substantially augmented at this time. There were still only two big carriers, one of them the British *Victorious* which replaced the battered *Enterprise* for a few months, but the strength in shipborne aircraft was increased by the arrival of four new escort carriers. At this time the surface forces included three new battleships, four old battleships, three heavy cruisers, nine light cruisers, and about thirty destroyers. The Japanese, however, still intent on resistance, were strengthening their position in New Georgia, centered on its airfield at Munda Point on the west coast, with another airfield at Vila on nearby Kolombangara Island. These two places, therefore, were the next American objectives.

Preparations for these invasions were made on a large scale and took time. Meanwhile there were night bombardments of the two Japanese airfields by cruisers and destroyers. These fields were never put out of action for long, but some damage was done and some trouble was caused, and in one raid two Japanese destroyers were sunk. With both sides building up their strength, the scale of air operations increased; on June 16, in a violent battle over Guadalcanal, an attacking force of 120 Japanese aircraft was almost annihilated by the defenders with little loss to themselves and only minor damage to the shipping attacked. During this period, too (in April), United States Army fighters shot down and killed Admiral Yamamoto, commander in chief of the Combined Fleet, who was on air passage near Bougainville. Foreknowledge of his movements had been gleaned from intercepted radio messages.

By the end of June 1943 all was ready for the next step. On the 30th Rendova Island, south of Munda Point, was occupied with few casualties, despite the loss of Admiral Turner's transport flagship, torpedoed by aircraft; two days later landings were effected on New Georgia itself, and operations were started to evict the enemy from their airfield.

From the naval point of view the situation was then not unlike that of the later stages at Guadalcanal. The enemy used the same technique of night passage in fast ships, usually troop-carrying destroyers escorted by others, to reinforce and supply their garrisons at Munda Point and Vila. Their route lay through Kula Gulf, which separates New Georgia from Kolombangara, and it was these waters that were soon to see further night actions.

The first of the two battles of Kula Gulf was fought during the night

of July 5–6. An American force of three light cruisers and four destroyers, commanded by Rear Admiral Ainsworth, had been bombarding in
support of a landing on the west coast of New Georgia on July 4, and
was returning to Guadalcanal when news was received that Japanese
reinforcements for Vila were en route. Though somewhat short of ammunition and fuel, Admiral Ainsworth's force was ordered to turn
again to the westward; by 1 A.M. on July 6 it was crossing the head of
Kula Gulf. At this time four Japanese troop-carrying destroyers escorted by three others had just entered the western side of the gulf
steering to the southward, and the leading Japanese destroyer with a
newly fitted search receiver obtained first contact. The Japanese commander then turned the escort to the northward to give battle while
ordering the troop carriers away to the southwestward.

Not until half an hour later, when the range was down to about
20,000 yards, did the Americans detect their enemies. After some
further delay the cruisers, with their destroyers somewhat out of touch,
turned together to close the range rapidly. They then turned to a
more parallel course, holding it steadily for a quarter of an hour and
opening fire when the range was 7,000 yards. The leading enemy destroyer was soon heavily hit and blew up, but meanwhile the Japanese
had fired their torpedoes, for which their opponents were presenting
an admirable and steady target. When at last the cruisers reversed their
course it was too late, for at that moment the *Helena* was hit by three
torpedoes and sank almost at once.

The *Honolulu* and the *St. Louis*, continuing to the southeastward,
found themselves crossing ahead of the destroyer transports, which
had turned to aid their comrades. When effective gunfire damaged the
two leaders, this force, too, had to retire. Thereafter the Americans
lost all touch with the enemy. With the need to get clear of the area
before dawn so as to avoid air attack, Admiral Ainsworth withdrew.

A second action a week later was hardly more successful, considering the strength of the American squadron. This time Admiral Ainsworth had ten destroyers with him in addition to three light cruisers,
the New Zealand ship *Leander* having replaced the lost *Helena*. Soon
after midnight (July 12–13) he was again standing across the head of
Kula Gulf to intercept a Japanese force of a light cruiser and four
destroyers which a night air search had reported approaching from the
northwestward. This time the Americans made the first radar contact,
at 1 A.M., when the two forces were approaching almost end on. Admiral Ainsworth ordered his five van destroyers to attack, while his
cruisers swung to port and opened fire from the enemy's starboard
bow, effecting surprise. None of the fifty torpedoes fired by the American destroyers hit, but the light cruiser *Jintsu* was soon disabled by

gunfire, to sink shortly afterward, and a destroyer was damaged. The Japanese destroyers had fired their torpedoes shortly after their opponents, but, as the Allied cruisers had by this time turned well away preparatory to coming round for a further engagement, it was rather a mischance that the *Leander* was hit by a torpedo that had been fired some seven minutes earlier.

For the next hour neither the remaining cruisers nor the van destroyers could regain touch with the enemy, and when the former at last got an echo they at first thought it was from their own destroyers. In fact, it was from the four undamaged Japanese destroyers which had withdrawn to reload their torpedoes and were returning to the attack. Within a few minutes of first contact they fired, and the American cruisers *St. Louis* and *Honolulu* were both hit, though without being vitally damaged. A destroyer also was hit, there was some resulting confusion and a collision, and the Japanese retreated unharmed. The American force then slowly withdrew, one damaged destroyer having to be sunk.

In these two night actions it is clear that the American Navy was not yet profiting to the full from radar, which should have given it an advantage over the still mainly radarless Japanese. This failure to make the best of their equipment was due not so much to the imperfections of the radar sets as to the difficulty of coordinating and applying the information derived from them. Discipline in the use of radiotelephony was still not so strict as experience eventually showed to be necessary, and thus there was delay in communicating information and orders from ship to ship. Furthermore, no efficient organization and equipment yet existed for giving a clear picture of the situation revealed by radar information combined with reports from other ships. These were matters in which much progress was soon to be made. Though the Americans did not realize at the time the extent of their failure (for they supposed the Japanese losses to have been much heavier than they were), they were determined to redress a state of affairs in which smaller Japanese forces, relying mainly on highly trained night lookouts and good tactical discipline, had inflicted heavy damage. So strenuous were the exertions of the campaign that there was little opportunity for the tactical training needed by the rapidly expanding United States Navy, except such as could be derived from battle itself. But to these difficulties, and to the severe strain of frequent torpedo damage in night action, officers and men rose superior, and a steady improvement in tactical methods and discipline resulted.

How much was possible was forcefully revealed in the next battle, when a small force of American destroyers, deriving full benefit from their radar advantage, fought a brief action that was a tactical masterpiece. The Battle of Vella Gulf took place during the night of August 6–7. The Japanese defenses of Munda Point airfield had been overrun on August 5, but the enemy were still holding on to Vila and were trying to keep it supplied by a route through Vella Gulf, which lies between Vella Lavella and Kolombangara, and then round the southern end of the latter island. As their attempts to supply Vila with barges and other small craft had been largely defeated by American motor torpedo boats, the Japanese determined to see what could be done by four destroyers. This force was sighted approaching by American air searches. Six destroyers under Commander Moosbrugger in the *Dunlap* were sent to intercept it, and these their commander organized in two divisions. Three ships were to attack with torpedoes by radar as soon as they could reach a firing position relative to any enemy encountered, while the other three were to turn at right angles to the torpedo attack course and open fire with guns at the same time as the torpedoes reached the target line.

The American destroyers rounded the south of Kolombangara and steered to the northward, and shortly before midnight they had radar echoes on the port bow showing an enemy force steering straight toward them. Only a few minutes were needed to reach a torpedo firing position on the enemy's port bow. The torpedo division fired, the enemy being still invisible to the eye, and then turned away 90 degrees together. The gunnery division, which had been to starboard of their consorts, crossed astern of them just before the torpedoes were fired, and a few minutes later their guns opened on the head of the enemy column. The Japanese, meanwhile, had seen nothing until the American torpedo division turned away after firing, when the white water of their wakes was sighted. No time was lost in firing torpedoes, but the Americans' tactics made them useless; before the Japanese could take any further action three of their four ships had been hit by torpedoes and were soon under fire from the gunnery division. In this action the torpedo division joined as soon as the danger from Japanese torpedoes was past. In a very short time the three torpedoed ships were sunk. The fourth escaped to the northward undetected by radar in the necessarily complex situation that had arisen; and the American force, on the not unreasonable supposition that the enemy had been annihilated, withdrew. That the surviving Japanese destroyer reloaded her tubes and returned, though fruitlessly, to the scene of the action shows how difficult it was to shake Japanese resolution; but it did not affect the result of this most satisfactory action.

After the capture of Munda Point and repair of the airfield there Japanese resistance progressively weakened. Vella Lavella was occupied by the Americans so as to threaten Kolombangara from both sides, and another attempt by four destroyers and some landing craft to run supplies to Vila during the night of August 17–18 was frustrated by four American destroyers, the enemy losing three landing craft and three small escort vessels. Then, on August 25, the last of the enemy were evicted from New Georgia, the attempted escape of the remnant to Kolombangara being badly cut up by motor torpedo boats.

Two days later Arundel Island, just south of Kolombangara, was occupied, and Vila airfield, well hemmed in and under shellfire, was no longer usable by the enemy. Within the next month the Japanese withdrew all their forces from Kolombangara, being much harassed by motor torpedo boats during the process. And so, by the beginning of October 1943, all that remained of the enemy in these islands were a few hundred men in northern Vella Lavella. The evacuation of these troops during the night of October 6–7 brought about the last naval action in these waters, the Battle of Vella Lavella.

Three American destroyers were concerned in this action, with six Japanese to oppose them. The Japanese destroyers were employed in covering a flotilla of small craft detailed for the evacuation. An American reinforcement of three more destroyers had been summoned, but could not reach the scene in time, and Captain Walker had therefore to take his division into action with the odds against him. Both sides were aware of the presence and the composition of the opposing force, and during their approach through the waters north of Vella Lavella the Americans were illuminated by Japanese aircraft flares. Although the Americans obtained an early radar contact (10:30 P.M.), both sides were in sight of each other before they had closed to action range. Because the Japanese were somewhat unsure of the American destroyers' identity when first sighted (for their own transport flotilla was in the neighborhood), there was some delay in opening fire, and a Japanese division of four ships was passing the Americans on opposite courses before the latter opened up with guns and torpedoes and the enemy replied. One American destroyer was hit by a torpedo and then rammed by her next astern, and eventually had to be scuttled; the leading American destroyer was also hit by a torpedo from the Japanese second division (two ships) which had now joined in, but she was able to withdraw. One Japanese destroyer was sunk. The approach of the American reinforcement caused the Japanese to retire to the northwestward, and the action was over. The Japanese small craft, however, succeeded in evacuating the 600 remaining troops from Vella Lavella without interference.

The central Solomons had finally been cleared. Only Bougainville and its off-lying islands at the northwestern end of the group remained in Japanese hands. Once more it would be necessary to deprive the

195

enemy of airfields and to occupy territory in which airfields for future operations might be developed; but this advance would be bound up with the next step, elimination of the important base at Rabaul and a gradual advance along the north coast of New Guinea, already in progress, which was to preface one of the two streams of assault against the Philippine Islands. As such it is the subject of a later chapter.

14

THE CONVOYS TO NORTH RUSSIA

IT IS NOT WITHIN the province of this book to appraise the relative heroism of the participants in the many heroic operations of the war; but it would be generally agreed that nowhere was courage shown under conditions of such prolonged strain, seemingly adverse odds, and intense climatic discomfort as on the convoy routes to North Russia.

As soon as Russia was attacked by Hitler in June 1941, Britain, and later America, were concerned to help her armies with all the much-needed munitions and equipment that could be made available. Access by two of the possible routes (Vladivostok and the Persian Gulf) was sharply restricted by long and difficult railway hauls. The route through the Arctic Sea to Archangel and Murmansk had, therefore, the greatest potential capacity for supplying the Russian front, and it was along this route that many ships had to be sent despite the inherent difficulties of protecting them from German forces working from northern Norway.

At the outset there was not much opposition, and during the autumn of 1941 several small convoys got through without loss. Assembling at Loch Ewe, they kept as far to the northward as the position of the polar ice pack allowed, passing round Iceland (where escorts could refuel) as long as ice conditions made it worthwhile. At this time the German submarine campaign in the Atlantic was passing through one of its least successful phases, a lull before the great expansion and intensive efforts of the following year, and there were no submarines to spare for northern waters. But during the spring of 1942 the situation was profoundly changed. The Germans, having failed to conquer Russia at the first dash, realized how important were Anglo-American supplies in stiffening Russian resistance, and they determined to do what they could to stop them. A flotilla of submarines was sent north and soon rose to a strength of twenty. More aircraft were sent to northern Norway, par-

197

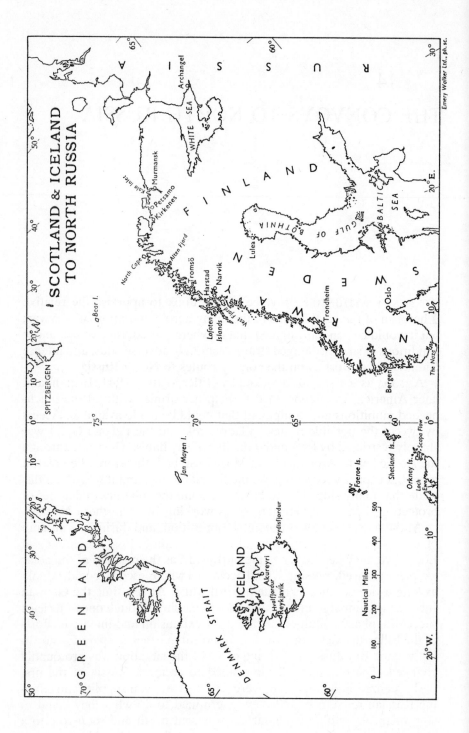

SCOTLAND & ICELAND
TO NORTH RUSSIA

RUSSIA

Archangel

WHITE SEA

Murmansk

Petsamo
Kirkenes

FINLAND

Kola Inlet

North Cape

Alten Fjord

Tromsö

Harstad
Narvik

Lofoten
Islands

Vest Fjord

GULF OF BOTHNIA

Luleå

BALTIC SEA

SWEDEN

NORWAY

Trondheim

Oslo

Bergen

The Naze

Bear I.

SPITZBERGEN

Jan Mayen I.

Faeroe Is.

Shetland Is.

Orkney Is.
Loch
Ewe
Scapa Flow

GREENLAND

DENMARK STRAIT

ICELAND

Seydisfjordur

Akureyri

Hvalfjordur
Reykjavik

Nautical Miles

0   100   200   300   400   500

20° W.

Emery Walker Ltd., ph. sc.

ticularly long-range dive-bombers and torpedo aircraft. Also, the main strength of the German surface navy began to gather in these waters. The primary reason for the latter move was Hitler's obsession that an Anglo-American army would invade Norway, a contingency he much feared. But, as the ships were there, he agreed that they should be used to attack the Russian convoys whenever possible. The newly commissioned *Tirpitz* and the *Scheer*, the *Hipper*, and all available fleet destroyers went north early in 1942. It was with a view to reinforcing this fleet that the *Scharnhorst*, the *Gneisenau*, and the *Prinz Eugen* made their dash upchannel in February, though in fact the *Scharnhorst* did not join up till a year later and the *Gneisenau* was never again ready for service. By March 1942, then, the convoys, which had increased considerably in size, to fifteen or twenty ships, with sometimes two convoys a month each way, were threatened by a powerful force.

Early in March the outward- and homeward-bound convoys were routed to pass fairly close to each other between Jan Mayen and Bear Island, with the Home Fleet (battleships, the carrier *Victorious*, cruisers, and destroyers) under Admiral Tovey covering them while they were passing through what seemed the most dangerous area. And danger there was, for German air reconnaissance had sighted the convoys and the *Tirpitz* had been sent out from Trondheim to attack them. The *Tirpitz* in turn was sighted by one of the British submarines that were now patrolling all the north Norwegian coast. Admiral Tovey therefore diverted the convoys and steered to intercept the *Tirpitz*.

Neither antagonist achieved his objective. The *Tirpitz* just failed to find either of the convoys, and the British battleships were unable to make contact with their enemy. On March 9, however, aircraft from the *Victorious* sighted the *Tirpitz* on her way back to Trondheim and an air striking force was sent against her. Unfortunately the strike aircraft made their first contact when they were well to leeward of the quarry, and therefore the approach, with slow Albacores, took a long time; in a gallant but unsuccessful attack, the *Tirpitz* succeeded in avoiding all torpedoes. Despite failure, however, the effect on the Germans was considerable. Hitler agreed with Raeder, his naval commander in chief, that the heavy ships must not be employed without adequate air reconnaissance and air protection, and this called for negotiation with the Luftwaffe to increase their strength and their willingness to cooperate in these waters—the latter usually more vocal than practical, here and elsewhere. The immediate danger from heavy ships, therefore, was somewhat reduced; but before long the air forces were in fact further increased, reaching their peak that summer and autumn, and with the lengthening days grave danger was to be apprehended from their attacks.

199

Meanwhile, late in March, in an attack by three German destroyers, the cruiser *Trinidad* was damaged by a torpedo.[1] But the Germans were unable to attack the convoy she was covering, and one of them was sunk by the covering force. Losses were suffered, however, by this and later convoys from submarine attack, which now took a regular toll, the weak escorts being unable to do more than hamper the attackers.

A month later there were additional cruiser casualties when the *Edinburgh*, covering a homeward-bound convoy, was torpedoed by a submarine, and later, while trying to regain Kola Inlet in tow, escorted by two destroyers, was attacked by three German destroyers. A hot action ensued in snow squalls and bitter Arctic weather, in which one enemy destroyer was sunk and the remaining destroyers on both sides were severely damaged. But the *Edinburgh* had been torpedoed again, and had to be scuttled. Then, in mid-May, the repaired *Trinidad*, returning from Kola Inlet with the destroyers that had escorted the *Edinburgh*, was also lost, suffering so much damage from aircraft torpedoes and bombs that she had to be sunk.

By this time the period of greatest danger had arrived. Daylight was continuous, and, as the polar ice pack had not yet receded, convoys had to pass within easy striking distance of the enemy's northern airfields. The Germans planned an attack on the next outward-bound convoy with all available forces—the *Tirpitz*, the *Hipper*, and six destroyers from Trondheim, the *Scheer*, the *Lützow*, and six destroyers from Narvik, and strong forces of aircraft and submarines. Late in June this convoy, PQ17, sailed; with thirty-four ships, it was the largest yet.

The strongest available forces were provided for its protection. An escort of six destroyers, two antiaircraft ships, and two submarines, with corvettes, minesweepers, trawlers, and rescue ships, was to accompany it for the whole passage, while squadrons of the Home Fleet under Admiral Tovey were to afford cover as far as their endurance would permit, roughly to the meridian of North Cape. The main force comprised the *Duke of York*, the USS *Washington*, and the *Victorious*, with cruisers and destroyers, and in close support of the convoy escort there was another squadron of cruisers (two British and two American) under Admiral Hamilton. With this protection, PQ17 pursued its way in comparative safety (only one ship was lost to air attack) until July 4, by which time it was just north of Bear Island.

There the position was one of serious difficulty. Aircraft had established the fact that the *Tirpitz* and the *Hipper* had left Trondheim, presumably on their way north, but there had as yet been no reports of their

[1] Subsequent investigation revealed that it was one of the *Trinidad*'s own torpedoes which had hit her.

being sighted at sea. It appears, however, that Admiral Pound at the Admiralty had some grounds on which to predict their movements, for soon after midday Admiral Hamilton was authorized to go farther to the eastward than originally planned, subject to Admiral Tovey's approval. Six hours later the Admiralty "informed him [Hamilton] that further information was expected shortly and instructed him to remain with the convoy pending further instructions."[2] From what followed it seems that this additional information was of a kind that could not be received directly by forces at sea.

By this time the covering forces were already some 1,200 miles from their base, and had insufficient endurance to go farther east and operate there for two more days against an enemy with bases close at hand. Only the escort could continue to defend the convoy, and it was clearly inadequate against heavy surface attack. With continuous daylight and no likelihood of evasion, there was every indication that if, as expected by the Admiralty, the German heavy forces emerged and met this body of ships it would be wiped out. Further, if such a disaster was to be prevented by scattering the convoy, action had to be taken well before the danger point was reached, so as to ensure that by then the ships would be well spread out.

Presumably on these grounds (his views have never been made known) Admiral Pound at 9 P.M. ordered Admiral Hamilton to retire and the convoy to scatter. These instructions forestalled the danger of annihilation which might otherwise have been the fate of both escort and convoy. It could not have been predicted that the German sortie of the following day would be as halfhearted as it was brief and profitless merely because "there was uncertainty as to the position of the British carrier [*Victorious*], and therefore the Luftwaffe was not in a position to attack her. Hitler's order stated categorically that the surface ships were not to attack until the carrier had been put out of action."[3] But in these submarine-infested waters, within easy air range of Norway, the chances of escaping attack were not good, even for individual ships or for ships that had formed themselves into small groups protected by escorts. Submarines and aircraft harried them without ceasing, and only eleven of the merchant ships reached harbor. Twenty-three were sunk.

The abortive passage of PQ17 made it evident that convoys could not be sent through while daylight was continuous and the enemy was in a strength that could not be matched so far from British bases. But the

[2] Admiral Tovey's Despatches on Convoys to North Russia, 1942, published in the *London Gazette*, October 13, 1950.
[3] Friedrich Ruge, *Sea Warfare, 1939–1945: A German Viewpoint*, trans. from German by M. G. Saunders (London: Cassell, 1957), p. 214.

political and military urge to support Russia was so compelling that further attempts would have to be made as soon as there was a change in conditions sufficient to hold out some hope, even a slender one, of success. Such changed conditions, it was considered, would obtain in September. There would be several hours of darkness each night and long periods of twilight, and by then, too, the polar ice would have receded to its farthest-north position so that the convoy could pass well north of Bear Island and more than 300 miles off Norway, while escorts could refuel from oilers sent to Spitsbergen. Because of these conditions and the Home Fleet's admitted inability to operate for long enough in these waters, particularly while it temporarily lacked an aircraft carrier, it was determined that reliance for protection should be placed solely on a numerous close escort. Though the latter could not be strong enough to defeat a concentration of German surface forces, it was believed that, should contact be made, the escort could at least make the enemy's attacks risky—and risking their big ships was not part of the German plan.

The escort given to this convoy of forty ships (PQ18) to protect it against all forms of attack, surface, submarine, and air, included the *Scylla* (with very effective antiaircraft armament) wearing the flag of Rear Admiral Burnett, the escort carrier *Avenger*, whose twelve Hurricanes might do much against air attacks, and sixteen destroyers. There was also the normal force of smaller vessels. In addition, thirteen Catalinas and twenty-three torpedo-carrying Hampdens were sent to North Russia to help in defense against submarines and surface craft on the last lap, and on the first lap of a returning convoy which the main part of the escort was to take over.

The convoy passed Jan Mayen on September 6, and at that time the German heavy forces, having been warned by submarine reconnaissance, sailed from Narvik. Nevertheless, despite this early warning, their blow missed and they had to return empty-handed. Not so the submarines and aircraft, however. Submarines attacked on the 10th and 13th, and two ships were lost. And on the afternoon of the 13th air attacks started, just as Admiral Burnett in the *Scylla* with six destroyers was rejoining after fueling in Spitsbergen. Three attacks were made, in the second and strongest of which (nearly fifty aircraft) eight ships were sunk. Next afternoon there were four more attacks, but this time the defense was more effective. The *Avenger* had given up an unsuccessful attempt to conceal the convoy's movements by driving off shadowing aircraft, and her fighters were now kept ready for direct defense. Twenty aircraft were shot down for the loss of three Hurricanes, and only one ship was sunk. Two days later, when some further scattered air attacks were made, the convoy was unharmed. Only one more ship was lost; it succumbed to air attack on September 18, when the convoy was nearing harbor with a reduced escort backed up by Catalinas and Russian destroyers. By this time the main body of the escort had joined the homeward-bound convoy. In thicker weather the latter escaped air attack, but three merchant ships, a destroyer, and a minesweeper were sunk by submarines.

This hard and sustained fighting had shown how much could be achieved in adverse circumstances by courage and skill; and to these qualities must be added the impelling force of the Prime Minister, determined the attempt should be made, and the bold face that was in part responsible for the failure of the enemy's heavy ships to attack. For these perilous summer passages, however, the price was too high. And, though the nights were lengthening, the strain imposed on Allied resources by the casualties and the wear and tear of these operations and of those for supplying Malta, in addition to the heavy calls being made by the North African expedition, made it impossible for the moment to provide sufficient escorts. Because of these heavy obligations, attempts were made in the early part of the winter to pass through individual ships under cover of darkness. Little success was achieved in the outward-bound traffic, as only five of thirteen ships reached Archangel; but the return home of empty ships that had accumulated in Russian ports was more satisfactory, for twenty-two of twenty-three got through.

By the end of the year escorts were again available, and a new convoy routine was started. The policy was to attempt the passage only during the winter, when hostile aircraft were unlikely to attack effectively and there was more chance of eluding or staving off submarines and surface vessels. The organization was a complex one with double convoys (the halves separated by about a week) each way. There was some transfer of escorts between outward- and homeward-bound convoys, and a cruiser force in the Bear Island area covered each convoy during the most dangerous part of its passage, sometimes refueling in Kola Inlet during the interval between the covering operations. A battleship force of the Home Fleet also gave support west of Bear Island, but was prevented by fuel limitations from making itself felt farther east unless the timing of the operations was unusually accurate.

It was in defense of the second (half) convoy of the new series (JW51B) that the next battle was fought. This convoy included fifteen ships escorted by five destroyers, two corvettes, and a trawler, another destroyer and a minesweeper having parted company as a result of trying to round up stragglers after a gale. The convoy's progress was reported to the enemy by an aircraft and a submarine, and on December 30, 1942, the *Hipper*, the *Lützow*, and six destroyers set out from Alten Fjord to attack it. Meanwhile Admiral Burnet in the *Sheffield* with the

Jamaica in company, having covered the previous convoy and fueled, was returning from Kola Inlet to cover JW51B.

First contact was made in the dim forenoon twilight of December 31, when three German destroyers had a brush with an escorting destroyer astern of the convoy. Captain Sherbrooke in the *Onslow* with two other destroyers (leaving one with the convoy) joined in the action, soon finding that he had not merely destroyers but the *Hipper* to deal with. For the next three hours, in a series of dogged actions in the half-light of a midwinter day, the British destroyers sometimes threatening the enemy with torpedo attack and sometimes drawing him off, kept the *Hipper* and her consorts from reaching the convoy. Captain Sherbrooke was himself disabled by a head wound, and one of his destroyers was put out of action, but at 11:30 A.M. pressure was relieved by the arrival of Admiral Burnett's two cruisers from the northward. They had been delayed by their investigation of a radar contact which proved to be only a straggling merchant ship, but they now surprised and hit the *Hipper* which at once withdrew to the westward. Later they engaged three destroyers, the *Sheffield* sinking one, and then were again in intermittent action with the *Hipper* and also with the *Lützow*, the enemy still retiring and eventually making good their escape. All danger from surface attack had been eliminated, and the convoy continued on its way without further molestation.

In this action the Germans had clearly been routed by an inferior force—inferior, that is, in weight of broadside. This occasioned bitter and justified criticism by Hitler, and the outcome was Raeder's supersession as commander in chief by Dönitz, previously admiral of submarines. In Raeder's view the big ships were justified in refusing to accept the risk of damage when engaged in these operations, and in fact they had been given orders to that effect. Hitler claimed that there was little sense in sending out a fighting force that was not prepared to take risks, even though he had always stressed the defense of Norway against invasion as the primary role of these ships and had imposed restrictions on the use of the *Tirpitz* during the convoy attacks of the summer before. In the new regime he agreed to Dönitz' proposals for operations by heavy forces against the convoys in favorable circumstances, in the hope that they would show more enterprise; but he reiterated his opinion that they were not likely to achieve much. Such lack of confidence and such halfheartedness undoubtedly diminished the dangers from surface attack which faced the convoys; but grave danger still obtained, and it could not be known to the Admiralty how unenterprising was the enemy's outlook.

In 1943, as had been planned, operations were suspended at the end of February and convoys were not run again till the following November. By that time the enemy had withdrawn the bulk of his air striking forces from these regions, but submarines were there in greater strength than before. Most of the passage was outside the range of Allied shore-based aircraft, which were proving so valuable in the Atlantic for breaking up submarine concentrations, and for this reason the convoys were severely threatened. But fortunately there were now sufficient small carriers for at least one to be included in each escort. Working under arduous conditions of extreme cold and bad weather, their Swordfish aircraft did much to keep the submarines at a distance and achieved several kills with rocket projectiles, while fighters were constantly available for the now less likely event of an air attack. In fact, so successful was the combination of air and surface protection that only 3 of 191 ships outward bound during the winter of 1943–44 were lost, despite an intensive effort on the part of the enemy in which he lost twelve submarines.

Even more completely successful was the security achieved against surface attack; this winter was to see the virtual elimination of any further danger in that respect. Much thought had been given to the problem of dealing with capital ships at so long a distance from British naval and air bases; and even before the convoy season started a resounding success had been scored. In the attack on the *Tirpitz* on September 22, 1943, by midget submarines, two of the six that set out on the exploit penetrated the defenses thickly surrounding her berth at the head of Alten Fjord and dropped their charges under her.

These six midgets had been towed the 1,200 miles or so to the scene of operations by submarines of normal type, the towed midgets remaining submerged except when ventilating, so as to keep steady in a seaway. One foundered on passage after parting her tow, and one had to be scuttled because of defects; but the other four, after slipping their tows some 30 miles to seaward of the entrance to Alten Fjord, closed the land and proceeded up the fjord. All these penetrated the further 30 miles to the head of the fjord, but one had then to retire because of multiple defects and one was sunk just short of her goal. The other two, with heroic perseverance, succeeded in their mission despite the *Tirpitz'* being berthed close to the shore with antitorpedo nets round her.[4] Both were then sighted and sunk or scuttled, the majority of officers and men (there were four in each submarine) being taken prisoner. The *Tirpitz* thus had some idea of the danger in which she was placed, and there was just time to warp her bows away from the position in which it was rightly assumed that timed charges had been dropped on the bottom.

[4] The position of the defenses was, of course, known to the submarines from air photographs.

Yet the damage was very severe when, half an hour later, the charges exploded.

The story of the *Tirpitz* may as well be completed here, for she was never again fit for service. It was decided to repair her locally, partly on the score that her presence in northern Norway continued to keep the Home Fleet occupied, which in fact it did. But no other benefit was derived from the decision. When after months of work the *Tirpitz* was nearly ready for sea, she was again attacked (April 3, 1944), this time by bombers from Home Fleet carriers, and again several months were needed for patching her up. A similar though not so successful attack followed on August 23, and in October the ship was moved to Tromsö to increase her distance from the Russian armies threatening the extreme north of Norway. There, without adequate air defense, she was within reach of Royal Air Force bombers, and on November 12, 1944, two specially trained squadrons of Lancasters (twenty-nine aircraft in all) attacked her with 12,000-pound bombs. This was her end. Weakened by previous attacks she was unable to stand up to the terrific explosions of hits and near misses. A few minutes after the attack she rolled over and settled on the bottom.

The end of the *Scharnhorst*, though shrouded in Arctic dusk, was hardly less spectacular. For this story we must return to 1943 and the last attempt by surface forces to interfere with a convoy, an operation for which the *Scharnhorst* and five destroyers were the only ships still effective. Several convoys had already been run each way that winter without loss, and for the first December convoy the heavy cover provided had been extended farther east than usual, the commander in chief, Admiral Fraser, in the *Duke of York* with the *Jamaica* and four destroyers continuing to Kola Inlet to fuel. From there Admiral Fraser's force had returned to Iceland to refuel preparatory to covering the next convoy, JW55B. Meanwhile a cruiser squadron (*Belfast, Norfolk*, and *Sheffield*) under Admiral Burnett, which had also visited Kola Inlet, was on its way back to the crucial Bear Island area, covering the homeward-bound convoy RA55A which passed through unmolested. This was the setting as JW55B approached. It had been reported by enemy aircraft and submarines, and on December 25 the *Scharnhorst* and her five destroyers sailed from Alten Fjord, bent on attacking it.

First contact was made at 8:40 A.M.[5] on December 26. At that time Admiral Burnett's cruisers were 50 miles east-southeast of the convoy, closing in at 24 knots, while the convoy itself had been ordered to steer

[5] British summer time, that is, the time of longitude 15° E. As the longitude of these operations was about 28° E, the brightest midday twilight occurred about 11 A.M., when the sun was approximately 5 degrees below the horizon.

to the northward of its normal course so as to increase the enemy's difficulties in finding it should he in fact be at sea. The wind was blowing hard from the southwest. The heavy following sea was causing some trouble for the destroyers of Admiral Fraser's force, which was approaching from the westward at 24 knots; this sea was also an important factor in Admiral Burnett's operations, for his cruisers could not steam at full speed if they headed into it.

When, at 8:40 A.M., the *Belfast's* radar picked up a large ship 17 miles ahead, Admiral Burnett continued on his course. Forty minutes later the stranger, which had been steering to the southward, was sighted at 13,000 yards and recognized as the *Scharnhorst*.[6] The British cruisers then engaged, illuminating with star shells. Their formation at this time, on a line of bearing at right angles to the direction of the enemy, would have given them an advantage had the enemy turned to engage on a similar course. But the *Scharnhorst* turned to the eastward, passing the British cruisers on an opposite course so quickly that their line of bearing could not be adjusted in time and they fouled one another's range. Only the *Norfolk* with her 8-inch guns (the other cruisers had 6-inch guns) continued in action for any length of time and scored some hits. The *Scharnhorst* did not reply, but made away to the southeastward at high speed, later hauling round to the northeastward. Admiral Burnett at first turned and followed her, but when she settled down to a northeasterly course at nearly 30 knots he declined to be led farther from the convoy. He believed that if the *Scharnhorst* had had an air report of the convoy's position, as was probable, and turned later to approach it at high speed steaming to the southwestward, he might well be left to leeward with no hope of helping the destroyer escort to protect the merchant ships. And even if he succeeded in keeping touch with the enemy's capital ship, rightly considered the first duty of a cruiser in most circumstances, there was little apparent likelihood that the *Scharnhorst* could be brought to action if she wished to avoid it. In the prevailing rough weather she was the fastest ship present, and she had ample sea room to the eastward. Moreover, there were no aircraft to slow her down. Only if she blundered, or entangled herself with the convoy, was there a reasonable probability that the *Duke of York* would be able to engage her. In these circumstances Admiral Burnett decided that his main duty was to place his squadron where it would most likely be able to protect the convoy, and with this objective in view he left the *Scharnhorst* and steered to the northwestward.

[6] The German destroyers, which had been spread to look for the convoy, had lost touch with the *Scharnhorst*. Failing to find their quarry, they were later ordered back to harbor.

This maneuver achieved just what had been hoped of it. Reinforced by four destroyers detached from the escort, Admiral Burnett's force took up a position about 10 miles ahead of the convoy, zigzagging across its front; there, at noon, about two hours after the *Scharnhorst* had disappeared, radar contact was made on a ship 15 miles away approaching from the eastward. Twenty minutes later the stranger was sighted in the half-light at 11,000 yards, and, as expected, proved again to be the *Scharnhorst*. This time there was no passing on opposite courses, for the enemy immediately turned away and fled to the southeastward, working up to full speed. On the earlier encounter she had withdrawn because she did not wish to become involved with cruisers before locating the convoy; but now, when she may have had better information of the convoy's position and might have been expected to force her way through to it, she assumed (on what score can never be known since no officers survived) that her way was barred by heavy ships. Hence her precipitate retreat and her apparent confidence that she could return to harbor without further trouble. The chasing action that ensued lasted about twenty minutes, and some hits were sustained by both sides while the British destroyers strove hard to reach positions for torpedo attack. But they were not fast enough, and before long the situation settled down, with the *Scharnhorst* running to the south-southeastward at 28 knots and Admiral Burnett keeping in touch with her from a position about 7 miles astern.

This state of affairs continued for more than three hours, during which time Admiral Fraser's force was coming in from the westward at 24 knots, heading to cross the *Scharnhorst*'s bows. He had been shadowed by aircraft for some time, but the *Scharnhorst*, continuing on a course that allowed her to be intercepted, apparently did not receive their reports. The situation, therefore, was developing as Admiral Fraser wished it to, and at 4:17 P.M. the *Duke of York* made radar contact with the *Scharnhorst* 23 miles to the northward, the British force being then on the enemy's starboard bow. The range continued to close rapidly, and at 4:48 P.M. the *Duke of York*, illuminating the enemy with a star shell at 12,000 yards, engaged her with main armament.

That the *Scharnhorst* had run so surprisingly into the arms of the main British force is almost certainly to be attributed to the shortcomings of her radar. The Germans had adopted radar range finders in naval gunnery before the war, and it was natural to assume that they had advanced far enough by this time to put their navy on a par with the British and American navies. But, in fact, the Germans had seriously neglected the development of naval warning radar, with the result that their ships were at a great tactical disadvantage by night or in thick weather. Though their gunnery sets might sometimes give them warning, they could not rely on this possibility, and therefore were constantly liable to being outmaneuvered and surprised. That is what happened on this occasion. The *Scharnhorst*, suddenly finding herself in the situation she most feared, a close engagement with a British battleship, at once turned away to the northeastward and made off at full speed. A few minutes later she returned the *Duke of York*'s fire, and the action settled down to a gunnery duel in chase with Admiral Burnett's cruisers joining in from the northward for a time.

Though hit several times by the *Duke of York* and inflicting only one hit (through the mast, without exploding) in reply, the *Scharnhorst* gradually increased the range. Admiral Fraser's four destroyers were ordered ahead to attack with torpedoes, and with the wind and sea moderating and the *Scharnhorst* swinging off her course from time to time to fire her broadside, they slowly gained on her, but only very slowly. Then, when the action had lasted nearly two hours and the range had increased to 20,000 yards, making radar-controlled fire of doubtful efficiency, another hit by the *Duke of York* brought down the *Scharnhorst*'s speed, and the destroyers began to forge ahead. After that the end soon came. Gallant torpedo attacks by the destroyers at close range reduced the enemy's speed still more; the *Duke of York* was soon in action again at 10,000 yards; and Admiral Burnett's cruisers and destroyers closed in from the northward, the latter having hauled ahead for a synchronized destroyer attack which miscarried through a failure of radio. By 7:30 P.M. the enemy ship was surrounded, stopped, and silenced. Additional torpedoes were fired by cruisers and destroyers, and at about 7:45 P.M., unseen in the dense smoke which defied illuminants, the *Scharnhorst* sank.

With the *Tirpitz* out of action, the main surface threat to convoys had been eliminated. The three destroyers that had accompanied the *Scharnhorst* had failed to find the convoy or to take any part in the action, and there was little doubt of the ability of the normal convoy escorts to fight off any future attempts at interference by destroyers alone. In these circumstances it was practicable to substitute full-sized convoys of thirty ships or more for the system of half convoys which, though called for by the grave surface threat, had been complicated and arduous for the covering forces and extravagant in escorts. There were still many submarines to contend with, but the protection given by the escorts was increasingly effective. As already noted, very few ships were torpedoed during the winter of 1943–44, and on three separate occasions, in March, April, and May, 1944, three submarines were sunk within a period of three days, all save one of the nine being sunk by aircraft from the escorting carrier.

So efficient had the system become that the summer recess in 1944 was only a short one. Monthly convoys, started again in August, continued through another bitter Arctic winter till the end of the war. There were still many battles with submarines, and in December 1944 and February 1945 the Luftwaffe again took a hand with attacks in some strength (about twenty-five aircraft) on homeward-bound convoys, though without success. But with escorts including two carriers, and with continuous flying day and night, it was increasingly hard for the submarines to close in. Ten were sunk during the last winter of the war, four of them by carrier-borne aircraft. It was only when they took to inshore work off Kola Inlet, using the snorkel, that they inflicted any damage. Then some merchant ships and escorts were torpedoed. But, by the time the war ended, the surface escorts had learned how to deal with these tactics and no further damage was sustained. During this last convoy season (August 1944 to April 1945) more than 250 ships had been safely escorted to Russian ports and only two had been lost.

15

THE INVASIONS OF EUROPE

IN THE DECADE before the war it was often remarked that mechanization of the army, increasing so greatly its mobility on land, had on
the other hand seriously diminished its aptitude for amphibious operations. For this view there was much justification. In former days an army
of men, horses, guns, and vehicles could be embarked in merchant ships
that had quickly been converted into transports; and they could be
landed in almost any part of the world in the transports' lifeboats, sup-
plemented by the boats of warships and a few special craft (such as
horse boats) which could be carried without difficulty. With the support
of warships' guns such a landing might even be effected on a hostile
shore against considerable opposition. But mechanization had changed
all that. Armored fighting vehicles weighing many tons could not be
put ashore in ships' boats, nor were large quantities of gasoline easy to
handle. At the same time the increased mobility of the enemy and his
probably greater strength in artillery and machine guns made it less
likely that infantry could be landed in open boats against opposition.

A further bar to amphibious operations might be imposed by aircraft.
Unless the attacker could bring more powerful air forces to bear than
were available to the defense (and some said they must be overwhelmingly powerful), it was clearly going to be difficult to land and to consolidate a beachhead.

It seemed, then, that with existing equipment a large army could
operate overseas only if there were friendly ports for disembarkation.
To achieve more, even in an area where sufficient air superiority could
be assured, there must be a large number of special craft (not yet in
existence) for landing tanks, guns, vehicles, and infantry on beaches,
and also special craft for providing fire support. To meet these requirements would be a heavy burden. It would, moreover, be an uneconom-

211

ical expenditure of effort, in that a large fleet of landing craft must be built, manned, and trained for a function that might operate during only one short episode of a campaign. But as time went on it became clear that invasions on a large scale and against opposition would be essential for winning the war, both in Europe and in the Pacific, and that the burden of providing landing craft must, therefore, be borne. It was a long time, however, before all concerned realized how large were the numbers and how intensive was the effort needed.

A start had already been made in time for the Guadalcanal and North African landings, but there the landing craft were mostly of the small types that could be carried in specially fitted transports, such as the British infantry landing ships (LSI) and the attack transports (APA) of the Americans. Bigger craft would be needed, and they were now being turned out. Most important were the tank landing craft (LCT) and infantry landing craft (LCI), which were intended primarily for short crossings (though also to be used between ship and shore), and the larger tank landing ships (LST) capable of long passages.[1] There was urgent need of the latter in the Pacific, but they were also to be used extensively and successfully in Europe. With their larger size they were necessarily more limited than the small vessels in the choice of beach (gradient and depth offshore) to which they could discharge directly, even when the vehicles to be unloaded were waterproofed; but their capacity, speed (10 knots, as against the 7 or 8 of the LCT), and seaworthiness made them valuable components of any amphibious force. The LST in the form finally adopted and built in large numbers was an American product, and so too were the large infantry landing craft (LCI(L)) which formed the great majority of that type of craft.

The first test for Allied amphibious forces on a large scale was to be the invasion of Sicily. This invasion had been determined upon as the sequel to the North African campaign, partly with a view to drawing German troops to southern Europe and perhaps detaching Italy from the Axis, and partly because the troops and landing craft for the more difficult business of invading northern Europe were not yet available on a sufficient scale. Planning for the operation had been started in February 1943. When, in May, the enemy armies in Tunisia surrendered, it was decided that two more months were needed for preparations, and July 10 was chosen as the day for the assault.

To conquer Sicily two armies were to be employed, the British Eighth

[1] Some early tank landing craft (LCT) were used in the raid on Dieppe on August 19, 1942, which had afforded some experience in cross-channel operations, but at a cost in lives which was probably disproportionate to the benefit derived.

under General Montgomery and the American Seventh under General Patton, with General Alexander exercising overall command of the land forces. The naval and air forces were commanded by Admiral of the Fleet Sir Andrew Cunningham (who had resumed the naval title of commander in chief, Mediterranean) and Air Chief Marshal Tedder. As in the North African campaign, the whole operation was under the supreme command of General Eisenhower. The forces to be landed comprised some 250,000 men with a full equipment of artillery and armored fighting vehicles. This strength was judged ample for the task, but there was as yet no large-scale experience under modern conditions of the jump from the water to the land against determined opposition, an operation that has always been one of the most difficult an army is called on to perform. A heavy concentration of effort, notably air support, was therefore called for. It was decided to land all forces in the southeast part of the island, which was nearest to the Malta airfields, and to disregard the attractions of another landing in the west with only a short sea passage from Bizerta.

Preliminary operations caused the island to be more weakly held than would have been supposed from a count of the defending forces, for the intense bombing of Italian ports and railways by Allied aircraft from North Africa, combined with the incessant activities of British submarines, had made it impossible for the enemy to keep his forces in Sicily fully supplied. The bombing of Sicily itself, particularly its airfields, was also causing much damage calling for additional supplies. Furthermore, the enemy could have no certainty that Sicily was to be the point of attack. Hitler himself believed that Sardinia and the Balkans (via the heel of Italy) were the most likely thrusts—a belief strengthened by bogus English letters, ingeniously conveyed via a corpse.[2] To foster such ideas Allied bombing was aimed almost as persistently at objectives in Sardinia and southern Italy as at Sicily, and it was thus possible to exploit the great asset of amphibious attack—the enemy's uncertainty as to where the blow will fall.

The role played by the Allied navies in the invasion was mainly one of organizing the passage and the landing of this large force and its equipment, and supporting the landing with gunfire. To stave off any possible interference by enemy warships was a comparatively simple requirement, and the Allied air forces could be relied on to keep enemy aircraft from attacking in strength. But much intricate organization was needed to marshal so large a number of ships and craft from almost every port on the Mediterranean coast of Africa, as well as some direct

___

[2] See Ewen Montagu, *The Man Who Never Was* (London: Evans Brothers, 1953).

from Britain and America; escort them all through a rendezvous off Malta; and then bring them to the chosen beaches. These duties were divided between the Western Task Force and the Eastern Task Force, for the American and British armies, respectively. The former, under Vice Admiral Hewitt, operated from Bizerta and the Algerian ports, the latter, under Admiral Ramsay, from Malta, eastern Tunisian ports, Tripoli, and Alexandria. The headquarters of the whole operation was at Malta.

So that the Western Task Force could be brought safely past Cape Bon to the rendezvous and thence to the assault, a preliminary operation was needed. The small, mountainous island of Pantelleria, 8 miles by 4, with a garrison of 15,000, had an airfield with underground hangars and also rock-hewn shelters for motor torpedo boats. Lying 50 miles east of Cape Bon, it was clearly an impediment to Allied operations; if captured, it could provide further air support for the landings. To effect its seizure, the island was subjected to an intensive pounding by aircraft from May 29 to June 10, and to a bombardment by five cruisers and eight destroyers on June 8. When an assault was launched against it on June 11, under cover of another naval bombardment, there was no resistance to the landings and the stunned garrison surrendered. On the small island of Lampedusa, 100 miles to the southward, which was also severely bombed, the garrison of 3,500 surrendered the following day.

A month later all was ready for the invasion. Despite some justifiable anxiety caused by bad weather on July 9, the assault on the Sicilian beaches was made as planned before dawn on the 10th. The American forces were landed on the south coast between Licata and Scoglitti and the British on the east coast from the Pachino peninsula (which ends in Cape Passero) as far north as Syracuse. Only at Gela in the center of the American position was substantial opposition met—a counterattack by German armor which was driven back with the help of gunfire from the cruisers *Boise* and *Savannah* and the British monitor *Abercrombie*. Firm beachheads were soon established at all points, including the almost undamaged port of Syracuse.

Next day the armies started to advance, the British up the east coast, where, with the help of bombardments by the 15th Cruiser Squadron and destroyers, they soon captured Augusta; the Americans drove north, across the island, so as to capture Palermo and isolate the western part. In its preliminary movements along the coast to the northwest, the American army was aided by bombardments by the *Abercrombie* and the cruisers—five in all—of the Western Task Force.

Although an attempt at interference by the Italian fleet was an unlikely contingency, full protection had, of course, to be given to these large and vulnerable bodies of transports and landing craft. Both to the eastward and to the westward powerful forces cruised. The former included the battleships *Nelson, Rodney, Warspite,* and *Valiant* and the carriers *Formidable* and *Indomitable,* while in the waters southeast of Sardinia were the battleships *King George V* and *Howe,* temporarily replaced in the Home Fleet by two new American battleships. Whatever may previously have been in the mind of the Italian naval command, these dispositions were fully sufficient to prevent any action from being taken.

Despite some stubborn resistance to the Eighth Army in the plain of Catania, the conquest of Sicily was completed in five weeks. With plans already made for the next moves, the breathing space this time was to be a short one. These plans were attuned to some extent to Italian political changes brought about by the invasion of Sicily. On July 25 Mussolini had been unseated and imprisoned, and control of Italian policy had passed to Badoglio. Secret negotiations had then been started, and it was agreed that if an Allied landing could be effected within reach of Naples there would be a simultaneous surrender of all Italian forces. This landing had been intended for September 15 (four weeks after completion of the Sicilian campaign), but in view of the instability of the position in Italy as between the Italian and German armies it was agreed to antedate the attack to September 9.

Landings on the mainland of Italy were effected even before the next long stride to the northward; on September 3 the Eighth Army crossed the Strait of Messina in landing craft, under cover of a heavy artillery and naval bombardment, and advanced through Calabria. There was little opposition and progress was steady, but it could not be rapid because of the nature of the country; and, although this operation might be of indirect assistance to a landing farther north, it was clear that the latter must rely on its own strength for gaining a foothold.

The amphibious operation now to be launched was a landing by the American Fifth Army, which included some British formations, on the east shore of the Gulf of Salerno, just over 30 miles from Naples. General Mark Clark commanded the Fifth Army and Vice Admiral Hewitt commanded the naval task force engaged in transporting the army and supporting the landing. Under these officers two assault forces were formed, the Northern and the Southern, in which the naval commands were held by Commodore G. N. Oliver, R.N., and Rear Admiral J. L. Hall, U.S.N., respectively. Determined German resistance was expected, and an assault so far in advance of Allied airfields (150 miles) was a bold stroke which could be made practicable only by using shipborne aircraft to supplement the fighter patrols from Sicily. At such a distance the latter could work only to a prearranged program. Any heavy air attacks on the beachheads or other urgent calls must, therefore, be met by aircraft closer to the assault area. To this end a special force was formed under Rear Admiral Vian, comprising five escort carriers (*Unicorn, Battler, Attacker, Hunter,* and *Stalker*) protected by three cruisers and ten destroyers. During such time as was available the aircraft carried were trained in what for them were unusual duties. To relieve Admiral Vian's carriers of the need to provide aircraft for their own defense, it was arranged that the latter duty should be taken over by aircraft of the naval covering force which, under Vice Admiral Willis, included the large carriers *Illustrious* and *Formidable* as well as six battleships and a number of cruisers and destroyers.

On September 8, while the expedition was on passage, Italy's surrender was announced to the world. This capitulation enabled elements of the Eighth Army to be landed at Taranto two days later, the Italians cooperating, and thus ensured that operations on the east side of Italy would be able to keep pace with those planned for the west. But it had no such immediate effect on the Fifth Army's operation. The Germans suppressed all attempts at Italian resistance in the vicinity of Rome and Naples, and the Allied expedition stood on for the Salerno beaches.

The initial landings were effected before dawn on September 9, and good beachheads were soon established. Thereafter progress was fairly satisfactory, though the capture of an airfield free from shellfire was not made as soon as had been hoped, and Admiral Vian's carriers had to operate for four days while landing strips were being prepared near the beaches, instead of the two days that had been planned. By September 13, however, the Germans had assembled powerful forces and launched a heavy counterattack which was within measurable distance of throwing the Fifth Army back into the sea. Fierce fighting and a determination to hold on saved an ugly situation, the Allied navies giving strong assistance. Cruisers and destroyers and the monitors *Roberts* and *Abercrombie* bombarded incessantly; and at the crisis of the battle, on September 15, the battleships *Valiant* and *Warspite* were brought close in to deliver a tremendous weight of fire which broke up the main German attack. By September 16 the Fifth Army could again advance. After further hard fighting, Naples was entered on October 1. The port had been thoroughly broken up and obstructed by the retreating enemy, but the highly skilled and forceful American salvage corps and port engineers soon enabled some ships to be unloaded. Within a few months the discharging capacity was higher than it had ever been, and the Fifth Army had a firm base for its future battles.

Among the trials endured by ships during the fighting at Salerno, one that gave some trouble was a radio-controlled glider bomb which the Germans used for the first time, sinking a transport and scoring

216

two hits on the *Warspite*; damaged badly, the latter had to be towed back to Malta. This type of attack was to some extent mastered, mainly by dealing with the parent aircraft, but it remained a menace. It was also at this time that the Luftwaffe, using another type of controlled bomb, sank the new battleship *Roma* which, with other ships of the Italian Navy, was en route for Malta to surrender. But in general Allied superiority in the air was sufficient, with the help of several special anti-aircraft ships (including the converted cruiser *Delhi*), to prevent any serious damage to shipping. From the strategical point of view, too, the Allied air situation was notably improved early in October by the Eighth Army's capture of the country round Foggia, an important air-field center.

With both Allied armies well established astride the peninsula, based on the ports of Naples and Bari, the advance to the north could pursue what proved to be its sanguinary course. The operations of the Eighth Army were somewhat handicapped for a time by a devastating air raid on Bari during the night of December 2–3, in which an ammunition ship exploded with terrific effect and, in all, sixteen ships full of supplies were sunk. But the losses were made good in a few weeks and the campaign continued. It was to be mainly a land and air war, but direct naval assistance on a large scale was needed for one more amphibious bound—to Anzio on January 22, 1944, with the object of hastening the capture of Rome. But this operation fell far short of what had been hoped. Though the landings were effected without much difficulty from the naval point of view, and were afforded air cover from shore-based aircraft, the situation ashore did not develop as planned. It was not till four months later that a junction was made between the forces in the Anzio beachhead and the troops advancing from the southward. Meanwhile the Luftwaffe's glider bombs had again proved troublesome, sinking the 5.25-inch cruiser *Spartan* a week after the landing and a destroyer a month later. The *Penelope*, too, veteran of the Mediterranean war, met her end during this operation, torpedoed by a submarine in February.

Even though it was not, strictly speaking, an invasion of Europe, space must be found here for the British attempt to weaken the enemy position in the Aegean by seizing the Dodecanese Islands when Italy surrendered. It had been agreed that the main object of the Allied forces in the Mediterranean was to defeat the Germans in Italy, and little could be spared, therefore, for an operation that would contribute only indirectly to this end. But so glittering appeared the prospect of ousting the Germans from this region, perhaps bringing Turkey into the war on the Allied side and contributing substantially to the defeat of the enemy in the east, that the Middle East commanders were told to see what they could do with the weak forces available. In the event the disastrous result served only to underline once more the unlikelihood of achieving success without adequate air superiority. In the years when Great Britain had her back to the wall it was often necessary, lest worse should befall, to attempt operations with forces of doubtful adequacy. But to stage an operation in so clearly unfavorable a strategical situation as was presented in the Aegean could no longer be sound, a fact that should have been almost as evident at the time as it is in retrospect.

When the Italian forces surrendered on September 8, the Germans were in full possession of Crete (with four airfields) and quickly established their ascendancy over the Italians in Rhodes (with two airfields) and Scarpanto (with one). Only in Cos, with one airfield, in nearby Leros with its naval base, and in Samos could British forces be established with Italian cooperation. Thither were sent such forces as were available, in the hope that the fighter squadron sent to Cos would be able to give sufficient protection for the consolidation and extension of the British hold, despite the fact that it had to work from a position 70 miles beyond the Crete-Scarpanto-Rhodes line of airfields. This hope was soon disappointed, and it was only a matter of time before the enemy assembled sufficient forces to evict the invaders and bring the whole enterprise to a close. Cos fell early in October, Leros and Samos a month later. In addition to the losses sustained by the army and the air force, these operations cost three destroyers sunk by aircraft and two by mines.

Tentative planning for the culminating invasion of the war against Germany, the landing in northern Europe of an Anglo-American army which was to penetrate eventually to the heart of the enemy country, had been in hand ever since the summer of 1942. It had been decided before long that the initial landings must be somewhere between Cherbourg and the mouth of the Seine. Nowhere else were there practicable beaches that provided sufficient breadth of front for the assault combined with suitable terrain for airfield construction and sufficient room to maneuver after the forces ashore had been built up to full strength —that is, beaches that were at the same time near enough to England for substantial fighter cover to be provided. Or nowhere, at least, that was not bristling with coast and beach defenses in apparently unbreakable strength. Even apart from the question of coast defenses, it is probable that the stretch of coast east of the Cherbourg peninsula would have seemed the most suitable, save in so unlikely a contingency as, say, the Flanders coast being inadequately defended. But it also happened that until a few months before the landing the Germans paid less attention to this part of the coast than to any other, a remarkable instance of how differently a problem may be viewed by attackers and defenders. In addition to its other assets, the stretch of coast chosen, extending from 10 miles north of the river Vire, which debouches at the eastern base of the Cherbourg peninsula, to the mouth of the Orne, 40 miles east of the Vire (see map, p. 46), had the advantage of being protected to a useful extent from the westerly and southwesterly winds which are in general the most frequent in the unpredictable Channel weather. This was an important factor when so much depended on the landing craft's being able to discharge onto open beaches.

Once the Italian campaign was well under way, detailed planning, preparation, and training for the invasion of Normandy could begin. The supreme command, originally intended for General Marshall, was again given to General Eisenhower, whose unequaled success in commanding Allied forces had been so signally displayed in the Mediterranean, and whose inspiring leadership was to make itself felt at every step of preparation and execution of the grand design. General Montgomery commanded all army forces for the assault and the initial stages of the land campaign, Admiral Ramsay, the naval forces, and Air Chief Marshal Leigh-Mallory, the air forces. Originally it had been intended to launch a simultaneous invasion of the south of France, but it was soon found that there were not enough landing craft to permit this undertaking. The strength of forces that could be carried in the initial passage of landing ships and craft was the main limiting factor in the whole enterprise, and the southern operation was not important enough to be allowed to jeopardize the landings in the north.

It should perhaps be emphasized here how awe-inspiring were the risks of this enterprise. As the years pass it becomes increasingly difficult to realize that the great and decisive victory that crowned this operation and has now passed into history might, had fortune looked the other way, have been a disastrous defeat. The tasks of planning and preparation were immense. The hazards, though everything possible was done to discount them, were many and formidable—the vagaries of the weather, the difficulties of effecting a lodgment should the beach and coast defenses prove more formidable than was estimated, and the danger of being held close to the beaches and perhaps even thrust back into the sea if the enemy was able to counterattack in strength before the Allies had built up enough forces to resist him. The last was perhaps the gravest danger of all. Surmounting it depended primarily on the Allied air forces' being able to break up all bridges on roads and rails leading to the lodgment area and so make the movement of enemy formations excessively slow and laborious. The general superiority of the Allies in the air was immense; but whether it was sufficient to achieve this essential interdiction could be proved only in the event.

The tasks of the Allied navies in the assault had three main aspects: first, to marshal the huge fleet of landing ships and craft, load them with troops and equipment, and sail them in flotillas and groups so that all would arrive off the enemy beaches at the appointed time; second, to protect the passage from interference by enemy warships, including submarines, and to ensure that it was clear of mines; third, to land the army on the beaches, under cover of a bombardment by warships and close support by various special craft. With the landing of the assault divisions, five in number, the most obviously hazardous part of the operation would have been accomplished, but thereafter the army's strength had to be increased sevenfold in the shortest possible time, a feat that would require additional heavy naval commitments in organization and protection.

To carry out these duties, the naval forces were divided into two sections: the Eastern Task Force under Rear Admiral Vian, concerned with landing the British and Canadian armies, and the Western Task Force under Rear Admiral Kirk, to land the American army. Each of these admirals had under his orders flag officers commanding the assault forces (three British and two American) who would embark in specially fitted headquarter ships carrying also the military headquarters of the assault divisions and air officers to control local air support and fighter defense. Also under the task force commanders were flag officers commanding the bombarding squadrons. In addition to the landing ships and craft and a vast number of small craft of many types, particularly minesweepers, the two task forces included in all seven battleships, two monitors, twenty-two cruisers, and ninety-three destroyers.

Safeguarding the passage against interference by enemy naval forces, often the navy's most important task in an oversea expedition, was in this instance perhaps the most straightforward and least anxious part of its duties. Little interference need be expected from enemy surface forces. Cover and escort must be provided against any such attempt, but with sufficient forces available there was not much anxiety on that score.[3] More important seemed the danger from submarines, enhanced by the fact that some of them were equipped with the snorkel device, which enabled them to remain submerged continuously. Escorts would no doubt do much to prevent submarines from attacking successfully,

[3] In fact, the only such attempts were those made by three torpedo boats from Le Havre on the morning of June 6, by motor torpedo boats after the landing, and by three destroyers from Brest which were intercepted on June 9 off the north coast of Brittany by eight destroyers (British, Canadian, and Polish) and turned back with the loss of two of their number.

but it would be better still if they could be prevented from reaching the area of operations. To this end intensive patrols by the aircraft of Coastal Command were planned, with the aim of plugging the mouth of the Channel and, though less danger was expected from the east, the Strait of Dover. These aircraft could not stop the snorkel submarines, but they should be able to prevent the large number of older-type submarines which were in the Biscay ports and the Atlantic from concentrating on the lines of passage of reinforcements and supplies (the "buildup"), and they could make the progress of the snorkel submarines to the scene of action very slow by keeping them down.

The other important protective task, minesweeping, required an intricate organization for the large numbers of sweepers that must be employed, as well as faultless handling of ships and sweeping gear. Enemy minefields were known to have been laid in mid-channel, and they could not be swept until the assault forces were on their way, lest surprise be forfeited. Moreover, the lowering areas for the infantry landing ships (where the assault infantry would transfer to landing craft), and subsequently the anchorages for the vast number of ships of all types which would soon be off the Normandy beaches, must be swept and kept swept.

Though the navy was chiefly concerned with organizing and protecting the passage of the army and assisting it to assault the enemy-held beaches, a major factor in the problem of landing subsequent supplies and reinforcements was causing both navy and army deep concern. It had hitherto been an accepted principle that no large-scale invasion by a modern army could succeed unless it quickly secured the use of a major port—or possibly a sufficient number of small ones, though dependence on smaller ports would restrict the size of ships used. Realization of this necessity was, in fact, one of the main causes of the enemy's neglect of the coast about to be assaulted. It was planned that the American army, on the right flank, should quickly get astride the peninsula on which Cherbourg stands and then, within a few weeks, capture the town and harbor, 20 miles distant from the landing beaches. But there was no doubt that the port would have been effectively wrecked by the time it fell into American hands, and that many weeks would be needed to put it into working order. To make good the lack of a port in the early months, therefore, the bold expedient of constructing two artificial harbors, known as "mulberries," off the Normandy beaches was determined on. One was to be at Saint-Laurent in the American sector and the other at Arromanches in the British sector. Close secrecy was essential, and it had to be achieved despite the inevitable bulkiness of the preparations. The breakwaters were to consist initially of blockships, to be sunk at these two places (and at three others) immediately after the assault, to form shelters for small craft in onshore winds; these were to be extended by concrete caissons towed across the Channel and flooded down in place. Inside the breakwaters there were to be floating piers and landing stages for stores and vehicles. In addition, outer break-waters were to be made of floating units moored with anchors, and it was hoped that they would give some protection to the bigger storeships and motor transport ships which were of too deep draft to unload inside.

The main initial naval task, the marshaling, loading, and sailing of the vast number of ships and craft for the assault and immediate follow-up, was one of great complexity. The difficulties of finding room for all vessels not too far from the cross-channel line of passage were formidable. In general, the American assault sailed from Portland and West Country ports; the British, from inside the Isle of Wight and the Sussex ports. But, despite the closest stowing and most intricate organi-zation for loading (much of it from specially constructed hards), not all the vessels concerned could be sailed from the south coast. The Thames and the Bristol Channel had to be used for the immediate follow-up, and the bombarding squadrons sailed from the Clyde.

It had originally been intended to launch the invasion in the first week of May 1944, but it soon became apparent that preparations, particularly the supply and training of landing craft, could not be com-pleted as early as that. Early June was therefore accepted, and a date had then to be fixed which would meet requirements as regards tide and moon. These were complicated.

The first point to be considered was the time of day for the assault. The generally accepted doctrine was that, although as much as possible of the approach should be by night, a landing on a strongly defended coast needs all the help it can get from bombardment immediately prior to the assault. It should be preceded by enough daylight for the gunfire of supporting ships to take effect. The resulting decision was to make the landing soon after sunrise. The next question had to do with the state of the tide. Here the decision was unorthodox. Normal practice would have been a landing an hour or two before high water, where on most beaches the gradient is steepest and where the assaulting infantry have least distance to advance over a probably fire-swept beach; and, with the tide still rising, it should be easy for the landing craft to be refloated. But in this instance it was decided that the mined obstacles with which the beaches were strewn would sink landing craft attempting to come in near high water. An earlier landing must therefore be ac-cepted so that the first landing craft could touch down short of the majority of obstacles. The latter would then be cleared by special parties of men before the arrival of subsequent landing craft on the rising tide.

The prescribed conditions of time and tide were fulfilled on three

mornings in each fortnight, but with the variation that during one of
these periods each month it would be nearly full moon and during the
other the nights would be moonless. June 5, 6, and 7 were the dates
on which a landing half an hour after sunrise could follow a moonlight
night, and this was the period chosen. Moonlight was essential for the
parachute troops, which were to be dropped before dawn on the flanks
of the assault area. Moonlight would also facilitate the movements of
the assault flotillas and their escorts and the minesweepers, and this
advantage was considered to override the more serious risk of discovery.
If, however, the weather made it impossible to land during that period,
a delay of a fortnight and moonless conditions might have to be accepted.

As June 5 approached, the weather and its probable trend were
scanned with much anxiety. During May conditions had been above
reproach, but June came in with stormy weather which darkened the
outlook and seemed to deprive the enterprise of its reasonable share of
fortune. On June 4 there was a temporary lull, but the forecast for the
next day was so bad that a twenty-four-hour postponement was ordered.
In the early morning of June 5 there was a ray of hope; though the
weather was then stormy it was probable that there would be a lull and
that the cloud layers would break up during that night and the next
morning, though with the likelihood of inferior conditions returning
thereafter. Should the probability of this lull, by no means a certainty,
be accepted and the expedition launched? Or should there be a postponement for a fortnight or a month, with a possible lowering of morale
in this great multitude of all three services now tuned up to concert
pitch? This fateful decision, which might well have daunted the stoutest
heart, had to be made by General Eisenhower on his sole responsibility.
After hearing all that the weather forecasters could tell him and listening to the final views of his three subordinates, he passed some moments
in intense concentration and then his mind was made up. The expedition was to go ahead.[4]

The following day, June 6, was to be D day and all movements were
put in train accordingly. Those forces that, having far to go, had already sailed (the bombarding squadrons from the Clyde and the west-

[4] This episode is vividly described in Major General Sir Francis de Guingand,
Operation Victory (London: Hodder and Stoughton, 1947). Had the invasion
been postponed to the first day of the next tidal period (June 19), the expedition
would have sailed on June 18, in good weather and in full confidence that favorable conditions would continue. The assault troops would no doubt have landed
successfully, but immediately afterward would have sprung up the unheralded
northeast gale that blew for three days and made all beach work impossible. The
outcome would almost certainly have been a disaster.

ern of the two American assault forces, from Devonshire ports) were told to carry on; the remainder swarmed out of their harbors during the afternoon. With the short nights of summer, the distance to be traversed, and the slow speed of the tank landing craft, there could be no question of darkness hiding the sailing of the expedition from hostile aircraft. But in fact no word reached the enemy. His inferiority in the air combined with weather (and, in his estimation, tidal conditions), so apparently unfavorable to the Allies, had resulted in his not attempting reconnaissance at this time. And not only did he lack air reports, but he was also largely deprived of radar information of the approaching forces, as a result of earlier attacks of low-flying aircraft on his radar stations. The tactical surprise achieved was, in fact, greater than the most sanguine estimate, and such short warning as the enemy received was confused for him by the maneuvers off Boulogne of some light craft and some aircraft dropping "window," acting in such a way as to simulate a body of ships, so organized as to represent themselves to the radar stations still in action as an important part of the invasion. In the event, therefore, the enemy could do nothing to alter his standing dispositions, and could meet the attack only with such forces as were already in place. On the front assaulted, these were, for the most part, of inferior quality.

During the night of June 5–6 there was little of the lulling of the wind which had been forecast, and the sea was rough; but the flotillas battled through, only two or three craft out of many hundreds having to turn back because of damage sustained. The clouds, however, had broken up as predicted; and while the seaborne expedition was making its slow passage, airborne troops landed on either flank and the Allied air forces were putting in the full weight of their blows—Bomber Command before dawn, followed by the Eighth Air Force and the Tactical Air Force as soon as there was sufficient light. Coast defense gun positions and beach defenses were so heavily pounded that the defenders were dazed, and, although little material damage was done to the concrete gun positions, it was some time before the crews could recover sufficiently to take action. By that time the naval bombarding squadrons had come into play. With the start given them, they were able to keep the coastal batteries subdued and in some instances to knock out guns by direct hits through the gunports.

In this bombardment many hardened warriors took part. The *Warspite*, the *Nelson*, the *Rodney*, and the *Ramillies* and the monitor *Roberts* were in the eastern bombarding squadron (under Rear Admiral Patterson), and the *Texas*, the *Nevada*, and the *Arkansas* were in the western (under Rear Admiral Deyo), as well as many cruisers and destroyers in both sectors. The British, with a larger number of ships in these waters than their allies, provided five cruisers to join three American and two French ones in support of the American assaults. The flagships of the task force commanders (Admiral Vian's *Scylla* and Admiral Kirk's *Augusta*) also joined in the attack. The weight and effectiveness of the fire from this great body of ships proved all that had been hoped. Such spasmodic return fire as the enemy was capable of was aimed, ineffectually, at the bombarding ships, and the amphibious assault was virtually unmolested.

Though enemy opposition at the moment of landing had been reduced at most places to meager proportions, the dangers of the sea took their toll of the assaulting forces. As already noted, the wind had not lulled as much as had been forecast, and the sea and surf were heavy for small craft. Many of the assault landing craft broached to, sometimes onto the mined beach obstructions, and some of the infantry were drowned while wading ashore. Some of the amphibious (DD) tanks, which had been relied on for close support, foundered while swimming ashore; off two of the five beaches it was considered too rough to launch them into the sea, and they had to wait until the landing craft carrying them could be beached. But despite these difficulties firm beachheads and considerable penetrations inland were effected at four of the five beaches. At the fifth, the eastern of the two American beaches, round about Saint-Laurent, there was serious resistance from a German division recently arrived in this sector and of better quality than most of the defenders. This resistance, combined with heavy breakers and the fact that the defensive positions could not easily be subjected to observed fire from ships' guns, resulted in heavy casualties and a dangerous situation. For twenty-four hours there was a clear possibility that the assault on this beach would fail; but at last a firm footing was gained, and after another twenty-four hours the attacking force (the American 5th Corps) had linked up with the British on their left.

As soon as beachheads had been secured, the landing of reinforcements and supplies went ahead at the fastest rate achievable. Because of the sea and surf, however, this operation proceeded far more slowly than had been planned. In particular, the transfer of vehicles and stores from tank landing ships to the shore by means of pontoon ferries proved impracticable; and as the beaches were not steep enough for these ships to discharge direct to the shore over their ramps, the risk was taken of grounding them on the falling tide and letting them dry out. This expedient, as a way of discharging cargo onto beaches with a large tidal range, had long been regarded as a useful one for coasters, which are strongly built and accustomed to grounding in tidal harbors. But there were grave doubts whether the lighter scantlings of tank landing ships

225

would withstand the strain of settling down, heavily laden, on a probably uneven beach. If the ships were made unseaworthy in this way, the loss of their services for the buildup of the army would have been serious. Fortunately, however, no damage resulted, and thereafter drying out was frequently resorted to. After the gale of June 19, to be recounted later, it became the standard practice. Although there might be some apparent delay in the turnaround of shipping because of having to wait for the tide, both in grounding and in floating, this disadvantage was found to be more than offset by the ease with which ships could be unloaded.

In addition to the vessels waiting to ground and dry out, there was soon a mass of shipping of all descriptions in the fifty-mile-long anchorage off the beaches. Only by using large storeships and motor transport ships in addition to the smaller vessels could the required bulk of equipment be carried across the Channel, and these had to be unloaded by landing craft and the invaluable amphibious DUKW's. To protect all this shipping was no small task, despite the paucity of the enemy's resources for attack. Some coastal batteries that could reach the eastern part of the anchorage were still in action, and they had constantly to be neutralized by the fire of battleships, monitors, and cruisers. By night motor torpedo boats from Havre and Cherbourg sought to attack the anchorage with both torpedoes and mines, and also to torpedo ships on the cross-channel passage.

Though they achieved some successes, particularly against ships on passage, the German motor torpedo boats were prevented from doing substantial harm by the successful operations of British destroyers and coastal craft working in conjunction with frigates which directed their movements by means of radar information, in much the same way as fighter aircraft are directed. But some mines were laid by these vessels and many more were laid by aircraft, for no degree of air superiority could prevent individual planes from entering the area by night when conditions were favorable. A serious situation resulted, and there were some casualties, for the mines were of a new type worked by a ship's pressure wave ("oysters"), and against them the sweepers were powerless unless the mines had been ripened by waves of a sufficient height. Only by very slow movements could explosions be avoided.

Despite the handicap imposed by mines, the landing of men and equipment was being effected at a rate such as had never been seen before. Though the surf and the consequent damage to craft had retarded the immediate follow-up of the assault, more than 300,000 men, 50,000 vehicles, and 100,000 tons of stores had come ashore in the first six days of the operation. With shelters for small craft ("gooseberries") off each beach completed by June 16, and the mulberries at

Saint-Laurent and Arromanches half-finished about that time and handling approximately 2,000 tons of stores a day each, operations seemed to be somewhat less at the mercy of the weather. But what the mulberries could take, or even what they should be able to take when finished, was less than half the stores that were going in over the open beaches and only a small proportion of the men and vehicles. That so much proved possible without a port, despite previously accepted views, was indeed fortunate, for partial disaster was soon to overtake the mulberry plan, which originally had seemed essential to success.

The near disaster to the mulberries, and an appreciable setback to the campaign, was a northeasterly gale that sprang up without warning on June 19 and blew for three days. All beach work was stopped except for the landing of some essential ammunition by venturesome DUKW's. Hundreds of damaged landing craft, thrown up beyond high-water mark, could not be refloated until the next spring tide. After two days of the gale the mulberries started to break up. The floating outer breakwaters at both places dragged their moorings and were of no further value. The main breakwater of blockships and caissons at Saint-Laurent, too, settled down and began to disintegrate; and many components of the floating piers both there and at Arromanches were wrecked. But at Arromanches, where reefs to the eastward did something to alleviate the force of the sea and the scour of the tides, the blockships and caissons stood up to their work, and on June 23, when the gale had abated but there was still too much surf for work on the exposed beaches, 4,500 tons of badly needed stores were landed there. When the gale ceased and stock was taken of the rather discouraging situation, it was decided to complete this mulberry, repairing the damaged piers, but to abandon the Saint-Laurent harbor, using its available material in the repair and completion of the other. This work was finished by July 20, and a valuable harbor resulted. Throughout the summer it averaged nearly 7,000 tons of stores a day, and it was capable of landing 4,000 men and 400 vehicles a day in addition.

On June 26 Cherbourg fell to the American army. To help in forcing the surrender, a naval squadron under Admiral Deyo had heavily bombarded the more important forts the day before. For the best part of three hours the three American battleships (*Texas, Nevada,* and *Arkansas*), with the cruisers *Tuscaloosa* and *Quincy* (new) and the British cruisers *Glasgow* and *Enterprise*, hammered at the enemy's gun positions, sustaining some damage from return fire. Not all guns were silenced, but the defense had been weakened.

It had, of course, been recognized that Cherbourg, when it fell, would be as unusable as the enemy could make it. British minesweepers had a difficult task before the waters of the harbor could be judged safe for shipping; American port engineers and salvage parties under Commodore Sullivan, who had already done wonders at Naples, had an immense work of clearance and reconstruction before them. Not till July 19 could the first cargoes be landed, and it was the end of August before the port capacity had risen to 10,000 tons a day. But by the end of October reconstruction was complete, and more cargo was being handled than would have been possible before the war.

Meanwhile, with the bulk of these huge armies and their equipment going in over the beaches (the millionth man landed on July 6 and another million were to follow), the Germans continued to attack the shipping with all means at their disposal. Human torpedoes were brought to the Bay of the Seine, and early in July they succeeded in disabling the cruiser *Dragon* (manned by the Polish Navy) and sinking three British minesweepers. Later they sank two destroyers and a merchant ship. All these casualties were on the exposed eastern flank, and it was here, too, that some interference by enemy shelling had still to be suffered despite all that could be done by battleships and monitors, though three of the four guns of the principal offender, a heavily protected battery at Houlgate, had in fact been put out of action by direct hits. It was decided, therefore, to forgo the use of the eastern beach (lying just west of the mouth of the Orne), and after July 19 supplies to the British forces on the left flank were landed on the other British beaches or in the Arromanches mulberry, thereby simplifying the problems of protection. Bombarding ships continued to be employed in this area, but more in direct support of the army than in neutralizing enemy coastal batteries. On occasions some very effective help was given in breaking up concentrations of enemy armor, sometimes as far as 15 miles inland, additional range being obtained by listing the ship to the disengaged side and so giving the guns increased elevation.

A word must be said here about the cross-channel supply of gasoline for the armies, a commodity that bulked so large in their requirements. After the first few days the greater part of this fuel was pumped from tankers at offshore moorings through submerged pipelines to storage tanks ashore. It had been hoped that two 3-inch pipelines laid from special vessels (one of which was a mammoth floating drum) from the Isle of Wight to Cherbourg would provide an additional capacity of 250 tons a day each. But serious difficulties were encountered, and, although these two pipes were laid during August, it was many weeks more before they could be used. Later, however, a number of the pipelines laid between Dungeness and Boulogne provided the main supply of gasoline for the winter and spring campaigns.

By the end of August, when a decisive victory had been won in Nor-

228

mandy and the remnant of the enemy had been driven across the Seine, the immediate naval tasks of the invasion were ended.[5] Help was given in opening up the small Channel ports as the army advanced, and of these Dieppe, proving capable of handling a remarkable amount of cargo for its size, was of particular value in supplementing the lines of communication from Cherbourg and the Normandy beaches, now drawing out to several hundred miles. But it was on the use of the great port of Antwerp that all plans for an advance into Germany were based, and here the navy had once more to play its part. Antwerp itself was captured by the British army on September 4; so rapid had the advance been that the port installations had not been demolished. But enemy positions lower down the Scheldt, and particularly on Walcheren, still prevented access from the sea. It was not till early November that these positions could be reduced, the final operations including an amphibious assault on Walcheren which secured its footing with the support once more of a bombardment by the *Warspite*, but only after much hard fighting at close quarters and heavy casualties. By November 4 more than fifty mines, ground and moored, had been swept in the Scheldt, and soon afterward all opposition was rapidly overcome and sweeping could go ahead unimpeded. By November 26 the port of Antwerp was open for shipping.

After the high tensions of General Eisenhower's great assault on the Normandy coast, with the main issue of the war depending on it and success by no means a foregone conclusion, the straightforward landings in the south of France in August 1944 had about them an air almost of anticlimax. Postponed because of shortage of landing craft from the original project of a double blow, the Mediterranean invasion was put in train at a time when the German army was already hard pressed in the north and could no longer attempt to hold southern France. How little resistance there would be could not, however, be fully known beforehand, and this attack, like that in the north, was therefore mounted with every available resource and planned to counter any possible opposition. But the anxieties preceding it were relatively inconsiderable.

Under General Maitland Wilson as supreme Allied commander in

[5] In this victory the inherent strength of amphibious operations had played an important part. Throughout June and July the Germans continued apprehensive of landings in the Pas-de-Calais and retained strong forces in that area, unaware that the Allies were in fact putting everything they had into the Normandy campaign. The idea of a second landing farther east was, of course, fostered by every possible deception.

the Mediterranean, this invasion was the task of the American Seventh Army under Major General Patch, with naval forces under Vice Admiral Hewitt and air forces under Brigadier General Saville. Points of embarkation were widespread. The transports and storeships sailed mainly from Algiers, Bizerta, and Tunis, while the tank landing ships were given the somewhat shorter passage from Naples, and the smaller craft (infantry and tank landing craft) sailed from Corsica and Sardinia and had a crossing of only about 100 miles.

From the naval point of view the principal interest in the operation lay in the employment of naval aircraft as the main tactical air support of the army, not only for the assault but for the subsequent advance inland. The majority of aircraft carriers for this purpose were supplied by the British Navy, and the force was commanded by Rear Admiral Troubridge. Under him were seven British and two American escort carriers, organized in two groups and specially trained and equipped for their task, the British with Seafires and the Americans with Hellcats. This force provided air support for the first eleven days of the operation, the groups being given short rest periods alternately from time to time.

The first wave of assault troops were landed at 8 A.M. on August 15 on three stretches of the coast from just east of Hyères to just west of Cannes. At most points there was little or no opposition. Conditions of sky and sea were perfect, and the seaborne landings had been preceded by airborne landings in strength before dawn some 15 miles inland, and by massive bombardments of the beach and coast defenses from air and sea. The air bombardment was both by heavy bombers and by the aircraft of Admiral Troubridge's squadron. Being, in the event, quite free from interference by enemy aircraft, the bombardment could be effected at high efficiency and with maximum intensity. From the sea, in addition to the close-range covering fire provided by destroyers and various types of supporting craft armed with guns or rockets, heavy bombarding fire was provided by the already experienced battleships *Ramillies, Texas,* and *Nevada,* by the French battleship *Lorraine,* and by sixteen cruisers, seven British, four American, and five French.

Under these favorable conditions and with such a wealth of support the invasion was overwhelmingly successful, being checked temporarily only at one point. In a few days the American Seventh Army was advancing up the Rhone Valley with aircraft from Admiral Troubridge's carriers harassing the retreating enemy. Toulon held out for some days longer, its principal forts being bombarded from time to time by the *Lorraine,* the *Nevada,* the *Augusta,* the *Quincy,* and the *Aurora.* But

230

on August 25 it was captured from the land side, and four days later Marseilles also fell, the forts on the off-lying islands surrendering to an American cruiser. Except for salvage and minesweeping in these two ports, naval participation in the invasion of southern France was at an end.

16

LAST MOVES IN THE GERMAN
SUBMARINE CAMPAIGN:
From June 1943 to the End

I T WILL BE REMEMBERED that in May 1943 the German submarine flotillas had suffered a devastating defeat. Although submarines had been at sea in larger numbers than ever before and had attacked with vigor, they had sunk only a third of the tonnage destroyed in some previous months while losing no less than thirty-six of the hundred or so operating in the North Atlantic (i.e., north of the Canaries) as well as five elsewhere. In these circumstances Dönitz withdrew all submarines from the northern routes until he could discover some way of redressing the handicaps under which they worked in that area. He left at sea only those in outlying waters: the Indian Ocean, where there were also some Japanese submarines based on Penang; and the more southerly route between the West Indies and the Mediterranean where the convoys, though more difficult to find, would be without the protection of shore-based aircraft.

As already noted, one of the enemy's main troubles at this time was his inability to detect the radar transmissions of Allied ships and aircraft and his consequent liability to surprise. His other main difficulty, partly due to this radar blindness but to some extent independent of it, was the problem of making the hazardous passage through the Bay of Biscay in face of the increasingly bold and intensive operations of Allied aircraft. Dönitz felt, though perhaps too optimistically, that if these two difficulties could be surmounted pack attacks could once more inflict heavy damage on the Atlantic convoys without incurring disproportionate losses. Strenuous efforts were made, therefore, to solve the radar problem by producing a search receiver that could be trusted not to reveal its presence by radiation (an unjustified stigma that attached to all the instruments developed so far), and there seemed no reason why success should not be quite close at hand. It was also hoped to solve the problem of breaking through the air blockade partly by technical means, that is, by increasing the number and power of the close-range weapons with which submarines had already been trying to fight off attacking aircraft.

It was not only on the above means, however, that German hopes of renewed success were founded. Though some improvement in these respects was to be looked for before many submarines could gain contact with a convoy, once they were there it was expected that great play could be made with a new weapon being developed, the acoustic torpedo. With this it seemed quite possible that a winning battle could be fought against surface escorts, and the way could thus be made clear for unhampered attack on merchant ships, for aircraft could do little to defend them once the submarines were close in. Previously it had been very difficult to hit back at destroyers, sloops, frigates, and corvettes; but a torpedo that, if fired in approximately the right direction, would "home" on the escort vessel and destroy her put a different complexion on affairs. The new weapon had its limitations. It could not "hear" vessels that were steaming very slowly and could not catch them if they were going too fast—12 knots in the case of the original type, but it was soon to be succeeded by one that was effective up to 18 knots. It was at medium speeds, however, that escorts had to do most of their work, and the effect of this form of attack on them might well be startling. The German command, therefore, planned for a resumption of submarine warfare on the grand scale in September, when there would be sufficient acoustic torpedoes available, whether or not their other difficulties had been overcome.

Meanwhile the more restricted battle continued throughout the summer, the submarines constantly suffering heavy losses, mainly while on passage through the Bay of Biscay. It was by no means a bloodless battle on the Allied side; the blockading aircraft were sometimes exposed to attack by long-range fighter formations while outside the range of their own fighter protection, and the return fire from the submarines themselves was often damaging. At one time, too, the submarines tried to increase the effectiveness of their self-defense by making their passage in company in close order; but these tactics also were defeated by the boldness of the Allied aircraft and the increasing number available. With many consorts in the area, an aircraft could call for support and a concentration of submarines could be met by a concentration of aircraft.

At this time, too, new vigor was given to the blockade of the bay by the operations of Captain Walker's sloops working on the western edge of the aircraft area, mainly off the northwest of Spain, with a cruiser in support in the event of attack by German destroyers. Here, as a result of long periods of strenuous hunting, they added three kills to the seventeen scored by aircraft in these waters from June to August.

Though the Bay of Biscay was the area of most intensive operations against submarines, the losses inflicted on them elsewhere were severe and widespread. During this same period (June to August) fifty-nine were sunk in addition to the twenty mentioned above. Of these, the activities of American naval aircraft, both shore-based and carrier-borne, were responsible for twenty-nine in the Atlantic south of the Azores and in Caribbean and Brazilian waters; of particular value were the attacks on tanker submarines by escort carrier aircraft and the destroyers working with them. The usefulness of these submarines depended on radio traffic between them and their combatant confreres, and the indications of their whereabouts which resulted often justified the detachment of a carrier from her convoy to strike at a tanker. So successful were these attacks that the tanker submarines could no longer be relied on, and the campaign in southern waters perforce came to an end.

The first trial of strength with the new torpedo was staged in September. Handicapped as they now were by aircraft over almost the whole North Atlantic, the submarine packs could do far less than formerly to choose their victims; they had to do the best they could against any convoy with which they made contact. Their first encounter was with an outward-bound convoy, or rather with two convoys that had amalgamated in the face of danger so as to concentrate the defense. Though shipping sunk outward bound was a regrettable loss, the loss was not, of course, so serious as when homeward-bound cargoes were lost as well.

The battle round this convoy, fought over a period of four days, was severe, and the victory on points lay with the submarines. Most of the convoy got through, only six merchantmen of a total of sixty-six being sunk; but of the seventeen escorts (including a support group) three were sunk by acoustic torpedoes and a fourth was severely damaged. Only one of the attacking submarines had been sunk (by the escort commander's ship), with another submarine in the vicinity sunk by an aircraft. Air activity had been hampered by thick weather, and to this factor much of the enemy's success must be attributed, but he had nonetheless been given a clear encouragement to renew the main onslaught on the convoy routes.

This encouragement, however, was short-lived. In October and November, 1943, the enemy's mean monthly haul of shipping was only 80,000 tons, while the loss of submarines went up again to more than twenty a month, with the North Atlantic once more their principal graveyard. Of the twenty-six sunk in October, no less than twenty were on or near the convoy routes, sixteen of them falling victims to aircraft. These aircraft sinkings are a measure of the submarines' difficulties in getting to grips with the convoys; but even when they succeeded, and could engage the surface escorts with acoustic torpedoes, they found that their initial success was not to be easily repeated. An antidote to this weapon was soon introduced in the form of a noise-making machine towed astern, which confused the torpedo's listening mechanism. There was still some danger that an escort vessel would be surprised before the "foxer," as it was called, was streamed; and it was at best a troublesome device that made the escort's task of engaging a submarine more difficult. But there was no repetition of the September battle. A Polish destroyer in October and two frigates and a corvette early in 1944 were the acoustic torpedo's only additional victims.

Two further changes affected the war in the Atlantic in the autumn of 1943. One was the agreement with Portugal for the use of airfields in the Azores, a measure that allowed long-range aircraft to cover the whole area of the North Atlantic. There was no longer a "mid-Atlantic gap," and, although aircraft from escort carriers still played an important part in the battle, help usually came from shore-based aircraft within call. Much useful work was done by the two types of aircraft in conjunction, the escort carrier directing operations by radar and radio. The other change, which had in fact started in July, was a revival by the enemy of the use of long-range aircraft from Bordeaux, both in direct attack on merchant ships and, less successfully, in scouting for submarines. This change was brought about by the increasing volume of traffic between Britain and the Mediterranean and the risks that were being taken in routing it only 200 miles west of the Portuguese coast. As some casualties were suffered, it became advisable to keep the convoys farther to the westward, a setback for the Allies in that it increased considerably the length of passage. With the route farther from the enemy air bases and within range of aircraft working from the Azores, however, the defense was much strengthened.

With the spring of 1944 there came a lull in the submarine campaign except in the Indian Ocean, where the handful of German and Japanese submarines based on Penang continued to inflict damage in the face of inadequate opposition. The German command had again to admit itself defeated in existing circumstances, and was once more pinning its hopes to a new device, this time the snorkel, a breathing pipe protruding above the surface which admitted enough air for running the diesel engines at slow speeds. With this device a submarine could keep submerged continuously and could thereby rid herself completely, or almost completely, of the menace from the air.

The effect of the snorkel on submarine tactics and strategy was revolutionary, and it was not difficult for the enemy to persuade himself in the first instance that the revolution was in his favor. For the last year and more it was from aircraft that he had suffered the greatest handicaps, and it was aircraft that had been responsible for the majority of his losses. Now at one stroke the aircraft would be rendered impotent; and Dönitz was even able to gain comfort from the fact that in concentrating his attacks in the inshore waters of the British Isles, which he would now be able to do, he would be annoying the British by bringing the war so close to their doorstep, a theory he had to recant a few months later when noting, correctly, the advantage it gave his enemies in being able to concentrate their defense. But there was, of course, another side to the business of being always underwater. Though submarines could now go almost anywhere they liked with impunity provided they lay low, they could move only at slow speeds. In relation to a convoy they were virtually immobile, and in consequence they could no longer concentrate their attacks. They had come close to defeating the Allies in 1942 by using their high surface speed and by concentrations that almost flooded the defense. Now that advantage had to be given up, and submarines had, in effect, gone back to the old individual tactics of 1917–18. Then they had charged their batteries while lying in wait on the surface; now they had to lie in wait submerged. But in essence the situation was the same. The surface escort of a convoy could deal with each attack as it occurred, and should have been able to deal with it much more effectively now than in the pre-asdic days of 1918. Although a submarine might sometimes get its shot in, it was thereafter in grave danger. Even if it escaped, it was unlikely to have a second chance for some days.

Though in principle the change in strategy which had been forced on the enemy was retrograde, the task of the defense was at first no easy one. When, after the failure of the first snorkel submarines to affect the invasion of Normandy, their numbers increased and they began to be used intensively all round the coasts of the British Isles, British escort forces encountered many difficulties, only partially offset by the submarines' withdrawal in August from the Biscay ports. Their main operating base was now at Bergen, where concrete shelters had recently been built despite the efforts of the Royal Air Force to hamper their construction; from there to the southwestern approaches, once more the main artery of supplies to England, was a long passage at a very slow speed, which was the best that could be achieved at that time with the snorkel. (At one time in April 1945, for example, there were thirty-seven submarines on passage out and sixteen on passage home, as against twenty-five in the attacking areas.) Nevertheless, the scale of attack was severe and at first difficult to combat. When this inshore campaign started, the main handicap of the defense lay in the inexperience of escort and support groups in working in shallow water. All their training and energies had been concentrated on deepwater tactics, in which one of the problems had been the increasing depths to which submarines were diving to escape attack. (In these tactics an important recent step had been the introduction of the squid, an ahead-throwing weapon that was a marked improvement on the previous hedgehog and many times more deadly than the dropped or sideways-thrown depth charge.) But now all this was changed. The chief difficulty was no longer, as it had been in the Atlantic, to kill a located submarine, but to locate an enemy that lay on the bottom among rocks and wrecks whenever in danger of pursuit. And so it was that in the last few months of 1944 few submarines were sunk, while in December the shipping losses were 59,000 tons. This figure was not important in itself, but it was not to be accepted willingly with nothing to offset it; and it evidently threatened to increase as more snorkel submarines became available, unless more could be done to check them.

As time went on, however, experience, combined with new devices and the accurate charting of all wrecks and rocks that gave asdic echoes similar to those of a submarine, overcame the enemy's tactics of concealment. The chances that an attacking submarine would escape became less and less. In December only two submarines were sunk in home waters, but in January the number increased to six, four by surface vessels and two probably by deep minefields which were being laid in increasing numbers in the focal areas of shipping. In February the score rose to nine, and in March to fifteen. Fifteen were also sunk in home waters in April, with another eight in the North Atlantic and off the east coast of the United States. The majority of these submarines had revealed themselves by trying to attack shipping, and with the number at sea maintained at about sixty they could still inflict an average monthly loss of approximately 70,000 tons in all seas. But even when not attacking, they were no longer safe. Some were being hunted successfully on their slow passages between Bergen and the Shetlands, and in addition to those enumerated above six were sunk while making surface passages through the Skagerak, some of them by British submarines and some by Coastal Command Mosquitoes.

An offshoot of the inshore campaign of early 1945 was an attempt to intercept the Allied army's supply line, running between the Thames and Antwerp, with a large number of quickly built "Seehund" midget submarines working from Texel. German hopes had again been raised

237

by a new weapon, this time on the very reasonable grounds that it would be extremely difficult for the defense to detect it. But its slow speed, lack of seaworthiness, and restricted vision, and the difficulty of ensuring an effective number in the right place at the right time, resulted in well-nigh complete failure. Only three Allied ships were sunk.

In the last months of the war the German Navy was keeping its spirits up with the thought of what could be done with the new submarines of higher submerged speeds than the existing types, which were now coming into service. There were the small Type XXIII and the large Type XXI, with submerged speeds of 12.5 knots and 17 knots, respectively. It was not difficult to argue that submarines that could, at need, go nearly as fast underwater as escort craft could steam when operating asdics would be able to achieve much more than their predecessors. The little experience that was gained with Type XXIII in the North Sea, however, brought these expectations down to the lower key of the advantage gained, not in attacking, but in escaping after attack. Experience of this question may be said to have ended there, for the threat of operations in the Atlantic by large numbers of Type XXI was countered by intensive attack on their building and fitting-out yards by Allied bombers,[1] and by the increasing difficulty of "working up" new submarines in the mine-strewn Baltic. As a result only one of these submarines put to sea for operations.

The course of events, had this threat developed, can be only a matter of conjecture. Conjectural, too, is the outcome of another design that was still in the experimental stage. This was a submarine with a new type of machinery for high submerged speeds (25 knots was aimed at), but able to use this high speed for a few hours only during a whole cruise, that is, before replenishing with the special fuel needed. There would no doubt have been some difficulties to overcome in contending with the new tactics that the enemy would have evolved. But the use of high submerged speed would by no means have been a straightforward matter for the submarine (it would have rendered her blind and deaf, for one thing); and it seems probable that, though convoys might again have been attacked with partial success, shipping losses would not have risen to such a point as seriously to affect the course of the war.

On May 4, 1945, Dönitz, seeing the end near at hand, ordered all submarines at sea to return to harbor. On the 8th those still at sea

---

[1] These Allied raids also sank not less than forty-two completed submarines during the last six weeks of the war.

238

were told to proceed on the surface to stated Allied ports, in conformity with the terms of surrender, and there to give themselves up. By the end of May, 49 had surrendered in this way. In all, including those in German ports, 156 submarines fell into Allied hands, while 221 more had been scuttled or otherwise destroyed.

As in 1918, the submarines were the last German forces to maintain themselves in full fighting trim and with their aggressiveness little impaired. But despite this ability to survive, which must be counted to their credit, they had been defeated, and defeated more completely then their predecessors of the earlier war. In the battles of 1943 they had been eliminated as a vital danger; their campaign of 1945 had failed to do more than inflict slight losses on shipping and had incurred a steadily rising rate of casualties. From July to October, 1918, an average strength of thirty-eight submarines at sea sank about 230,000 tons of shipping a month. From January to April, 1945, though the mean number at sea was nearly sixty, the average monthly loss inflicted on Allied shipping was only 63,000 tons. It is possible, though by no means certain, that the Allies had had to expend a larger proportion of their total effort in defeating the German submarine campaign than the proportional German expenditure in sustaining it. But wars are decided, not on a mathematical basis, but on achieving victories and incurring defeats. Here the Allied victory was an overwhelming one; and, despite the effort that had been needed to gain it, sufficient resources had remained available for defeating Germany and Japan in other fields.

17

HARASSING GERMAN SHIPPING IN NORTH EUROPEAN WATERS

I N THE DAYS OF TRIBULATION after the fall of France, attack on German shipping plying along the coasts of northern Europe was one of the few forms of offensive action open to British forces. It was also the one that seemed the most likely to yield appreciable results in the near future. It will be remembered that the iron ore trade from Narvik was of great importance to Germany, particularly in the winter and spring when the Gulf of Bothnia was frozen. It may be remembered, too, that in 1939 it had been Raeder's rather pessimistic view that this trade would be more difficult to protect with Norway in German hands than it was when shipping could take advantage of Norwegian neutrality. Also, the iron ore carried from Lulea in the Gulf of Bothnia came through the western Baltic, where it might perhaps be accessible to mines laid from the air. Moreover, much of the shipping from Narvik and Lulea, as well as east- and northbound cargoes of coal, must ply to and from Rotterdam, in effect the chief port of the Ruhr, and so offer chances of attack off the German North Sea coast and the Dutch coast. In addition to the routes that were essential factors in Germany's normal economy, the seaborne supply lines to the ports of western France were becoming increasingly important as bases for German submarines and surface warships. All these sea routes were necessary to the enemy, and the importance of a heavy flow of traffic along them, particularly in the North Sea and the Channel, would be increased by any damage the Royal Air Force could do to the railways and canals that afforded partial alternatives.

Even before the German invasion of France, a start had been made. From the Norwegian campaign of April 1940 onward, submarines had worked on the Norwegian coast, and Bomber and Coastal Command aircraft had laid magnetic mines in the western Baltic, in the Kiel Canal,

240

and off the Frisian Islands. After the fall of France this air mining campaign had extended to the Channel and the Bay of Biscay, and from 1941 onward mines were also laid there from time to time by the new fast minelayers of the *Abdiel* class. These operations caused the enemy some losses and required him to employ minesweeping forces that were later to grow so large and complex as to put a severe strain on his resources. But it was not till the German invasion of Russia in June 1941 that opportunities arose for worthwhile results in direct attacks on shipping. Then the situation changed in two major aspects. First, the bulk of Germany's air power was transferred to the east, leaving little for the protection of the North Sea and Channel coasts. Second, the sea route to the extreme north of Norway, for supplying the German armies striking toward Murmansk, became an important point of attack for British forces, concerned as they were to keep open the supply routes through the northern Russian ports.

The campaign in the Channel and off the Dutch coast was waged mainly by Coastal Command aircraft by day and by motor torpedo boats and motor gunboats by night. These light surface forces, now growing in strength, were beginning to show their worth in the hands of young officers of enterprise and daring. The vessels themselves were not so reliable as could be wished, and they suffered from the danger of gasoline as a fuel. They were in fact technically inferior to the German motor torpedo boats, equipped with high-grade diesel engines, which made them less vulnerable and gave them a higher speed. But, despite these handicaps, the attacks of the British forces were soon found to be effective, imposing on the enemy a severe effort to provide a large number of small craft of all sorts to protect his convoys.

Coastal Command attacks were mainly by Hudsons bombing from low altitudes, though a beginning was being made with torpedoes carried by Beauforts. These attacks, too, were putting a severe strain on the escorts, for little help was available from the Luftwaffe, and often the escorts themselves as well as the merchant ships suffered. The scale was a small one compared with the output of later years; but in September 1941 Raeder was already reporting to Hitler that attacks by motor torpedo boats and aircraft were causing regrettable losses, and in November that British air superiority in the western area was making sea transport difficult.

In the far north the operations of British submarines, handicapped in the summer by lack of darkness for charging their batteries, were stepped up as autumn advanced, several merchant ships being sunk. Meanwhile some attempts to influence the situation had been made by aircraft carriers and cruisers. On July 30, 1941, aircraft from the

Victorious and the *Furious* were ordered to attack shipping in Kirkenes and Petsamo (though the latter was found to be empty)—attacks that could achieve little, while proving regrettably expensive in aircraft and lives. On September 7 the cruisers *Nigeria* and *Aurora* penetrated an inlet near the North Cape where some ships were destroyed.

At the end of the year two further operations aimed in part at disturbing the enemy's sea communications along the coast. These were the commando raids on Vågsöy (100 miles north of Bergen) and the Lofoten Islands, both of which did some damage to shipping at trifling cost and provided small-scale experience in amphibious operations, a form of warfare evidently destined to have increasing importance. The Vågsöy raid on December 27, 1941, conducted by Rear Admiral Burrough, was given cover during the brief period of daylight by long-range fighters of Coastal Command, and some support was afforded by a Bomber Command attack on the nearest airfield, which was close to Bergen. Simultaneously Rear Admiral L. H. K. Hamilton was making his raid on the Lofotens, where he operated for three days in the Arctic darkness and twilight and then withdrew unscathed.

The year 1942 saw a marked increase in the activities of British motor torpedo boats in the Channel and off the Dutch coast; throughout the year they were constantly attacking convoys and battling with the enemy's motor torpedo boats and escort craft. At this time, too, the intensity of the aircraft mining campaign was stepped up. Mines were being manufactured in larger quantities and with a wide variety of subtle firing mechanisms, designed to confuse the enemy's sweepers. And, whereas previously the laying had been done mainly by one group of Bomber Command, three other groups now took a hand. In November 1942 Raeder reported to Hitler: "Our effort to sweep these mines is taxing our forces to the limit."

Much the same in these southern waters was the story of 1943. The offensive effort was increasing at all points, and destroyers as well as motor torpedo boats were being used to strike at the convoys on the Breton coast, two of the Hunt class fighting a very successful night action off Ushant on April 28. There was a setback to this strategy later in the year when a mixed force, composed of the light cruiser *Charybdis*, some fleet destroyers, and some destroyers of the Hunt class, were sent on a similar operation with little preparation and no previous experience of working together. Attempting to intercept a convoy by night, they were outmaneuvered by the division of German destroyers which was covering it, and the *Charybdis* and a Hunt destroyer were torpedoed and sunk. It was not until the following April (1944) that revenge was taken for this disaster when four destroyers of the Tribal class, supported by the light cruiser *Black Prince*, routed four enemy destroyers, sinking one. But throughout this period motor torpedo boats had continued to score some successes. Coastal Command aircraft now had less opportunity, for the enemy moved his Channel traffic only by night. But there were from time to time some successful night attacks by Fleet Air Arm aircraft working under Coastal Command; and Hudsons and Beauforts were still able to do important work off the Dutch coast, not only against merchant ships but also against the minesweepers, whose burden of keeping the shipping routes clear was becoming increasingly onerous. These waters were being mined by motor launches as well as by aircraft.

Even in the waters where the German minesweepers could work undisturbed, the volume and subtlety of aircraft minelaying were causing serious difficulty and severe losses. Dönitz, who had succeeded Raeder as commander in chief of the navy early in 1943, had made strong efforts throughout that year to increase minesweeping resources. Nevertheless, he had to report early in 1944 that the mine situation was a cause of deep anxiety, and that ore imports from Sweden were seriously threatened. So it continued to the end. In all some 400 merchant ships and 100 minesweepers were sunk by British mines, and many more were damaged. Most of them were sunk in the western Baltic and the southeastern North Sea in 1943 and 1944, and about 80 percent fell to mines laid by aircraft.

Though in a different category from the shipping plying on the coastwise routes, mention must be made here of the German blockade runners that attempted to reach the French Atlantic coast. It will be remembered that early in the war the British blockade had put a stop to Germany's oceanic trade. As time went on, however, the need of certain raw materials (notably natural rubber) became acute; and from autumn of 1941 onward several ships were employed in trying to bring these supplies from the Far East. When this fact became known, special operations to intercept the German ships were put in hand, usually with cruisers and Coastal Command aircraft in cooperation. Some of the valuable cargoes got through; but in 1942 and 1943 the majority of ships were intercepted, some of them between Africa and South America by the joint action of British forces working from Sierra Leone and American ships and aircraft working from Brazilian bases. These operations culminated on December 27 and 28, 1943, when not only was a blockade runner sunk by aircraft on the outskirts of the Bay of Biscay, but a flotilla of eleven German destroyers, which

243

had been sent to meet her, was intercepted by the 6-inch cruisers *Glasgow* and *Enterprise*. The enemy force was routed in a running fight, three destroyers being sunk. After that the venture was given up. Submarine blockade runners were also tried; but, with their comparatively small capacity and, by that time, the almost equally hazardous passages into the Bay of Biscay, they too were eventually found to be hardly worthwhile.

Turning again to events on the Norwegian coast, the story is one of growing intensity of attack as more and more forces became available, while at the same time the importance of these routes to the enemy was substantially increased by the course of the war. More forces were available for attack, because the withdrawal of German submarines from mid-Atlantic released escort carriers for other tasks and also allowed the steadily expanding Coastal Command to devote a higher proportion of its resources to attacks on enemy shipping. The importance of the Norwegian routes was increased because, after the Allied invasion of France, Bergen became the enemy's principal submarine base. In addition, as the pressure on land increased, the transport of troops from Norway back to Germany was an urgent requirement.

Not much was done in these waters during 1943. The spring of that year saw the beginning of some daring incursions by motor torpedo boats of the Royal Norwegian Navy, working from the Shetlands, into the leads north and south of Bergen, where from time to time they sank some ships. But for the most part operations in Norwegian waters were concerned with the protection of the convoys to Russia. The following year, however, shipping was harassed continually from the air. On March 30, 1944, Beauforts, attacking by night, torpedoed a 14,000-ton transport, and from then on the pressure was seldom relaxed. Coastal Command attacked on the west coast (i.e., southward from Stadland) and in the Skagerak, and even, as the German air forces weakened, right into the Kattegat. To the north, along the 400-mile stretch between Stadland and the mouth of Vest Fjord, there were constant raids by carrier-borne aircraft of the Fleet Air Arm. The *Victorious* and the veteran *Furious* of the Home Fleet launched many of these attacks, and several escort carriers worked with them—*Searcher, Striker, Pursuer, Fencer, Trumpeter,* and *Emperor*—from time to time. Some of these vessels were withdrawn in the summer to provide close support for the invasion of the Riviera; but on completion of that successful operation they returned once more to the north, and the scale of attack was again increased. That winter, 1944-45, the situation in these waters as regards the iron ore trade and the withdrawal of heavy military equipment from the north (the troops could go by train to Oslo) seemed to Dönitz to be almost beyond hope. Appeals to the Luftwaffe for more aircraft to find and attack British ships and oppose Allied aircraft could not be met, and suggestions by the High Command that the British aircraft carriers be driven off by submarines were opposed by Dönitz as hopelessly ineffectual, at least in the absence of good air reconnaissance which was evidently not forthcoming. He agreed in December 1944 to order a concentration of snorkel submarines round Scapa Flow in the hope of intercepting the carriers there, but nothing was achieved.

Coastal Command attacks in the south gained in effectiveness, not only by a steady increase in numbers opposed to a declining Luftwaffe, but also by the addition of the fast and admirable Mosquitoes to the Beauforts which, since the Hudsons had become obsolete, had provided the bulk of the striking force of the command. In addition, aircraft now fired rockets which, armed with solid shot, were found to be very effective against unarmored ships. As compared with bombs, their accuracy was remarkable, even in face of the intensive close-range fire to which the aircraft were subjected by escorting craft, and which made these operations always hazardous despite the decline of the Luftwaffe. They smashed holes so effectively right through a ship, coming out under water, that she was unlikely to remain afloat for long after an attack.

In the autumn of 1944 the pressure on the enemy was further increased by sending cruisers and destroyers to attack shipping by night. On November 12 Rear Admiral McGrigor in the *Kent*, with the light cruiser *Bellona* and some destroyers, virtually annihilated a northbound convoy off Egersund (70 miles south of Stavanger), sinking nine ships out of eleven. On January 12, 1945, a similar operation, Admiral McGrigor being on this occasion in the *Norfolk*, was not quite so successful, some of the enemy gaining the shelter of the Egersund defenses. A fortnight later German destroyers made a last effort to stem the tide by engaging two British cruisers in a night action in these waters, but soon had to retire. For the enemy the situation was past recovery, and the night of April 4 saw the last surface action of the war in European waters. On that occasion Captain Browning in the *Onslow*, with three other destroyers, intercepted a convoy of four ships with three escorts 30 miles southeast of Egersund. One ship was sunk and several others were damaged before the enemy reached shelter close under the shore.

Air attacks and air mining in the Skagerak and the Kattegat con-

245

tinued throughout this period in a crescendo that took increasing toll of such troop transports and supply ships as the enemy still ventured on the routes from Norway. He struggled almost to the end to withdraw his remaining troops. But all was now over and Hitler was dead. On May 4, 1945, the Allied attacks were called off, and by May 8 the armies of the British Commonwealth, the United States, and Russia had forced unconditional surrender on what remained of the Wehrmacht.

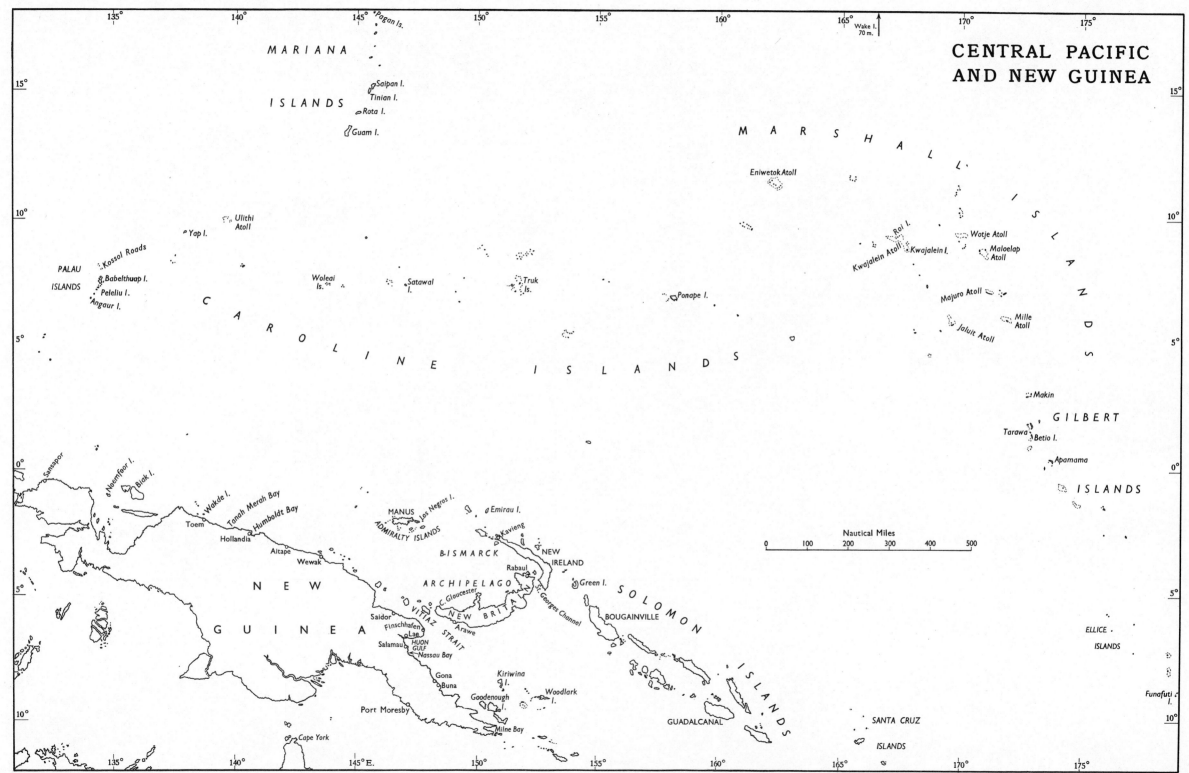

CENTRAL PACIFIC
AND NEW GUINEA

MARIANA

ISLANDS

MARSHALL

ISLANDS

Pagan Is.
Saipan I.
Tinian I.
Rota I.
Guam I.

Eniwetok Atoll

Ulithi
Atoll
Yap I.

Roi I.
Wotje Atoll
Kwajalein Atoll
Kwajalein I.
Maloelap
Atoll

PALAU
ISLANDS
Kossol Roads
Babelthuap I.
Peleliu I.
Angaur I.

Woleai
Is.
Satawal
I.
Truk
Is.
Ponape I.
Majuro Atoll
Mille
Atoll
Jaluit Atoll

CAROLINE   ISLANDS

Makin

GILBERT

Tarawa
Betio I.

Apamama

ISLANDS

Sansapor
Naemfoor I.
Biak I.
Wakde I.
Tanah Merah Bay
Humboldt Bay
Toem
Hollandia
Aitape
Wewak

MANUS
Los Negros I.
Emirau I.
ADMIRALTY ISLANDS
Kavieng
BISMARCK
NEW
IRELAND
Rabaul
ARCHIPELAGO
C. Gloucester
NEW BRITAIN
Arawe
Georges Channel
Green I.
SOLOMON
BOUGAINVILLE

ELLICE

ISLANDS

Nautical Miles
0   100   200   300   400   500

NEW

Saidor
Finschhafen
VITIAZ
STRAIT
Lae
HUON
Salamaua
GULF
Nassau Bay

GUINEA

Gona
Buna
Kiriwina
I.
Woodlark
I.
Goodenough
I.

ISLANDS

Funafuti I.

Port Moresby
Milne Bay

GUADALCANAL
SANTA CRUZ

ISLANDS

Cape York

135°   140°   145° E.   150°   155°   160°   165°   170°   175°

Emery Walker Ltd., ph. sc.

18

ADVANCE IN THE PACIFIC, SOUTHERN ROUTE: *Lae to Biak Island*

F OR THE THREADS leading to the great Pacific campaigns of 1944–45, we must go back to the Solomon Islands operations (see chap. 13) and, even further, to the defeat of the Japanese in the Coral Sea on May 7 and 8, 1942. Because of that defeat the enemy recalled the seaborne expedition that was heading for Port Moresby, the Allied base on the south coast of eastern New Guinea. Three months later another amphibious attempt, this time to get a footing at Milne Bay at the extremity of New Guinea's eastern peninsula, was frustrated (August 25–29) by Australian troops already established there and American air forces. Once more the enemy withdrew, and the Allies continued to develop Milne Bay as a base for eventual offensive operations. After that the Japanese resigned themselves to an advance on Port Moresby overland through a difficult country of mountain ranges and dense forests.

For this land attack the Japanese started, not from Lae and Salamaua in Huon Gulf where their previously established bases and airfields were located, but from Buna and Gona, some 150 miles down the coast to the southeastward and more directly opposite Port Moresby. In September 1942 the advance began. In October it was held and thrust back by General MacArthur's Australian and American army advancing from Port Moresby; the Allied troops then drove on with increasing strength until they had forced the enemy to retreat to his starting points and pinned him there with his back to the sea. Gona was captured on December 9, and all Japanese in the Buna district had been mopped up by the end of January 1943. It was at this time, it will be remembered, that the enemy was giving up hope of keeping a foothold in Guadalcanal, 600 miles to the eastward.

During this period there was no interference by surface forces with the sea communications on either side of New Guinea (the Allied routes from Australia and the Japanese from Rabaul), for both navies were fully occupied in the struggle for the Solomon Islands. But something could be done by air. The Japanese were not strong enough in this respect for more than an occasional raid on Port Moresby, but the Allied air forces were steadily growing and were now able, not only to support the ground forces, but to harass shipping with increasing effect off the New Guinea coast, while on passage thereto, and in Rabaul itself. These Allied air forces comprised the Fifth United States Army Air Force and some formations of the Royal Australian Air Force, the whole working as a single organization under Lieutenant General Kenney, who was General MacArthur's air commander. They were to provide the principal air component in the maritime operations of the New Guinea campaign during the coming eighteen months, but their most resounding victory at sea was achieved in March 1943: the annihilation of a convoy bound for Lae, an operation that became known as the Battle of the Bismarck Sea.

This Japanese convoy, comprising six troopships and two supply ships, was escorted by eight destroyers. It had sailed from Rabaul and was first sighted on March 1 off the north coast of New Britain. On the two following days it was assailed by all the aircraft at General Kenney's disposal, bombers and fighters, some 300 in all, while it was passing through the strait between New Britain and New Guinea on March 2, and while the remnant was entering Huon Gulf on March 3. From Lae and from subsidiary airfields in western New Britain the Japanese put up a substantial number of fighters in defense, a force that was comparable in size with the attack. But the Allied aircraft went through them, inflicting severe casualties on the Japanese fighters with little loss to themselves and attacking the shipping with devastating effect. During these two days all eight ships of the convoy and four of the escorting destroyers were sunk.

The Battle of the Bismarck Sea, in conjunction with continuing hazards to all shipping entering Huon Gulf, decided the Japanese army command, in May, to withhold further reinforcements from their advanced positions in New Guinea. It was their intention to delay the Allied advance by holding on with the troops already there, particularly near Finschhafen on the peninsula north of Huon Gulf; but for the future their main defensive position was to be in the area round Wewak, 300 miles west of Finschhafen, where they were building up a strong army and air force. This activity, however, was not the immediate concern of the Allies, who first had to turn the enemy out of his nearer

248

positions and advance their airfields to points from which they could support operations farther to the westward.

The Allied amphibious offensive in New Guinea opened at the end of June, concurrently with the attack on New Georgia in the central Solomons (see p. 191, above). These two offensives were in fact two prongs of a thrust destined to threaten and eventually to encircle Rabaul. To ensure full coordination between them, Admiral Halsey's South Pacific Force (of which the naval component was the Third Fleet) was put under the control of General MacArthur, commanding the Southwest Pacific Force. The naval organization under General MacArthur's direct command was the Seventh Fleet. In the initial stages this fleet comprised only an amphibious force, the cruisers and destroyers of the Australian squadron, eight American destroyers, usually an American cruiser or two, and some submarines; but it was to grow in strength as the army advanced in successive seaborne bounds to western New Guinea and beyond, until eventually it included large numbers of almost every type of warship. It was, then, with the Seventh Fleet Amphibious Force under Rear Admiral Barbey, recently formed and still in process of expansion, that the first amphibious operations of the New Guinea campaign were effected. These were landings on Kiriwina Island, lying 100 miles north of Milne Bay, and on Woodlark Island, 100 miles farther east, the aim being to establish airfields that would enable fighters to escort bombers to Rabaul, 300 miles away. Little opposition was met and both islands were soon in American hands. At the same time a small American force was put ashore by night at Nassau Bay, 10 miles short of Salamaua, to link up with Australian troops fighting in the interior and so keep up a steady pressure on the enemy positions round Huon Gulf.

These operations were only preliminaries; more time was still required for building up and training a substantial amphibious force. But at the beginning of September all was ready, and the first real step forward was taken—the landing of an Australian division on the north shore of Huon Gulf on September 4. Thereafter events moved rapidly. The enemy forces withdrew from Salamaua to concentrate at Lae, but could not hold the latter position against this new thrust from the north. Their depleted numbers were soon overwhelmed by Allied troops (some of them airborne) and aircraft, and on September 16 Lae was occupied. A further amphibious stroke quickly followed, a landing a few miles north of Finschhafen, 50 miles east of Lae. Here, however, the resistance was fiercer, for the enemy was not yet prepared to give up this peninsula jutting out toward New Britain. Finschhafen itself was taken on October 2, but soon afterward the Japanese counterattacked in strength, and fighting was to continue in this area for another four months.

It is convenient here to turn to the parallel advance in the Solomons, 500 miles to the eastward. On the night of October 6–7 the battle of Vella Lavella (see p. 195, above) had marked the end of the campaign in the central Solomons, and at that time Admiral Halsey was already preparing for his next step. This was to be the occupation of an area in Bougainville, the large northern island, 100 miles long, which would give him airfields within 250 miles of Rabaul. The Japanese had strong positions with airfields at Buin at the southern end and Faisi in the off-lying Shortland Islands, and also at Bonis at the northern end and Buka Island just opposite it. From these positions, however, it was not intended to dislodge the enemy. Instead, a landing would be effected in Empress Augusta Bay on the west coast, and ground, sea, and air forces would be established there which would eventually neutralize the enemy to north and south of them by throttling their communications with Rabaul. The main landing, timed for November 1, was to be preceded by diversionary landings, on October 27 in the Treasury Islands, south of Bougainville, and on Choiseul Island to the eastward, and also by air and sea bombardments of the airfields in the Buka-Bonis and Buin-Faisa areas.

For these operations Admiral Halsey's naval forces were on a smaller scale than the extensive fleet that had been assembled for the New Georgia invasions; but they included a carrier force under Rear Admiral Frederic Sherman (the *Saratoga* and the new light carrier *Princeton*, with cruisers and destroyers) and a force of four light cruisers and eight destroyers under Rear Admiral Merrill, as well as the Third Amphibious Force, now commanded by Rear Admiral Wilkinson.[1]

Admiral Sherman's and Admiral Merrill's forces carried out the preliminary air and sea bombardments to the north and south, and on the morning of November 1 Admiral Wilkinson's force landed 14,000 marines in Empress Augusta Bay with little loss, under cover of local sea and air bombardment. Resistance afterward stiffened; but in time the marines established an extensive perimeter, and airfields were constructed as planned.

On the night after the landing the Japanese made their first attempt to interfere, sending all available ships from Rabual. This force—two heavy cruisers, two light cruisers, and six destroyers—advanced to-

---

[1] Admiral Turner had been transferred to take charge of the amphibious force being formed for the Central Pacific campaign.

ward Bougainville, but it was intercepted during the middle watch by Admiral Merrill's light cruisers (*Montpelier, Cleveland, Columbia,* and *Denver*) and destroyers and engaged with radar-directed gunfire. The result was a notable victory. The Japanese, believing themselves to be engaged by a far stronger force, were driven back with the loss of the light cruiser *Sendai* and a destroyer, several other destroyers being badly damaged. An American destroyer was crippled and had to be towed away, and in its slow retreat Admiral Merrill's force suffered a heavy air attack the next morning. Some damage was sustained, but gunfire, rendered many times more effective by the use of the new proximity fuses,[2] shot down more than a quarter of the attackers and no ship was lost.

The Japanese had used the forces immediately available for this interference. But even before the Empress Augusta Bay landing, their naval command was beginning to react strongly to the threat to Bougainville. Though they may not have realized it at the time, the Japanese had in fact reached a crisis, and the action they now took resulted in losses that crippled the striking power of their main fleet and thus profoundly affected the course of the war. Admiral Yamamoto had always, rightly or wrongly, judged it necessary to fight to the death in the Solomons, believing that if the Americans succeeded there they would gain such confidence as would inevitably carry them forward to further victories. Now he was dead, and his successor, Admiral Koga, foreseeing an American advance in the Central Pacific when enough of the new carriers were ready, believed that it was there and not in the Solomons that he should fight the decisive battle. With the shore-based aircraft on the Marshall Islands to augment his carrier forces, he thought that victory was well within his reach. But, if it was to be achieved, there must be no more heavy expenditure in the Solomons. Delaying actions must be fought there and in the Bismarck Archipelago, but liabilities must be strictly limited.

Events, however, overrode Admiral Koga's reasoned views. He had twice advanced from Truk into the Marshalls in anticipation of an American move. But nothing had happened; and, since the Japanese position in southern Bougainville had been bypassed and Rabaul was more directly threatened, he consented to the use once more of the Combined Fleet's striking power in the Solomons. The carrier-borne fighters of the Japanese Third Fleet had already been ordered to Rabaul,

---

[2] Proximity fuses are fuses actuated by radar which explode the shell as it passes close to an aircraft, instead of at a preset time. The type in use were also known as VT fuses.

and now that the blow had fallen and the Rabaul surface forces had been repulsed by Admiral Merrill, Koga ordered the remainder of the Third Fleet's carrier aircraft and the cruisers and destroyers of the Second Fleet to follow.

This was a move for which Admiral Sherman's carriers had been waiting. The Japanese forces were reported approaching Rabaul on November 4, and on the 5th Sherman struck. Fighters from the Solomons provided his force with a combat air patrol, enabling him to attack with the full strength of his carrier-borne aircraft, and the blow he delivered left the enemy reeling. Many of the Japanese aircraft were destroyed, with a loss of only eight American planes, and many ships were hit. None were sunk, but the heavy cruisers *Maya* and *Mogami* were so badly damaged that they had to return to Japan for repairs, and many other cruisers and destroyers were damaged and forced to return to Truk as soon as they could be made seaworthy.

A week later, on November 11, the attack on Rabaul was repeated; for this second blow Admiral Sherman's force was joined by another carrier force from the Central Pacific Command, the new big carriers *Essex* and *Bunker Hill* and the light carrier *Independence* under Rear Admiral Montgomery. There were now fewer Japanese ships to strike at, but a destroyer was sunk and once again the Japanese aircraft, some of which were on the point of returning to Truk, were severely handled, and many were destroyed with slight loss to the Americans. A return blow at Montgomery's carriers during the afternoon resulted only in further severe losses to the Japanese striking force, nearly fifty aircraft being shot down by guns and fighters without any damage being sustained by the ships.

These heavy losses spelled the end of Admiral Koga's hopes of opposing the Americans in the Marshall Islands. With the destruction of the Third Fleet's air squadrons, the Combined Fleet was virtually impotent; it could only look on from its base at Truk while Admiral Spruance started his victorious assaults on the atolls of the Gilbert and Marshall groups (see chap. 19). By February 1944 it was no longer advisable even to remain at Truk. On February 10, therefore, the Third Fleet was sent to Singapore to train the air squadrons being formed to replace those destroyed, and the Second Fleet withdrew to the Palau Islands.

Meanwhile the American position in Bougainville was becoming fully secure. The Japanese positions to north and south were being deprived of seaborne supplies, and from time to time their airfields were bombarded. American surface forces could move with increasing freedom in the area between Bougainville and St. George's Channel (separating New Britain from New Ireland), and on the night of November 23, 1943, a last incursion of Japanese destroyers into these waters was driven back with heavy losses. Five American destroyers under Captain Burke intercepted an equal number of Japanese off Buka Island. Three of the enemy were sunk without loss to the Americans, and the other two were chased to within 60 miles of the airfields of Rabaul before Captain Burke felt impelled to haul off.

We return now to New Guinea. After the capture of Finschhafen in October, General MacArthur's next aim was to deprive the Japanese of their airfields at the western end of New Britain, so that his ships could advance more freely through Vitiaz Strait, which separates that island from New Guinea. To accomplish this objective, two separate operations were needed, one at Arawe on the south side and the other near Cape Gloucester at the western extreme.

The Arawe airfield was only a subsidiary and was not heavily defended. The landing there on December 15, 1943, was therefore on a comparatively small scale, employing only a regimental combat team. One part of this assault, attempted as a surprise before dawn (but in moonlight), was driven back with severe loss, with the consequence that thereafter attempts at night landings without supporting fire were eschewed, and all future assaults of the Seventh Amphibious Force took place in daylight and were preceded by heavy bombardments. The main landing, however, supported by destroyers, was successful, and the position with its airfields was soon captured.

The Cape Gloucester operation was on a heavier scale, employing a marine division with some additions; there were about 12,000 men in the assault, and an equal number following up. Bombardment by Rear Admiral Crutchley's cruisers (two Australian and two American) and destroyers preceded the landing, and there were few casualties in the assault itself. Some loss, however, was suffered from a heavy air attack which got home on the tank landing ships and some destroyers, sinking one of the latter. After the landing there was hard fighting for the two airfields, but by December 30 the marines had captured both. The American position was then firmly established, though the marines had to continue to fight for many weeks to enlarge their lodgment area to a more comfortable size.

To eliminate the remaining Japanese forces on the peninsula that ends at Finschhafen, so as to establish complete domination of Vitiaz Strait, another landing followed as soon after the Cape Gloucester assault as the landing craft could be reorganized. This was at Saidor, 90 miles west of Finschhafen, where a regimental combat team was landed

253

on January 2, 1944, encountering little opposition. A considerable remnant of the Japanese who were retreating before the Australian advance from the eastward were trapped, and some of those who tried to escape by barges were frustrated by American motor torpedo boats. On February 8 the advancing Australians joined hands with the Saidor force; by that time all organized resistance in the area had been broken up, the majority of the enemy having been killed.

Freedom of passage through Vitiaz Strait was an important step forward in the encirclement of Rabaul and the subsidiary enemy base at Kavieng (in New Ireland), 150 miles to the northwest. The Japanese were in fact already hard put to it to maintain their forces in the Bismarck Archipelago; their strength was waning, and, if an island could be captured to the westward of them which afforded a harbor and airfields, they would be rendered impotent and would have no more influence on General MacArthur's advance. Such an island was Manus, the largest of the Admiralty Islands, 350 miles west-northwest of Rabaul. It was well placed, and its harbor was the most commodious in all these seas.

Manus, then, was the next major objective; but further pressure on Rabaul and Kavieng did not await its capture. The Fifth Army Air Force was constantly attacking both the ports themselves and their sea communications, scoring a notable success against a southbound convoy 100 miles northwest of Kavieng on February 15. From the other wing Admiral Halsey's forces, which included a powerful component of land-based aircraft, were constantly hammering at the enemy, and they now so dominated the waters west and north of Bougainville that they could bombard by gunfire as well as from the air. Admiral Sherman's carrier aircraft struck at warships in Kavieng on January 1 and again on January 4; and on February 18 two groups of destroyers bombarded Rabaul and Kavieng, respectively. Meanwhile the isolation of the Japanese remaining in Bougainville was made even more stringent by the occupation of the Green Islands, 50 miles north-northwest of Buka, on February 15.

The capture of Manus Island did not prove so straightforward an operation as had been expected. It was originally planned for April, but because air reports indicated that it was only lightly held it was decided to anticipate the planned attack by a landing on a comparatively small scale at the end of February. Amphibious scouts, who had landed a few days in advance, brought back news of Japanese strength far greater than had been reported from the air; but nevertheless the enterprise went forward, and on February 29 a brigade of the First Cavalry Division (dismounted) was landed on Los Negros, one of the islands bounding the extensive harbor. The assault, covered by a destroyer bombardment, was effected with few casualties; but soon afterward the situation was found to be one of serious difficulty. The scouts' reports of Japanese strength had been fully justified, and the Americans were hard put to it to avoid being driven back into the sea. Improvised reinforcements from New Guinea were rushed forward, hard fighting restored the situation, and finally the enemy was overcome. By March 16 his main resistance had been broken, and on the 24th the last position interfering with the use of the harbor was captured. Thereafter the harbor and airfields of Manus were rapidly developed into the principal naval base on the southern route to the Philippines.

While the occupation of Manus was being completed, Admiral Halsey was delivering his last blows to the northward. On March 20 Emirau Island, 100 miles west-northwest of Kavieng, was seized by marines landed by the Third Amphibious Force, and at the same time Kavieng itself was bombarded by battleships and destroyers.

With the elimination of all danger from the Bismarck Archipelago, General MacArthur could continue his advance along the New Guinea coast. He was confronted by a strong Japanese force (perhaps 50,000 men) centered on Wewak, 250 miles west of Saidor; but he intended to bypass this opposition, striking at Hollandia, 250 miles farther along the coast, 12 miles inland of which were some useful airfields.

This operation was by far the largest and boldest yet undertaken by the Seventh Amphibious Force. The troops to be landed comprised two divisions of the Sixth Army with ancillaries, amounting to 70,000 men in all with 25,000 in the assault; the troops must embark at Finschhafen and at Goodenough Island (north of Milne Bay), entailing a passage of 700 miles and more by the route that must be followed. Because the landings were to be so far ahead of any American airfields, special measures were needed for air support. Hitherto this support had been provided by the Fifth Army Air Force, fighter protection being effected through fighter direction officers in the cruisers and in specially equipped destroyers, the latter sometimes stationed well to seaward to intercept Japanese formations before they could reach the scene of the landing. But for this new move aircraft carriers were needed. Eight escort carriers, under Rear Admiral Davison, were therefore provided for close support. In the offing, both to assist with further air support and to provide cover against any attempt at interference by the Japanese fleet, was to be Vice Admiral Mitscher's Fast Carrier Force whose operations (recounted in chap. 19) were beginning to dominate the Central Pacific. Three landings were planned, the two main ones in Tanahmerah Bay and Humboldt Bay (the site of Hollandia) and a subsidiary one at Aitape, 100 miles to the eastward (i.e., toward

Wewak), to hold back any Japanese forces that might try to interfere from that direction. Under the general direction of Vice Admiral Kinkaid, now the commander of the Seventh Fleet (i.e., General MacArthur's naval commander), the amphibious and supporting forces were commanded as before by Rear Admiral Barbey, who also had the immediate direction of the Tanahmerah Bay assault.

After passing through Vitiaz Strait, the fleet of warships (including a supporting force of five cruisers and ten destroyers under Rear Admiral Crutchley), transports, fast troop carriers (converted destroyers), landing ships (LST), and landing craft (LCI) steered to the northward to keep well clear of Wewak. It passed close to Manus and turned in toward the coast only when almost abreast of the landing places. Complete strategical surprise was achieved, the Japanese being prepared only for an attack on Wewak, and on the morning of April 22 all landings were quickly effected with slight loss. The Fast Carrier Force bombed the airfields but found few Japanese aircraft to engage, for heavy damage had been inflicted some weeks previously in long-distance raids by the Army Air Force. Soon the whole position was safely in American hands. The large enemy forces at Wewak were virtually isolated. Fighting was needed to keep them hemmed in between the American forces at Aitape and the Australians advancing from Saidor, and a remnant continued to hold out till almost the end of the war. But they were no longer an obstacle in General MacArthur's path, and, with supplies dwindling and without aircraft, they soon ceased to cause anxiety.

After the occupation of Hollandia further landings succeeded one another with remarkable speed. On May 17 a regimental combat team was landed at Wakde Island, 70 miles farther along the coast, and at Toem inshore of it; ten days later the next step was taken, an assault on Biak Island, 200 miles farther on.

Biak was needed because it was important to have airfields well forward from which bombers could strike at the Moluccas, and it had been found that the Hollandia airstrips could not be made usable for heavy bombers for several months. But to move so soon so far in advance of the Central Pacific operations involved some evident risks. The Japanese Third Fleet (aircraft carriers) had returned from Singapore, and the Combined Fleet was concentrated in the southern Philippines, with strong land-based naval air forces in the Palau Islands. Unless, therefore, a powerful covering force could be provided, this new thrust would be exposed to attack from seaward in great strength. But no covering force was available. The Fast Carrier Force, fully occupied in the opening moves of the Marianas campaign, could not be spared.

Nonetheless, General MacArthur decided to advance, knowing the risk and accepting it.

Though there were some justifiably anxious times during the days that followed, the result was a complete success, vigorous action by Allied forces and an erroneous air report on the Japanese side combining to prevent interference from seaward. The landing of about 7,500 men was effected on May 27 without much opposition, but thereafter not only did resistance stiffen but the enemy attempted reinforcement from the Philippines. Admiral Toyoda,[3] commander in chief of the Combined Fleet, ordered a cruiser squadron carrying an amphibious brigade to proceed to Biak, arranged for air cover from the Palau Islands (500 miles north of Biak), and prepared to support the move with stronger surface forces. Fortunately for the Allies, the initial enemy moves were followed by a signal from a Japanese aircraft reporting Admiral Crutchley's cruisers (the Australian *Australia* and *Shropshire* and the American *Phoenix, Nashville,* and *Boise*) as a carrier force. Because of this report, on June 2, the Japanese movements were countermanded.

Meanwhile the fighting ashore was heavy, the Allied cruisers and destroyers assisting the army with flanking gunfire. A few days later there was again a threat from seaward, for the Japanese were making another attempt to send reinforcements, this time in destroyers. The approaching enemy forces, sighted by air reconnaissance on June 8, were heavily attacked by bombers of the Fifth Air Force, one destroyer being sunk. The remainder came on, but that night they were intercepted and driven back by Admiral Crutchley's force as they were approaching the land, a hasty retreat saving them from serious damage. Still not willing to give up hope, and perhaps realizing by this time that there were no American carriers in the neighborhood, Admiral Toyoda ordered the battleships *Yamato* and *Musashi* with three cruisers and three destroyers to the scene. But before they had gone far they too were recalled. The shape of the American design against the Marianas was now beginning to reveal itself, and the Combined Fleet had to be concentrated to meet it.

On Biak Island hard fighting continued, but by June 21 all airfields were in American hands. Though resistance continued here and there throughout July, American aircraft were being brought forward in large numbers. To provide wider scope for the powerful air forces at General

---

[3] Admiral Toyoda succeeded to the command after Admiral Koga had been lost while on air passage between the Palau Islands and the Philippines on March 31, 1944.

MacArthur's disposal (a new formation, the Thirteenth Air Force, had recently been added to the Fifth), two more amphibious operations followed. These were landings on Noemfoor Island (west of Biak) on July 2, and at Sansapor on the north coast of New Guinea's western peninsula on July 30. Neither landing was seriously contested. Although there were still isolated Japanese garrisons in several areas, western New Guinea now provided General MacArthur with firm bases for air attacks on the Moluccas and the Philippines, and for the seaborne expeditions that were soon to follow.

19

ADVANCE IN THE PACIFIC, CENTRAL ROUTE: *Tarawa to the Marianas*

THE CENTRAL PACIFIC operations, which were to employ the main fighting strength of the United States Navy during the first half of 1944, developed along lines shaped by the interaction of several major factors. Hitherto, during the period covered by the first part of chapter 18, the principal thrusts had been made in New Guinea and the Solomons. The former had seemed the only route by which the Philippines, the supposed key to the Asiatic position, could be approached with the step-by-step support of strong land-based air forces. An offensive in the Solomons had first been essential for guarding the communications to New Guinea, and had later developed into something of a trial of strength between the opposing navies. But as the New Guinea offensive was getting into its stride and an advance to the western end of that island and beyond was in sight, further naval operations were needed to cover the seaward flank of General MacArthur's forces. The comparatively local threat from Rabaul might be dealt with from the Solomons, but beyond that was the possibility of interference by the Japanese Combined Fleet from its base at Truk or from other bases farther to the westward.

The problem of advancing to the westward in the face of increasing resistance might, perhaps, have been grappled with on the lines of throwing the main weight of the navy onto the southern route, where all forces would then advance in what would be in effect one massive concentration. But the alternative strategy of an advance through the Central Pacific, though necessarily starting much farther from the Philippines, had several possible advantages. For one thing, if increasing strength in carrier-borne aircraft made it possible to take longer steps, it might prove a quicker form of progress than could be achieved in the New Guinea campaign. For another, there would probably be

259

difficulty in deploying the whole massive strength of American arms in the southern theater, with its comparative paucity of good harbors and its still roundabout supply routes from the United States. Moreover, if the American forces in the Pacific could indeed deploy sufficient strength to advance rapidly along both routes, they would keep the enemy in uncertainty as to the direction of the vital stroke and so confuse his strategy, for an advance in the Central Pacific would bring American forces, and particularly land-based aircraft, within striking distance of Japan itself.

It was with these general ideas in mind that the first steps were taken in the autumn of 1943. By the end of the year the strategy of mutually supporting advances north and south of the equator had been accepted by the Combined Chiefs of Staff, and early in the new year a provisional plan to carry the former via the Marianas to the Palau Islands was prepared. An important feature of the early stages was to be the destruction of the Japanese Combined Fleet at Truk, or at least its eviction therefrom if it could not be brought to battle. But before this could be achieved there must be an assault on Japan's eastern bastions in the atolls of the Gilbert and Marshall groups.

The overall control of Central Pacific strategy was the province of Admiral Nimitz, who had been designated commander in chief of the Pacific Ocean Areas as well as commander in chief of the Pacific Fleet, a post that gave him control of all forces outside General MacArthur's Southwest Pacific Command.[1] Always accessible to advice, though with clear views of his own, Admiral Nimitz handled his subordinate commanders with a tactful firmness, well salted with humor, which never failed to win their support and always elicited the best from them and their men. Only in the ambiguous orders he gave to the Third Fleet before the invasion of the Philippines (see chap. 20) did he seem to lack his habitual sureness of touch. Fortunately there were no ill effects, and he continued to receive the trust and admiration of the whole navy, as well as of the soldiers and airmen in his command, until the end of the war and after.

Under Admiral Nimitz, the forces engaged, including land-based aircraft and the joint expeditionary force, were allocated to the Fifth Fleet,[2] commanded by Vice Admiral Spruance who had the immediate responsibility for conducting the operations. Though it was to grow

[1] The South-West Pacific Area comprised the central and northern Solomons, the Bismarck Archipelago, New Guinea, the Moluccas, the Philippines, Borneo, Celebes, and everything to the southward thereof.

[2] At this time the United States Navy was organized into numbered fleets, odd numbers in the Pacific and even numbers in the Atlantic.

steadily, Admiral Spruance's fleet was at first not a large one, barely reaching parity with the Japanese in aircraft carriers. But new carriers were rapidly coming forward. By October the *Essex*, the *Yorktown* (new), the *Lexington* (new), and the *Bunker Hill* were ready for service, as were also the light carriers (built on cruiser hulls) *Independence, Princeton, Belleau Wood, Cowpens*, and *Monterey*.[3] With these, supported by the new battleships, all six of the *Washington* class, and now the larger and faster *Iowa* and *New Jersey*, a start could be made. The first step, the seizure of Tarawa and Makin in the Gilbert Islands, was therefore planned for November 1943.

Islands in the Gilbert group were chosen as the first objective because they were the only ones within effective bombing range of American-held airfields. In general, the Marshall and Gilbert Islands lie about 2,000 miles from Pearl Harbor, but the Gilberts are only 700 miles from Funafuti in the Ellice Islands where bombers of the Seventh Army Air Force were already stationed; additional airstrips were constructed on other islands of this group. At this time it was considered important that any positions to be attacked by the amphibious force should be subjected to preliminary air bombardment over a period of days or even weeks, a task it was thought could not be assigned to carrier-borne aircraft alone. It seemed, also, that prolonged preliminary bombardment might be very effective, for the targets were concentrated and well defined. Though the diameter of an atoll lagoon might be anything up to 40 miles or more, usually only two or three islands on the surrounding reef were habitable, and on these there was often only just room for the airfield, to which the position owed its importance, and the defenses. The latter, it was hoped, might be pounded to pieces, and the troops should then be able to land from the smooth water of the lagoon without difficulty. But there was a countervailing disadvantage: there could be no tactical surprise. If any enemy survived the bombardment and held on resolutely, as the Japanese would certainly be expected to do, the inevitable frontal assault would be an expensive one.

After several days of preliminary air raids, culminating in heavy bombardments by carrier aircraft and battleships (old as well as modern, thirteen in all), Tarawa and Makin, lying 100 miles apart, were assaulted on November 21.[4] On Makin there were only about 400 de-

---

[3] Carriers of the *Essex* class normally carried ninety-seven aircraft; light carriers had between forty and sixty, depending on the proportion of fighters to bombers and torpedo planes.

[4] November 21 is the eastern hemisphere date. Some accounts of the Gilbert and Marshall operations assign them to the western hemisphere, i.e., the Pearl Harbor, date, and thus place the Tarawa and Makin assaults on November 20.

fenders, and an assault by 6,500 infantry soon had the position in hand. But at Tarawa there were some 4,500 Japanese, most of whom had survived the preliminary bombardment in their dugouts; they defended the small islands of Betio, where they were concentrated, with great vigor. To add to the difficulties of the invading marines, an irregular tide caused their landing craft to ground on the edge of the reef, half a mile offshore, whence they had to wade or be ferried by the few amphibians of the initial assault which had not been knocked out.

The resulting casualties were very heavy. Few of the initial assault got as far as the defensive seawall, and very few penetrated beyond it. But once more the invincibility of the United States Marines pulled them through. All reserves were thrown in, and after nearly four days of heavy fighting, during which more than 6,000 marines were landed, the defenders were at last exterminated. The cost to the marines had been nearly 1,000 killed and more than 2,000 wounded, and there had been many naval casualties in addition.

During this operation the Japanese fleet, destitute of carrier aircraft because of its heavy losses at Rabaul at the beginning of the month (see p. 252, above), had been unable to interfere. Land-based aircraft and submarines had done what they could. One of the latter sank the escort carrier *Liscome Bay* with heavy loss of life. Of the many aircraft that tried to attack from airfields in the Marshalls, mostly at dusk, one succeeded in torpedoing the light carrier *Independence*, though without damaging her vitally. But these were the only ship casualties.

Once the fighting was over, the object of these operations was soon achieved: rehabilitation of the airfields on these islands and on Apamama (80 miles south of Tarawa), which had been seized without opposition. Before long bombers of the Seventh Army Air Force were established there in preparation for the next step, the attack on the Marshall Islands.

For the advance into the Marshalls it was decided to strike boldly nearly 200 miles beyond the Japanese-held atolls of the eastern edge (Wotje, Maloelap, Mille, and Jaluit) and to capture the large Kwajalein atoll, which included defended islands at its northern and southern ends (Roi and Kwajalein Island), 40 miles apart. At the same time forces would be landed at the unoccupied atoll of Majuro (250 miles southeast of Kwajalein), which had a particularly good anchorage for a large number of ships and room for airstrips. During and prior to the amphibious attack on Kwajalein, the Japanese airfields on the other atolls would be neutralized by air attack. The attack would also extend to Eniwetok (350 miles west-northwest of Kwajalein), through which reinforcing aircraft might be staged to the eastern atolls. The task of neutralizing the Japanese airfields in this way was divided among three organizations. Mille, Jaluit, and some other islands to the southward would be the care of the Seventh Army Air Force working from their new bases in the Gilberts. Wake Island, which lies 600 miles north of Kwajalein, would be hit by aircraft from Hawaii routed via Midway Island. All the above would be directed by Rear Admiral Hoover, Admiral Spruance's commander of land-based aircraft. The middle islands, Wotje, Maloelap, and later Eniwetok, would be the targets of the carrier force. The latter would, of course, also provide the aircraft for bombarding Kwajalein prior to the assault.

As in the Gilbert operations, the amphibious force was commanded by Rear Admiral Turner; it included some 50,000 assault troops, marine and army, under Major General H. M. Smith of the Marine Corps, a conspicuously forceful officer who had also been in command of the landing forces at Tarawa and Makin and was to continue to make his mark in two further assaults. Sailing from Pearl Harbor, the two parts into which the force had been divided arrived off their objectives on February 1 (eastern hemisphere date) for the preliminary bombardment and the landing of advanced artillery on adjacent islets. Next morning the assaults went in; and so well had the lessons of Tarawa been learned that neither at Roi nor at Kwajalein Island were there heavy casualties. Each of these two bastions of the lagoon had been subjected to more than twice the weight of bombardment put into Tarawa, and steps had been taken to ensure that the battleships' shells (eight 16-inch battleships took part) hit at a steep angle of descent, as opposed to the close-range flat-trajectory fire of the earlier operation. The artillery that had been landed on adjacent islets also proved its value: a large number of the defenders, probably more than half, were killed before the assault troops landed, and most of the rest were too dazed for effective resistance. The assaulting forces, too, had now been provided with a larger number of landing vehicles, that is, amphibious tanks and armored troop carriers. As a result, Roi was secured on the day of the assault, only a remnant of the original 3,500 defenders holding out on a neighboring islet. Kwajalein Island, garrisoned by 5,000 men, took a few days more to clear up, but by the afternoon of February 5 all resistance was at an end there also, and the airstrips on both islands were soon in operation. With Majuro, too, in American hands and an airstrip being rapidly constructed there, the Japanese islands to the eastward were now dominated, and thereafter they were no more than a minor annoyance.

Up to this time the important matter of fulfilling the supply requirements of the large number of warships engaged in the operations had
been met mainly by the expedient of fueling at sea from a fleet train
of oilers which moved round from one prearranged mid-ocean position to another. Additional supplies came from, and all repairs were
made at, Pearl Harbor. But with a further advance to the westward in
prospect, returns to the main base could no longer be afforded, and
a mobile service squadron had therefore been formed which was
eventually to fulfill almost every requirement of the fleet. This squadron
was brought to Majuro, which for the next few months was to be the
fleet's advanced base. There it provided all that was needed by warships returning to harbor, including replacement aircraft for the carriers, and from there it could send out the ships needed as a train for
supplying the fleet at sea—oilers, ammunition ships, escort carriers with
spare aircraft, and store carriers.

So successful had been the Kwajalein operations that it was decided
to follow them by capturing Eniwetok, the northwestern of the Marshall
atolls, and so rounding off the position preparatory to the next major
step. This would be either to Truk (650 miles west-southwest of Eniwetok) or to the Marianas (1,000 miles west), a point that had not
yet been decided. But whatever the eventual objective, an immediate
air bombardment of Truk by the Fast Carrier Force was indicated, to
cover the Eniwetok operation and perhaps to deal a heavy blow at
the Combined Fleet if it remained in those waters, either in harbor or
at sea.

The American Fast Carrier Force, which had grown to six large and
five light carriers, with eight fast battleships, six or eight cruisers, and
some thirty or forty destroyers, was becoming as powerful a fleet as
has ever dominated an ocean. Though its title was merely Task Force
58,[5] it was in fact the main fleet of the United States Navy—in British
parlance of earlier days, the Grand Fleet. Command of this force
was exercised by Vice Admiral Mitscher, a veteran naval aviator who
had been captain of the *Hornet* at the Battle of Midway; except for a
three-month period at the end of the year, he was to continue in command, under Admirals Spruance and Halsey alternately, until the

[5] The American task force system was used originally for the temporary organization of ships drawn from various formations and working in company for
a particular task. By this time, however, the organization had in many instances
become a semipermanent one. Sometimes both semipermanent and temporary
systems were in use simultaneously, a force retaining its semipermanent number
while assuming another force or group number temporarily for a special phase.
The first figure in the number denoted the fleet; the second, the force; and the

end of May 1945. But as it was the main fighting strength of the Fifth Fleet, general direction of the operations of the Fast Carrier Force fell to the fleet commander, Admiral Spruance, who flew his flag in the heavy cruiser *Indianapolis*. Task Force 58 was organized in four groups, each under a rear admiral, and as a rule the battleships were divided among these groups, where their heavy antiaircraft fire was an important additional protection to the carriers. But whenever there was a probability of surface action against strong Japanese forces, all eight battleships, with some cruisers and destroyers, worked as a separate force under Rear Admiral Lee.

For the bombardment of Truk, Admiral Spruance took with him three of the four groups of Task Force 58, leaving the fourth to cover the assault on Eniwetok.[6] Sailing from Majuro, he reached a position 8 miles northeast of Truk at dawn on February 17. From there Admiral Mitscher's aircraft struck. First were the Hellcat fighters, which surprised the Japanese and shot down more than a hundred of the defending fighters with little loss to themselves. Then, with more fighters to escort them, came the Avengers, some with torpedoes and some with bombs, to attack the Japanese ships. But here, as we know, they were disappointed. The loss of Kwajalein and the resulting American domination of the Marshalls had caused Admiral Koga to withdraw the Combined Fleet just a week before. The ships that remained, however, were heavily punished; nearly all were destroyed, some that tried to escape receiving their *coup de grâce* from Admiral Spruance's battleships and cruisers. A light cruiser, a training cruiser, and three destroyers were sunk as well as many minor vessels and cargo ships; and next morning an additional air striking force, sent in to complete the business, sank another destroyer. In the intervening night the Japanese had done what they could with their few remaining aircraft, and had succeeded in hitting the carrier *Intrepid* with a torpedo that put her temporarily out of control. But they had no other success.

From Truk, after fueling in mid-ocean, the Fast Carrier Force next headed for the Marianas, 600 miles to the northwest, to probe the de-

---

third, where necessary, the group. Thus Task Group 58.3 was the third group of the eighth force of the Fifth Fleet. When, as recounted later, Admiral Halsey alternated with Admiral Spruance as fleet commander, it was thought convenient that he bring with him the fleet designation assigned to him in the Solomons campaign, namely, Third Fleet. The result was that, though the composition of the fleet remained unchanged, the numbers of all forces were altered and the Fast Carrier Force became Task Force 38 instead of Task Force 58, possibly to the mild confusion of the enemy.

[6] For the Truk operation Admiral Spruance flew his flag in the battleship *New Jersey*. When in company with the Fast Carrier Force, the flagship (whether *New Jersey* or *Indianapolis*) usually took station in Task Group 58.3.

fenses of Saipan, Tinian, and Guam. In particular, aerial photographs were needed if these islands were later to be assaulted, for at this time there was no information about them other than that obtainable from prewar charts and maps. With the enemy thoroughly on the alert, the approach was not unhampered; during the afternoon of February 22, while still eighteen hours short of its launching position, Admiral Mitscher's force was discovered by a Japanese aircraft which succeeded in reporting it before being driven off. That night aircraft from Saipan and Tinian made many attempts to attack, all of which had to be, and were, staved off by the gunfire of the screening battleships, cruisers, and destroyers, since the Americans could not afford the delay of constantly turning into the wind, a northeast trade, to operate night fighters. A further attack soon after daylight got partly home on Rear Admiral Montgomery's group (*Essex* and *Yorktown* and the light carrier *Belleau Wood*), but most of the attackers were shot down and no serious damage was done.

By this time the air striking force, Hellcats and Avengers, had taken off, bound for Saipan and Tinian. Many Japanese aircraft were shot down over the islands or destroyed on the ground for the loss of only six Americans; shipping was sunk and damaged; and photographs were taken of the defenses of these islands and of Guam, 100 miles southwest of Tinian. This done, the strike aircraft were recovered and the Fast Carrier Force returned to its base at Majuro, 1,500 miles to the eastward.

While this raid was in progress, the attack on Eniwetok, directed by Rear Admiral Hill, had proceeded as planned. After a heavy air and ship bombardment the main island of this large atoll was captured within a few hours, on February 18; and within a few days all the other islands round the lagoon, assaulted by marines and infantry, were in American hands. Seabees at once started to develop an advanced base for further operations, whatever form they should take. Before long the decision on this point was made; the next step would be to the Marianas, with Saipan as the first objective.

So rapid and successful had been the advance in the Central Pacific that a strong current of naval opinion was questioning the existing plan of an approach to Japan via the Philippines. It seemed that, once the Marianas were occupied, a more northerly route might well be feasible and that, by the close investment of the enemy's homelands which this occupation could bring about, the war might be concluded more quickly and with less bloodshed. This view was strongly supported by the Air Force, for with Saipan in American hands the new Superfortress bombers could devastate the Japanese economy. As a matter of theoretical strategy there was much to be said for such a plan, and it was in fact supported by the Strategical Survey Committee, comprising one retired officer from each of the three services. But on more general grounds it could not be justified. For nearly eighteen months General MacArthur's army, navy, and air forces had slogged their way forward, and a triumphant return to the Philippines, which he had left in such tragic circumstances, was ever in the General's mind. To tell him and his men that they were no longer wanted for this purpose would have dissipated a fund of *esprit de corps* which could not be directly employed elsewhere, as well as putting a severe strain on their fighting spirit. And no one could yet be sure that the northern route could achieve all that was needed. The decision, therefore, of the President was that the two advances were to continue on their parallel routes until they united for the invasion of the Philippines. There Nimitz' fleet would support MacArthur's army.

During the next three months, while preparations were being made for the assault on Saipan, there was a lull in amphibious operations. But there was little leisure for the Fast Carrier Force. Late in March it again left Majuro, this time to strike at the Palau Islands, 2,200 miles to the westward.

As in the preceding operation, the approach of the Fast Carrier Force from the eastward was reported, and the enemy tried to attack during the evening before it reached its launching position. But this time the delay involved in keeping defending fighters in the air was accepted, and all attacking aircraft were either shot down or driven off. On the next two days (March 30 and 31) the American aircraft struck. Again, as at Truk, the Japanese ships had not awaited their arrival. The Second Fleet (battleships) had been stationed at the Palau Islands, while the Third Fleet was training new aircraft pilots at Singapore, but it had been withdrawn on March 28 on news of the American approach, a battleship being torpedoed (but not sunk) by an American submarine during the withdrawal. So again the American aircraft found only the defending aircraft and some shipping to hit at. But much damage was done. A destroyer and many cargo ships and tankers were sunk, and the harbor was thickly sown with aircraft mines. About 150 aircraft in all were destroyed here and during subsequent strikes against Yap and Ulithi (300 miles to the northeastward) on March 31 and against Woleai, in the western Carolines, on April 1; these operations cost the Americans in all some twenty-five aircraft lost in combat.

The effectiveness of the attack on the Palau Islands convinced Admiral Koga, who was present, that the Combined Fleet could no longer be based there. At the same time it inclined him to the opinion that the main American thrust would be from New Guinea against Mindanao, and he believed that it might come soon. He therefore ordered his fleet to concentrate in southern Philippine waters despite the still incomplete training of the Third Fleet's aircraft, and he also ordered more aircraft to be flown to the Palau Islands so as to give him the strongest possible concentration of ships and aircraft in the New Guinea–Moluccas–Mindanao–Palau Islands area for a decisive battle. He then left by air for Mindanao but never arrived, his aircraft being lost on passage from some cause unknown. As already noted (see p. 257 n. 3), he was succeeded a few weeks later by Admiral Toyoda.

In mid-April Admiral Mitscher again set out from Majuro with his Carrier Force, this time to cover General MacArthur's Hollandia operations (see chap. 18). This cruise was comparatively uneventful, though there was again some hard fighting over Truk which was raided on April 29 and 30, while the force was on its return passage. The raid was a heavy one but against land installations only, for there was practically nothing left afloat. At the same time (April 30–May 1) battleships, cruisers, and destroyers bombarded installations on Satawal (300 miles west of Truk) and Ponape, in the eastern Carolines.

The capture of Saipan in the Marianas, now to be undertaken, differed in some important respects from the previous amphibious operations in the Central Pacific. The defenders of Saipan, an island of normal formation, 15 miles long by 7 broad, were not so concentrated as on the atoll islets, and when captured the island would give more room for airfields that would take heavy bombers. On the other hand it did not provide the spacious sheltered anchorage of an atoll, and would be of little value as an advanced base for ships. Fortunately a shelf off the southwest coast provided an anchorage, though a deep one, sheltered from the northeast trades, which could be used while the island was being captured and rehabilitated. But it afforded no protection from submarines.

The value of Saipan, when captured, would be that it could be used as an air base to threaten Japan itself, distant 1,300 miles, with constant attack by heavy bombers; this activity would create an important diversion while the main thrust was being made at the Philippines. At the same time it would deny to the Japanese the freedom to move their aircraft along the chain Japan–Iwo Jima–Marianas–Palaus–Moluccas, at present their main lateral communication for the defense of Asia. Though an American footing in the Marianas did not directly endanger the Philippines, still 1,200 miles distant, so important did this point on their outpost line seem to the Japanese that Admiral Toyoda intended to meet any American attack with the full force at his disposal, fleet- and land-based aircraft, knowing that the resulting battle

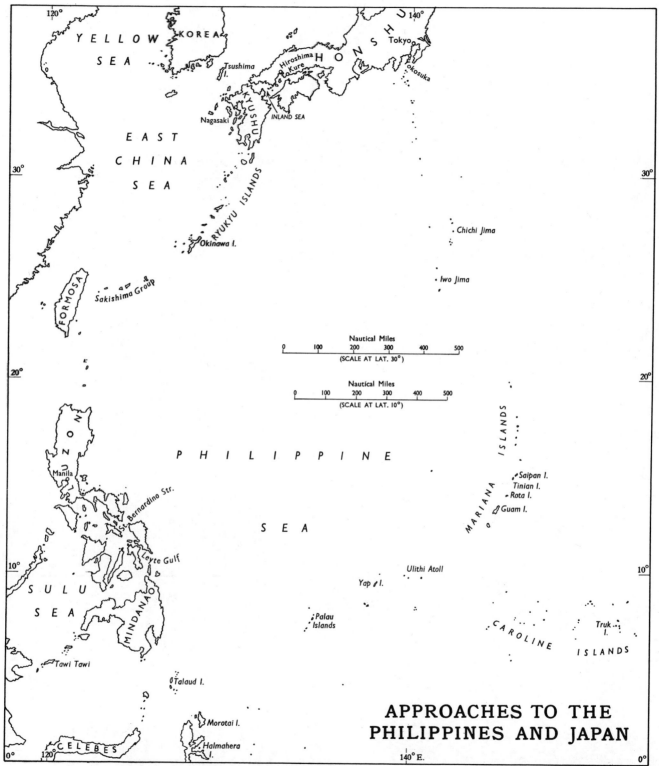

YELLOW SEA
KOREA
Tsushima I.
HONSHU
Tokyo
Hiroshima
Kure
Yokosuka
KYUSHU
Nagasaki
INLAND SEA

EAST CHINA SEA

RYUKYU ISLANDS

Chichi Jima

Okinawa I.

Iwo Jima

FORMOSA
Sakishima Group

Nautical Miles
0   100   200   300   400   500
(SCALE AT LAT. 30°)

Nautical Miles
0   100   200   300   400   500
(SCALE AT LAT. 10°)

LUZON

Manila

Bernardino Str.

Leyte Gulf

PHILIPPINE

SEA

MARIANA   ISLANDS

Saipan I.
Tinian I.
Rota I.
Guam I.

Ulithi Atoll

Yap I.

SULU SEA

MINDANAO

Palau Islands

CAROLINE   ISLANDS

Truk I.

Tawi Tawi

Talaud I.

Morotai I.

CELEBES

Halmahera I.

APPROACHES TO THE PHILIPPINES AND JAPAN

140° E.

Emery Walker Ltd., ph. sc.

would have a decisive effect on Japan's future. He thought it more probable that the American attack would come from the south, and it was therefore in the Palau Islands that, following Admiral Koga's policy, he had concentrated the majority of his land-based aircraft; but he hoped for sufficient warning of the impending blow to enable him to move strong forces to the decisive point in whichever area the attack materialized.

For the invasion of Saipan, and the capture of Guam and Tinian which was to follow, Admiral Turner's amphibious force carried nearly six divisions—three divisions and some additional regiments of marines and two army divisions, all under Lieutenant General H. M. Smith. The force would be supported and covered by the full weight of the Fifth Fleet, which included many old battleships and numerous escort carriers in addition to the ships of the Fast Carrier Force. Early in June these extensive forces sailed from Eniwetok, Kwajalein, and Majuro on the biggest enterprise they had yet undertaken. At the same time the Mobile Service Squadron moved from Majuro to Eniwetok, which now became the fleet's principal advanced base.

The first blows were delivered by Admiral Mitscher's Task Force 58, including seven big carriers (the new *Hornet* and *Wasp* had joined recently) and eight light carriers, with seven fast battleships (under Admiral Lee) and many cruisers and destroyers. On the afternoon of June 11, while the carriers were still 200 miles from the objective, Hellcats raided the airfields of Guam and Rota (the latter a small island between Guam and Tinian), destroying a number of Japanese fighters. For the next two days Hellcats and Avengers struck at airfields on all four islands (Saipan, Tinian, Rota, and Guam), and at such minor shipping as was present. On the second of these days (June 13) the fast battleships bombarded the defenses on the west coasts of Saipan and Tinian for long periods. At the same time General MacArthur's aircraft, working from New Guinea, started a series of heavy attacks on Yap and the Palau Islands to prevent Japanese air reinforcements being moved in from the south.

The next morning (14th) two of Admiral Mitscher's four task groups were sent to the northward to attack Iwo Jima, an island halfway between Saipan and Japan with good airfields which the enemy might use for staging reinforcements from the north. These attacks were made on the following afternoon (15th). Meanwhile the rest of Task Force 58 took up a position just west of Saipan, while the advanced elements of Admiral Turner's amphibious force—old battleships, escort carriers, and minesweepers—were clearing the way for landing. Heavy bombardments on June 14 were followed by a further pounding at daylight on the 15th, under cover of which the assault went in, four regimental combat teams of marines landing simultaneously on the southern part of Saipan's west coast. Despite all the preliminary bombardment, resistance was tough and the casualties were not light; but steady progress was made against a stubborn garrison which totaled some 30,000 men. By June 18 the principal airfield had been captured (it was ready for use by American aircraft two days later), and by June 20 most of the southern part of the island was in American hands. It took, however, nearly three weeks more to overcome organized resistance in the remainder of the island, and many additional weeks before all pockets of Japanese were exterminated.

While this heavy fighting was in progress ashore, all available Japanese naval forces were advancing from the Philippines in a determined attempt to frustrate the invasion. On June 13 the Second and Third fleets had sailed from Tawi Tawi (between Mindanao and Borneo) under Vice Admiral Ozawa of the Third Fleet; this force of three battleships, nine carriers, ten cruisers, and twenty-seven destroyers had then steamed through the central Philippines to San Bernardino Strait. They were not unobserved, for twenty-eight American submarines had been stationed off and to the eastward of the Philippines in readiness for such a move. One of these had reported the fleet's departure from Tawi Tawi; on June 16, as it emerged through San Bernardino Strait into the Philippine Sea (i.e., the waters between the Philippines and the Marianas), another submarine stationed there reported that heavy Japanese forces had passed. In addition the *Yamato* and the *Musashi* with three cruisers and three destroyers, just recalled from the south (see p. 257, above), were on their way to join Ozawa east of the Philippines, and they also were reported by a submarine. The Americans knew, therefore, that for the first time in their Central Pacific operations their covering force of carriers and battleships was to be called on to fight the enemy's main fleet.

The Japanese plan, directed by Admiral Toyoda from his headquarters in Japan, was a very simple one. It was that Ozawa's fleet should advance straight toward Saipan; that its aircraft (some 450), in cooperation with 500 shore-based aircraft working from the Marianas and the Palaus, should then attack Admiral Mitscher's carriers and battleships; and that the surface forces should thereafter break up Admiral Turner's amphibious force and so cripple the land operations. It was hoped that the air battle would be fought near the Marianas so that Ozawa's aircraft would be able to attack at long range, landing thereafter on Guam or Rota for refueling, while the Japanese fleet was still too far from Admiral Mitscher's force for a return stroke.

Had this simple plan been known to Admiral Spruance, it would evidently have been to his advantage to go and meet the Japanese fleet as far from the Marianas as possible. He knew that the main fleet had sailed from Tawi Tawi on June 13, and that some, though not necessarily all, of these ships had emerged through San Bernardino Strait on the 16th. But as to Japanese intentions, he had clearly in mind that on previous occasions (Coral Sea, Midway) they had approached in two bodies converging from widely separated directions, and he believed such tactics to be an established Japanese doctrine. He could not rely on getting long-range warning of the enemy's approach because it was difficult to operate flying boats from the open anchorage at Saipan at the time of the assault; in consequence only four of these craft with one small tender were available. In these circumstances, therefore, Admiral Spruance's main concern was to guard Admiral Turner's ships from attack, whether the blow came from the westward or the southward or both. To this end he recalled the two task groups (58.1 and 58.3) that were operating off Iwo Jima, reinforced Task Force 58 with some of Admiral Turner's cruisers and destroyers, and sent all unwanted shipping of the amphibious force back to the eastward. With the concentrated and reinforced Task Force 58 (groups 58.1 and 58.3 rejoined soon after daylight on the 18th), Admiral Spruance took up a position about 200 miles west of Saipan to await events. Three of the carrier groups were disposed 12 miles apart on a north–south line; the seven battleships with their destroyer screen took station 15 miles to the westward, that is, toward the enemy; and the fourth carrier group was 12 miles north of the battleships.

On the afternoon of June 18 Admiral Spruance received news from a submarine, the *Cavalla*, that she had sighted heavy forces the preceding night approaching from the westward; and there were further indications of the enemy in that direction in the shape of radio jamming signals (presumably to jam the *Cavalla*'s further reports) and a signal believed to emanate from the Japanese flagship. From this information it was estimated that at sunset these ships would be about 300 miles to the westward, and the question arose as to whether the American fleet should close during the night for a concentrated attack at dawn well away from the Marianas airfields. This Admiral Spruance decided against. No certainty existed that there was not another Japanese force to the southward, and his primary aim was to ensure the success of the battle on Saipan. Fighting there was hard and continuous, and any serious damage to Admiral Turner's ships might turn the scale. Admiral Spruance decided, therefore, to retire to the eastward during the night, which would bring his fleet to within 100 miles of the Marianas in the morning. He could then steam to the westward again during the

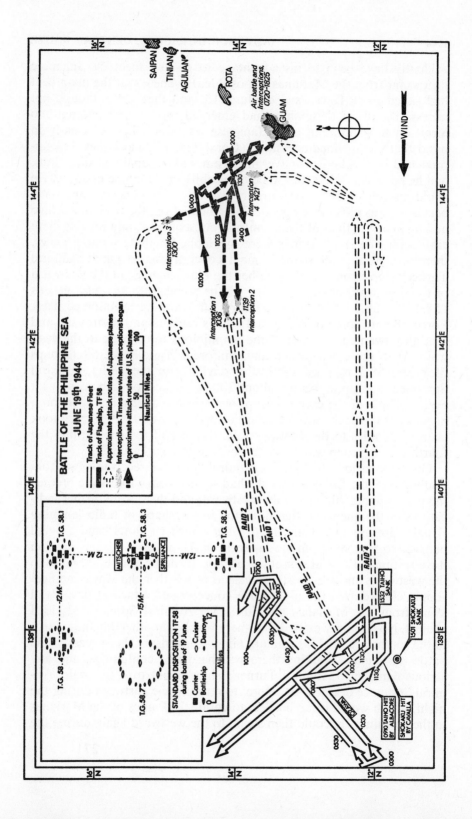

BATTLE OF THE PHILIPPINE SEA
JUNE 19th 1944

Track of Japanese Fleet
Track of Flagship, TF 58
Approximate attack routes of Japanese planes
Interceptions. Times are when interceptions began
Approximate attack routes of U.S. planes

Nautical Miles
0   50   100

SAIPAN
TINIAN
AGUIJAN
ROTA
GUAM
Air battle and Interceptions, 0720-1825

Interception 3 1300
Interception 1 1036
Interception 2 1139
Interception 4 1421

WIND

0400
0200
1023
2000
1330
2400

STANDARD DISPOSITION TF-58
during battle of 19 June
Carrier
Battleship
Cruiser
Destroyer
Miles

T.G. 58.1
T.G. 58.3
T.G. 58.2
T.G. 58.4
T.G. 58.7
MITSCHER
SPRUANCE
12M
15M
12M
12M

RAID 1
RAID 2
RAID 3
RAID 4

1200
0630
0530
0430
1030
1130
1000
0900
0500
0790 TAIHO HIT BY ALBACORE
SHOKAKU HIT BY CAVALLA
0530
0300
1550 SHOKAKU SANK
1532 TAIHO SANK

day, though, being in the trade-wind belt, he would be handicapped in this plan if air attacks developed: when carriers are engaged in battle the constant turning into the wind for launching and landing on makes it impossible to gain much ground to leeward. Perhaps the decision to steam to the eastward till dawn might have been modified had a report been received from a flying boat that gained radar contact with the Japanese fleet at 1:15 A.M. on the 19th; but because of faulty communications, her signal did not get through to Admiral Spruance till eight hours later.

During the same night (18th–19th) Ozawa had marked time, knowing the American fleet's position from reports of shore-based air reconnaissance and hoping, justifiably, that his carriers might be able to send in their air attacks next morning (to refuel at Guam) while the ships remained out of range of a return stroke. Early in the morning his striking forces were launched. But now he was to meet with his first mishap. The *Cavalla* had succeeded in trailing the Japanese fleet during the 18th and the night following, and another submarine, the *Albacore*, was also in touch. At 9 A.M. the latter torpedoed the new carrier *Taiho*, Ozawa's flagship. The damage did not seem to be serious, but six hours later there followed a tremendous gasoline explosion, tearing the ship apart. Ozawa was able to shift his flag, but the ship went down with three-quarters of her crew. Three hours earlier the *Cavalla*, untiring in her efforts to get at the enemy, had reaped her reward by hitting the *Shokaku* with three torpedoes and sinking her. Two of the best Japanese carriers had gone, leaving only the *Zuikaku*, the two converted liners *Hiyo* and *Junyo*, and four smaller carriers.

Meanwhile the air battle was in progress. Admiral Mitscher's dawn searches to a depth of 300 miles had not reached the enemy, but about 10 A.M. the first Japanese striking forces began to appear on the American radar screens. They were met by strong forces of Hellcats, and most were shot down before reaching the fleet. Other forces of Hellcats and Avengers attacked the Guam airfields, thus both damping down the activities of land-based aircraft and hampering the refueling of such carrier aircraft as had survived. All day long the air fighting continued, the Japanese attacking in progressively smaller groups. Of the few that got through the fighter defenses, a small remnant sometimes got past the guns. The battleships *South Dakota* and *Indiana* were hit (the latter by a crashed aircraft), but did not sustain serious damage, and later the carriers *Bunker Hill* and *Wasp* were slightly damaged by near misses. But that was all, and it was of little importance compared with the air battle. In this the Japanese lost in all some 400 aircraft shot down out of about 545 engaged (carrier-borne and land-based), and in addition some had been destroyed in the *Taiho* and the *Shokaku*.

Once more the Japanese carrier air squadrons had been virtually annihilated. In inflicting this heavy punishment, the American fleet had lost in action only 16 of nearly 300 fighters engaged.

Constant maneuvering into the easterly wind had prevented Admiral Spruance from closing the enemy during the day, but at nightfall, leaving one carrier group to cover Saipan, he headed west with the remainder at 23 knots (fuel was becoming a serious consideration), hoping to find the Japanese fleet next morning. In this he was disappointed. Though Ozawa, despite his heavy losses, had not yet abandoned hope of returning to the attack, he had retired to the northwestward with a view to refueling from his fleet train. Once more, therefore, the American dawn search found nothing, and it was not till 3:20 P.M. (June 20) that the enemy ships, which had started fueling, were discovered nearly 300 miles to the northwestward. Despite the lateness of the hour and a distance that was only just within their reach, Admiral Mitscher at once launched striking forces from all carriers. They reached the Japanese fleet, now with only a thin fighter defense, just before sunset, and they hit it hard. The *Hiyo* was sunk and her sister ship the *Junyo* was badly damaged. Many other ships were hit, and the Japanese were at last convinced that they could not resume the attack. Toyoda ordered Ozawa to retire and the fleet once more drew away.

Only twenty American aircraft had been lost during the attack, but the return of the striking forces after dark was hazardous and resulted in many calamities. Few of the pilots had had any recent practice in night landing, and nearly all the aircraft were at the end of their fuel. The inevitable result, despite full landing lights being switched on, was that many were damaged on landing and eighty came down in the sea. Intensive rescue work by destroyers, however, picked up nearly all the crews.

The recovery occupied two hours (9 P.M. to 11 P.M.), during which time Task Force 58 was again heading to the eastward into the wind. Admiral Spruance decided not to send on the battleships in pursuit of the enemy while the recovery was in progress, preferring to keep his force concentrated in the hope of hitting with more air strikes next day. Though he realized that the Japanese air squadrons had been hit hard, he did not yet know that the *Taiho* and the *Shokaku* had been sunk and that there were almost no aircraft remaining. So the whole of his force continued the pursuit in company, and during the night flying boats from Saipan were able to keep in touch with the enemy. Their reports, however, were discouraging: the Japanese were still making a good speed to the northwest, and at dawn they were about 340 miles from Task Force 58. They were evidently slipping out of Admiral Spruance's grasp, and many of his ships were very short of fuel. The chase was continued for a few hours in the hope of picking up stragglers, but then, at dusk on June 21, the whole force turned back to fuel.

It was natural that the Battle of the Philippine Sea should have caused some disappointment in the American Navy. A victory had been won. The enemy had been prevented from interfering with the conquest of Saipan, and his fleet had been sent reeling back to Japan with the loss of three of its five big carriers and nearly all its aircraft. But this result had been achieved in the main, not by the aggressive action of the superior American fleet, but partly by the prowess of two submarines and partly by a defensive battle in which the enemy air squadrons, still not fully trained, battered themselves to pieces, overwhelmed by the superiority of the American fighters in performance, fighting power, and tactical skill. It seemed, in the light of afterknowledge, that more might have been done.

In seeking to judge events, however, it is important not to allow afterknowledge to falsify the contemporary picture. It has always, and rightly, been the traditional view of naval strategy that the destruction of the enemy's main fleet, where such exists, is the most important aim of naval forces. But there is no recorded case of a fleet commander putting his immediate objective into what seemed to him serious jeopardy in order to achieve this wider aim. Surrounded as he is by the fog of war (so quickly dispersed by afterknowledge), his chief difficulties have always lain in deciding what is or is not an undue risk to the affairs for which he is immediately responsible. And so it was here. Admiral Spruance rightly believed that the capture of the Marianas was an important step toward the defeat of Japan, and that a setback there would have delayed victory, perhaps for a long time. And with America's power still growing while Japan's waned, there seemed no reason to suppose that the Japanese fleet, if it avoided a fight to a finish now, could offer more effective resistance later—a view that was justified by events. Admiral Spruance therefore stood on the defensive, refusing to lay open the Saipan operations to a possible thrust from the southward. Had he been able to pierce the fog and clear up his uncertainties about Japanese movements, and had he in consequence advanced to the westward during at least part of the night of June 18–19, and so brought the enemy to decisive action the next day, the Battle of the Philippine Sea would in all probability have ranked with Quiberon Bay (where grave risks were taken), Trafalgar, Tsushima, and Midway as one of the most famous victories of naval history. To that preeminence it did not attain. But the enemy had been defeated and the campaign went forward unchecked.

There was no further serious interference with the conquest of Saipan. In sporadic air attacks by night, the old battleship *Maryland* was damaged by a torpedo and a few minor vessels also received damage. But this did not affect the fighting ashore, which went on unabated until all resistance had been overcome. To damp down the possibility of any heavier air attacks from the northward, one group of Task Force 58 continued at sea, bombarding Pagan Island, 200 miles north of Saipan (June 24–25), Iwo Jima (June 24 and July 4), and Chichi Jima, 150 miles north of Iwo Jima (July 4).

Once the position on Saipan was fully secured, attention could be turned to the other main islands, Guam (the American outpost which had fallen on December 12, 1941) and Tinian. The original intention had been to assault Guam with one marine and one infantry division within a few days of the landing on Saipan. But the sortie of the Japanese fleet, together with the fierce battle ashore, for which the Guam divisions were being held as a reserve, caused this operation to be postponed. Now it was once more put in train, under Rear Admiral Connolly with Major General Geiger in command of the troops, but experience had led to a revised plan which included a fortnight of heavy and almost continuous bombardments. From July 8 to July 21 battleships, cruisers, and destroyers fired daily at the defenses; air attacks from Saipan, from escort carriers, and from Task Force 58 were incessant. On July 21 the troops landed. Between that date and July 30 the fighting was intense. Thereafter resistance was still stubborn, but by August 10 it had been overcome and the Americans held the whole island. As in Saipan, however, it was many weeks before all pockets of Japanese had been eliminated.

Tinian, the last of the large Mariana Islands, was assaulted three days later than Guam (July 24) by the marine divisions that had conquered Saipan. As Tinian was separated from Saipan by only 5 miles of water, much of the preparation could be done by land artillery. The operation, directed by Rear Admiral Hill, was brilliantly carried out. By August 1 the island was secure, and on the 8th the occupation was completed, insofar as organized resistance was concerned.

In view of the important part played by American submarines in the Battle of the Philippine Sea, it is perhaps appropriate to say something about the general course of submarine operations up to this time, mid-1944.

It will be remembered that the operations of submarines in defense of the Philippines in December 1941 had been a severe disappointment (see p. 122, above). But in the two and a half years since then great strides had been taken. Something had been done even in 1942, particularly in the Eastern Archipelago, by the submarines of General MacArthur's Southwest Pacific Command based on Freemantle (Western Australia); and since 1943 the more numerous submarines of the Pacific Fleet, controlled by Vice Admiral Lockwood, had waged an increasingly effective campaign in the Pacific Ocean Area, including the home waters of Japan. The time spent on passage was necessarily long. It was at least 3,200 miles from Pearl Harbor to Japan. (Midway Island, 1,200 miles closer, could be used for fueling but lacked amenities.) And it was nearly 3,000 miles from Majuro, which became a fully equipped submarine base, to the Philippines. But despite these distances strong patrols were maintained in enemy waters, even right into the Sea of Japan, that is, between Japan and the mainland of Asia.

Numbers had, of course, been much increased. To the 112 submarines in the United States Navy at the beginning of the war, 132 had been added up to June 30, 1944. During the same period 29 had been lost through enemy action, 8 of them in Japanese waters (including the Ryukyu Islands and the East China Sea) and the other 21 in the Philippines, the Eastern Archipelago, and the Pacific Islands—proportions that show roughly the distribution of their activities. This cost, though considerable, had reaped a rich reward. Japanese shipping was harried with increasing vehemence, both ships bringing essential materials from the tropics and Manchuria to Japan and those supplying the widespread Japanese outposts in the southwest Pacific. In 1942 the submarines of both commands (i.e., Pacific Ocean Area and Southwest Pacific) had sunk 134 ships totaling 580,000 tons; in 1943 the number had risen to 284 ships totaling 1,342,000 tons; and in the whole of 1944, 492 ships of 2,388,000 tons had been sunk.

Perhaps more spectacular, because more unexpected, were the successes against destroyers, usually regarded as the submarine's most dangerous foes. Almost as severe casualties had been inflicted on the destroyers as were suffered by the submarines, for during this same period (i.e., to June 30, 1944) twenty-eight Japanese destroyers had been sunk. At need the submarines' operations against them were concentrated and irrepressible; for example, in June 1944 four destroyers were sunk in the Sibutu Passage (between Tawi Tawi and Borneo) within a period of four days (one on the 6th, one on the 7th, and two on the 9th).[7]

[7] Destroyers had, of course, been sunk by submarines in other theaters: Italian destroyers by British submarines, and British destroyers by German submarines. But in these instances the relative loss of submarines was on so much higher a scale as to present an entirely different picture. Compare the above figures (which for a period of eighteen months, from January 1, 1943, to June 30, 1944, should be adjusted to 23 Japanese destroyers against 23 United States submarines) with

Some of the submarines' successes against other surface warships have already been recorded: two fleet carriers on June 19, 1944, and the heavy cruiser *Kako* off Kavieng in August 1942. Besides these, submarines had sunk an escort carrier and four light cruisers. Finally, they had contributed to the safety of American surface forces by sinking ten Japanese submarines.

Though this bare array of figures can do no more than give a general idea of a widespread success compounded of a large number of individual examples of courage, enterprise, and efficiency, they should do something to show how important thus far had been the contribution of this numerically minor arm of the United States Navy in hastening Japan's defeat. This contribution it was fully to maintain during the next few months.

---

the following figures for double the time (the years 1941, 1942, and 1943) in the Mediterranean and the Atlantic. In the Mediterranean a relatively small force of British submarines sank 10 Italian destroyers and torpedo boats, against a loss of 34 of their own number. In the Atlantic and the Mediterranean a very large force of German submarines sank 23 British destroyers, against a loss, from all causes, of 357 submarines. These figures are not meant to imply that this form of warfare is simply a contest between submarines and destroyers, but they do illustrate how profoundly Japanese antisubmarine measures were failing to deter United States submarines from striking when and where they pleased.

20

RECONQUEST OF THE PHILIPPINES, I:
Preliminary Operations and the Battle for Leyte Gulf

EVER SINCE 1943 it had been the intention that General MacArthur's Sixth Army (Lieutenant General Krueger) and Seventh Fleet (Admiral Kinkaid), supported by the Far East Air Force (Lieutenant General Kenney), should reconquer the Philippines by means of a steady step-by-step advance with land-based air support. These Southwest Pacific forces, it will be remembered, had completed the occupation of western New Guinea in July and August, 1944. From there the next steps were to be: 300 miles to Morotai in September; 150 miles on to the Talaud Islands in October; another 150 miles to southern Mindanao in November; thence 400 miles (but less by air) to Leyte Gulf in December; and thereafter by similar steps to the northern Philippines. During these operations ships and aircraft of Admiral Nimitz' command would protect General MacArthur's right flank from interference by sea or air. Their first task would be to capture or neutralize enemy bases to the west of the Carolines (the Palau Islands and Yap), and it was arranged that an assault on Peleliu in the Palau group should coincide with General MacArthur's seizure of Morotai, planned for September 15.

In Admiral Nimitz' area there was now a change in the command. The rapid succession of operations on the largest scale, both amphibious and blue water, which were evidently to continue until Japan was conquered, called for the frontline commander to be given periodical spells for relaxation and further planning. On completion of the conquest of the Marianas, therefore, Admiral Spruance and his amphibious commander, Vice Admiral Turner, withdrew to Pearl Harbor to plan the operations that were to follow the Philippines campaign, and their places were taken by Admiral Halsey and Vice Admiral Wilkinson, who had completed their task in the South Pacific Area (Solomons and

Bismarck Archipelago) and had been engaged since June in planning the forthcoming Palau operations. As already noted, the change in command brought with it a change in fleet designation. The Fifth Fleet became the Third Fleet, Task Force 58 became Task Force 38 (still under Vice Admiral Mitscher), and Admiral Wilkinson's command was the Third Amphibious Force.

As an overture to the assaults on Peleliu and Morotai, Admiral Halsey conducted a series of widespread air strikes by Task Force 38 which, starting on August 31, extended for the first time to the Philippines.[1] Working in groups, the carriers sent in their striking forces against Iwo Jima and Chichi Jima away in the north (cruisers and destroyers bombarding as well), against Yap, and against Mindanao. On September 10 cruisers and destroyers closed the coast of Mindanao and annihilated a convoy of thirty-two small cargo ships. Here in the south there was so much less air opposition than had been expected that Admiral Halsey shifted his points of attack to the central Philippines (September 12 to 14), while at the same time some of his groups were engaged in final bombardments before the assaults of September 15—the Palau Islands themselves, Talaud Island, and, in the south, in coordination with General Kenney's forces, airfields in Celebes.

The Palau Islands form an almost continuous chain of islands and reefs, 70 miles long, from the partly reef-enclosed Kossol Roads in the north to the island of Peleliu, some 5 miles by 2, in the south. Six miles farther south in clear water lies the island of Angaur (2 miles by 1). It was only these last two islands that were to be captured, Peleliu having the only airfield in the group and Angaur being needed for airfield development. The large and heavily garrisoned central island of Babelthuap (25 miles by 10) would be left alone. Therefore it would not be possible to use the principal Palau harbors, but steps would be taken to sweep Kossol Roads clear of mines by September 15, thus affording sufficient anchorage for ships waiting their turn to discharge to the beaches in the south.

After three days of air and surface bombardment, the assault troops, a division of marines under Major General J. C. Smith, were landed by the Third Amphibious Force at dawn on September 15. They secured their footing, and by the evening of the following day they had captured the airfield. Fighting continued to be hard, despite the smallness of the island and the support of warships' guns; it was several weeks before the Japanese were finally suppressed, though the outcome had

[1] Admiral Halsey had hoisted his flag in the *New Jersey*, the newest of the battleships which normally worked in company with Task Group 38.2.

never been in doubt. Meanwhile, on September 17, Angaur had been attacked by part of an infantry division, and its relatively small garrison was overrun in three days. The remainder of this division was then sent to seize Ulithi Atoll, 300 miles to the northeastward, where minesweeping had already started. It was found to have been abandoned by the enemy and was occupied on September 23. From then on, as soon as it could be developed and the Mobile Service Squadron brought forward, Ulithi, 850 miles east of Leyte, was to be the principal forward base until American forces were once more established in the Philippines. Ulithi was not ideal either as an anchorage or in its position; but with the Palau Islands harbors ruled out by the enemy's hold on heavily defended Babelthuap, it was the best available. Experience showed that there was little difficulty in neutralizing the airfield of Yap, 100 miles to the westward, with carrier aircraft and long-range bombers.

The simultaneous assault on Morotai Island by the Seventh Amphibious Force under Rear Admiral Barbey met with no opposition from the enemy. There had been a widespread neutralization of airfields in Ceram, Halmahera, and Celebes by General Kenney's bombers, and, as already mentioned, in northern Celebes by Admiral Mitscher's aircraft. Close support was given by six escort carriers and some American and Australian cruisers and destroyers. Difficult beach conditions had to be surmounted, but 50,000 troops were soon landed and airfields were quickly made.

A day or two before landings on Peleliu and Morotai a major change was made in the plan for the reconquest of the Philippines. No doubt it had gradually been growing apparent that the strategy of short steps with strong land-based air support, already dispensed with at Hollandia and in the Central Pacific, need no longer be employed even in operations on the largest scale. The available strength—eight big carriers, eight light carriers, and eighteen escort carriers—might well be able to provide almost all the air power needed for a landing in the Philippines; and when, during the Fast Carrier Force strikes at Mindanao and the central Philippines (September 9 to 14), it was found that the Japanese air forces there were much weaker than had been expected, Admiral Halsey suggested that the intermediate steps of Talaud Island and Mindanao be cut out and that Leyte be assaulted with carrier-borne support in October. With this proposal General MacArthur at once agreed; the approval of the Combined Chiefs of Staff, then in conference at Quebec, was given within a matter of hours; and on September 15 the change of plan was ordered. Two army corps, with four divisions

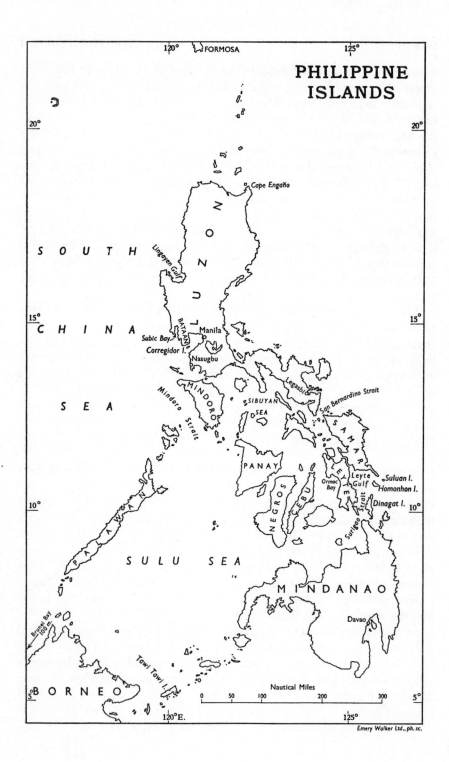

PHILIPPINE
ISLANDS

FORMOSA

Cape Engaño

LUZON

SOUTH

CHINA

SEA

Lingayen Gulf

BATAAN

Subic Bay

Corregidor I.

Manila

Nasugbu

MINDORO

Mindoro Strait

SIBUYAN

SEA

Legaspi

San Bernardino Strait

SAMAR

LEYTE

PANAY

NEGROS

CEBU

Ormoc

Bay

Leyte

Gulf

Suluan I.

Homonhon I.

Surigao Strait

Dinagat I.

SULU SEA

MINDANAO

Davao

Brunei Bay
100 m.

PALAWAN

Tawi Tawi I.

BORNEO

Nautical Miles

0   50   100   200   300

120° E.

125°

Emery Walker Ltd., ph. sc.

assaulting, were to be landed in Leyte Gulf, and October 20 was to be the day of the main attack.

With this change of plan there was an immediate transfer of forces from the Central Pacific to General MacArthur's command. Troops already en route for an attack on Yap were diverted to the Sixth Army; Admiral Wilkinson's Third Amphibious Force reported to Admiral Kinkaid, to work in partnership with Admiral Barbey's Seventh Amphibious Force; Admiral Kinkaid's bombarding and supporting forces were increased to a total of six old battleships, five heavy cruisers (two Australian), six light cruisers, eighteen escort carriers, and eighty-six destroyers (two Australian). With all these forces Admiral Kinkaid set about preparing an expedition that would sail from such distant points as Hollandia, Manus, and Finschhafen, the central and principal of these (Manus) being some 1,600 miles from the Leyte beaches.

What of the Japanese Navy's reactions to these events and prospects? As will have been noticed, there was no attempt to interfere with the attacks on Peleliu and Morotai. After the loss of the Marianas, the Japanese High Command had decided that no further steps would be taken to meet the Americans in the off-lying islands. But an assault on the Philippines, now an obvious probability, was another matter. It was the decided naval opinion that if the Philippines were lost the navy would no longer be of any real value; it would not be able to operate effectively from Japan because of lack of fuel,[2] and if it remained in the south, where the fuel was, it would be cut off from Japan and unable to influence events. In defense of the Marianas, Toyoda had been willing to fight a decisive battle, believing there was a fair chance of a victory that would bring the Americans to a halt. In defense of the Philippines he felt compelled to fight, but with little hope that the decision could be in Japan's favor. The incalculable fortunes of war might bring some success, though it was difficult to see just how such success could come. The Japanese fleet would fight, as ever, with courage, but it would be mainly the courage of despair.

After the Battle of the Philippine Sea, therefore, every effort was made to prepare to defend the Philippines against an attack that it was hoped would not materialize before November. The Second Fleet went

[2] By this time United States submarines had sunk so many tankers as not only to prohibit the building up of stocks of fuel in Japan, but also to make it difficult at times to find the oilers needed for the fleet train. This circumstance tended to limit the fleet's mobility when embarked on an operation, as well as to affect the question of its base.

to Singapore,[3] but Ozawa could not for the present join it there, as some of his carriers needed dockyard repairs and all required new aircraft. The Third Fleet therefore remained in the Inland Sea, once more training an entirely new complement of air squadrons. When ready, probably early in November, it would move to Singapore, and Ozawa would once more take command of the Second and Third fleets. Toyoda, the commander in chief, would give general directions from Japan. As we know, however, events were moving too fast for these Japanese plans.

The operations of the Fast Carrier Force prior to the Leyte landings were prolonged and extensive. It had already put in a heavy and destructive attack on Manila Harbor and airfields (September 21 and 22) and the central Philippines (September 24); after returning to Eniwetok for a brief spell, Admiral Mitscher's four groups resumed the attack with a raid on Okinawa on October 10, followed next day by a fighter sweep over northern Luzon. These were preliminaries, and it was on the next two days that the main air battle was fought over and to the eastward of Formosa. The main strength of Japanese shore-based naval aircraft (the Second Air Fleet) was concentrated in Formosa; to break up this force and hamper enemy reinforcement from the north when the Leyte attack developed, Admiral Halsey operated with the whole weight of his fleet. October 12 and 13 saw heavy attacks on all the Formosa airfields. Many aircraft were destroyed, both in the air and on the ground. But the Japanese hit back with all the strength they could muster. On the evening of October 13 the heavy cruiser *Canberra*[4] was torpedoed and crippled so badly that she had to be towed away. The next day, while the whole force retired slowly to seaward, covered by fighter sweeps over the Formosa airfields as well as combat air patrols for direct protection, the Japanese sent in new attacking forces, including 300 aircraft from Kyushu which struck at the fleet on the evening of the 14th, to land thereafter on Formosa. In this attack they succeeded in torpedoing the light cruiser *Houston* (new) and slightly damaging three of the big carriers. Not only were all normally land-based aircraft put into attack, but once more the Third Fleet carrier aircraft were thrown into the breach, adding to the numerical strength but crippling the carriers for effective action later.[5]

[3] The Japanese operating base in the Singapore area was an anchorage off Lingga Island, 100 miles southeast of Singapore.

[4] The *Canberra* was a new American ship named to commemorate the Australian cruiser sunk at the Battle of Savo Island.

[5] It is said that the pilots of these aircraft were not yet sufficiently trained for carrier work, so it is possible that they would not in any event have affected the Battle of Cape Engaño twelve days later.

Misled, apparently, by the reports of their aircraft in this dusk battle, the Japanese thought that grave damage had been inflicted on Admiral Halsey's fleet, and they sent out a small force of three cruisers and four destroyers to pick up stragglers. On receipt of further air reports next day (15th), this force quickly retired. But the enemy continued to send air attacks, again hitting the *Houston* but having many aircraft shot down. When all was over the Japanese had lost perhaps 600 aircraft in six days, as against an American loss of 90.[6] Clearly this damage would greatly reduce the risk to Admiral Halsey's and Admiral Kinkaid's ships during the critical period ahead, though still the Japanese were able to fly some 350 aircraft from Formosa to Luzon when the call came a week later, joining there the First Air Fleet (perhaps 150 strong) which had never been brought up to strength since its losses in the Marianas battles in June.

After a short respite on October 16 and 17, Task Force 38 was at it again on the 18th and the three following days with strikes at Luzon and the central Philippines to cover the Leyte landings.

On October 17 Admiral Kinkaid's advanced forces, approaching through the backwash of a typhoon, landed rangers on Suluan Island and, on the following day, on Dinagat and Homonhon islands, all lying in the entrance to Leyte Gulf, some 45 miles to seaward of the main beaches. At the same time minesweeping and the demolition by night of underwater obstructions off the main beaches were started. At 10 A.M. on October 20, after a furious bombardment by battleships, cruisers, and destroyers as well as air attacks from escort carriers and close support by many special craft, the four assaulting divisions went in. The Japanese, with so many possible landing beaches in the Philippines to defend, were unable to meet an attack on so large a scale, and such local resistance as there was was quickly overcome.

As was to be expected, there was some reaction in the air. Even that was on only a light scale, thanks to the widespread preparatory bombing by General Kenney's forces from Morotai and American aircraft from China, as well as Admiral Halsey's strikes. But some Japanese aircraft reached the scene of action, and they could not all be staved off by the fighters of the escort carriers. The light cruiser *Honolulu* was torpedoed, and the *Australia* was hit and severely damaged by an aircraft that dived into her. Nonetheless, the landing went forward substantially unhampered.

Two days earlier (October 18) the Japanese fleet had been put in motion to meet a clearly impending invasion. It had for some time been evident that Ozawa's Third Fleet would not be able to concentrate with

---

[6] One account puts the Japanese loss at 807 aircraft.

the Second Fleet at Singapore, and Admiral Kurita, commanding the latter, would in consequence work directly under Admiral Toyoda. On the 18th, therefore, Kurita was ordered from Lingga Roads to Brunei Bay (North Borneo) to fuel and stand by. By the time he arrived there General MacArthur's forces had landed, and on October 22 he was ordered to sail again to carry out his part in the plan to break up Admiral Kinkaid's transports and supporting ships. With him were the mammoth battleships *Yamato* and *Musashi*, the 16-inch ship *Nagato*,[7] the old battleships *Kongo* and *Haruna*, ten heavy cruisers (the *Atago* flying Kurita's flag), two light cruisers, and fifteen destroyers. This force was to proceed west of Palawan, thence through Mindoro Strait and the Sibuyan Sea to San Bernardino Strait. There it would turn south down the east coast of Samar, headed for Leyte Gulf. Meanwhile a detached force under Vice Admiral Nishimura, the battleships *Yamashiro* and *Fuso*, one cruiser, and four destroyers, which had sailed from Brunei Bay later than Kurita, would try to burst through to Leyte Gulf via Surigao Strait, which enters it from the south. For these forces, Kurita's and Nishimura's, the only air support for countering attacks from Admiral Halsey's carriers would be provided by land-based aircraft, for, as already indicated, the Japanese carriers had few aircraft, and those they had were only half trained. Nevertheless, Toyoda decided to send Ozawa's Third Fleet into the battle. It was rightly supposed that the Americans would look on this carrier force as the Japanese main fleet, and it might therefore be able to hold Admiral Halsey's force in play while Kurita went through to attack Admiral Kinkaid. On October 20 Ozawa sailed from Japan and headed south for a position east of Luzon where, with such aircraft as he had, he could fight in cooperation with the shore-based air fleets.

This plan, even though hardly more than a counsel of despair, derived, perhaps, some slight advantage from the system of command under which the American forces were working. The question of command in combined operations is one that has often been debated by the rival supporters of unified command, on the one hand, and of joint command, on the other, by the heads of the two (or three) services, the usual practice in former wars. Latterly the trend of opinion had been toward unified command, and this system had worked well in the New Guinea campaign, as also in Europe. But in the present operation a large-scale invasion would have to be covered by the full battle strength of the United States Fleet, a situation that was clearly outside the scope of a single commander in the field, whether soldier or sailor,

[7] The *Nagato*'s sister ship, the *Mutsu*, had been destroyed by an internal explosion in June 1943.

however able. At some point, therefore, situations had to be dealt with by cooperation (subject to general directions from higher commanders and the Chiefs of Staff) rather than by orders. Traditionally this cooperation would have been between the naval and military commanders who, besides coordinating their actions, would have been charged with a joint responsibility for the success of the enterprise, similar to the joint responsibility borne by the Combined Chiefs of Staff for the general direction of the war. But in this instance the line of cooperation was not between the land and sea commanders, but between two parts of the naval forces—between Admiral Kinkaid, working under General MacArthur, and Admiral Halsey, who was under Admiral Nimitz. This cooperation would be as good as it could be made, subject to the limitations imposed by the different communications systems of the two fleets; but the fact remained that there was no one admiral wielding all the resources and bearing all the responsibility for protecting the passage and landing the army. The orders given to Admiral Halsey by Admiral Nimitz were to "cover and support" Southwest Pacific forces "in order to assist in the seizure and occupation of all objectives in the central Philippines, and to destroy enemy naval and air forces in or threatening the Philippines area." But Halsey was also told: "In case opportunity for destruction of major portion of the enemy fleet is offered, or can be created, such destruction becomes the primary task."[8]

Whether this alternative aim would have been so worded if all naval forces had been under Admiral Nimitz can only be surmised. Probably it had its roots in the disappointments of the Battle of the Philippine Sea, and no doubt it was welcomed by the navy. No attempt, however, had been made to define "major portion," nor was allowance made for the fact that information about the enemy fleet might be far from precise. It is seldom that a double aim can be justified, and in this instance a lack of clarity made the expedient even more dubious than usual.[9]

It was not long before Kurita's movement was reported. The Seventh Fleet submarines *Darter* (Commander McClintock) and *Dace*, patrolling in company in the South China Sea to the northward of Borneo, gained radar contact with heavy forces soon after midnight (October 22–23) and proceeded to shadow the two columns of the enemy from

[8] Samuel Eliot Morison, *History of United States Naval Operations in World War II* (15 vols.; Boston: Little, Brown, 1947–1962), XII, 58.

[9] It has recently been suggested (S. L. Falk, *Decision at Leyte* [New York: Norton, 1966], p. 77) that Halsey had himself written these orders and then persuaded Nimitz to approve them. For Nimitz, however, to have put his signature to so vital a document unless he was in full agreement would have been quite out of character; there can be no doubt that his was the full responsibility.

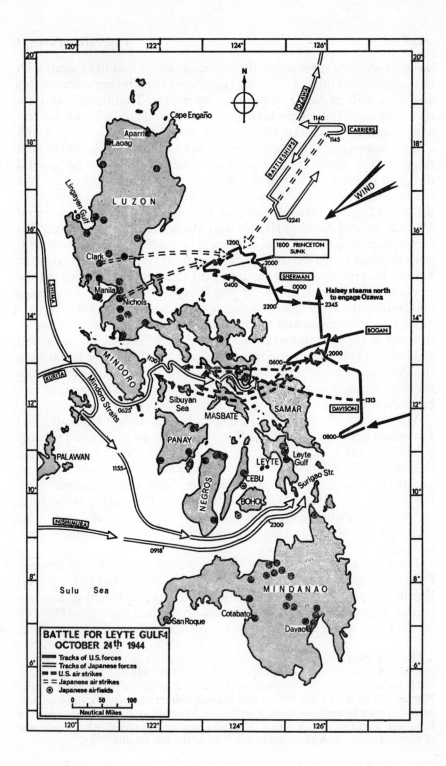

BATTLE FOR LEYTE GULF
OCTOBER 24th 1944

Tracks of U.S. forces
Tracks of Japanese forces
U.S. air strikes
Japanese air strikes
Japanese airfields

0   50   100
Nautical Miles

LUZON
Cape Engaño
Aparri
Laoag
Lingayen Gulf
Clark
Manila
Nichols
MINDORO
Mindoro Straits
PALAWAN
PANAY
NEGROS
CEBU
BOHOL
Sibuyan Sea
MASBATE
SAMAR
LEYTE
Leyte Gulf
Surigao Str.
San Roque
Cotabato
Davao
MINDANAO
Sulu Sea

SHIMA
KURITA
NISHIMURA
OZAWA
CARRIERS
BATTLESHIPS
WIND
SHERMAN
BOGAN
DAVISON

1140
1145
2241
1200
1800 PRINCETON SUNK
2000
0400
0000
2200
2345
Halsey steams north to engage Ozawa
2000
0600
1313
0800
1130
0625
1155
2300
0918

ahead as they steamed up Palawan Passage, a channel between the
shoals fringing Palawan and the many unmarked reefs in the South
China Sea. Having reported the enemy force, though underestimating
its strength and importance, they dived at dawn and attacked. The
Darter hit the leader of one column, the *Atago*, with four torpedoes
which caused vital injury, and then with her stern tubes she hit and
severely damaged another heavy cruiser, the *Takao*. Twenty minutes
later, just as the *Atago* was sinking, the *Dace*, attacking the other
column, put four torpedoes into the heavy cruiser *Maya*, which sank
within a few minutes. After these heavy losses the fleet increased speed
and zigzagged more drastically for a while, and it was not till 4:30 P.M.
that it was thought justifiable to slow down for Kurita, who had been
taken off the *Atago* by a destroyer, to transfer his flag to the *Yamato*.
Thereafter the Japanese force proceeded as planned, being reported by
submarines as it cleared the northern end of Palawan Passage soon
after dark, and again as it stood southeastward through Mindoro Strait
at midnight.

From the *Darter*'s reports Admiral Kinkaid had already, early on
October 23, concluded that strong Japanese forces were being launched
against the shipping off the Leyte beaches and would probably approach
through the central Philippines; he had so informed Admiral Halsey.
The latter had on the day before temporarily withdrawn Task Force 38
to the eastward. One of the groups (38.1, Vice Admiral McCain) had
been ordered to Ulithi for replenishment, while the other three groups
were due to fuel at sea on the morning of the 23d. This they did. Then,
in view of the gathering threat, they moved in toward the Philippines,
spreading as they advanced. The southern group (38.4, Rear Admiral
Davison) headed for Leyte; the central group (38.2, Rear Admiral
Bogan), accompanied by Admiral Halsey in the *New Jersey*, headed
for San Bernardino Strait; and the northern group (38.3, Rear Admiral
Sherman), including Admiral Mitscher's flagship, the *Lexington*, stood
in toward central Luzon. At dawn on the 24th the three groups would
be about 150 miles apart and some 50 miles off the coast, and from
these positions they would send off widespread and strongly armed
searches which would cover the Philippines from Lingayen Gulf in the
north to the north coast of Mindanao in the south.

As they stood to the westward during the night (23d–24th), Admiral
Sherman's group was constantly shadowed by enemy aircraft, but the
other two escaped attention. At dawn the searches flew off, and during
the next few hours the situation developed much as surmised. Kurita's
force was sighted in the Sibuyan Sea and evidently contained the bulk
of the Japanese battleships. Two more forces, hitherto unreported,
were also sighted, both in the Sulu Sea heading for Surigao Strait. One

of these, coming from the southwest, was Nishimura with his two battleships, one cruiser, and four destroyers; the other was Vice Admiral Shima, sent from Japan to join Nishimura in his attack from the southward.

Knowing that Admiral Kinkaid had sufficient force to deal with the attack through Surigao Strait, Admiral Halsey decided to put all he had into attacks on the force in the Sibuyan Sea, which was evidently heading for San Bernardino Strait. To that end he ordered Davison's southern and Sherman's northern groups to close on the center, attacking as soon as they could, while Bogan's carriers at once sent off the best striking force they could muster.

The attacks resulting from these orders were neither so heavy nor so concentrated as might have been hoped. It so happened that Bogan's group was the weakest of the three, with only one big and two light carriers;[10] Davison was still out of striking range; Sherman, having been shadowed all night and appearing to the enemy no doubt as the main fleet, was being subjected to the full weight of air attack from Luzon. These assaults were successfully repelled with heavy loss to the enemy, most of them being turned back while still a long way from the group; but all the carriers' fighters were needed for this operation, and striking forces were therefore delayed till 11 A.M. During a lull in the attacks a lone undetected Japanese plane dropped a single bomb on the light carrier *Princeton* which started large fires and led eventually to the loss of the ship; but this was the only damage suffered.

Despite the piecemeal nature of the American attacks, Kurita's force was hit, and hit hard, in a succession of strikes which continued till about 4 P.M. Fortunately for the striking forces, the Japanese battleships had been given only a small handful of shore-based fighters to protect them, everything else having been thrown into the attacks on Sherman's force. But their antiaircraft fire was very heavy, shooting down several planes and doing something to impair the accuracy of the attacks; this fact, plus considerable cloud, made assessment of damage by the Americans very difficult. The result was that the reports of the striking forces presented a misleading picture. They stated that they had made many hits on many ships and that the enemy had eventually turned tail. But in fact the damage had not been so extensive. The great battleship *Musashi* had been sunk, having been hit by nineteen torpedoes and many bombs; and a heavy cruiser had been torpedoed and forced to retire. Before the last attack Kurita had, as reported, turned

[10] Admiral McCain's group (38.1), which was no longer heading for Ulithi but had turned back and was preparing to fuel at sea, contained three big and two light carriers. Each of the other two groups had two of each type of carrier.

to the westward, withdrawing temporarily in the hope that the Luzon air fleets would succeed in driving off the American carriers. But, though every battleship had been hit by one or more bombs, none of the four remaining was seriously impaired in speed or fighting power, and the force as a whole could still steam at 24 knots.

To Admiral Halsey it naturally appeared from the reports he had received that the force opposed to him had been thoroughly broken up and was retiring. To him, therefore, the situation seemed not unsatisfactory, the only worrying feature being the whereabouts of the Japanese carrier fleet, which was still unlocated. This question had also been troubling Admiral Mitscher, in the *Lexington* with Sherman's group, particularly as one attack on that group had come in from the northeastward. He had ordered a search in that direction, but the many other activities of the day had caused delay, and it was not till about 4:40 P.M. that anything was revealed. At that time several reports from searching aircraft, when sifted, led to the conclusion that there was a Japanese fleet about 190 miles northeast of Sherman's group, and that it was in two parts, one with three or four carriers and one with, perhaps, four battleships. The latter seemed unlikely in view of the number of battleships reported in Kurita's and Nishimura's forces, but it was accepted as a possibility.

On this information, in conjunction with the supposed crippling of Kurita's force, Admiral Halsey decided to take his whole fleet to the northward, leaving San Bernardino Strait unguarded. He has said of this decision that "it preserved my fleet's integrity, it left the initiative with me and it promised the greatest possible surprise. Even if the Central Force meanwhile penetrated San Bernardino and headed for Leyte Gulf it could hope only to harry the landing operation. It could not consolidate any advantage because no transports accompanied it and no supply ships. It could merely hit and run."[11] For Halsey to write off in this way the probable effect of Kurita's appearance was clearly to treat his orders to "cover and support Southwest Pacific forces" in a somewhat offhand manner. It is true that danger to the landing operations was no longer so serious as it would have been a day or two earlier, for the whole of General MacArthur's two army corps, totaling 200,000 men, were now established ashore and had with them 130,000 tons of equipment including stores for thirty days. But though there were only some thirty freighters and twenty LST's remaining in the anchorage, there was still some hard fighting not many miles inland which bombardment of Japanese ships might have checked, and to accept without

[11] William F. Halsey and J. Bryan III, *Admiral Halsey's Story* (New York: Whittlesey House, 1947), p. 217.

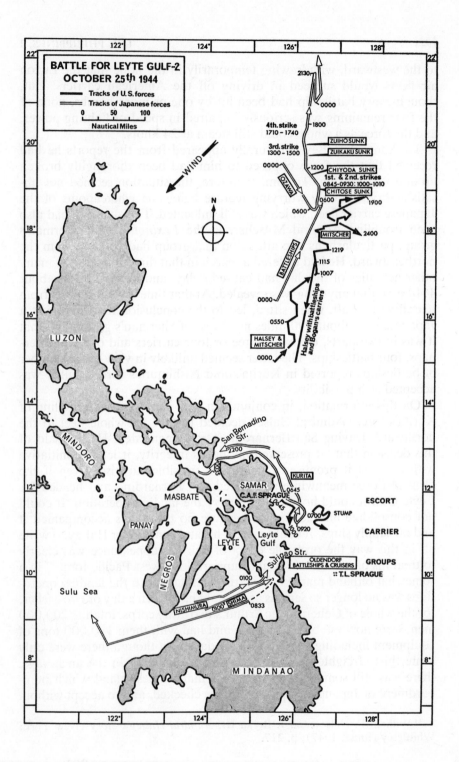

BATTLE FOR LEYTE GULF-2
OCTOBER 25th 1944

— Tracks of U.S. forces
⟶ Tracks of Japanese forces

0   50   100
Nautical Miles

WIND

N

22°
20°
18°
16°
14°
12°
10°
8°

122°   124°   126°   128°

2130
0000
1800

4th. strike
1710 – 1740

3rd. strike
1300 – 1500

ZUIHO SUNK
ZUIKAKU SUNK

1200   CHIYODA SUNK
1st. & 2nd. strikes
0845-0930: 1000-1010
CHITOSE SUNK

OZAWA
0000
0600   1900

MITSCHER   2400

BATTLESHIPS   1219
1115
1007

Halsey with battleships
and Bogan's carriers

0000
0550

HALSEY &
MITSCHER

0000

LUZON

MINDORO

San Bernardino
Str.
2200

SAMAR

MASBATE

KURITA
0645

C.A.F. SPRAGUE
0645
1000   0920

0700   STUMP

ESCORT

PANAY

NEGROS

LEYTE

Leyte
Gulf

CARRIER

GROUPS

Surigao Str.

OLDENDORF
BATTLESHIPS & CRUISERS
∷ T.L. SPRAGUE

0100

Sulu Sea

NISHIMURA   0100   SHIMA   0833

MINDANAO

122°   124°   126°   128°

some compelling cause any risk to the ever hazardous business of a
seaborne invasion is not the way in which sound strategists have conducted such affairs. Nonetheless the problem facing him was indeed a
difficult one. No doubt his thrustful temperament welcomed the clause
in his orders which gave destruction of a major portion of the enemy
fleet as his primary task. But orders they were, given to him by Admiral
Nimitz, and the decision as to what constituted a major portion had
been left to him.

In this instance it is difficult to divest oneself of afterknowledge. It
is so evident now that what seemed to Halsey to be the Japanese main
fleet was in fact only Ozawa's half-trained force, an almost pitiful
remnant—one large and three light carriers equipped with only 120
aircraft in all (most of which had already been expended in attacks on
Sherman's group), two 14-inch battleships with launching platforms
aft depriving them of four of their original twelve guns (but with no
aircraft), three light cruisers, and ten destroyers. We know, also, that
Kurita, far from being crippled, was heading at 20 knots for San
Bernardino Strait with four battleships (one 18-inch, one 16-inch, and
two 14-inch), six heavy cruisers, and eleven destroyers, and that the
only forces between him and Leyte Gulf were Admiral Kinkaid's six
battleships, eight cruisers, and about thirty destroyers, already saddled
with the task of confronting Nishimura's and Shima's approach from
the southward, and his escort carriers, which were not primarily concerned with attacks on warships. But these things were not clear to
Halsey, and even his general information about the number of Japanese
ships fit for service was by no means precise. There were at this time
four new big Japanese carriers in commission or just commissioning.
Had they been in Ozawa's force with full aircraft equipment (as well
they might, for all Halsey knew to the contrary), this northern force
would certainly have qualified as a major portion of the enemy fleet.

Having made his crucial decision, Admiral Halsey signaled his orders
about 8 P.M. Davison's and Bogan's groups were to close with Sherman's, and Admiral Mitscher was told to deliver a concentrated strike
against the enemy carrier fleet at dawn. At the same time Halsey informed Admiral Kinkaid of what he was doing, and told him that
Kurita's force was in the Sibuyan Sea but badly damaged. Finally he
ordered McCain's group to steam toward the expected scene of action
when his ships had finished fueling.

Some inkling of the real danger from Kurita's force reached Halsey
a few hours later, when a night shadower from Bogan's group reported
it steering east at 20 knots and nearing San Bernardino Strait. But night
reports could not be fully reliable, and to Admiral Halsey this appeared to be the suicidal action of a few ships "with battle efficiency

greatly impaired by torpedo hits, bomb hits, topside damage, fires and casualties."[12] Although informing Admiral Kinkaid that part of the enemy force had been reported as still coming east, Halsey was not to be moved from his resolution to engage Ozawa's force with the whole of his fleet. Throughout the night of October 24–25, he stood to the northward, away from San Bernardino and away from Leyte.

During all this time Admiral Kinkaid had been taking steps to oppose the enemy's advance from the southward through Surigao Strait. This he felt able to do without any need to look over his shoulder, despite the reports that there were still Japanese ships in the Sibuyan Sea, for he had intercepted a Third Fleet signal indicating the withdrawal of the battleships and some of the cruisers from the groups of Task Force 38 and their formation as Task Force 34, the normal procedure in preparation for a surface action. This re-formation would in fact be done during the night. But Admiral Kinkaid assumed that it had already been done; and when, later, he received a signal from Admiral Halsey saying that the latter was going north with three groups, he came to the conclusion that Task Groups 38.2, 38.3, and 38.4 were going north and that Task Force 34 was remaining to watch San Bernardino Strait.

This view seems also to have been formed by Admiral Nimitz at Pearl Harbor, but it was quite contrary to Admiral Halsey's conceptions. He was firmly of the view that the battleships should not be exposed to possible shore-based air attack without having a carrier group in company to provide protection, a view that one would suppose had general acceptance; and his reason for refusing to divide his fleet was not that the battleships were essential to the northern operation, but that he wanted his full strength of aircraft there. Admiral Lee, commanding the battleships, said after it was all over that "he would have been only too glad to have been ordered to cover San Bernardino Strait without air cover,"[13] but this opinion should surely not be taken as justifying tactics that had long been considered unsound.

For the operations in Surigao Strait, Admiral Kinkaid put the available forces under the command of Rear Admiral Oldendorf, whose flag was in the heavy cruiser *Louisville*. There were no doubts that these forces were adequate for the task of stopping and destroying enemy formations, which were known to comprise two battleships and an uncertain, but not large, number of cruisers and destroyers. The American forces were not, perhaps, so overwhelmingly powerful as appeared

---

[12] C. Vann Woodward, *The Battle for Leyte Gulf* (New York: Macmillan, 1947), p. 84.
[13] Morison, *op. cit.*, XII, 194n.

on paper, for of the six old battleships only three had the radar equipment needed for fully effective blind firing, and none of them, since their primary duty was bombardment, had more than a small outfit of armor-piercing shell. It was decided, therefore, that everything possible was to be done first with torpedoes, the battleships coming into action to crush what was left. The plan, then, to oppose the enemy's passage through Surigao Strait, which was some 30 miles long by about 15 wide, was to station all motor torpedo boats (thirty-nine of them) in sections of three, in and beyond the southern entrance to the strait, and to send in the destroyers, twenty of which, organized in seven divisions, were available for attack, as soon as the Japanese were well committed to the passage. What was left of the enemy would be engaged at the northern end of the strait by the six battleships and eight cruisers, which would stand to and fro in the southern part of Leyte Gulf on 10-mile legs at slow speed.

That was the plan and that, to a large extent, was the outcome. The motor torpedo boats sighted, reported, and attacked Nishimura's force off the southern end of the strait about midnight (October 24–25). By 3 A.M. Nishimura was well committed to the passage, and Admiral Oldendorf sent in his destroyers to attack by divisions. The flagship, *Yamashiro*, and a Japanese destroyer were sunk. The remnant—the *Fuso*, perhaps already torpedoed, the *Mogami*, and three destroyers—stood on, to be received by the fire of the battleships and cruisers. By about 4 A.M. the *Fuso* was out of action, to sink shortly afterward, and one of the destroyers had been sunk; and the crippled and blazing *Mogami* and two remaining destroyers had turned to the southward.

By this time, with so much movement in such confined waters, there was naturally some confusion which not even the most efficient radar could clear up, and one American destroyer was put out of action by the fire of her own cruisers. To add to the confusion, Admiral Shima approached from the southward with the vague knowledge that Nishimura was ahead of him, but with no other coordination of their movements. At 3:20 A.M. Shima's light cruiser, the *Abukuma*, was torpedoed by a motor torpedo boat and retired. Shima stood on with his two heavy cruisers, and about 4:30 A.M. his flagship, the *Nachi*, collided with the retiring *Mogami*. With his speed reduced by the resulting damage, Shima decided to retire, firing his torpedoes at what he believed to be the American battle line.

The Japanese had been routed, and Admiral Oldendorf led his cruisers down the strait in pursuit, once more engaging the burning *Mogami*. No further stop, however, was put to the retiring remnant of enemy ships, and by daylight they were clear to the southward. A few hours later striking forces sent by the Seventh Fleet escort carriers finished off the *Mogami*, and on the following day (October 26) the *Abukuma* was sunk by Army Air Force bombers as she tried to limp home. The *Nachi* and the *Ashigara* escaped to Manila, the former to be sunk by carrier aircraft ten days later.

At dawn on October 25, while Shima was emerging from the southern end of Surigao Strait and Admiral Halsey was 300 miles to the northward steering north, Kurita with his four battleships, six heavy cruisers, two light cruisers, and eleven destroyers was within 80 miles of the entrance to Leyte Gulf, steaming down the east coast of Samar at 20 knots, his presence entirely unsuspected. He had passed through San Bernardino Strait at midnight, his movements unknown to his enemies and only surmised by his colleague Ozawa. He knew that his reversal of course in the Sibuyan Sea the afternoon before had made him too late to synchronize his attack with Nishimura's, but he intended nonetheless to attack the shipping in Leyte Gulf. Of what forces to expect there and of the whereabouts of the American fleet, he had little or no knowledge. He was actuated mainly by Admiral Toyoda's signal of the preceding afternoon: "Trusting in divine aid the entire force will attack."

These were the circumstances when, at 6:45 A.M., he sighted the northern group of the escort carriers which were operating about 40 miles to seaward of Leyte Gulf to provide the army with support and the shipping with protection from air attack. These escort carriers were in three groups, the whole under the command of Admiral T. L. Sprague, who also commanded the southern group. In the latter group, which was about 120 miles south of the present scene of action, there were only four carriers, two having been detached to make good defects. In each of the other two there were six. Rear Admiral Stump commanded the middle group, which was about 30 miles south of the northern group. The latter, now to be brought to action, was commanded by Rear Admiral C. A. F. Sprague.

The surprise on both sides was complete. Kurita, though he must have had some idea that there were escort carriers supporting the landing operations, did not expect to meet any of Admiral Kinkaid's forces so far from Leyte Gulf, and believed that at least some of the ships sighted were big carriers and therefore part of the Amerian main fleet. On the American side, the escort carriers, in common with all Seventh Fleet forces, believed themselves to be well protected to the northward by the Third Fleet. But it was soon clear that they were in the presence of the enemy, and at 7 A.M. all four battleships opened fire on them.

What followed was a remarkably successful retreat by Admiral C. A. F. Sprague's ships, a success mainly attributable to the dash and reckless courage displayed by their escort, by their aircraft, and by the aircraft of the other groups. The carriers first retreated eastward into the wind (the enemy had been sighted in the northwest), flying off everything on board. Then they hauled gradually round to the south and southwest, obtaining some cover from smoke made by themselves and their escorts, as well as from rain squalls. Then, from 7:30 A.M. on, the escort went in to attack with torpedoes. There were only three destroyers and four destroyer escorts (the latter with three torpedoes apiece), but they pressed their attacks home despite heavy gunfire. The heavy cruiser *Kumano* was hit and turned for home, the *Yamato* and the *Nagato* were forced to turn away for a time, and the whole Japanese force, already much spread out in endeavors to bring the carriers under effective gunfire, was considerably disorganized. Two of the American destroyers and a destroyer escort were sunk; but they had given the enemy pause. And now followed an amazing series of attacks from every Avenger and Hellcat that could be flown off the carriers, both from this northern group and from their comrades in the other two groups.[14] There were not enough torpedoes for all the Avengers, and some of the bombs with which the rest were loaded were not suitable for attacking ships; but they went in with everything they had and sometimes with nothing but their machine guns. Though many paid for their temerity, the result was a notable success. Two heavy cruisers (*Chokai* and *Chikuma*) were crippled and had to be sunk, and Kurita was convinced that he was in the presence of a powerful carrier force. As his fleet was becoming ever more spread out and the battleship *Haruna*, having sighted the middle group of carriers, was speeding away toward them, he concluded that something must be done to put a stop to growing disorganization. At 9:20 A.M., therefore, though two hours and twenty minutes of gunfire had succeeded in sinking only one of these 18-knot carriers (the *Gambier Bay*), Kurita recalled all forces to his flag and stood to the northward and westward at slow speed.

During the next three hours, while his forces were re-forming and later, Kurita virtually marked time. He was not yet retiring, but nor did he try to make ground toward Leyte while re-forming. He seems to have been a man whose firmness of purpose had broken down under the

---

[14] The first strikes sent by Admiral Stump's group, which, from proximity combined with freedom from attacks, was able to contribute most, consisted of thirty-one Avengers and twenty-eight Hellcats.

long series of trials and perplexities to which he had been subjected. Though the whole object of the operation had been to attack shipping in Leyte Gulf, he persuaded himself that the American army had been so long ashore that there would no longer be anything worth attacking, a view that, as we have seen, was not without some substance. He felt that perhaps he ought to look for the main American forces to the northward (for he had heard nothing from Ozawa), though with what eventual object is not clear. All this time small forces of Avengers, backed up by Hellcats, were continually attacking; another heavy cruiser, the *Suzuya,* was badly damaged and had to be sunk; and he intercepted a plain-language message telling some aircraft to land and refuel on the newly made Leyte airstrips. In fact, this was an emergency measure, for the airstrips were barely usable; but Kurita conjured up pictures of hosts of shore-based aircraft attacking him if he went any farther south. At 12:30 P.M., therefore, in the midst of another air attack, he finally decided to go to the northward, still with some vague idea that he might engage Admiral Halsey in night battle, but no longer menacing the Seventh Fleet.

Kurita's was not the only attack that the escort carriers suffered during the day. The situation was evidently so critical for the Japanese that the commander of the First Air Fleet at Manila sent in numerous suicide attacks, the so-called Kamikaze[15] corps, to assist Kurita; they struck at Admiral T. L. Sprague's and Admiral C. A. F. Sprague's groups during the forenoon. Suicide attacks there had been before, some in the heat of action by damaged aircraft and some, perhaps, premeditated; but this was the first time they had been ordered and directed. On this occasion the southern group (T. L. Sprague) was attacked first by four or five Kamikaze shortly before 8 A.M. Two carriers were hit but both survived, despite the fact that one of them was also hit by a torpedo from a submarine a few minutes later. Then, no sooner had the hard-pressed northern group (C. A. F. Sprague) had its unexpected deliverance from the onslaught of Kurita's ships than it too was assailed by six or seven Kamikaze. Three ships were hit and one, the *St. Lo,* sank. Later the southern group was again attacked but without success. At last the hard-pressed escort carriers were to be free from further molestation. Nearly all the northern group had sustained

[15] Kamikaze ("Divine Wind") was the name traditionally given to the typhoon of August 1281, which destroyed two fleets sent by Kublai Khan from Korea and South China to conquer Japan. Most of the invading army were drowned, and those already ashore were exterminated or enslaved by the Japanese at their leisure.

damage from gunfire and some from Kamikaze as well, and casualties had been very heavy; but in the situation in which they had found themselves it was scarcely believable that only two carriers had been lost.

During all, or nearly all, this time Admiral Halsey's fleet had been steering to the northward. During the night he had formed Task Force 34 (six battleships, including his own flagship, two heavy cruisers, six light cruisers, and eighteen destroyers), and by the morning this force had hauled ahead of Admiral Mitscher's three carrier groups, closing the enemy as quickly as possible, ready to engage any ships slowed down by the air striking forces. At this time Ozawa was standing off and on about 200 miles east of Cape Engaño, the northeast point of Luzon. Earlier in the night, when he had received delayed news of Kurita's afternoon withdrawal in the Sibuyan Sea and had supposed that the battleships were retiring for good, Ozawa had decided to withdraw to the northward, since there was no longer anything to be gained by sacrificing his fleet. But later, realizing from further signals that Kurita was again advancing, he came round to the southward and everything was shaping for a battle in the morning. To Ozawa it was clear that the battle would be one-sided in the extreme, for his only remaining air resources were twenty half-trained fighters, and there was little hope of effectual help from the shore. But his mission was to draw the American fleet away from Kurita at whatever cost, and to this mission he adhered.

Admiral Mitscher's dawn searches were at first unsuccessful in finding the enemy; the night shadowing had been partial and somewhat misleading, and in consequence he was searching only between north and west, whereas Ozawa was bearing north-northeast. But his misunderstanding was soon rectified. At 7:35 A.M. some fighters sent on an additional search found the whole of the Japanese Third Fleet 140 miles from the American carriers. A large striking force—fifty-five Avengers with torpedoes, sixty-five bombers (Avengers and Helldivers), and sixty Hellcat fighters—already in the air and waiting about 50 miles north of Task Force 38 was at once directed at the enemy. About 8:20 A.M. it struck. The few Japanese fighters shot down one Avenger before being routed, and antiaircraft fire accounted for some more, but these losses could do little to halt the attack, and heavy damage was inflicted. The light carrier Chitose was crippled, to sink an hour later, her sister ship Chiyoda was reduced in speed, the Zuiho was hit, and a destroyer was sunk. This damage was all caused by bombs. In addition, the light cruiser Tama was torpedoed and had to steer for home, and so was the one big carrier, the Zuikaku, which was flying

299

Ozawa's flag. Though not otherwise seriously injured, her steering engine was put out of action, and in hand steering she could not go more than 18 knots. As a result Ozawa shifted his flag to the light cruiser *Oyodo*. Before doing so he had sent a signal to Kurita telling him of his success in luring the Americans to the northward, but like some earlier signals from the *Zuikaku*, this one never got through; Kurita remained, as we have already seen, completely befogged as to his enemies' dispositions. Having succeeded in their diversionary role, the Japanese carriers and their supporting forces made off to the northward at their best speed.

It was at this dramatic juncture, at about 8:25 A.M., when the first striking force had just reached the enemy's supposed main fleet and Admiral Halsey seemed to have the ball at his feet, that the drama was intensified by the receipt of Admiral Kinkaid's news that his escort carriers were being attacked by battleships. But as the scene of that action was 350 miles away, any immediate help by surface forces was clearly out of the question. Admiral Halsey had previously made his decision to concentrate on the northern force despite some risks to the general situation, and, since there was now no thorough way of rectifying affairs in the south, to this decision he adhered. The battleships, still intent on bringing Ozawa to action, increased speed to 24 knots, and Admiral Mitscher's three groups prepared for further strikes.

Admiral McCain's group, however, now fueling at sea away to the eastward, was ordered to do everything possible to help the Seventh Fleet. It was too far away from the scene of the southern action for an immediate strike, but by dint of closing at 30 knots McCain's three big carriers were able to launch a force of ninety-eight aircraft at extreme range (340 miles) at 10:30 A.M. At this range torpedoes were too heavy a load, so all Avengers as well as Helldivers carried bombs. Soon after 1 P.M. they arrived off Samar and found Kurita's force steering north. Their attacks, however, did little to add to the damage he had already received, and, as we know, the danger in the south was now past. Nor was there much more success from some further strikes sent by Admiral McCain in the course of the afternoon. Kurita continued to stand to the northward, still at this time with some vague idea about engaging an American fleet in that direction.

All this, however, is well ahead of the situation as we left it in the north, where, though the battle was continuing, events were slowly getting the better of Admiral Halsey's strategy. A small strike about 10 A.M. had brought the damaged *Chiyoda* to a halt, and more striking forces were being prepared. But the appeals from Admiral Kinkaid for help were incessant and urgent, and Admiral Nimitz at Pearl Harbor sent a signal showing that he too had supposed that the battleships were to the southward guarding Leyte Gulf from Kurita. So heavy was the pressure that Admiral Halsey at length came to the reluctant conclusion that part of his fleet must give up the chase of Ozawa and return to the southward—so reluctant that he has recorded: "The orders I gave now, I gave in rage."[16] Because of the distance and the need to replenish the destroyers' fuel from the big ships, he could not intervene in the Leyte area till the following morning; but if the situation was indeed as serious as seemed to be implied in some of the messages he had received, his help might still be required even at so late an hour. At 11:15 A.M., therefore, Task Force 34 (less two heavy and two light cruisers) reversed its course, taking with it Admiral Bogan's group (38.2) and slowing down to 16 knots to fuel destroyers. Later, about 4:30 P.M., unwilling to be tied down to the slower battleships and the carrier operations, Admiral Halsey went ahead at 28 knots with the *New Jersey* and the *Iowa*, three light cruisers, and eight destroyers, prepared if necessary to engage Kurita's four battleships in night action. But the danger in the south had already passed, and the possibility of engaging the enemy was just passing. Kurita was close north of Samar, still without any clear aim, and at dusk, deciding that there was nothing more to be done, he headed for San Bernardino Strait. The bulk of his force had passed through by midnight, leaving one crippled destroyer to be intercepted and sunk by Admiral Halsey's cruisers and destroyers about 1 A.M.

The feeling of relief in the Seventh Fleet when the outcome of Kurita's hesitations was at last realized was, of course, intense. To face this powerful Japanese force Admiral Kinkaid had, since 7 A.M., been doing all he could to prepare and deploy his battleships, cruisers, and destroyers for defense of the Leyte anchorages and beaches. But they were woefully short of ammunition, particularly armor-piercing shell, and most of the destroyers' torpedoes had been fired in Surigao Strait the night before. What the outcome of a resolute Japanese advance would have been no one can now say. How much can sometimes be achieved in defense by inadequate but aggressive forces had just been shown by Admiral C. A. F. Sprague's destroyers and all the aircraft of the escort carrier force. But the Seventh Fleet and the shipping still in the gulf might well have suffered damage, including some loss of army

[16] Halsey and Bryan, *op. cit.*, p. 221. His rage sprang largely from the faulty handling of Nimitz' signal. With the aim of baffling enemy cryptographers, signals had padding added to them which was to be lopped off in the cipher office on receipt. In this instance "Where is Task Force 34" was padded with "the world wonders," and these words were erroneously left on the message that was handed to Halsey—conveying, not unnaturally, an air of sarcastic reproof.

equipment. It is clear that this danger would not have arisen had Admiral Halsey, when he received news from his night shadowers that Kurita was still advancing, toned down, rightly or wrongly, his views on the virtues of concentration and guarded San Bernardino Strait with his battleships and a carrier group.

It remains to relate the last stages of the battle off Cape Engaño during the afternoon of October 25, and the last blows at Kurita's force on the following morning.

In the north Admiral Mitscher was left with only two carrier groups (with cruisers but without battleships) to continue the chase of Ozawa's force, still retreating to the northward at its best speed. Striking forces were sent in from 1 P.M. on. Soon after 2 P.M. the *Zuikaku*, last of the carriers that had attacked Pearl Harbor, succumbed to bomb and torpedo hits and went down, to be followed an hour later by the *Zuiho*. About 4:30 P.M. the crippled *Chiyoda* was overtaken by cruisers and destroyers which Admiral Mitscher had sent ahead, and she too went to the bottom. There remained only the battleships *Ise* and *Hyuga* and the light forces. Although additional strikes, employing ninety-six aircraft, were aimed at them between 3 P.M. and 6 P.M., the only hit was one bomb on the *Ise* which did only superficial damage. The past days and weeks of incessant and intense activity were no doubt beginning to tell on the American pilots, and accuracy suffered. So at last the Japanese remnant could draw clear, though a destroyer that had been picking up survivors was overtaken by light cruisers and destroyers about 10 P.M., to be sunk an hour later. American submarines had been disposed to intercept the retreat, but their only success was to sink the damaged *Tama*. The rest, two battleships, two light cruisers, and eight destroyers, after one more turn to the southward for a time in response to the appeals of the stricken destroyer, made the best of their way to Japan.

The two carrier groups with Admiral Mitscher now shaped course for Ulithi to refuel and replenish, and could take no further part in the battle; but by 6 A.M. the next day Admiral Halsey had with him off San Bernardino Strait McCain's recently refueled group (38.1) and Bogan's ships (38.2) which, despite their intensive operations of the past two days, were still capable of another effort. From these two groups, as soon as daylight permitted, strikes were launched at Kurita's force as it retreated through the island.[17] About 8:30 A.M. the Japanese battle-

[17] The light carrier *Independence* of Admiral Bogan's group, whose aircraft, specially trained in night flying, had been doing the searching and shadowing during the two preceding nights, sent in a small striking force about 4 A.M. (October 26), but widespread thunderstorms prevented its finding the enemy.

ships were found and attacked as they were steaming south between Mindoro and Panay islands. The *Yamato* was hit by two bombs, and the light cruiser *Noshiro* was first crippled and then sunk by a later wave. Later, too, a damaged destroyer was sunk. But no further serious damage was done to the main body of Kurita's force, either by the carrier strikes or by a force of twenty-four Liberators of the Thirteenth Air Force which attacked about 11 A.M. and succeeded only in inflicting some casualties in the *Yamato* by splinters from near misses. Throughout these attacks the antiaircraft fire from the Japanese ships was still heavy, and at last they were receiving a certain amount of help from their shore-based fighters. Kurita continued to stand to the southward and then to the westward, and by 6 P.M. he was passing north of Palawan and out into the South China Sea. From there he made a wide detour to the westward. Two days later he anchored once more in Brunei Bay.

Last scene of all in this long series of fierce battles is of further trials and successes for the Seventh Fleet's gallant escort carriers. The two damaged groups, those of Admiral T. L. Sprague and Admiral C. A. F. Sprague, had to retire to Ulithi, leaving Admiral Stump's group to continue supporting the Leyte operations. But the former were not yet out of the wood, for about noon (October 26) six or more Kamikaze aircraft made for the southern group. Four were shot down by defending aircraft and one by gunfire, but one hit the *Suwannee*. Damage was severe and casualties were heavy, but fire fighting succeeded in averting destruction.

As if to avenge this damage, Admiral Stump's group was once more showing that escort carriers could achieve far more than their regular tasks. On the evening of October 25, four Japanese transports from Mindanao, escorted by a light cruiser (*Kinu*) and a destroyer that had joined them from Manila, had succeeded in landing 2,000 troops at Ormoc Bay, on the west coast of Leyte, to reinforce the hard-pressed defenders. Next morning these ships were sighted by Admiral Stump's scouting aircraft as they steamed north between Leyte and Cebu islands. Thereafter they were attacked with every aircraft Admiral Stump could make available. All torpedoes and heavy bombs had been expended in the battle off Samar the day before, but with no more than rockets and relatively small bombs the American pilots achieved a near annihilation. By the afternoon two transports and the destroyer had been sunk, and about sunset the *Kinu* too went down.[18]

[18] The *Kinu* had been attacked by aircraft from Admiral Bogan's group as she was leaving Manila on the morning of October 24, and may have received initial damage then.

The trial of strength between the American and Japanese fleets, covering four days of activity at the highest pitch, had come to an end. The Japanese fleet, though prepared to risk all in defense of the Philippines, had not, in the event, fought to the last man. Of the nine battleships that had taken part, six were still afloat and could be repaired before very long. And, though all four carriers had been sunk, there were four new ones in Japan. But the losses sustained by the Japanese in battleships and carriers had nonetheless been devastating, and in addition they had lost six heavy cruisers, four light cruisers, and nine destroyers, as well as a large proportion of the First and Second Air fleets. The Americans had lost only one light carrier, two escort carriers, two destroyers, and one destroyer escort; and, though the continuous activity of their striking forces had cost them some ninety aircraft, their reserves of planes and pilots were ample. It was clear to the Japanese that any attempt to dispute command of the sea with their remaining surface forces would be futile, and this judgment had to extend even to carrier-borne aircraft, for once more there were no pilots available, and new ones took a long time to train.[19]

From this point on, therefore, the Japanese Navy had to rely almost solely on its land-based aircraft for resisting the further step-by-step advances of the United States forces, which were evidently to be expected. Here too their losses had been so heavy and their reserve of pilots was so scanty that not much could be expected of orthodox operations. But the Japanese had one powerful asset remaining: the patriotic fervor and highly developed self-control of many of their officers and men, which permitted the formation of the "special attack corps," the Kamikaze aircraft, on a wide basis. In this activity they were joined by the army's air forces. Although the latter had not previously been trained in attacking ships, the technique was comparatively simple to learn.

This, then, was the situation that the United States Navy and the seaborne expeditions with whose safety it was charged had to face. No longer was there any appreciable danger from surface ships; and Japanese submarines had not shown themselves of much account. But from now on American forces must constantly guard against thrusts that only the complete disintegration of the attacking aircraft could prevent from striking home. For the present the damage inflicted, though a destructive mixture of fire and explosion, did not penetrate armor; but

[19] If any further emphasis was needed on this aspect of the situation, it was soon to be given. Two of the new carriers were sunk by American submarines during the next two months: the *Shinano* on November 29 off the Japanese coast, and the *Unryu* on December 19 in the East China Sea.

there was no reason to believe that some form of armor-piercing would not be developed in specially designed machines. Though, as events were to show, it would take more than such last-hope methods to halt or even to slow down the massive and superbly equipped American forces, there was no doubt that the Japanese had introduced a form of warfare calling for a scale of defense out of all proportion to the size of the attack. Particularly at the start, these new tactics put a severe strain on all officers and men in warships and transports.

21

RECONQUEST OF THE PHILIPPINES, II:
From Leyte to Luzon

THE CONQUEST OF LEYTE proved a stiff undertaking, owing partly to the heavy seasonal rains to which the eastern islands of the Philippines are subjected, and partly to the reinforcements that the enemy managed to bring up from time to time. When invasion of the Philippines was clearly imminent, the Japanese army had built up a reserve in central Luzon; now that the blow had fallen, some of these troops were sent to the front via Ormoc Bay on Leyte's west coast. But they suffered casualties en route, for the ships carrying them were attacked whenever sighted—notably by aircraft of Task Force 38 on November 11, when four transports, five destroyers, and one destroyer escort were sunk while entering the bay, and by Seventh Fleet destroyers on the night of December 2–3, when each side lost one destroyer. To put a permanent stop to these operations, it was decided to seize a position ashore, and on December 7 an amphibious force under Rear Admiral Struble, consisting mainly of destroyer transports and infantry landing craft, supported by destroyers, landed about 7,000 men. There was little opposition ashore, but Kamikaze aircraft came into action, sinking a destroyer and a destroyer transport, and another destroyer a few days later.

Throughout November, while the stubborn fight for Leyte was in progress, Task Force 38 had been actively engaged at frequent intervals; five strong attacks were put in, some of them lasting two days. By this time Vice Admiral Mitscher had hauled down his flag for a spell, and Vice Admiral McCain was in command. Because of the more intensive defense needed to oppose Kamikaze tactics, the force had been reorganized in three groups instead of four. And since it was now clear that the main future danger would be from the air, whether Kamikaze or more orthodox attack, the striking forces were aimed

306

mainly against the airfields in Luzon. Warships and other shipping in Manila Bay were hit when opportunity offered, and during the month three cruisers and eight destroyers were sunk, as well as many transports, tankers, and freighters. But air supremacy was the most important factor, and the Japanese air forces in the Philippines were being worn down faster than they could be replaced. Occasionally they were still able to hit back with vigor. On November 2 they caused some damage and casualties to one carrier group, and again at the end of the month (November 25) they counterattacked in strength. But some 700 aircraft had been destroyed, and their numbers were dwindling. Despite the patent superiority of American aircraft and pilots, both individually and in the strength in which they could operate, all this hard fighting in the air and attack on heavily defended ground targets could not, of course, be engaged in without casualties, and during the month ninety-seven aircraft of Task Force 38 were lost in combat. But, as before, these could be quickly replaced at Ulithi or at sea by aircraft that had been transported forward in escort carriers.

Because of the rains it soon became evident that, even when cleared of the enemy, Leyte could not in itself provide the airfields needed for the next main step, whose objective was Luzon. The central plain of Luzon, running from Lingayen Gulf to Manila Bay, was the core of the Philippines and the chief center of Japanese air forces. Some intermediate airfields had to be provided, therefore, and the Americans decided to capture sufficient ground on Mindoro Island for the purpose. Here, south of central Luzon and on the west side of the islands, the rainfall was less heavy and airstrips would be easier to make. When constructed, they would be only 100 miles from Manila.

For this operation, again under Rear Admiral Struble, some 20,000 troops were to be landed to hold the territory needed for airfields. Although strong ground opposition was not expected, the expedition was given full support, both locally and by Admiral Halsey's covering operation. Three old battleships, seven cruisers, six escort carriers, and many destroyers accompanied the amphibious force for the assault, which went in on December 15. On December 14, 15, and 16 Task Force 38, operating east of the Philippines, struck heavily at Luzon airfields. Although the latter operation gave a large measure of local air control, it could not put a stop to all Kamikaze attacks, some of which succeeded in hitting Admiral Struble's flagship (the light cruiser *Nashville*) and several tank landing ships, causing heavy casualties. But the operation went forward. As had been surmised, there was little opposition ashore, and work on airfield construction was at once put in hand.

On withdrawing to the eastward to refuel on completion of the covering operations, Admiral Halsey's ships encountered a heavy and unexpected typhoon. The main body of the force escaped with a severe battering, but three destroyers that were riding light from lack of fuel capsized and sank.

Within a few weeks of the Mindoro landings, General Kenney's aircraft were established there, and the invasion of Luzon could go ahead. In organization and scale it was a replica of the assault on Leyte. Under General MacArthur were the Seventh Fleet, the Sixth Army, and the Far East Air Force. Admiral Kinkaid's Seventh Fleet comprised much the same ships as before, and once more the Third and Seventh Amphibious forces of Vice Admirals Wilkinson and Barbey each carried an army corps, each with two divisions in the assault. Only the army formations were new, these two corps having recently been added to General Krueger's Sixth Army. As in the attack on Leyte, this expedition was staged from western New Guinea, 2,000 miles to the rear.

The plan was to pass by the heavily defended mouth of Manila Bay and land in Lingayen Gulf, 110 miles north of Manila, as the Japanese had landed three years before. Covering operations were started by Task Force 38 on January 3, 1945, with strikes at airfields in the Ryukyu Islands and Formosa, whence the point of attack was shifted on January 6 to Luzon, and then back to Formosa. Meanwhile, on January 6, Vice Admiral Oldendorf's battleships, cruisers, and destroyers, and Rear Admiral Durgin's escort carriers, started their local bombardments which were to last for three days, pounding the beach defenses and covering the minesweeping. Two hours after sunrise on January 9, after further furious bombardments, the assaulting forces landed with little opposition to confront them.

Despite the great superiority of the American forces and the weight of Admiral McCain's air attacks, the Kamikaze corps again succeeded in striking some blows during the preliminary operation. An escort carrier (*Ommaney Bay*) and three minesweepers were sunk, three of the bombarding battleships and a cruiser were hit and suffered many casualties, and the *Australia*, with her Leyte damage repaired, was again hit. But with these attacks the Japanese had, for the time being, shot their bolt, and within a few days nearly a quarter of a million troops were landed.

While General MacArthur's forces were landing in Lingayen Gulf, Admiral Halsey was taking Task Force 38 on a raid into the South China Sea. Passing close south of Formosa he stood toward Indochina, and on January 12 Admiral McCain sent in the striking forces against shipping in Saigon and Camranh Bay and on the trade route from the south to Japan, which passed close to the coast. Three convoys were hit, one of them being annihilated. Such slight air opposition as was encountered was easily disposed of. Turning back to the northeastward, Task Force 38 attacked Formosa on January 15, and Hong Kong, Canton, and Hainan on the 16th. On January 20 the force reentered the Pacific, striking once more at Formosa. Here, for the first time during the cruise, substantial opposition was met. One of the big carriers (*Ticonderoga*) was hit by two Kamikaze and badly damaged, as was also a destroyer. After a final strike at Okinawa on January 22, Task Force 38 returned to Ulithi.

The American army's advance from Lingayen to Manila progressed steadily against stubborn resistance. The main fighting was out of reach of naval support, but amphibious operations were still needed to prevent the enemy from taking up the strong Bataan position and to assist in forcing an entrance into Manila Bay. These operations were mounted by the Seventh Amphibious Force in rapid succession, air support being provided by the Far East Air Force. On January 29 some 40,000 men were landed just north of Subic Bay, and there was a subsidiary landing the following day on an island in the bay, which thus became available as an anchorage. On January 31, 8,000 men were landed at Nasugbu, which lies on the peninsula southwest of Manila, that is, south of the entrance to the bay.

On February 4 General MacArthur's troops reached the outskirts of Manila, and a fierce battle commenced which was to lay most of the city in ruins in the ensuing month. While the fighting was in progress, amphibious and airborne forces were breaking down the powerful defenses at the bay's mouth. After several days of heavy bombardment by cruisers, destroyers, and army aircraft, troops went ashore at Mariveles on Bataan Peninsula on February 15; the next day seaborne and airborne assaults secured a footing on the fortress island of Corregidor. Losses were high, and it was some days before the garrison of 4,000 Japanese could be wiped out. They had in fact outnumbered the assault troops, which were limited by the room available for landing. But by the end of the month all was over, the entrance channels had been swept, and American shipping was once more able to enter Manila Bay.

Thereafter the reconquest of the Philippines (i.e., the elimination of the Japanese troops still in action) was the affair mainly of the Sixth Army, which was to continue fighting till the end of the war. But many further amphibious operations were needed, and troops were landed on various islands under cover of ship and army air bombardments, which were always sufficient to prevent any serious opposition. In February a position was secured in Palawan. In March there were landings on Mindanao (the large southern island where the initial assault on the Philippines had originally been intended—and expected by the

Japanese), on Panay, and on Cebu. In April there were further landings in Mindanao and in southeastern Luzon, at Legaspi. These were the main operations, and no less than twelve minor landings took place during the same period. Finally, its task in the Philippines completed, the Seventh Amphibious Force was transferred to Borneo. Here Australian troops were landed, at Tarakan (May 1), Brunei Bay (June 10), and Balikpapan (July 1), and Japanese occupation of Borneo oil fields was at an end.

22

THE LAST PHASE: *Southeast Asia, Iwo Jima, Okinawa, and the Bombardment of Japan*

WITH SHIPS AND aircraft firmly established in the Philippines and an increasing number of Superfortresses working from the Marianas, American forces could exert a pressure on Japan itself which was gradually becoming lethal. The vital supplies of oil and aviation fuel from the south had to run the gauntlet of air as well as submarine attack as they passed up the China coast; the Marianas aircraft could bomb continuously, if as yet but lightly, all the industrial areas of the home islands. But much more was still needed. Only an invasion of Honshu, the main island, could guarantee surrender, and other footholds were required both for exerting preinvasion pressure and for supporting the invasion itself. With these footholds gained, however, there would also be the hope that the pressure brought to bear from them on seaborne imports and on industry would in itself prove decisive, and would obviate the need for the final stroke.

To gain these objects two main steps were determined on. First, the Marianas aircraft must be enabled to hit harder. With not less than 1,300 miles to their objectives, they had to keep an ample margin of fuel and had to work without fighter escort, flying high; thus they were restricted to relatively small bomb loads. Halfway to Tokyo lay the small island of Iwo Jima (5 miles by 2) with two airfields. The island in itself was not a serious nuisance, for it had been kept under restraint by frequent air attacks and ship bombardments. But its capture would radically alter the situation. With these airfields in American hands, Mustang fighters based there could join the Superfortresses and escort them on their raids. The latter could then bomb more accurately, and at the same time could carry heavier bomb loads, for they would not need to keep so large a margin of fuel: any returning bomber that found itself

311

short would be able to land on Iwo Jima and replenish. The capture of the island, therefore, was to be the next amphibious operation.

While this step would ensure a thoroughly effective campaign by the heavy bombers of the Twentieth Army Air Force working from the Marianas, more pressure still could be exerted if airfields nearer the mainland of Asia were occupied. For this purpose the island of Okinawa in the Ryukyus was the obvious choice. It already had airfields, and there was plenty of scope for further development. From these airfields, with the great strength of United States aircraft which could be established there, and with the dwindling resources of the enemy, it should be possible to cut down Japan's seaborne supplies to a mere trickle. Not only would the route from the south be cut, but even the short passages from Korea, Manchuria, and North China (whence came some special coal essential to industry as well as important supplies of food) would be severely harassed. Air forces in Okinawa, too, would be able to provide powerful support for the invasion of Kyushu, intended as the last step before the Honshu campaign. It was planned, therefore, that the capture of Okinawa should follow closely on the Iwo Jima operation.

Before describing these two amphibious operations, the last of the long series that brought United States forces to the threshold of Japan, some account must be given of the genesis of the British Pacific Fleet, which was to play a subsidiary part in the Okinawa operation and was thereafter to contribute its share to the final air and sea bombardments of Japan. For this story we must turn back to operations in the Indian Ocean in 1944.

As that year progressed, and as the campaigns in the Mediterranean and later in northern Europe had less and less need of naval collaboration, reinforcements could be sent to Admiral Somerville's Eastern Fleet which would allow it to take a more active part in the Southeast Asia campaign. Hitherto, though there had been some aircraft carriers, old battleships, and cruisers, the number of destroyers had been insufficient to enable the fleet to act offensively; for a long time it had been based as far away as Kilindini, in East Africa. Only the submarines, based on Trincomalee, had been able to keep up the attack, harassing shipping in the Strait of Malacca and to the northward thereof. This was an important enemy supply line to Burma, for the overland communications from Siam were inferior and often were interrupted by bombing. It was also by this route that the Japanese had to supply their outposts in the Andaman and Nicobar Islands. Here the British submarines had taken a considerable toll, which increased as time went on; and now surface ships and their aircraft were to take a hand as well. In March 1944 the first destroyer reinforcements arrived, as did also the American carrier *Saratoga*, lent from the Pacific Fleet. On April 19 the first operation was staged. It was a strike from the *Illustrious* and the *Saratoga*, with battleship and cruiser escort, at the port of Sabang (on an island close to the northwest point of Sumatra) and at a nearby airfield on Sumatra itself. Damage was inflicted, while a light enemy counterattack was warded off without casualties.

This operation, despite its small scale, gave valuable experience to a fleet so long compelled to be relatively inactive, and a month later the *Illustrious* and the *Saratoga* struck farther afield, this time at Surabaya in Java, some 2,200 miles from Trincomalee, which was now the fleet's base. Crossing Java from a launching position off the south coast, nearly 100 aircraft attacked Surabaya on May 17, sinking some ships and putting out of action an important oil refinery nearby. There was some opposition and several Japanese aircraft were destroyed, but no damage or casualties were sustained by the Allied forces, which included Australian, Dutch, and French ships in addition to the British and American carriers. A month later (June 21) a smaller force under Vice Admiral Power, second-in-command of the Eastern Fleet, struck at Port Blair in the Andamans with aircraft from the *Illustrious*.

Further operations gave scope to the guns of battleships, cruisers, and destroyers, as well as to the carriers' aircraft. On July 25 Sabang was bombarded with devastating effect at a very small cost in casualties, and in October there were similar bombardments of Japanese positions in the Nicobar Islands. Meanwhile, on August 24 and September 18 (*Victorious* and *Indomitable*), and again on December 20 (*Indomitable* and *Illustrious*), there were more carrier-borne air attacks under Rear Admiral Moody, commanding the Eastern Fleet aircraft carriers. On these occasions the attacks were launched against industrial targets in northern Sumatra.

By this time the Eastern Fleet had been further reinforced, and the decision had been taken to divide it into two sections: the Pacific Fleet and the East Indies Fleet. The former would comprise all the newest ships and would work with the United States Pacific Fleet as soon as arrangements could be made for keeping it supplied at so long a distance from any existing British base. The East Indies Fleet, consisting of some old battleships (eventually the *Nelson*, the *Queen Elizabeth*, and the French *Richelieu*), escort carriers, cruisers, destroyers, and submarines would continue to support the Burma campaign and the amphibious operations against Malaya which had been planned to follow it. Admiral Fraser, who had recently relieved Admiral Somerville, would command the Pacific Fleet, and Admiral Power, the East Indies Fleet.

The first move under the new organization was made in December 1944, when Admiral Fraser sailed for Australia in the *Howe*. In January 1945 he was followed by the aircraft carriers *Indomitable*, *Inde-*

fatigable, Victorious, and *Illustrious,* with the battleship *King George V,* five cruisers, and ten destroyers. These formed the majority of the ships that would cooperate with the American Fast Carrier Force from the Okinawa campaign to the end of the war. Vice Admiral Rawlings in the *King George V* was second-in-command to Admiral Fraser, and commanded the seagoing fleet as a whole. Rear Admiral Vian in the *Indomitable* commanded the aircraft carriers and, in conformity with American practice, took tactical command whenever flying was in progress. Like their American counterparts, the carriers were equipped with Avengers (to be used mainly as bombers since torpedoing of ships had become a secondary matter), and their fighters were mainly Hellcats and Corsairs, the latter also an American machine, but not quite so handy as the Hellcat and more difficult to land on a carrier. They also carried a few Seafires, valuable in defense but of insufficient endurance for striking forces, and some Fireflies, two-seater fighter reconnaissance aircraft. Though about the same size as the *Essex* class, the British carriers were differently constructed in that they had armored flight decks and closed-in hangars, and as a result they could carry only about half the number of aircraft. It was therefore difficult for them to keep pace with the intensive operations to which the Fast Carrier Force was accustomed, and the closed-in hangars, invaluable in stormy northern seas, were a handicap to rapid operations, particularly in the tropics. But the armored flight decks were to stand them in good stead when assailed by Kamikaze aircraft, and, as noted later, they came through these ordeals with remarkably little damage in comparison with that suffered by the American ships.

While on passage to Australia, the carriers launched two strikes, on January 24 and 29, at oil refineries in the Palembang district of southern Sumatra. These refineries were the main Japanese source of aviation fuel, some of which was still getting through to Japan, and as such they were the most heavily defended positions south of the Philippines. The strong resistance encountered inflicted considerable casualties on the striking forces, but the attacks were pressed well home and the refineries received such severe and lasting damage as to make them of little more use to the enemy.

On February 10 the force arrived at Sydney, which was to be the home base of the British Pacific Fleet. When operating in the forward areas it would be maintained by a fleet train stationed at an advanced base; and from the fleet train would be detached, when needed, a logistic support group (including escort carriers) to replenish the fleet at sea. Much had to be learned by the British fleet to enable it to keep pace with a system that the American fleet had built up in two years of strenuous experience; the provision and equipment of suitable ships for the train had not been easy. Particularly was it handicapped by having to make do with slow tankers. But with some American help in fueling in the early stages, these difficulties were surmounted.

At the end of February Admiral Rawlings with the whole British force, to which the *Howe* had been added as a private ship, sailed from Sydney for Manus. At the same time Admiral Fraser joined Admiral Nimitz at Guam, where the latter had established his forward headquarters. Arrived at Manus, Admiral Rawlings' force was able to spend a few days in exercising and completing with stores before sailing again (March 18) to play its part in the campaign.

We must return now to the proceedings of the American Fast Carrier Force and to the assault on Iwo Jima, which, as already noted, was to be the next important step after the Luzon operations.

At the end of January Admiral Spruance, having planned the next moves, had relieved Admiral Halsey, and the Third Fleet had once more become the Fifth Fleet. Vice Admiral Mitscher was again in command of the Fast Carrier Force (now Task Force 58) and Vice Admiral Turner of the Joint Expeditionary Force, the latter command approximating the amphibious force commands of the Philippine campaign. Most of the old battleships, escort carriers, cruisers, and destroyers of the Seventh Fleet had also been transferred to the Fifth Fleet, and were formed into the Amphibious Support Force under Rear Admiral Blandy.

On February 16 and 17, Task Force 58 struck for the first time at the main island of Japan, hitting airfields and aircraft factories in the Tokyo area. Despite very unfavorable weather, some damage was done which was an important supplement to the work of the Superfortresses, and at the same time helped to prevent interference with the Iwo Jima operations.

The attack on Iwo Jima started on February 16, opening with a three-day aerial and gunnery bombardment by Admiral Blandy's ships and by army aircraft. On February 19, after further bombardment, two divisions of marines were landed on the southeast coast, while a third division lay off in reserve. These forces, comprising some 60,000 men under Lieutenant General H. M. Smith, were opposed by 23,000 Japanese established in deep and elaborate defenses. As in previous landings, the intense preliminary bombardments prevented much opposition to the initial assault; nevertheless, the landing conditions were difficult. Because the beaches were composed of soft volcanic ash, the bows of grounded landing craft would not hold, and many broached to; even tracked amphibious vehicles had trouble in getting ashore. Notwithstanding this handicap, the two assault divisions were landed

315

during the day with relatively light casualties; the reserve division landed the following day. But thereafter the fighting was very severe; progress was slow and casualties were heavy. The advance was, however, continuous, help being given by Admiral Blandy's forces wherever possible. The first and main airfield was captured by the end of the second day, and the second airfield three days later. But much remained to be done and fighting continued till March 16. On March 3, however, a Superfortress returning from Tokyo had already made a successful forced landing, and thereafter repairs and improvements to the airfields were rapidly completed. The capture of Iwo Jima had cost the American forces 4,600 dead and 15,300 wounded, a high price for so small an island, but one that was found to have purchased fully the benefits expected of it. The bombing of Japan by the Twentieth Air Force was increased manyfold in intensity.

During these operations the supporting ships had not been seriously molested by air attack, most attempted raids being on a small scale and easily countered by the fighters of the escort carriers and by shore-based fighters which had been established as soon as the airfields were serviceable. But one raid in the early days (on February 21) had been larger than usual, and some Kamikaze succeeded in penetrating the defense. The Saratoga was hit by no less than five of these machines, but she was able to return to America for repairs. An aircraft that hit the escort carrier Bismarck Sea, however, started such bad fires that the ship eventually capsized with heavy loss of life.

While fighting was in progress ashore, Admiral Mitscher's carriers again (on February 25) attacked airfields and aircraft factories in the Tokyo district, coordinating their operations with an attack on Tokyo itself by more than 200 Superfortresses. Task Force 58 then moved southwest for a strike at the Okinawa airfields on March 1, and thence went to Ulithi to replenish before the next series of operations. The returns of the force to a base to replenish were being made at longer and longer intervals, for the extent to which the carriers could be supplied at sea by service squadrons was being constantly increased in scope, and even the largest types of bombs could be replaced in this way. It was in fact to be a long time before the Fast Carrier Force would again enter a harbor.

Though the island of Okinawa was not large in extent (65 miles long but averaging only 5 miles in width), its capture called for forces on the same scale as those used for invading the Philippines. Not only was its garrison large,[1] but its proximity to Japan made the problem of

[1] The Okinawa garrison numbered nearly 120,000 men, including local levies, though the American plan had estimated it at only 60,000.

preventing air interference from outside a difficult one. In the Philippines, even in the original Leyte landing, some degree of interdiction had been achieved by the strikes of the Fast Carrier Force at the Luzon and Formosa airfields, which had done much to keep the Japanese air forces occupied and their numbers down. But such a policy would not be able to accomplish so much at Okinawa. To the south, such aircraft as remained in Formosa would be prevented from being thrown into the battle in any strength if the airfields in the Sakishima group were kept in subjection by bombardments and fighter patrols. But, in the north, the airfields of Kyushu were little more than 300 miles away, and behind them were the many airfields of Honshu and the whole of the enemy's aircraft supply system. Defense against air attack from the north, therefore, would have to rely to a large extent on meeting the attackers in the air, and the hazards from Kamikaze aircraft, navigated and directed by aircraft of normal type, were clearly going to be grave.

The landing force assigned to this enterprise consisted of the Third Marine Amphibious Corps and the Twenty-fourth Army Corps (each of three divisions), the whole forming the Tenth Army, about 180,000 strong, under Lieutenant General Buckner. This force, embarking at many different ports throughout the Pacific, finally converged on its objective from Saipan, Ulithi, and Leyte. But before it was due to arrive on April 1, much preliminary work had to be done.

The first preparatory attack was by the Fast Carrier Force, which had sailed from Ulithi on March 14 and headed for Japan. On March 18 and 19, working from a position about 100 miles southeast of Kyushu, Admiral Mitscher's aircraft hit hard at the airfields in that island, with some side thrusts at Japanese warships in Kure. On the 19th a lone Japanese aircraft succeeded in bombing the *Franklin* just as she was launching aircraft, causing disastrous fires and the loss of more than 800 men. During the fleet's slow withdrawal on March 20 and 21, with the almost burned-out *Franklin* in company, the Japanese again and again tried to attack, but without success; all attackers were intercepted and shot down before reaching Admiral Mitscher's force. The latter, after replenishing with fuel, then took up its position for intercepting aircraft bound from the north for Okinawa, where preliminary operations were just starting. After the vigorous work of March 18 to 21, however, Japanese ability to interfere from the northward had been so damped down that the American aircraft found little to meet during these first few days.

At the same time Admiral Rawlings' force of carriers and battleships came up from the southward for its first turn of duty as part of Admiral Spruance's Fifth Fleet. Leaving Manus on March 18, it arrived at Ulithi two days later, fueled from American resources, and sailed again on March 23 as Task Force 57. On March 26 it was on station about

317

100 miles south of the Sakishima group and started a series of strikes against the airfields there, and occasionally against those in Formosa. These activities were to continue for the next month (and again later) with periodic withdrawals to seaward to replenish with fuel and aircraft from the logistic support group. During these latter periods the duty of neutralizing the Sakishima airfields was taken over by escort carriers of Admiral Blandy's Support Force.

With everything possible arranged to prevent air interference, the operations in the waters immediately round Okinawa went steadily ahead. Minesweeping had already started (on March 24) under cover of a bombardment by Admiral Lee's battleships of the Fast Carrier Force; on March 26 landings were effected against little opposition in the Kerama group of small islands lying 20 miles west of southern Okinawa. Its valuable anchorage was quickly netted and provided with the other defenses needed. Seaplane tenders and various types of supply ship were brought in, and the Keramas became an important advanced base during operations which, as will be seen, were to be more lengthy than had been expected. Some islets between the Keramas and Okinawa were also occupied as a preliminary move, and during the week beginning on March 24 minesweeping continued and positions ashore were bombarded by Admiral Blandy's ships and carrier aircraft.

Two hours after sunrise on April 1, after the customary intense bombardment from sea and air, the assaulting marines and soldiers landed on the west coast of the south end of Okinawa, sustaining few casualties. By that evening 50,000 men were ashore, and two airfields had been captured; and two days later the American forces were firmly astride the island, cutting off the main enemy force in the southern 12 miles from lighter forces in the north. The latter were steadily driven back and gradually eliminated; but in the south resistance was more powerful and stubborn than anything yet encountered, even on Iwo Jima, and for several weeks progress was negligible.

Meanwhile the Japanese were doing everything that remained in their power to interfere with the shipping of the expeditionary force and the supporting warships. Already, on April 1, the *Indefatigable* of Task Force 57 had been hit by a Kamikaze from Sakishima, fortunately without serious damage; but it was not till April 6 that heavy air attacks came in from the north. When they did come, they drove in more persistently and over a longer period than ever before.

With the opening of this attack, the tactics of the forlorn hope, now the uppermost idea in the Japanese mind, were extended to their surface ships. On April 6 the *Yamato*, with the light cruiser *Yahagi* and eight destroyers, left the Inland Sea with orders to attack shipping off Okinawa, and there was a clear understanding that they were not expected to return. When American shore-based aircraft sighted them that evening, Admiral Mitscher took Task Force 58 north to meet them. Again sighted by patrol aircraft next morning, being then in the East China Sea about 300 miles north of Okinawa, the Japanese ships were attacked throughout the day by carrier-borne aircraft. Bad weather handicapped the striking forces, but by the end of the day the *Yamato*, the *Yahagi*, and a destroyer had been sunk, and three more destroyers were badly damaged. Thus ended the last attempt of the Japanese surface navy to avert defeat. That the attempt was not followed by sorties of the other fighting ships still seaworthy was probably due, not to loss of spirit, but to lack of fuel. It had been difficult to collect enough fuel even for the *Yamato*'s operation, and no more was available for such purposes. During Admiral Mitscher's attacks on the *Yamato*, his force was subjected to air attacks, and one Kamikaze succeeded in hitting the carrier *Hancock*, causing severe damage.

From now on till the end of May, operations to stave off Kamikaze were almost continuous, though there were occasional lulls of a few days. From time to time Task Force 58 or some of its groups moved north for attacks on the Kyushu airfields, in the hope of diminishing the number of aircraft available for attack. But most of the time these carriers and the escort carriers of the support force were engaged in intercepting raids, which now included the additional menace of a piloted, rocket-propelled flying bomb, released from a parent aircraft. During April and May about 900 Kamikaze aircraft of various types, some navy, some army, effected their self-immolations; perhaps 200 of them hit their targets. The big American and British carriers, the most obvious marks, took their share of hits. On April 16, during an attack on the Kyushu airfields, the *Intrepid* was heavily damaged; on May 4 the *Formidable* (which had recently relieved the *Illustrious*) was hit off Sakishima, as was also the *Indomitable*, though the latter's assailant bounced over the side without causing damage; on May 9 the *Victorious* was hit and the *Formidable* was hit again. All these British carriers were again in action after a few hours for repairs, but they lost a number of aircraft, and in some instances their speed of handling was reduced. Then, on May 11, Admiral Mitscher's flagship, the *Bunker Hill*, was crashed by two aircraft almost simultaneously, starting fierce fires which cost nearly 400 lives and burned out much of the ship. Three days later, during another attack on Kyushu, the *Enterprise* was hit and damaged.

Though the carriers were no doubt thought by the Japanese to be their most important targets, smaller ships suffered severely. Destroyers, in particular, often took the brunt of the attacks, for it was the practice to protect the fleet and shipping by throwing out pickets to distances varying from 12 to 50 miles, each picket consisting of a destroyer equipped for fighter direction and a small force of fighters. It was on these destroyer pickets, as the first warships sighted, that the Kamikaze often tried to crash. Twelve destroyers and more than 20 smaller ships were sunk during the campaign, and when all was over there were nearly 200 ships of various types needing repair. A small amount of damage had been done by orthodox bombing, but most of it resulted from hits or near misses by Kamikaze. Fighting the Japanese at sea was still a dangerous enterprise despite their dwindling resources; during this period the United States Navy lost nearly 5,000 killed.

Ashore, in the southern part of Okinawa, the campaign was long-drawn-out, for the Japanese positions were exceedingly strong and their fighting could not have been fiercer or more resolute. Organized resistance did not cease till June 22, when, their resources at an end, the Japanese general and his chief of staff committed hara-kiri. General Buckner had been killed by a shell five days earlier while watching the decisive attack of the last phase.

Before this final victory ashore, local defenses, including land-based aircraft, had been sufficiently established for the Fast Carrier forces, American and British, to be withdrawn. The latter, less adapted as yet to prolonged periods of operations, had already had a brief spell in Leyte Gulf from April 23 to May 1; after a last day of strikes on May 25, it set course for Manus, and thence to Australian and New Zealand ports for repairs and replenishments. The American force remained on station for another fortnight, but under a different command. At the end of May Admiral Halsey again took over from Admiral Spruance, so that the latter could start planning for the invasion of Kyushu, and Admiral McCain again relieved Admiral Mitscher. Once more the main fighting force of the United States Navy was the Third Fleet, and the Fast Carrier Force was Task Force 38. As such it continued to operate between Okinawa and Kyushu for a few days longer. After striking at the Kyushu airfields on June 2 and 3, it was subjected to a severe typhoon in which the heavy cruiser *Pittsburgh* lost 100 feet of her bows, and two other cruisers, two carriers, and two destroyers were badly damaged. When the weather moderated, there was another air strike (June 8) and some gun bombardments of off-lying islands (June 8 and 9) before this sea- and battle-scarred fleet set course for Leyte Gulf. There, on June 13, it anchored, having been at sea continuously for ninety-one days.

One of the main reasons for capturing Okinawa was to provide airfields from which to attack such Japanese shipping as was still bringing supplies from China, Manchuria, and Korea. These operations were quickly put in train by the land-based forces established on Okinawa. In view of the intensity with which these air attacks could be conducted, the American submarines, hitherto the chief destroyers of shipping in all these waters, transferred their main activities to the seas least accessible to aircraft. In April and May, while the fighting on Okinawa was still in progress, they had been concentrated off the southern coasts of Japan and in the Yellow Sea; but now that aircraft could take over much of that area the submarine effort was shifted to the Sea of Japan, where there was still some traffic from northern Korea. In addition, with so many submarines available and relatively few areas to work in, some could be spared for the "lifeguard" duty of rescuing airmen who had come down in the sea. Submarines had already been employed extensively and successfully in this duty during carrier strikes, lying closer inshore than it was advisable for surface vessels to go, and now they were to perform the same services for the Okinawa aircraft when working against shipping in the Yellow Sea and Tsushima Strait.

It is convenient here to summarize the achievements of the submarines from June 30, 1944, when the matter was last considered (see p. 277, above), to the end of the war. During this period of a little more than a year seventy-one new submarines had been commissioned and seventeen had been lost, seven in Japanese home waters and ten elsewhere. As already noted, 1944 was a record year for sinkings of merchant ships, 492 aggregating nearly 2.4 million tons having gone down; of these the second half year probably claimed the majority. In 1945, for the reasons just mentioned (lack of targets and employment of American aircraft to attack many of the remaining routes), the sinkings were at a lower rate, 132 ships aggregating nearly .5 million tons being sunk from January 1 to the end of the war. But successes against warships had continued much as before. After June 30, 1944, submarines had sunk two big aircraft carriers (see p. 304 n. 19), three escort carriers, one battleship, two heavy cruisers (see p. 289, above), four light cruisers, fifteen destroyers, and eleven submarines. These are bare figures for many courageous exploits, but they will perhaps give the reader some idea of how notable an achievement was the part played by the United States submarines in the destruction of the Japanese surface fleet.

With the Allied forces closing in on Japan and the enemy's navy impotent to stop them, we must turn for a time to the southern theater of war. Here, based on Singapore, there were still a few cruisers, and for them, unlike their sisters in Japan, there was ample fuel available locally. But there was little they could do. In Burma, under Admiral Mountbatten's supreme command, the British Fourteenth Army under General Slim, assisted by minor but very effective amphibious operations on the flank, was steadily forcing back the Japanese army.

Admiral Power's East Indies Fleet was amply sufficient to cover these operations against Japanese ships, and to keep Japanese outposts in the Andamans, Nicobars, and Sumatra in subjection by air and sea bombardment. The eventual advance was rapid, and on May 2 Rangoon was occupied by a seaborne force. Though preparations had been made for a seaborne assault in strength, so as to close the campaign before the monsoon would prohibit further action, there was in fact no fighting, for the Japanese had withdrawn a few days earlier.

Soon after this operation came the enemy's last naval venture in these waters. The heavy cruiser *Haguro* and a destroyer had gone north from Singapore to assist in supplying their hard-pressed army in southern Burma, and on May 16, while on her return passage, the *Haguro* was sighted and bombed by an Avenger from the escort carrier *Shah*, though apparently without any reduction of her speed or fighting power. Vice Admiral Walker (second-in-command, East Indies), who was to the westward with the bulk of the fleet, sent in five destroyers to intercept the enemy in the Strait of Malacca. They succeeded in this mission, and there followed a brilliant night action in which the destroyers, under Captain Power of the *Saumarez*, countered the *Haguro*'s liberty of movement by attacking from all directions simultaneously, sinking the *Haguro* with torpedoes despite the superior weight of her gunfire.

Three weeks later another heavy cruiser, the *Ashigara*, was sunk between Singapore and Bangka Strait by one of the British submarines cooperating with the submarines of the United States Seventh Fleet. Only two cruisers remained at Singapore, both having been previously damaged by American submarines; one of these, the *Takao*, was soon to be put permanently out of action by a British midget submarine which penetrated the harbor defenses. In July, therefore, when the East Indies Fleet took the first steps in the intended Malayan campaign (minesweeping in the northern Strait of Malacca and the occupation of an island 350 miles north of Penang), there was no opposition at sea.

By this time the climax was approaching. The war in Europe had been brought to its victorious end two months before, and the forces that the Allies could bring into action against Japan were now limited only by the problems of transport and supply. In the Pacific the main American and British naval forces were once more refreshed and ready for action, and a start could be made with the operations that were to precede the invasion of Kyushu. For this coming campaign, and for the invasion of Honshu in the vicinity of Tokyo, which was planned to follow in 1946, the system of command had been altered. No longer was the theater of war to be divided into General MacArthur's South-

west Pacific Area and Admiral Nimitz' Pacific Ocean Area; in future
all army forces were to be under General MacArthur and all naval
forces under Admiral Nimitz. For the first time Admirals Halsey and
Spruance would be in active command simultaneously. The latter
would be responsible for direct support of amphibious operations,
while the former would use the Fast Carrier Force, working in coordination with the Twentieth Air Force, to neutralize the Japanese air
force and aircraft industry in Honshu, as well as to pound all other industries and means of existence. So as to give the vast invasion forces
full use of all bases to the westward, the Carrier Force would once
more be supplied from Eniwetok in the Marshall Islands.

After a spell at anchor in Leyte Gulf of less than three weeks, the
Fast Carrier Force, with Admiral Halsey in the battleship *Missouri*
directing its operations, put to sea again early in July, and by the 10th
it was in station off the Honshu coast. Here, from a position about 170
miles southeast of Tokyo, the full strength of its striking forces, some
1,200 aircraft, was launched against the airfields surrounding and to
the north of the enemy capital. This attack followed closely on heavy
raids by the Twentieth Air Force both here and against other industrial
cities, raids that were being made at frequent intervals in strengths of
as much as 500 Superfortresses. There was little resistance to these attacks in the air, and no attempt by Japanese aircraft to strike back at
the carriers. Nor was there any more resistance when the fleet moved
northward up the coast to strike at northern Honshu and southern Hok-
kaido on July 14 and 15, the chief aim being to destroy aircraft that
the Japanese might have supposed they had withdrawn out of harm's
way. So little had now to be feared that the battleships could indulge in
gun bombardments of steel mills and oil installations in two coastal
towns in this area.

By July 17 Admiral Halsey was back again off Tokyo, where he was
joined by Admiral Rawlings and the British force, which had sailed
from Australia on June 28. This move added four British carriers to
the American sixteen, as well as three battleships and the cruisers and
destroyers; the British ships, organized as a group of Task Force 38,
came under Admiral Halsey's tactical command. The junction of the
fleets was signalized the same day by a bombardment of coastal positions by American and British battleships, and on the following day by
further air strikes in the Tokyo area, particularly against the remnant
of warships at Yokosuka, the *Nagato* being damaged beyond repair.
During the week of July 24–28 the point of attack was shifted to the
Inland Sea, particularly to the main naval base at Kure, where the two
remaining big Japanese carriers were put out of action and the last

three battleships sunk. Then, on July 30, there was once more an air attack on targets near Tokyo and another battleship bombardment of a coastal town.

During the first week in August Admiral Halsey's force was battling with a severe typhoon which put a check on flying. But in the supreme councils of Japan, a realization of the hopelessness of continuing to resist these blows from sea and air and the impossibility of checking the creeping paralysis of the blockade was at last taking firm hold. For some time the Emperor had been urging his ministers to surrender on any terms acceptable to the Allies, but the chiefs of the army still believed that resistance to invasion and the casualties it would inflict on the American army would better the terms they could make. Now, however, the Emperor's views were given sudden and overwhelming backing. On August 6 a Superfortress flying from Saipan dropped the first atomic bomb on Hiroshima with devastating effect, and three days later a second bomb was dropped on Nagasaki. And in the interim Russia, in pursuance of a previous pledge to the Allies, had declared war on Japan and invaded Manchuria. The army's opposition to the Emperor therefore gave way, and negotiations for surrender were at once put in hand.

For these negotiations a few more days were needed, and during this time the Fast Carrier Force delivered its final blows: on August 9 and 10 against northern Honshu, with another battleship bombardment in addition to air strikes; on August 13 against Tokyo when Japanese aircraft made a last, unsuccessful attempt to hit back at the fleet; and on August 15 when a dawn strike was sent in just before receipt of the cease-fire order that put an end to all hostilities. This order followed the provisional acceptance of the Japanese surrender on the day before, and with it went directions for the first steps in the occupation of Japan and the formal surrender that were to follow.

The brief interval for preparation required for these steps was prolonged for two days by another typhoon. But on August 28 the first American airborne forces landed near Tokyo; on the 29th Admiral Halsey entered Tokyo Bay in the *Missouri* and anchored off Yokosuka; and on the following day General MacArthur arrived by air with additional army formations, and a seaborne force of United States Marines occupied Yokosuka Naval Base. Meanwhile Admirals Nimitz and Fraser had arrived from Guam in the battleships *South Dakota* and *Duke of York*. On September 2, 1945, the instrument of surrender was signed on board the *Missouri* by the Japanese Foreign Minister and a representative of the Japanese Army. With the surrender thus formally enacted, General MacArthur signed the document as supreme Allied commander. Representatives of all the Allied powers followed, Admirals Nimitz and Fraser signing for the United States and Great Britain respectively. On September 8 Tokyo was formally occupied by the United States Army, and within a few weeks General MacArthur was in effective control of the conquered nation.

In the six years of fighting now ended, sea affairs had played as large a part as in any previous war of comparable importance. In Great Britain and in the United States the proportion of national effort employed in providing and manning warships and maritime aircraft was at least as high as it had ever been in the past. In Japan it was probably higher, and in Germany it was very substantial despite the tremendous exertions on land and in the aerial war against industry. So large was the sum of these efforts, and so extensive the experience derived from hard struggles on, over, and under all the seas of the world, that the conduct of maritime warfare had attained an efficiency excelling anything hitherto known. In the Atlantic the hardest and most prolonged fighting had been needed to defeat a powerful, well-directed, and courageous submarine force menacing the communications on which victory in Europe depended. In the Pacific the United States Navy had shown itself able to bring forward the United States Army, together with its air force, in a fighting advance step by step to positions from which Japan could have been invaded. Never before had the sea power of a nation been exerted so overwhelmingly at so great a distance from its home against an enemy of comparable strength.

In a maritime war of such magnitude there had been, as would be expected, changes in equipment and technique which modified some of the previous conceptions of naval strategy. There were also, as is usual at the end of a long war, many developments in train which were expected to bring about further and more drastic modifications. These latter developments, including the atomic bomb, which had not yet been used at sea, are outside the scope of this history. The former, the changes that had already taken place, have been indicated in the course of the narrative, but it is perhaps worthwhile to conclude by summarizing very briefly the main developments.

Foremost among the changes were those relating to aircraft. That there would be many alterations of this kind had been realized before the war, but the lines they would take were at that time much disputed. Broadly, it may be said that in the outcome there were two main aspects: first, the eventual experience of the Pacific war showed that, in normal weather with normal periods of daylight, aircraft and their missiles (torpedoes, bombs, and rockets) had displaced big guns as the

325

dominant weapons in a contest between rival concentrations of maritime power; and, second, in such circumstances it was the carrier-borne and not the shore-based aircraft that had proved themselves of prior importance.

This latter fact brings us to the invention that had had a revolutionary effect in so many aspects of maritime warfare—radar. It was by means of radar that aircraft carriers were able to direct their fighters in defense of themselves and the fleet of which they formed a part, and so constitute that fleet a secure basis for attack despite anything that could be done by hostile aircraft, whether ship-borne or shore-based. Without radar there might have been more justification for those who had prophesied the doom of big ships at the hands of shore-based aircraft, for ship-borne fighters lacking radar direction could have done little against strong attacks. With radar, however, a fleet could operate against air forces of equivalent magnitude with no more than the risks normally acceptable in war. Not only had radar revolutionized defense by fighters, but it had also added enormously to the effectiveness of antiaircraft gunnery, both in the pointing of guns and by the use of radar-actuated fuses.

Experience had shown, then, that big warships were still an important ingredient of sea power, and in most instances they were still the basic ingredient. The core of naval power was now the aircraft carrier rather than the heavily gunned battleship, though in some circumstances a proportion of the aircraft needed in maritime operations might be provided from shore bases. But the latter, the shore-based aircraft, had not superseded the big ships.

Radar had played an equally important part in the other great contest of the war at sea, the battle with the German submarines which sought to disrupt transatlantic communications, not by one huge concentration, but by a number of smaller concentrations that would locally be too much for the defense. It was largely by means of radar that the wolf-pack tactics had been defeated, and it was through radar that aircraft had been able to hamper and take toll of submarines on passage. In almost every other field, too, traditional conceptions of strategy and tactics had had to be extensively modified. Hitherto the division of time into periods of daylight and darkness had been fundamental to nearly all strategical problems, as had also the effect of low visibility by day; now an enemy could be found almost as easily by night or in thick weather as by day in high visibility. Hitherto, also, gunfire could be effective only if the opponent was in clear sight, either from the firing ship or from a spotting aircraft; but by the end of the war guns could engage an unseen ship with full effect to the limit of their range. Darkness and thick weather still made it difficult for aircraft, even though equipped with radar, to attack a fleet. And there was already a development of countermeasures hampering the use of this device in some respects. Nevertheless, it would not be an exaggeration to say that, in 1945, radar was the most important of all the technical devices used in war at sea.

One other notable characteristic of sea fighting during these six years was the success achieved by torpedoes fired at warships. The experience of 1914–1918 had made it seem that, except perhaps as a defensive weapon in a fleet action, the torpedo was not so effective against warships as had previously been supposed, and the general feeling was that improved ship construction would make it even less effective in the future. But in fact the pendulum had swung the other way, partly because of the extensive use of torpedoes by aircraft and their more concentrated use by submarines (which often fired six or more in a salvo), partly because of the more frequent opportunities for destroyer attacks by night, and partly because of increases in the weight and power of the explosive head. All these factors in concert had put the torpedo on the highest plane as a crippler and a destroyer of warships.

Mention has already been made of the long distance from its home bases at which American sea power was exerted in the Pacific. Insofar as this separation of ship from base resulted from the way in which American, and later British, fleets were able to operate unrestricted by the need for periodical returns to advanced bases, it, too, must be noted as an outstanding change in the practice of naval warfare. The idea that a fleet must resort to a harbor for replenishment at frequent intervals, hitherto a basic factor in the strategy of steam-driven navies, was shown to be no longer tenable. Even in the less extensive waters of the North Atlantic, German warships had fueled undisturbed on many occasions. That there were risks in such a procedure was clear, and these were increased the more limited the area of operations; but in most circumstances the danger was no more than was acceptable, and the gain derived from being able to remain at sea almost indefinitely was immense.

Last there were the changes in amphibious warfare, in landings on hostile shores. There had been an extensive development of special craft and appliances and of the technique of welding navy, army, and air force together for the tremendous blow of the assault. But in the principles governing these operations, experience had shown the changes to be far less fundamental than might have been expected. A landing on a hostile shore had remained one of the most difficult of all forms of war; it required much preparation and a large amount of special equipment

327

which could not contribute to other operations. But it had retained the strength derived from the flexibility given to the attacker, the fact that the defense would often be unable to forecast where and when the blow would fall. In the strategical setting of the later years of the war, seaborne assaults had been, not merely natural ingredients of maritime warfare, as they had so often been in the past, but operations on which nearly all the main steps to victory had depended.

Bibliography

Official Publications Other Than Admirals' Dispatches
(Issued by H.M.S.O., London, unless otherwise indicated)

Admiralty. "Führer Conferences on Naval Affairs." Admiralty trans., 1947. In *Brassey's Naval Annual, 1948*.

———. *Loss of H.M.S. Glorious*. House of Commons Parliamentary Report. (Hansard), May 8, 1946.

———. *Ships of the Royal Navy: Losses during the Second World War*. 1947.

———. *U. Boat Casualties during the War: German, Italian and Japanese. Particulars of Destruction*. Cmd. 6843. 1946.

Admiralty and Air Ministry. *Battle of the Atlantic*. 1946.

———. *Report on the Escape of Scharnhorst, Gneisenau, and Prinz Eugen from Brest to Germany*. Cmd. 6775. 1946.

Eisenhower, Dwight D. *The Operations in Europe of the Allied Expeditionary Force, June, 1944, to May, 1945*. Report of the Supreme Commander to the Combined Chiefs of Staff. 1946.

King, Ernest J. *U.S. Navy at War, 1941–1945*. Official reports to the Secretary of the Navy by the Commander in Chief United States Fleet and Chief of Naval Operations. U. S. Navy Department. 1946. The appendixes list all United States and Japanese warships sunk or destroyed during the war.

British Admirals' Dispatches Published in the *London Gazette*
(Dates of publication are given in parentheses)

Barry and Creasy. Attack on the *Tirpitz* by Midget Submarines, September, 1943 (July 3, 1947).

Burrough. Final Stages of the Naval War in N.W. Europe (Jan. 8, 1948).

Collins. Battle of the Java Sea, 27th February, 1942 (July 7, 1948).

Cunningham. Action off Calabria, 9th July, 1940 (April 28, 1948).

———. Fleet Air Arm Operations against Taranto, November, 1940 (July 14, 1947).

———. Battle of Matapan, March, 1941 (July 31, 1947).

———. Action against a Convoy, 15/16 April, 1941 (May 12, 1948).

———. Battle of Crete, May, 1941 (May 24, 1948).

———. The Landings in North Africa, November, 1942 (March 23, 1949).

———. Control of the Sicilian Straits, July, 1943 (April 25, 1950).

———. Operations in the Gulf of Salerno, September, 1943 (May 2, 1950).

Cunningham, Somerville, Curteis, and Syfret. Mediterranean Convoy Operations, 1941–1942 (Aug. 11, 1948).

Forbes. St. Nazaire, March, 1942 (Oct. 2, 1947).

Fraser. Sinking of the *Scharnhorst*, December, 1943 (Aug. 7, 1947).

———. British Pacific Fleet in the Conquest of Okinawa, March to May, 1945 (June 2, 1948).

Halifax and Whitworth. First and Second Battles of Narvik, April, 1940 (July 3, 1947).

Harwood (Vian). The Battle of Sirte, 22nd March, 1942 (Sept. 18, 1947).

Hughes-Hallett. The Dieppe Raid, August, 1942 (Aug. 14, 1947).

Layton. Loss of the *Prince of Wales* and *Repulse*, December, 1941 (Feb. 26, 1948).

Power. Naval Operations in Ramree Island Area, January–February, 1945 (April 29, 1948).

Ramsay. The Evacuation from Dunkirk, May–June, 1940 (July 17, 1947).

———. Assault Phases of the Normandy Landings, June, 1944 (Oct. 30, 1947).

Somerville. Action off Cape Spartivento, 17th November, 1940 (May 5, 1948).

Syfret. Capture of Diégo-Suarez, May, 1942 (March 4, 1948).

Tovey. Raid on the Lofoten Islands, March, 1941 (June 23, 1948).

———. Sinking of the *Bismarck*, May, 1941 (Oct. 16, 1947).

———. Carrier Aircraft Attacks on Kirkenes and Petsamo, July, 1941 (May 25, 1948).

———. Raid on Vaagso Island, December, 1941 (July 5, 1948).

———. Convoys to North Russia, 1942 (Oct. 13, 1950).

Willis. Naval Operations in the Aegean, September–November, 1943 (Oct. 11, 1948).

Willis and Somerville. Actions against Raiders, 1941–1942 (July 12, 1948).

Lectures at the Royal United Service Institution
(In chronological order)

Rear Admiral G. E. Creasy. "The Navy's Part in the Victory in Europe." December 5, 1945.

Captain I. M. R. Campbell, R.N. "Russian Convoys, 1941–1945." January 16, 1946.

Admiral the Viscount Mountbatten of Burma. "The Strategy of the South-East Asia Campaign." October 9, 1946.

Admiral Raymond A. Spruance, U.S.N. "The Victory in the Pacific." October 30, 1946.
Rear Admiral G. N. Oliver. "Carrier Aircraft in Support of Major Landings." November 20, 1946.
Captain E. M. Evans-Lombe, R.N. "The Royal Navy in the Pacific." March 19, 1947.
Air Vice-Marshal A. B. Ellwood. "Coastal Command in the Victory in Europe." April 16, 1947.
Commander R. F. Jessel, R.N. "The Bismarck Operation: The German Aspect." November 19, 1952.

Selected Books

Chalmers, William S. *Max Horton and the Western Approaches: A Biography of Admiral Sir Max Kennedy Horton.* London: Hodder and Stoughton, 1954.
Churchill, Winston S. *The Second World War.* London: Cassell, 1948–1954. 6 vols.
Cowie, J. S. *Mines, Minelayers and Minelaying.* London and New York: Oxford University Press, 1949. Captain Cowie, R.N., was concerned with minelaying operations throughout World War II.
Cunningham, Andrew Browne Cunningham, Viscount. *A Sailor's Odyssey: The Autobiography of Admiral of the Fleet, Viscount Cunningham of Hyndhope.* London and New York: Hutchinson, 1951. Viscount Cunningham was commander in chief, Mediterranean, from 1939 to 1943, and first sea lord from 1943 to 1945.
De Guingand, Francis. *Operation Victory.* London: Hodder and Stoughton, 1947. An account of the invasion of Europe by General Montgomery's chief of staff.
Dönitz, Karl. *Memoirs: Ten Years and Twenty Days.* Trans. from German by R. H. Stevens. London: Weidenfeld and Nicholson, 1959. A personal history of the German Submarine Command by its commander from 1935 to 1943, with the stress still on submarine operations during Dönitz' subsequent service as head of the navy until the end of the war.
Eisenhower, Dwight D. *Crusade in Europe.* Garden City, N.Y.: Doubleday, 1948. London: Heinemann, 1949.
Falk, S. L. *Decision at Leyte.* New York: Norton, 1966. This account of the operations ashore, afloat, and in the air, from the initial planning to the final mopping-up of Japanese forces on the island, contains more information on the Japanese aspects than previous accounts.
Field, James A. *The Japanese at Leyte Gulf: The Shō Operation.* Princeton: Princeton University Press, 1947.
Halsey, William F., and J. Bryan III. *Admiral Halsey's Story.* New York: Whittlesey House, 1947.
Holmes, Wilfred J. *Undersea Victory: The Influence of Submarine Operations on the War in the Pacific.* Garden City, N.Y.: Doubleday, 1966.
Jacobsen, Hans Adolf, and Jürgen Rohwer, eds. *Decisive Battles of World*

War II: The German View. Trans. from German by Edward Fitzgerald. London: André Deutsch, 1965. Several chronicles in this volume touch on the naval aspects of the war. Of particular importance is Rohwer's chronicle, "The U-Boat War against the Allied Supply Lines," which gives a more complete narrative than does Dönitz' volume.

King, Ernest J., and Walter M. Whitehill. *Fleet Admiral King: A Naval Record.* New York: Norton, 1952. Although written by another hand, this is a true and illuminating autobiography.

Millington-Drake, Eugen. *The Drama of the Graf Spee and the Battle of the River Plate: A Documentary Anthology, 1914–1964.* London: Peter Davies, 1965. At the time of the incident of the *Graf Spee*, Millington-Drake was British minister at Montevideo; he prints information from all possible sources, British and German.

Morison, Samuel Eliot. *History of United States Naval Operations in World War II.* Boston: Little, Brown, 1947–1962. 15 vols. Though not an official history, this work is a definitive account; Professor Morison was given access to all official documents.

Pack, S. W. C. *The Battle of Matapan.* London: B. T. Batsford, 1961. This volume contains vivid impressions of Admiral Cunningham's personality, as well as a good account of the battle.

Puleston, William D. *The Influence of Sea Power in World War II.* New Haven: Yale University Press, 1947.

Raeder, Erich. *Struggle for the Sea.* Trans. from German by Edward Fitzgerald. London: W. Kimber, 1959. The Grand Admiral's apologia for his conduct of German naval affairs from 1928 until he resigned in 1943.

Roskill, Stephen W. *The War at Sea, 1939–1945.* London: H.M.S.O., 1954–1961. 3 vols. Captain Roskill's official history, published in the United Kingdom Military Series.

Ruge, Friedrich. *Sea Warfare, 1939–1945: A German Viewpoint.* Trans. from German by M. G. Saunders. London: Cassell, 1957. A short history from the German aspect. Vice Admiral Ruge served in several staff appointments during the war.

Taffrail [pseud. of Henry Taprell Dorling]. *Western Mediterranean, 1942–1945.* London: Hodder and Stoughton, 1947.

Wemyss, D. E. G. *Walker's Group in the Western Approaches.* Liverpool: Liverpool Daily Post & Echo, 1948. An account by one of the commanders.

Woodburn-Kirkby, S. *The War against Japan.* Vol. I. London: H.M.S.O., 1957. This volume in the United Kingdom Military Series of Official Histories gives a more complete account of the opening moves in Malayan waters than does Captain Roskill's earlier (1954) narrative.

Woodward, C. Vann. *The Battle of Leyte Gulf.* New York: Macmillan, 1947.

Zimmerman, John L. *The Guadalcanal Campaign.* Washington: U.S. Marine Corps, 1949. Zimmerman was official historian of the United States Marine Corps.

Index